To John Lusty, Class of 1942

David Tall

+

Graham Tall

Memories of Wellingborough Grammar School 1930–1975

David Tall
Graham Tall

With contributions from Joe Keep, Noel Pearson, Peter Wilson, Graham Sharp, Geoff Hodgkins, Peter Godfrey, David Wilson, & many other Old Boys

First published in 2006 by
Clock Tower Publications
21 Laburnum Avenue
Kenilworth
Warwickshire
CV8 2DR
UK

ISBN: 0-9548689-1-9

Front Cover: *Photograph taken in 1958 by old boy and master, Colin McCall. The combination of the old school and the new extension as yet unweathered symbolises the stable origins and long-term growth of the tradition of the school.*

Back Cover: *Photograph taken in the mid-fifties, from the collection in Miss Bavin's scrapbook. It represents Parents' Day and the parents who supported the school. Our mother, grandmother and father sit in the centre with our father resting his eyes after shift work at Stewarts & Lloyds Iron Co.*

Prepared by David Tall on an Apple Macintosh Computer in Adobe *InDesign®*, using 12 pt Palatino font; pictures processed in Adobe *Photoshop®*.

Manufactured in the EU by L.P.P.S. Ltd, Wellingborough, Northants, NN8 3PJ.

Contents

Foreword by Old Grammarian Sir David Frost

It is a pleasure and a privilege to be asked to write a few introductory words to this excellent book about Wellingborough Grammar School because WGS was an outstanding grammar school.

The grammar schools, and the whole post-1944 Education Act system, gave opportunities to children of my generation that our predecessors never had. At the same time, the priorities of the system meant that anything over and above the preparation for examinations depended more than ever on individual teachers' calibre and enthusiasm. And that is where we were particularly blessed.

There was one teacher at Wellingborough who really ignited my interest in words, and the use of words. He was my English teacher, Mr Cooksey, and he managed to transmit his passion for the written word in a way that was irresistible. He was also concerned to see that we could discern the difference between an accurate report in a newspaper and a loaded one. He urged us to read two newspapers rather than one. During its courageous opposition to the Suez invasion, he urged us to make the *Observer* one of those two papers. He made us more aware of the outside world. He introduced us to John Osborne and explained the significance of Jimmy Porter.

In addition to English, my other Sixth Form subjects were Latin and History. When it came to writing history essays at home I was very grateful for my father's treasured set of encyclopaedias, until one day when I was writing an essay on Gladstone. The encyclopaedia's profile of the great man concluded with the words: 'W.E. Gladstone retired from politics in 1892 and is now living at Hawarden Castle near Chester.' It dawned on me that perhaps I was not receiving the full benefit of the latest research on the subject!

I have many light-hearted memories of WGS. Producing plays in the House Plays competition and acting in the School plays, masterminded by Spike Jackson. My roles usually involved wearing a beard and meeting an untimely end early in the first act, as was the case with Banquo and Sir Roger Ackroyd.

When Bill Haley fever was at its peak, we got some soapy water, put it in small bottles and sold it at the corner of the street in Wellingborough as Bill Haley's Bath Water. Four or five people snapped up this bargain at threepence a time.

We had a very successful series of bogus letters printed by the Northamptonshire *Evening Telegraph* and on one memorable occasion, I "took a day off" – in order to watch Jim Laker complete his historic 19-wicket haul against the Australians.

On a more serious note, I remember the school's Toc H group and Jake Dunning's most treasured quotation from the founder, Tubby Clayton, "Service is the rent we pay for our room on earth".

Then there were the words of that outstanding Headmaster, H A Wrenn, to all new arrivals – that they should always have a book in their pocket so that they could study it whilst standing in a bus queue or on a journey and use all their time well. I always say that I don't like wasting money but I hate wasting time. So the influence of H A Wrenn lives on in my life to this day!

As you can tell, my memories of Wellingborough Grammar School are very happy ones. But my primary emotion – shared, as you will read, by the other contributors to this book – is one of gratitude. I do not think I could have achieved whatever I have achieved without WGS.

Sir David Frost

Foreword by French Master
Mr Richard 'Buzz' Temple

To be asked to write a few lines in a general preface to *Memories of Wellingborough Grammar School* is quite an honour, even though I am – just – the last of what the authors call "long-serving masters", which perhaps means that they had little choice.

The key to the whole exercise in recording what went on in the buildings in Doddington Road lies in the word in the book's title. And that word is "Memories".

You are about to read an all-embracing (I won't say "comprehensive") and thoroughly researched history of a highly successful Grammar School, its foundation in 1930, its growth and expansion in what it offered, its successes over all those years to 1975. All this was important to the school, and not least to the boys who benefited from "attending".

Yet their years spent there culminating in certificates, scholarships and places in higher education or business are not entirely the stuff that they remember, or are grateful for – it is the fact of being part of a system which offered friendships made for life, experiences in the classroom not understood at the time, tyrants who were human after all, being a member of a school with a spirit which will not die.

"Memories" – warmth, affection, respect: that was Wellingborough Grammar School's contribution to Northamptonshire.

R. H. Temple

19/6/06

Richard H. Temple

Preface

This book is based on memories of a school in the heart of rural Northamptonshire in the middle of the twentieth century. We two brothers were pupils at the school (1952–60 and 1955–63) and share a similar background with many others who were pupils during its life from 1930 to 1975. It is our goal to paint a picture of those times when Wellingborough Grammar School provided an academic education for the most able boys in Wellingborough and District for the first time in history.

Our parents saw the hope for our future through education and we left the town in the nineteen sixties to study at university and eventually to become university academics, one a lecturer in education, the other a professor in mathematical thinking.

In the new millennium, we both returned to celebrate the fiftieth anniversaries of our time at the Grammar School to meet old friends who were our contemporaries. We were moved by the warmth and affection that so many held for the school after such a period of time. We shared memories of our masters ('teachers' were 'masters' then) and of our experiences in all the activities provided by the school. These were stories that needed to be collected and told as a record of what it was that made our school so special.

To widen our knowledge of the school over its whole history, we contacted many generations of old boys through the Old Grammarians Association and more widely through the internet, collecting memories from the early days of the school in the ninteen-thirties through the war and the late forties, fifties, sixties and seventies.

It soon became clear that what united boys from all periods of its history were memories of a number of long-serving masters of whom almost everyone could tell a tale. 'Nick', 'Jake', 'Eddie', 'Chunky', 'Johnny B', 'Spike' and 'Beery' all stayed more than thirty years; several war-time arrivals including 'Danny', 'Hobo', 'Lennie', and 'Father' stayed for more than ten. The redoubtable Miss Bavin was an ever-present secretary presiding over the front office from 1931 to 1973. Then there was the sport, the clubs and the societies that we could choose to enrich our days: rugby, cricket, athletics, swimming, drama, music, the Railway Club, the Puppet Club and a host of others that waxed and waned as new generations with different aptitudes and interests passed through the system.

Here was a story we could tell, but it needed organising into a suitable narrative. We decided to begin with a group of long-serving masters who would be known to most boys as ever-present participants in the action to come. We then organised chapters on the development of the school from its opening with 64 boys in 1930 under the first headmaster, Mr Lay, through the reign of the second Headmaster, Mr Woolley, and on to the post-war period of Mr Wrenn. Where we could, we peppered the narrative with reminiscences from boys who were there at the time and inserted more substantial vignettes from boys with vivid memories of particular aspects of school life.

Writing about the period after the war, we introduced a second tranche of long-serving masters who coloured the post-war years alongside the pre-war and war-time veterans, including 'Ivor', 'Buzz', 'Tony', 'Ernie', 'Gus', 'Johnny H' and 'Herbie' (aka 'Terry'), all of whom served over twenty years. Then we gathered together aspects that occurred throughout the history of the school. The House system was set up in 1931 by Mr Lay: Dragons, Gryphons, Lions and Stags (conveniently in alphabetic order with our own House named first). The sport, clubs and societies, the school trips home and abroad, all started in the time of Mr Lay and, after varying fortunes during the war, were expanded with great vigour by Mr Wrenn. The Annual Prize Days were enhanced by increasingly interesting guests to present prizes, rising to a climax from the fifties onwards with many world-famous scientists, authors, war heroes and royalty.

Our purpose is to celebrate the Grammar School as it was. However, as old boys who became university academics, we also have a professional interest in looking at the achievement of the school and reflecting on the changes that led to comprehensive education and the transition to the Wrenn School.

In this book we take you back to those days that served us well when we were young, to reveal the school that we remember with respect and pride.

Graham Tall, BSc, MEd, PhD
(Lecturer in Education, University of Birmingham)
David Tall, MA, DPhil, PhD
(Professor in Mathematical Thinking, University of Warwick)

Acknowledgements

We acknowledge with grateful thanks the many old boys of Wellingborough Grammar School who have assisted us in the preparation of this book, in particular, those who provided written contributions that are acknowledged throughout the text.

We would never have had so wide a range of contributions were it not for the internet, *Friends Reunited*, and the magnificent pioneering work of old boy, Paul Titcomb, who set up the first Wellingborough Grammar School website at

http://www.wellingboroughgrammarschool.co.uk

Many old boys made themselves known through these pages and enabled us to begin the quest to gather together information for this book, which was placed on the web by Graham Tall at

http://www.wgs1955.org.uk

now also available through the address

http://www.wellingboroughgrammarschool.org.uk

This site also contains all the school panoramas with an invitation to identify everyone pictured, to build a visual archive of almost every boy who attended the school. The task is on-going and we welcome further information to make it as inclusive as possible.

We thank the Wellingborough Heritage Centre, in particular, Eileen Baxter, who introduced us to the two scrapbooks of cuttings put together by Miss Bavin that told the public story of school events.

Miss Bavin's collection provided us with the majority of illustrations that feature throughout the book. We acknowledge, with grateful thanks, the *Evening Telegraph* – who own the copyright of many of the photographs – for granting us permission to reproduce them.

The Wellingborough Old Grammarians Association – in particular Martin Layton – allowed us not only to make an electronic copy of the original scrapbooks, but also gave us access to the full set of School Magazines which we are in the process of turning into electronic form and placing on the web for others to study.

We have been given willing assistance by many individuals who have generously provided information, loaned us valuable materials, and given us immense positive support.

Keith Gennis was an invaluable source of information about the war years, David Wilson was ever-present in the preparation, filling in details, writing insightful reminiscences and continually giving us warm encouragement. The organisers of various reunions, including John Garley, Tony Bayes, David Spencer and Richard Bryan, all gave us access to their lists of e-mails for further gathering of information.

We received massive help from a huge array of old boys, and others, including:

> Richard Adkins, Tony Beadsworth, John Bergson, Roger Brown, Richard Bryan, Richard Buchta, Jim Buckby, Peter Buckey, Bob Buckler, Nick Butler, Bert Catlin, Roy Catling, Frank Chambers, Graham Chapman, Barry Clarke, Peter Clark, John Cook, Adrian Coombes, David Cooper, Brian Corn, Artin Cornish, Paul Cox, Richard Cox, Clive 'Dixie' Dean, Geoffrey Dean, Michael Eakins, Donald Franklin, Richard Frost, John Garley, Robert Gibson, Martin Gray, Keith Gennis, Peter Godfrey, Terry Gotch, Gary Griffiths, Richard Hall, Sam Harris, John Hobbs, Roger Hobbs, Geoff Hodgkins, (Alan) David Holder, Arend Hoogervorst, Brian Horn, 'Pedro' Howes, Pete Jackson, Tim Kearsley, Joe Keep, Norman Keech, Michael King, Ray King-Underwood, Martin Layton, David Lodge, David 'Perce' Long, John Maddock, Colin McCall, Gerald Neville, Richard Nobes, John 'Fred' Nutt, Richard Oberman, Ron Palmer, Lionel Parker, Richard Partridge, Derrick Pearce, Denis Pearson, Noel Pearson, Martin Percy, Roy Pettit, David Pope, Barry Reynolds, Terry Rice, Danny (David) Richardson, Ian Richardson, Paul Robinson, John Rodhouse, Alan Rudd, Paul Scroxton, Roland Sewell, Graham Sharp, Dave Shurville, Keith Shurville, Neil Sinclair, Dick Smart, David Spencer, Terry Stratton, Kevin Street, Chris Talbot, Barrie Tall, Frank Taylor, Tim Thompson, Paul Titcomb, Roy Tomlin, Jim Tompkins, Keith Tompkins, Nick Tompkins, Dave Toseland, Ivor Vincent, Barry Waite, Arthur Warner, Graham Willey, David Wilson, Jim Wilson, Peter Wilson, John Wittering, Colin Wright.

For specific information about earlier Grammar Schools in Wellingborough we are indebted to *Four Centuries: The History of Wellingborough School* by Neil Lyon.

In the final stages of production, we were assisted by Susan Tall in the editing and old boy Lionel Parker in the production.

We give special thanks to Sir David Frost as Old Boy and Mr Richard Temple as Master for writing the forewords. We also give our thanks to the many others who have helped us in producing this book, in particular, and in retrospect, to the late Miss Bavin, whose collection of memorabilia and photographs made our task so much easier.

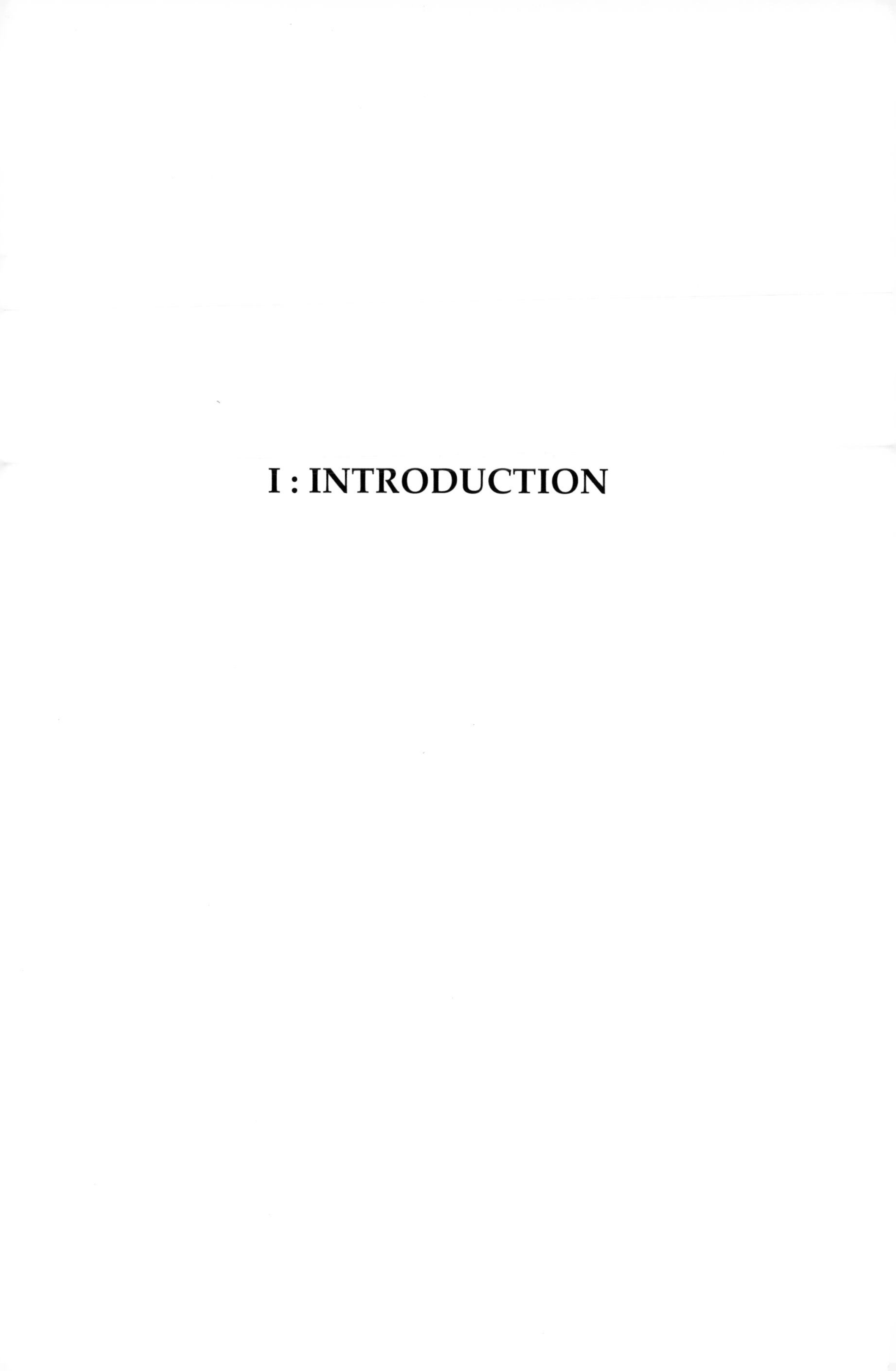

I : INTRODUCTION

What made our school so special?

Chapter 1

What Made Our School So Special?

For forty-five years between 1930 and 1975, Wellingborough Grammar School was a symbol of academic excellence to which all able boys in the town and surrounding district could aspire. It was created in a time of austerity when secondary education was not free, but scholarships were available to support exceptional pupils (see below). From 1930 to 1945 all pupils had to pass a test to enter the school, the majority paid fees but the most able in need of financial support had their fees provided by the local authority, effectively producing two different kinds of pupil: fee-payers and scholarship boys.

It was a school not only for Wellingborough, but for the communities in the surrounding area, including Rushden, Raunds, Higham Ferrers, Wollaston, Bozeat, Irchester, Irthlingborough, Finedon, Wilby, Doddington, Earls Barton, Ecton, and smaller villages in between.

A. S. E. 19.

NORTHAMPTONSHIRE COUNTY COUNCIL
EDUCATION COMMITTEE.

County Education Offices,
NORTHAMPTON,
13 JUL 1935

Dear Sir, or Madam,

Annual Schools Examination, 1935 : Special Places.

1. I have pleasure in informing you that the County Examining Board have decided to recommend that your son (daughter) be awarded a Special Place tenable at ......Wellingborough Grammar.......... School.

2. The Place entitles him (her) to payment of travelling expenses (if any). I enclose copy of the Committee's Regulations in the matter. If your home is more than two miles from the School or from the nearest available Railway Station, kindly let me know what the distance is and how you propose that your son (daughter) shall travel to and from School.

3. The Education Committee will in addition grant :-

(a) remission of School fees, either total or partial ;
(b) an allowance for out-of-pocket expenses - to meet expenses incidental to attendance at a Secondary School ;
(c) a maintenance allowance

if your means are such that all or any of these aids are in their opinion required. Appended to this notice is a Form (H. S.) on which, if you wish to apply for these aids, you should submit as soon as you can confidential information as to your circumstances. The submission of this Form, duly completed, is all that is necessary to ensure consideration for any of the aids for which, on the income shown, you may be eligible.

Offer of a place and financial support before the 1944 Education Act

The 1944 Education Act gave free grammar school education for all those who passed the scholarship at 11+. Those who passed felt a sense of privilege: they had 'won' a scholarship, which entitled them to a high-quality academic education which was now theirs by right.

As time passed, the perceived need for more equal educational opportunities for all led to the development of comprehensive schools large enough to encompass the whole cross-section of children under one roof. In 1975, the Grammar School for Boys amalgamated with the High School for Girls to become The Wrenn School, one of several mixed comprehensives in the town. The Grammar School was no more, yet some four thousand boys had passed through its portals and many remembered it with a sense of pride and affection.

What was it that made our school so special? The concept of a Grammar School has a long provenance in history, back to Tudor times and before. It was a school in which a boy could be given an education that included classical Latin, an essential requirement for entrance to the great universities of Oxford and Cambridge.

As the twentieth century progressed, it gave boys from working-class families the opportunity to begin a journey of personal improvement. It catered for the most academically-able going on to university and for a wider band of individuals who would take leading roles in the local community in business and the professions.

Wellingborough Grammar School flourished for a period of forty-five years, which—on the face of it—can be subdivided into three parts: pre-war, the war, and post-war. This coincides closely with the reigns of its three headmasters, Mr Lay 1930–37, Mr Woolley, 1937-45, and Mr Wrenn, 1946–75.

On academic grounds there is another sea-change that separates the time of the first two headmasters from that of Mr Wrenn: the 1944 Education Act. This changed the nature of the pupils educated at Wellingborough Grammar School from a combination of fee-payers and scholarship boys to just one class of pupil who passed the 11+.

Academically and socially, therefore, the 1944 Education Act divides the life of the school into two major periods, where the first period may be further divided into pre-war and war-time. The pre-war time starts with the opening of the school in 1930 with 64 boys to build into a full school with a sixth form in the latter part of the decade. This development set down the structure of the school with its academic and liberal tradition, the division into four houses for internal competition, the building of sport and school societies to broaden the education of the boys. When Mr Lay left in 1937 and Mr Woolley took over, the other ten members of staff remained and the growth of the school continued almost seamlessly. Once the war had begun in 1939, four senior staff (Messrs Pine, Butler, Phillips and Dunning) were called up to fight for their country, leaving Mr Woolley to cope with expanding school numbers with a changing group of teachers, including younger school mistresses and older men no longer fit for war service.

After the war, in January 1946, Mr Wrenn began to build on the foundations of his predecessors to establish a highly successful school with a burgeoning sixth-form and ever-increasing numbers going to university. The liberal education in the school was enhanced by the phenomenal growth of school clubs and societies; the annual Parents' Day saw a succession of internationally famous individuals to present the prizes and to give their names to laboratories, lecture rooms, and departments.

As the school went from strength to strength in the fifties and sixties, the national mood changed subtly as the Labour Government declared its desire to introduce comprehensive education in 1965. For a time the Grammar School continued as before, but as local moves towards comprehensive education began in the late sixties, reality began to dawn and the school passed through a brief final period as preparations were made for the change to comprehensive education.

In attempting to capture the essence of these years of the Grammar School, we found a number of sources of information to supplement our own memories. These include the School Magazines produced twice a year from the autumn of 1932, two scrapbooks of newspaper cuttings kept by the school secretary Miss Bavin from 1930 to 1973, and a previous book on the school assembled by Don Stratton in 1990.

All of these shared one thing in common: they presented the *public face* of the school to the community. However, the personal side of the school, as experienced by the boys themselves, remained unspoken. Here we were fortunate that the development of the internet and e-mail allowed us to make direct contact with old boys with vivid memories of their schooldays.

As we corresponded with boys from different periods of the school's history, several aspects became evident. First of all, it was the *boys* who saw most of the soul of the school as they encountered the teaching of many different masters at first hand, while the masters themselves were more confined to their own classrooms during the school day.

Even the headmaster had only a partial view of what went on in the day-to-day teaching. Each headmaster would teach the boys to get to know them personally, for instance, Mr Wrenn taught divinity to the first form to learn all the boys' names. He would also walk round the school during teaching periods, quietly observing the operation of the school to gain at least an external view from outside the classroom.

The organisation of the school separated into two quite different areas. At the front was the headmaster's office, guarded by the ever-present Miss Bavin. At the back of the school was the masters' common room containing the deputy headmaster and all the other masters. If the headmaster wished to enter the common room, he would always knock first, as a courtesy before entry.

The headmaster was in overall charge of the school. In Mr Wrenn's time, he was responsible for overall strategy and discipline, his number two, Mr Nicholas, took care of the timetable.

The teaching of the pupils was devolved to the masters. Many of them had studied at Oxford or Cambridge and came to the school without any further teacher training. They had experienced the subjects they were to teach both at school and at university, they knew about entry to Oxford and Cambridge, and the syllabus of the School Certificate was available to define the curriculum.

In this context, it was their responsibility to use their experience to teach the boys what they knew. Initially Mr Wrenn would invite new staff members to show him their weekly plans of work, but once settled in, unless there was a problem, each was left to his own devices to teach as he saw fit.

The subtle use of the name 'master' rather than 'teacher' suggests that it was masters who were, or who should be, in charge. The boys were known formally by their surnames and, by a perverse twist of fate, the masters were known to the boys either by their first name or a nickname that was strictly for private consumption and not for public use where the masters could hear.

Some masters operated a strong disciplinary regime, using a slipper, stick, knotted rope, or other implement to administer instant retribution. Some had a natural presence that enabled them to teach without any form of punishment, while a few were overcome by the natural exuberance of the boys and were unable to maintain control.

The headmaster had a subtle insight into what was going on, through the examination results of the boys and a sense of the atmosphere of different classes observed from outside the door. However, he was rarely given to interfering with *what* to teach; he appointed the best masters he could get and let them get on with it. This gave the school a special flavour as each master had his own personality and his own way of carrying out his duties.

Social pressures of the time had their influences. Working-class parents were in the main proud that their sons were having a grammar school education and would scrimp and save to give them the resources to enable them to benefit from their schooling. Most respected the headmaster and the staff of the school and expected their boys to do their best to succeed.

Boys, of course, would be boys, and had energy in plenty to pour into their work with masters they respected or in subjects that they grew to enjoy, but they were likely to make fools of masters for whom they had no respect, or who taught subjects they grew to despise.

Of course, the views of the boys were likely to be influenced by their own personal circumstances, seeing the positive side of masters teaching subjects that they liked and more negative aspects in those who taught subjects that were less pleasurable. Some masters presented very different personalities to boys in different circumstances. As one C-stream boy wrote (in a vignette that appears later in this book):

> *If the A-stream was probably where the staff got their professional gratification; the C-stream was certainly where they got their target practice.* *Graham Sharp (1958–64)*

The very same master might enjoy encouraging the intellectual pursuits of his most able charges, while believing it necessary that he must beat the information into those of lesser intellect.

To understand what made the Grammar School special, we must reconcile memories that vary between two considerable extremes:

The time we spent at WGS was one of those defining periods in our lives, although we were much too young to realise it at the time. We all have a great deal to be grateful for, not least those formative years spent with really fine teachers who had seen some of the worst aspects of humanity in the World War, yet did not lose their faith in the human spirit and passed on to us their hopes for a better and more compassionate world. I hope we have justified that faith. *Peter Godfrey (1955–60)*

Some terrible flashbacks of rulers, canes, slippers, tubes, pipes, ... anyone remember the psychopathic Halliwell (Latin, I think) who used to take running kicks at little lads' backsides? Frightening stuff.
John Bergson (1961–66)

The truth, as they say, probably 'lies' somewhere in between.

WGS was a unique institution (thank God!) — you either loved it or hated it, but apart from the public schools, there are not many schools that engender such a following, so long after its passing.
Richard Partridge (1967–73)

Those of us who benefited from an academic education certainly remember the Grammar School with affection, but there are also those who fell foul of the system, yet were still able to appreciate what it had to offer. Tony Beadsworth, a pupil from the swinging sixties, remembers his time with masters John Butler, 'Arthur' Bantoft and 'Carlos' Stevenson, as he and twelve others spent their final year in the school in a one-off class entitled 5X:

Beadsworth, Blagburn, Brawn, Edmunds, Gallagher, Hammond, Laughton, Merricks, Povey, Riddle, Robinson, Siddons, Sinclair. A fairly innocuous bunch of names you might think, but for anyone who was at school in the year '65–66 they could mean only one thing – 5X (X for extra, not excellent).

Thirteen (it had to be really) educational misfits who had squandered their earlier talents for a life of ease. We were treated either with contempt by our teachers or as a novelty by others. I asked John Butler, long after I had left the school, why he, one of the most respected of masters, ended up being our form master and he replied that he needed a challenge! He had us in the palm of his hand and he knew it, as for the others – well, it was kill or be killed.

I think we gave up trying when we were told of the formation of 5X. It was as if the door to further education had been slammed in our faces; we were in quarantine, isolated from those we would infect with our brand of rebellion, although, to be fair, had we been made of sterner stuff we could have knuckled down to work to prove everyone wrong.

In the mid-sixties it was too easy to find a job, qualifications or not, so why bother studying? We amused ourselves with simple pleasures like Gallagher, Robinson and myself carrying out a commando raid in the Fleming Lab and washing Hammond's head in dilute hydrochloric acid. The look on Mr Bantoft's face as he perceived a steaming-haired Hammond is never to be forgotten especially as, when asked how it happened, Hammond confessed his hair needed washing. We still got hit round the head by 'Arthur' anyway.

There was the time we stayed late after school mainly because we couldn't go until Laughton had woken up, and perhaps the one that remains in my memory most is the whole class getting 1000 lines from our dear friend Mr Stevenson, to be finished by the end of term. Our last day before Easter and 9 of the 13 suffering the agonies of writer's cramp whilst Gallagher, Laughton, Robinson and myself applied ourselves to obtaining extra holiday money from each other by playing nine-card brag. Oh how we laughed when Carlos popped his head round the door and uttered the immortal line: 'Imposition Cancelled.'

SEMPER JUVENTUTIS MEMOR: You can't beat it!

Tony Beadsworth (1961–66)

Our purpose in writing this book is to draw together a range of memories that paint a picture of Wellingborough Grammar School. We begin by introducing the *dramatis personae* in the form of the long-serving masters who put their own special stamp on the school for most of its history. They arrived in the thirties and forties and served for twenty to forty years, several of them through the reign of all three headmasters, many of them having highly individual characters that made them stand out from the ordinary.

We continue by tracing the history of the school, considering first its origins as part of a longer line of development starting from Tudor times to the first Grammar School founded in Wellingborough over three centuries ago.

Our school's first phase began with the foundations laid by Mr

Lay (1930–37) and the continuation by Mr Woolley (1937–45) through the austerity of the war. In between the narrative of the chapters we present several vignettes by old boys that give personal insights into different aspects of their school experience.

The post-war phase begins with a chapter on the masters who arrived after the war, leading into the years with Mr Wrenn as Headmaster.

At this point we take a look at those aspects that gave the school its special character. First we consider the academic curriculum, beginning with the School Certificate and the switch to the General Certificate of Education in 1951. We find significant increases in performance in the reign of each headmaster and follow the changes in examination procedures through to the General Certificate of Education. We then turn to the liberal curriculum that gave the school its special character, including the sport (especially rugby), the school societies and clubs that began back in the time of Mr Lay and were considerably expanded in the time of Mr Wrenn. Then we turn to the sequence of eminent guests that came to present prizes, rising to a crescendo in the later years as royalty, Nobel laureates, war heroes, and other great men left their mark on plaques in rooms named after them.

As the Grammar School maintained its high levels of performance, the shift to comprehensive education cut it down in its prime. The change was formulated in Circular 10/65 issued by the new Labour Government in 1965. The theory was that the separation of children into three school streams at 11+ was not beneficial for all and a fairer solution was to teach all children in large comprehensive schools to cater for all abilities. At first the national change of mood had little influence on the Grammar School which continued in unbroken style through to the end of the sixties. The change, when it came, came quickly. In the final two years the staff worked together to facilitate the change to the new Wrenn School.

The Grammar School is gone, as are most other schools of its type. But it existed in a golden age when it gave great benefits to many individuals who were able to take advantage of its special kind of education. It continues to be remembered by a dwindling band of old boys who adopted the Latin motto: 'Semper juventutis memor', meaning 'Always mindful of our youth'. Just as the Grammar School has adapted, so has the Old Boy's Association, opening up its doors to all who wish to join. Now there are new generations that may benefit from sharing an experience that meant so much to so many of us.

Our first headmaster, Mr Lay, encapsulated the spirit of the school in the very first School Magazine in an essay entitled "Who we are":

> *A school's status depends on two things:– firstly on the quality and character of the citizens it produces, and secondly on the scholastic and academic training imparted. By unselfishness and determination to put the school first, we shall achieve the former, and by hard work and clear honest thinking, the latter will take care of itself. We are living through a period of world-wide depression, but not despair. We can feel very thankful that our school was in being before the dark days set in, and it is for us to hold aloft a torch, and be foremost in lighting up the path of progress, convinced that the path of progress lies in the way of efficiency and honesty of purpose.* F. C. L.

We trust that the memories enshrined in this book will enrich not only those who shared the golden days of our youth, but also intimate to new generations precisely what it was that made Wellingborough Grammar School so very special.

The three headmasters meeting in 1952:
Mr Wrenn (1946–75), Mr Woolley (1937–45), Mr Lay (1930–37)

The Three Headmasters

Mr Lay (Autumn 1930 – Summer 1937) was a charismatic leader who built the school from 64 boys in four forms with five masters (including himself) in autumn 1930 to 220 boys in ten forms with eleven masters in the autumn of his final year at the school in 1936. He was responsible for setting up the House system, the first clubs and societies, a programme of sports including rugby, cricket, athletics, swimming and boxing, and an academic structure which, in his final term, led to 14 boys passing the School Certificate and four the Higher School Certificate.

Mr Woolley (Autumn 1937 – Summer 1945) continued to build up the school in difficult circumstances as senior masters were called up for war service, leaving a changing staff with a number of lady masters and older men who were often too old to be called to service. He built the school to a three-form entry, with 371 boys in thirteen forms and 19 masters in the summer of 1945. The number of passes in the School Certificate were increased to 39 in 1945 with four successful in the Higher School Certificate.

Mr Wrenn (Spring 1946 – Summer 1975) built on the work of his predecessors, complementing the academic curriculum with a wide range of clubs and societies and an enhanced Prize Day with guests of world-renown. The three-form entry remained constant, with a broadening to four forms from the second form onward and a three-year sixth form of over a hundred pupils. In 1974 the school had 580 boys in 23 forms and 37 masters; 93 out of 94 candidates passed O-level (61 with five or more subjects), and 47 passed at least one subject at A-level.

II : THE STORY OF THE SCHOOL

The Long-Serving Masters

Name	Degree	College/University	Start	End	Years
I. J. Nicholas	MA	Jesus College, Oxford	1932	1973	41
H. C. Phillips	ARCA	Royal College of Art	1934	1973	39
J. H. Butler	BA	Saint Catherine's Society, Oxford	1936	1975	39
C. A. Pine		Carnegie College, Leeds	1938	1975+	37+
J. G. Dunning	MA, FRGS	Peterhouse, Cambridge	1932	1966	34
R. V. S. Ward	BSc (Econ)	University College, Nottingham	1941	1975+	34+
A. Jackson	MA, PhD	University College, London	1939	1970	31
H. A. Wrenn	MA	Christ Church, Oxford	1946	1975	29
M. S. Cheale	BSc (Eng)	London University	1947	1975+	28+
R. H. Temple	MA	Queens' College, Cambridge	1948	1975+	27+
A. E. Sparrow	MA	Downing College, Cambridge	1949	1975+	26+
J. W. Huddart	BSc (Hons)	Manchester University	1952	1975+	23+
A. W. Leftwich	BSc, FZS	London University	1947	1969	22
J. P. Hyde*		Loughborough College	1954	1975+	21+
T. J. C. Sulch	MSc	Nottingham University	1955	1975+	20+
W. Holmes	MSc	Manchester University	1944	1963	19
B. R. Burrell	MA	Keble College, Oxford	1942	1958	16
C. J. H. Ward	BSc	London University	1946	1962	16
J. E. Barker	CBE, BA	Jesus College, Cambridge	1958	1974	16
A. J. B. Tussler	BA, FRGS	Keble College, Oxford	1959	1975+	16+
R. Bentley	BSc	Birmingham University	1960	1975+	15+
C. W. F. Laurie	BA	St John's College, Oxford	1931	1945	14
A. R. Chesters	BMus	Manchester University	1961	1975+	14+
E. L. Hole	BA	Emmanuel College, Cambridge	1930	1943	13
T. G. Cook	BA	St Catherine's College, Cambridge	1943	1955	12
L. E. Bratt	BA	Lincoln College, Oxford	1943	1954	11
R. B. Taylor		Winchester College	1964	1975	11
T. G. Tomlinson		Loughborough College	1964	1975+	11+
D. S. Wilson*	BA	Leeds University	1964	1975+	11+

* denotes Old Boys. The end date 1975+ indicates teachers staying on in The Wrenn School in 1975

Chapter 2

Long-Serving Staff

The backbone of Wellingborough Grammar School lay in its long-serving staff, including Miss Nora Bavin, who served as School Secretary for 42 years from April 1931 to April 1973.

In this chapter we focus on the characters who arrived in the thirties and early forties, including all of those who stayed for ten years or more. Three of them taught from the 1930s to the 1970s: Mr Ivor Nicholas (aka 'Nick' or 'Tinbum'), 'Eddie' Phillips and 'Johnny' Butler. These would be familiar both to many younger boys present when the school opened and to older boys at the school when it closed. With four other characters—'Chunky' Pine, 'Jake' Dunning, 'Beery' Ward and 'Spike' (aka 'Alf' or 'Doc') Jackson — they all taught at the school for more than thirty years. Two others ('Froggy' Hole and 'Uncle' Laurie) spanned most of the reign of the first two headmasters. Four more – 'Danny' Burrell, 'Hobo' Cook, 'Lennie' Bratt, and 'Father' Holmes – arrived during the war and stayed on for more than a decade. These are the fundamental *dramatis personae* in the first part of our story during the tenure of Mr Lay and Mr Woolley, together with a supporting cast of other characters who also made their mark. Those who arrived to take up the torch after the war will be considered in detail in a later chapter.

Nora Bavin: School Secretary Extraordinaire

As secretary from 1931 to her retirement in 1973, Miss Bavin will be remembered by virtually every boy who attended the school. In a nutshell, she exemplified the school and its highest qualities. She gave unstintingly to the life of the school, and yet was a rounded personality who knew, supported, and cared for every individual boy.

Miss Bavin was far more than the ever-present secretary, always available in the office at the front of the school. She not only stood in the corridor in the morning to make sure that no boy used the front corridor as a thoroughfare, she was there to receive late-comers, organise the registers, provide exercise books, type the letters, look after lost property, and minister to the sick.

She was willing to turn her hand to anything—as treasurer of the Parents' Committee, and as support for the Dramatic Society, Music Society, Railway Club and the Scouts. During the war she cooked meals for the boys at agricultural camp and refereed hockey matches between the Sixth Form and the Girls' High School. Year after year, she assisted in the make-up for the school play, giving special assistance to those boys playing female roles who needed to look the part.

She was also responsible for obtaining and organizing the prizes for Parents' Day—a service which Mr Wrenn was quick to acknowledge at the prize-giving of 1949:

> *Parents and boys should welcome the opportunity of thanking publically that lady without whom the school would cease to function. Nominally the School Secretary, she willingly undertook a host of other duties. The average small boy had a most intensive programme. He spent the school day assiduously losing every article he possessed while acquiring those of other people; he continually invented methods of lacerating his clothing, he stopped cricket balls with every possible part of his anatomy, and he developed a sick headache before any period for which he had not done the required preparation. From all these emergencies he was unfailingly rescued by Miss Bavin.*
>
> *Harold Wrenn (Parents' Day, 1949)*

Ever-present Miss Bavin and Mr Nicholas, always in support on Parents' Day, here with Sir Lawrence Bragg, presenting a prize to Peter Wooding in 1961

She was particularly well organised on the day when the examination results arrived from the Oxford Local Examination Syndicate:

> *Miss Bavin would be up with the Lark to meet the 4.30 am postal deliveries from Oxford to Wellingborough. By special agreement with the Post Office, she would take the exam results home, enter each boy's results in his own letter, and then rush the letters back to the post office. They would be posted by 6.00 am and reach the boys the same day.*
>
> *Evening Telegraph (1973)*

Miss Bavin knew the names of all the boys in the school and clearly remembered them long after they left, as noted by an old boy whose daughter later joined the Girl Guides:

> *When my daughter went from Guides to Rangers, Miss Bavin was in charge of the Rangers. The girls were all terrified of Miss Bavin, and when she came home, my daughter said, "we had to call her Nora and not Miss B.," and also, "what did Dad do when he was at school?", as Nora had said to her, "Ah, Gennis, I remember your father well at Wellingborough Grammar School!" I assured her that I did nothing that could possibly have affected Miss Bavin, (or did she see the boys running around the quad drying after showers?)*
>
> *Keith Gennis (1943–47)*

Miss Bavin became the Wellingborough District Commissioner for Guides and, in the year of her retirement, was elected President of the National Association of School Secretaries.

Celebrating her work at the 50th Anniversary of the Old Boys in 1988, Mr Wrenn said:

> *More than any other person Miss Bavin symbolises to Old Grammarians their schooldays. In addition to her secretarial duties, she was fully involved in almost every aspect of school life from the very beginning, especially in the Drama Club, the Music Society, the Railway Club and the Scouts. She was not only highly efficient but could work at phenomenal speed and had a fantastic memory. Even when the School reached 600, she not only knew all the boys by name but a great deal more about them than they suspected. Miss Bavin was equally well-known over the years to thousands of parents. She was treasurer of the Parents' Committee and, together with Mrs Webb, Mrs Wrenn and the parents, raised the larger*

part of the funds with which the Old Grammarians original memorial field was bought, and on which their present fortunes are founded.

Mr Wrenn (1988)

She also kept her own scrapbooks of the school, with entries from the opening of the school to events in 1973 when she retired. The two scrapbooks are hand-made and suggest the hands of Mr Phillips who had a talent for binding books.

Included in the scrapbooks are not only cuttings from local newspapers, such as this one of her studying the pages of the first book, but also many original photographs and proof copies from the press that provide most of the illustrations in this book. The influence of Miss Bavin lives on in this legacy she left to us. The scrapbooks are now in the safe keeping of the Old Boys Association.

MISS Bavin has two thousand names to draw on for her memories. And to help her she keeps this giant scrapbook about the school and its past and present pupils.

The Masters

The 'characters' that gave the school its own special flavour began arriving in the thirties. Two of the pioneers, 'Froggy' Hole and 'Uncle' Laurie served almost throughout the time of the first two headmasters. The first long-serving masters 'Nick' and 'Jake', arrived in 1932, followed later in the thirties by 'Eddie', 'Johnny', 'Chunky' and 'Spike'. During the war came 'Beery', 'Danny', 'Hobo', 'Lennie' and 'Father'.

All of them worked in a school typical of its time. In the thirties, forties and fifties, children were expected to be respectful of their elders, to work diligently and to do as they were told: "children should be seen and not heard." School was a place where the young were educated to take their place in society, enriched in mind, body and spirit.

Young boys were seen as full of energy that needed to be channelled into many activities to keep them fully occupied with their educational development. "The devil makes work for idle hands," so teachers kept their pupils busy to keep their natural exuberance from leading them astray.

The message, reiterated in countless speech days, was to work hard and play hard:

> *I'm sorry I cannot give you an easy way to success. ... Work and more work is the first step up the ladder.* *Sir Alexander Fleming (1954)*

> *Over-specialization ... industrial leaders complained that some boys came from fine grammar schools and universities excessively specialised without general interests and unaware of the world around them. They were only interested in chemistry, physics and mathematics.*
> *Mr Hallward, Vice Chancellor of Nottingham University (1956)*

> *There is no success that is complete unless integrity of mind can be added to it.* *Lord Birkett (1960)*

> *Avoid boredom ... you have the right to enjoy life, including work, play and hobbies, and I advise you all to have hobbies.*
> *Alderman W. Penn (1961)*

> *Education does not end with schooldays and the most important thing to carry from school is the ability to continue learning.*
> *Lord Mountbatten of Burma (1966)*

To provide a liberal education after this fashion required masters to set high standards and give freely of their time to run clubs, societies and trips both home and abroad. Corporal punishment was the norm and many masters had their own particular method of adminstering it. Some had sticks or slippers with names such as 'Twanker', 'George', 'Arthur' or 'Cuthbert', wielded as the automatic consequence of any misdemeanor, however, slight. Others used a slipper with a touch of humour to maintain both order and willing cooperation. A few used no physical punishment at all; some had the presence to command authority without effort, while others suffered the ignominy of losing control.

Most boys seem to remember the Grammar School with affection, but a few have bad memories of the school and the teachers:

I hated WGS with a passion. I remember doing cartwheels down Doddington Rd the day I escaped! Lately I've been curious to find out how people are. A lot of the comments trigger memories. Most of the teachers I couldn't stand seem to be highly thought of. Must be me!
David Lodge (1955–60)

My time at WGS was so awful that I must have blotted it out. ... Glad that I wasn't the only one persecuted by Cyril Pine, or who felt that Spike Jackson was a very silly old person. Who was that teacher (sorry, Master) who used to 'ruler' us? *Frank Chambers (1961–66)*

The great majority of old boys, however, were highly appreciative of their time at WGS and what they learned from the masters. The affection and esteem in which their old teachers were held is evident in the many fond memories recalled by pupils over fifty years later. This is exemplified in the many reunions organised by old boys who look back at their time at Wellingborough Grammar School in a positive light.

Masters from Thirties

Only two masters who arrived in the first two years of the school remained in the early forties: Mr Hole (1930–1943) and Mr Laurie (1931–1945).

'Froggy' Hole (French) 1930–1943

Mr E. L. Hole remained at the school longer than any other teacher present at its opening. Appointed to teach French in 1930, he brought with him a range of other talents, as a cricket coach, and as a musician with a fine tenor voice and the ability to play the piano. He was known as 'Froggy' or 'Wookey' (after Wookey Hole in the Cheddar Gorge). As Second Master from 1939–1943, he was a constant source of support not only to the School, but to the Old Grammarians, being present at its inauguration in 1934 and serving as its Chairman from 1943 to 1945.

He was a leading figure in establishing the standards of the school, enhancing the musical life in concerts, performing as tenor soloist, piano duettist, and also singing in choral and chamber groups.

His work with school cricket took time to develop, as the young boys in the school team struggled at first but then produced creditable performances in later years. He gave much of his time and energy in the week and on Saturday mornings. It was said that many local cricketers owed their forward defensive strokes to sound 'Hole' coaching.

He introduced Esperanto as the initial language learnt for a time at the beginning of the war, and for two years he shared the production of school plays with Dr Jackson. He supported the school camp in summer, sharing the cooking with Mr Dunning and Mr Wintersgill. He left in the Summer of 1943 to take up an appointment at the Merchant Taylors' School in Hertfordshire.

'Uncle' Laurie (Mathematics) 1931–1945

Mr C. W. F. Laurie arrived in 1931 to teach mathematics and retired in 1945 at the end of the war. He was considered by the boys to be one of the most eccentric individuals in the school, characterized by his catch-phrase "How much?" which regularly punctuated his conversation. His final years in the school culminated in the first students in mathematics and science to be awarded scholarships at Oxford and Cambridge.

He was of ample girth and was said to enjoy large helpings at dinner, washed down with a few beers at the Hind Hotel that were likely to cause him to fall asleep in the afternoon. In his time outside school he had a farm at Byfield near Daventry.

> *Laurie was reputed to be more interested in the pigs he raised than in his teaching – he was certainly very idiosyncratic. He and Mr Woolley were supposed to be competing in the size of their families.*
>
> *John Rodhouse (1940–45)*

On his retirement, he was fêted by the boys cheering loudly as he walked amongst them at morning assembly, declaring he would use the money collected for him to buy a new pig. We will hear more of his exploits later in stories related by the boys who knew him.

The Longest Serving Masters in the School

The longest serving masters arrived during the thirties in the following order: Mr Nicholas (41 years), Mr Dunning (34), Mr Phillips (39), Mr Butler (39), Mr Pine (37) and Dr Jackson (31). The only other master serving longer than 30 years was Mr R. V. S. Ward who arrived in 1941. The life and vitality of the school was very much driven by these highly individual originals.

Ivor J. 'Nick' Nicholas (Latin) 1932–1973

Mr I. J. Nicholas was the longest serving master at Wellingborough Grammar School. He arrived in 1932 to teach Latin, and the school was to benefit greatly from his sporting prowess, not only on the field in rugby and cricket, but also in his knowledge of the wider administration of the game. In those early years, Mr Clayton was in charge of rugby and 'Nick' made his presence felt by coaching at school and playing cricket and rugby in the town. When Mr Clayton left in 1939, he took over the school first fifteen and began a long-term development of school rugby.

While his colleagues, Messrs Butler, Dunning, Phillips and Pine were called to service in the war, Mr Nicholas, ostensibly one of the fittest on the staff, was declared medically unfit for service on the grounds that he had 'flat feet'. He responded by taking command of the school's newly-formed Air Training Corps (1941–1946), drilling his squadron of boys on the school playground. He and his fellow officer, Dr Adamson, soon became skilled in morse code, aircraft recognition and navigation and passed on their knowledge to the cadets. He was soon at home leading his squadron to Sywell for a flight in a Tiger Moth or to an American airbase to study a Flying Fortress.

When the Second Master, Mr Hole, left in 1943, with several of his experienced colleagues away at war, Mr Nicholas was the most obvious candidate to be appointed to the post. He remained the central bulwark of the school for the next thirty years, briefly as acting head in the autumn of 1945 between the reigns of Mr Woolley and Mr

Wrenn, organising the time-table and, when a gap appeared, he filled it, teaching not only Latin, but history, divinity and English.

His leadership on the rugby field took spectacular flight after the war as three boys successively played for the English Schools XV (Johnny Hyde, 1949; Bob Leslie 1950; John Whiffing, 1951) and two became full English internationals (Don White, 1947; Johnny Hyde, 1950).

As he grew older, he supported the Old Grammarians Association as an active member of their committee, as President (1945–7) and then as an ever-present influence in the Old Boys' Rugby Club. During his latter years, when his active engagement in school rugby finished, he remained a moving spirit in the school while becoming less evident to the boys who were not taught by him.

Boys, being boys, gave him an alternative nickname. His own name of 'Ivor Nicholas' in scatological boy's humour suggested 'I've a nickel-arse' and he became known for a time as 'Tin Bum', a name which seemed in no way to diminish his stature. For the rest of the time he was known as 'Nick' or 'Ivor'. He was always there at prayers in the morning, silently in support of the Headmaster, quietly getting on with his administration within the school.

He took Latin in a formal style:

He always addressed us as "O", as in "Pray continue reading, O Cook."
John Cook (1947–52)

Mr Nicholas taught Latin – and always translated "statim" as "in the nick of time."
John Rodhouse (1940–45)

If you had Tinbum for Latin you'll remember, "Most iniquitous, most reprehensible, Page 64!"
Graham Walden (1957–64)

In his Latin lessons he could sometimes seem on 'autopilot' as he repeated a lesson he had taught many times before: "Discipulae, picturam spectate", "amo, amas, amat, amamus, amatis, amant." Those needing Latin to enter Oxford or Cambridge were to benefit from his solid training and remain forever in his debt.

Throughout his career, he remained a stoic and essentially private character: solid and dependable, the rock on which the school was built. Indeed, as second master, he ruled his colleagues in the Common Room with a rod of iron. Even Beery Ward put down his hand of cards when the bell had gone and Nick ordered him to get to his classroom.

John G. 'Jake' Dunning (Geography) 1932–1966

It is difficult to know where to begin describing Jake. He was a martinet in the classroom, capable of tearing a boy's exercise book in half because he was disgusted with the standard of the work. He would then give the lad another book and tell him to re-enter everything properly.

On other occasions, to check how accurately a map had been traced, he would hold up the tracing paper to the light to see if the lines on the two sides coincided; if they didn't, the perpetrator was in serious trouble. He never told the boys precisely what they were required to do, like several other teachers, he simply assumed that a pupil should *know* what to do without being given detailed instructions.

Yet, probably more than any other, he gave his whole life to the school. Who was it that started off the School Magazine? Mr Dunning. Who organised the early school athletics schedules, the seating for the school photographs, the choices for the school excursions? Mr Dunning. When the first Scout Master, Mr Clayton, left in 1939, and his replacement, Mr Pine, and others, left for the war, it was he who took over and for the rest of his time in school, he spent his holidays leading the troop at camp, organising everything, including the cooking. When the Toc H Group started in the 1950s, he was there to guide it.

He never married, living at home with his sister. In essence he was wedded to the school, focusing on his vision of excellence, pushing ahead in a way which could be more than many others could take, both staff and pupils. He was an unstoppable force, driven incessantly by an inner demon seeking nothing but the best.

One tactic he used with new classes was to start by asking the boys to work out the time in one part of the world, given the time somewhere else. Having said once that the world revolved 360° in 24 hours, so that it turned 15° every hour, he then gave the latitude of one town and the time there and asked for the time at a given latitude elsewhere. He never explained again, but simply gave the test every time he took the class until every boy got it right.

He left indelible images on his pupils long after they had left:

Jake Dunning wasn't one of my favourite teachers. I could never understand why we had to rush from PE to Geography for one of his tests and why I could only manage to arrive there in time for question 9. As a result of my tardiness I was given a detention. I was the only detainee that evening and, having set me my task, Jake left the room. After about 20 minutes I needed a pee but, to my amazement and anger, Jake had locked the classroom door. My feelings were really confused as my mind flipped between physical necessity and a sense of outrage that he had not trusted me to stay in the room and fulfil my detention.

I am amazed that this 46-year-old incident can still raise such a strong emotion and it indelibly colours my view of a man who, to many, was an inspiration. *Pete Jackson (1955–62)*

No-one in their right mind crossed Jake. Yet those who knew him in his capacity as a leader in Scouts or in his support for the school Toc H group saw a completely different character. He used his car to help Toc H members collect jumble for the annual sale and helped them assign prices to the items (two shillings for a coat, with baby clothes priced slightly higher than children's). He organised classes of boys as his 'printing press' to write out notes requesting jumble which would then be slipped into letterboxes prior to the collection.

He was always decisive when action needed to be taken:

At a summer fruit picking camp at Evesham, three or four boys and I went to climb Bredon Hill. On our return, we were accosted by some youths from the village of Elmley Castle who took various things off our bikes – bike lamps etc. Returned to camp we at once told JG who was galvanised into action. Dressed in his standard camp gear of rugger shirt and shorts he leapt into his faithful Hillman Minx and motioned to us to join him. We were soon back in Elmley Castle and Mr Dunning pulled up outside the house of the village Bobby. Based on our descriptions and the latter's obvious knowledge of his patch, he soon rounded up the ringleaders and found the stolen items. The gang leader was a young soldier and the policeman demanded to see his Army Pay Book which he then studied in great detail and made notes. The soldier lad was obviously much discomfited and crestfallen by this action. (I was to learn of the significance of Pay Books some seven years later when I was called up for National Service.) The miscreants were given a stern lecture. *Michael King (1942–49)*

Many boys eventually realised his true worth. As a relentless force in teaching he had a fine record of getting weaker boys through their O-level examinations and, as boys looked back on their whole experience, they were more likely to see him in a different light:

One of my lasting memories is how scared I was of Jake Dunning in my first term at the school and how precise we had to be in our work and knowledge. I really saw what a fine man he was when I joined the school Scout Troop which he ran with Mr Stanley, the music master.

Jake was a man of unimpeachable integrity who always worked hard for the boys and only really became annoyed when people fell below the highest standards of honesty, openness and hard work. I actually still have my exercise book from that first term, it must be a museum piece.

He must have influenced me, because when I went to London University, what did I do? Geography of course, and then spent the next 35 years teaching it. Perhaps a little bit of Jake resides in the knowledge that some of my past pupils have now? Peter Godfrey (1955–60)

A great geography teacher who kept us on our toes but still imparted an enthusiasm for his subject. He was also rumoured to have a strong influence on the running of the school. Tim Thompson (1956–61)

H. C. 'Eddie' Phillips (Art) 1934–1973

Mr H. C. Phillips arrived in 1934 from the Royal College of Art to teach at the school. Known as 'Eddie' to all schoolboys, his names were actually Horatio Cornelius. In common with other masters, he had several aspects to his character. As a Baptist Lay Preacher, he saw service to the community as a priority, and as an art teacher he combined mastery of art history with a practical technique in painting, drawing, woodwork, book-binding and various other aspects of art.

Super chap. He influenced me greatly in art and gave me a love of Gothic architecture. He ran the Puppet Club and was a very sincere man. He had a fabulous italic handwriting style. Norman Keech (1963–70)

I remember after doing a painting, he told me off for drawing the outline of everybody before shading them in. I never understood his criticism, after all Frank Hampson always had outlines around his Dan Dare characters and, what was good enough for Digby, was certainly good enough for me. *Graham Tall (1955–63)*

He had a range of advice to instil sensible ways of working with materials. For instance, he showed us how to cut with a Stanley knife by using a ruler or other guide held down firmly and to cut in towards the guide, making several light strokes of the knife.

Mr Phillips always gave good advice: "Measure twice, cut once ..."
Gary Griffiths (1952–58)

He was responsible for a range of clubs and activities, overseeing the boxing with Mr Page and founding a Model Aeroplane Club before the war. In 1947 he founded and ran the Puppet Club (with a little help from Mr Pine in constructing the stage for puppet shows). Those of us fortunate enough to work in the club learned to construct string puppets with *papier mâché* heads and wooden bodies which were used in puppet shows for local schools and organisations, especially in the Christmas period.

He used his own mode of punishment to bring errant boys into line:

To think I shall never again be invited by my favourite art master, Eddie Phillips to stand in the middle of the quad for an hour or so to reflect on my recent misdemeanour and to ponder on the progress of my academic career.

1. How clever I had been to get sent out from what I considered was a useless art lesson?

2. How not so clever had I been to choose the early stages of a double lesson so that I had to stand there feeling an absolute prat whilst the rest of the school wandered by sniggering from 15 paces as they changed classes?

*3. How bl***y stupid had I been to get sent out on a *** cold November morning instead of a nice summer's day?*

4. At least I know how a rain gauge works.

David Spencer (1955–59)

'Johnny' H. Butler (Mathematics) 1936–1975

John H. Butler was the mathematics master who spent the whole of his teaching career at Wellingborough Grammar School. He arrived straight from Oxford in 1936 and retired as Head of Mathematics in 1975 when the school became comprehensive. He was an enigmatic and gentle soul who needed only his love of mathematics and his firm sense of purpose to maintain discipline in class. Physical punishment was not an option for him. While he took pleasure in teaching the most able boys preparing for open scholarships at Oxford and Cambridge, he also took his responsibilities seriously as Head of Mathematics by helping the less able boys in the C-stream to prepare for the Ordinary Level General Certificate of Education.

> *'Johnny' Butler took us for maths and I have always been grateful for his encouragement which did wonders for my O-level. Mind, he did hit the buffers with us when he tried to teach the sixth-form biologists calculus, of which none of us could make head nor tail.*
>
> *Richard Hall (1946–54)*

In later years, he volunteered to be form master for the most unruly boys in the one-off class 5X mentioned earlier. While they would play havoc with other teachers, he was said to hold them "in the palm of his hand." One of them later explained that he succeeded because he saw the good in every one of them and could see that they were capable of achievement when everyone else had written them off.

One of us (David Tall) is a viola player and had the special joy of working with him both as mathematician and musician. He was an accomplished musician, playing the clarinet with a clear, liquid tone that was especially suitable for his beloved Mozart, be it in the Clarinet Concerto, the Clarinet Quintet, or the Trio for Clarinet, Viola and Piano. This latter item featured regularly in concerts throughout his career as others passed through the school and had the privilege of playing with him. He also started a thriving recorder group.

While 'Johnny', as we knew him (but always 'Mr Butler' to his face), was an inspiring teacher, he always focused on the things that needed doing and refrained from giving his more able pupils praise for partial achievement. David Tall writes:

> *Mr Butler praised me only once. In the sixth form I finished the two years of calculus in a term for Mr Mardell, but Mr Butler was not convinced of my commitment to the full range of my study in mathematics because I spent more time on Chemistry and Physics, which I found more demanding. In my lower sixth report he wrote, "If his effort matched his enthusiasm, he could be a competent mathematician." My mother was furious. Everyone else, including Mr Wrenn, gave me glowing comments. I defended him by declaring, "he is the only one with any standards." Events proved he was right.*
>
> *When I first took entrance examinations at Cambridge, he refused to give me papers to practice, saying that I should not expect to be successful at this stage, as I had not covered enough of the syllabus. After the exam, the Master of Magdalen College wrote to the Headmaster, Mr Wrenn, saying of my attempt, "If this man expects to go to university, he should try places other than Oxford and Cambridge." He considered me inadequate to study maths at Oxbridge.*
>
> *Mr Butler's vision was longer-term. Although he gave praise to encourage less able boys, he gave me absolutely no praise for travelling part of the way; he could see the longer journey and there was so much to do. A year later, under his tutelage, I gained an Open Scholarship to Oxford. I rushed to the school with my acceptance letter and showed it to Mr Wrenn who beamed and said, "Well done, David." This made me feel strangely out of place; it was the first time he called me by my first name and I found it over-familiar!*
>
> *Outside, I met Johnny Butler in his gardening clothes and Wellington boots, pushing a wheelbarrow of potatoes from his allotment on the school ground to his house in Croyland Road. I showed him the letter. He smiled and said, "I'm pleased." Then he turned and went on his way.*
>
> *After three years at Oxford I was awarded the University Mathematics Prize given to the top three students in Finals. It was a singular success. Yet when I saw Mr Butler many years later and commented on his lack of praise, he responded by telling me of another boy from the school whom he considered to be even better!*
>
> *When he died, I recalled that brief moment of praise and treasured it more than all the easy gestures from others. As I commiserated with his*

wife, Peggy, sometime later, I mentioned to her that he never gave any praise while I was at school. "Oh, but he wouldn't," she said, "it wasn't his way." *David Tall (1952–60)*

Cyril A. 'Chunky' Pine (PE and Physics) 1938–1975+

The nickname was very apt, Chunky was a short—one could never call him small—man who was extremely solid. He was one of only a handful of the long-serving teachers who didn't have a degree—a fact that was very evident at speech days, when he was one of the very few who didn't have a gown to wear. He was, however, responsible for the sound system and if anything failed to work, it was he who went into action.

In the mid-fifties, he shifted from teaching PE to concentrate more on Physics. In the sixth form he clearly read the book just a lesson ahead of having to teach it—yet he never seemed inadequate as a teacher.

He had a reputation as someone over-fond of using Bunsen burner tubing to punish miscreants and his sense of humour was clearly misunderstood by many.

A superb teacher of physics who had a most wonderful sense of humour. A truly lovable little guy! *Tim Kearsley (1973–75+)*

The only master I can remember is Chunky Pine, who regularly thwacked me with his bunsen burner tube.
Clive 'Dixie' Dean (1967–70)

Each year he illustrated Newton's third law of motion, "For every action there is an equal and opposite reaction," by lining up a row of boys and charging them from the left. The audience could then see that, whilst all the boys on the left and middle stayed stationary, there was an equal and opposite reaction on the right with one or two boys bouncing off into the corridor.

Chunky was well-known as a square-dance caller and ran a country dancing club after the war.

"We have always been looking for something to help shy boys to mix more easily with girls," said the Grammar School headmaster Mr H. A.

Wrenn. "Then we thought of square dancing which doesn't put the boy in the embarrassing position of having to ask a girl to dance." Mr C. A. Pine, the school's physical training instructor said, "about 50 boys meet about 50 girls for dancing once a week after school, between 4.00 and 5.45 pm. Occasionally there is a later 'social evening' with party games. There are no rules for the club ... If boys like to escort girls home they may. They are all well-behaved and we never have complaints."

Newspaper cutting 1950/51

He regularly called at public dances in Northampton and in the surrounding villages. Even when performing for paying customers, he refused to accept expenses when the takings were nominal.

There was an apocryphal story that his short stature resulted from his feet being blown off during the war, then re-attached minus a portion of his legs! Unlikely. But I remember his motorbike. He took us for swimming over at Wilby. Those of us that normally travelled in by United Counties Bus were supposed to cycle in on swimming days, so as to then be able to cycle over to Wilby. If we failed to cycle in, the choice was between walking to Wilby or hoping for a lift with his motorbike. Since he had rather a large sidecar attached, he could normally manage one on the pillion and two in the sidecar with him driving kitted out in goggles, white helmet and long riding coat. Without his lift, the walking option gave about 5 minutes in the pool before having to change and walk back again.

Paul Robinson (1955–62)

Dr A. 'Spike' Jackson (English) 1939–1970

Everyone remembers Dr Jackson; his appearance and voice were so distinctive that, in his absence, he was *the* teacher to imitate. He awarded 'goods' for anything and everything, and stories of his behaviour and his use of his 'Twanker' called 'George' abound. At first the boys called him 'Alf', 'Jacko', or 'Doc', but as time past, he became universally known as 'Spike'; the reasons are lost in the eons of time, but they may have had something to do with the black homburg hat and overcoat that he wore which made him look like a Cockney spiv. To describe his presence and his effect on his pupils, the only possible way is to recount some of the stories.

Dr Jackson came to the school at the beginning of the war, full of Cockney cheer and ready to negotiate to make the best of the privations that were part of everyday life:

> *The first impression of Dr Jackson was his making the acquaintance of a new intake by asking if anyone kept a shop, or knew anyone that did, who might be able to provide a bit of butter or a pot of jam.*
>
> *Jim Tompkins (1944–48)*

> *When he first met my class we were introduced to acting — Doc called this 'Drama'. It was done by first moving the desks to provide room and then asking each group to perform a 'Tableau', 'Mime', or 'Action' for a subject of his choice, banging his 'tocsin' (bell) to start them off, and awarding marks at the end.*
>
> *At the close of each drama lesson the desks had to be lined up and extra marks would be awarded to the group whose row was the straightest.*
>
> *He always referred to us boys as 'gents' in that nasal cockney accent of his. I remember there was a boy who sat at the back corner seat on the right looking forward who had a book and if you spoke he entered your name in it for punishment. Dr Jackson's system was three 'whacks' on the backside with what he called 'the Twanker'. This was made of wood and was off the front of a school desk which acted as a buffer against other desks. I think it was about 15 inches long 4 inches wide and three eighths of an inch thick.* *Keith Gennis (1943–47)*

To deal with the fines that were collected during the term, Spike used his experience as a gambler to dispense the ill-gotten gains back to the pupils. He would invite the boys to bet on which direction a pointer would end up when he spun it and the winners got portions of the money until it was exhausted.

His classes were always unpredictable. He would award 'goods' for almost anything: "Jones, I like your knees. Three goods for Jones's knees." When he got excited as he spoke, he often covered the front few rows with a fine spray of spittle. Whatever he did was always unexpected and always intriguing.

He would give his pupils nicknames and use them throughout their school career.

I went to the Grammar School in September 1942. Having mysteriously won a 'Free Place' in the annual exams (this was before the 1944 Education Act), I was allocated a place in Form 2A1 so our Form Master was Dr Jackson. He made us feel welcome and initiated us into the mysteries of Grammar School life. His accent seemed to be very east London. His common opening gambit at the start of a lesson was to say "Well gents." His opening address to me was to say "Well König." That was about the only German word I knew so I was able to respond appropriately. There was, I'm sure, no motive to catch me out and I felt quite pleased to show my knowledge in front of my classmates.

Michael King (1942–49)

Despite, or because of, his great eccentricity, Dr Jackson could have a remarkable effect on the development of his pupils, using a mixture of humour, good-natured banter and positive encouragement:

I owe my nickname 'Squatter' to Spike Jackson, though I suspect that my brother Chris resented being called 'Squatter Jr' two years later. Spike was one of my WGS heroes. If you could avoid 'George', the tocsin, and the inevitable spray, his classes were always enjoyable, even though his drama classes were total chaos. As a child I had problems with public speaking — I had a severe stutter when I was nervous. Spike helped me to overcome my anxieties. Public speaking is now my profession.

Paul Scroxton (1965–72)

Dr Jackson substantially reduced his marking workload by the simple expedient of getting boys to mark their neighbour's books. At other times, a whole set of books would be given to a boy in the A-stream — and he didn't moderate the marking! There is some evidence that, on at least one occasion, Mr Wrenn became aware of this, and asked boys if they had been marking work for Dr Jackson, but in traditional protective mode, the boys never admitted the deed and Spike carried on, uninterrupted. As one of his pupils was to observe:

It could be said that he tort us to deligate but not to spel.

Richard Adkins (1950–57)

Mr Wrenn coped manfully with his head of English. When Dr Jackson retired, Mr Wrenn invited David Wilson to take over as subject head. David was somewhat taken aback as he understood that Dr Jackson had another candidate in mind. "Doctor Jackson," said Mr Wrenn, "is a cross I've had to bear for the last twenty-five years."

Whatever his weaknesses and strengths, Dr Jackson remains one of the true characters who made Wellingborough Grammar School one of the most remarkable experiences a boy could have. Everyone who knew him has a 'Spike' story to tell:

> *Spike Jackson's lessons were memorable, not least in my case. When we were reading out loud around the class I would get out less than half a dozen words before Spike would call out, "Blimey, that's aw'l – next." It wasn't that there was anything wrong with my reading ability, but I must have learnt to speed read at quite an early age and this doesn't reflect well in audible reading and makes one painfully slow in order to pick out all of the words to enunciate.* Richard Hall (1946–54)

Peter Jackson recalls:

> *I've dozens of memories of Spike, including the misfortune of being his namesake which, apparently, entitled me to two strokes from 'George' when my less lucky classmates only received one. However, the most memorable was a story he told against himself, the images from which still make me chuckle.*
>
> *Not long after the M1 had opened, Spike decided to take his family for a ride on this exciting new road in his recently acquired Vauxhall. He had on some previous occasions suggested that his young brood were not always easily controlled and this proved to be one such time. Taken with the novelty of the journey and the vehicle, they delighted in rolling down the windows, sounding the horn, flashing the lights and generally creating a degree of mayhem which he found intolerable, so he stopped! In the centre lane of the M1.*
>
> *First period: Maths for class 4B with Charlie Ward in Room 2. Jake and Ernie have just parked when Spike turns into the drive. Ernie has put his briefcase on the ground behind his car and is having a word with Jake. Spike seeks to park his car behind Ernie's but there is only a relatively small space into which to manoeuvre. So comical are these attempts that Maths is forgotten and even Ernie and Jake appear enthralled. Eventually success seems imminent when there is a shout from Ernie who rushes to the rear of his car but, alas, too late: Spike has crushed his case. Class 4B collapses into gales of laughter to be*

silenced by, "Alright, joke over," from the wonderful Charlie Ward. "I think it's a record, Mr Pine."

If you were fortunate enough to have Spike in a period coinciding with any major horse race, you could guarantee his absence for a large chunk of that lesson.

Caricature of Spike
by G R (Roy) Pettit 1955–59
aided and abetted by art master
'Eddie' Phillips

He had a free-standing cupboard in his room which I never saw him open until, in the 6th form, he suddenly remembered that he might have some relevant notes on Thompson's 'Winter' therein. After some difficulty with the lock he triumphantly flung wide the doors only to be deluged with paper. He took one look at the resulting chaos and decided to rely on his memory. A wonderful man. *Pete Jackson (1955–62)*

While all the other teachers at least related to other men we knew, Spike was a one-off:

A regret that schools today are increasingly lacking some of the characters on the staff who were so vivid and eccentric. I suppose 'Spike' stands head and shoulders in my memory — the 'goods', the fines, the glorious drama in one of the prefabs, an ability to wipe the board with the tail of his gown whilst remaining seated, the rusting Vauxhall Velox — and the English somewhere amongst all that! *Kevin Street (1963–70)*

There was the irrepressible — and what is often forgotten, highly intelligent — Dr Jackson — Spike — the imitation of whom has become a cottage industry among even those who never went to the Grammar School. His most famous moment came when he stamped in the staff common room one day to announce, "I've just been doing Edgar Allen Poe's 'The raven' with 2B. You know the poem — Spake the raven, 'Nevermore', Saith the raven,'Nevermore', Quoth the raven, 'Nevermore'. Well, I said, 'Jones, what's the name of the bird in the poem?' 'Owl,' he said! Bloody owl!" *Richard Oberman (1953–61)*

For all his individuality, Spike was a warm person inside:

There are indeed all sorts of stories about Spike and he's given us a lot of laughs over the years but there was just one moment when I saw a different side of him. Spike was making me up in Room 8 behind the stage in December 1957 when I was Sir Wellington Hacker MP in 'The Party Spirit' (the reviews said my voice had not had enough years of port to give it the required crustiness – I've tried to put that right since). My father had died very suddenly and unexpectedly in early November. Spike was chatting away about nothing in particular but then suddenly he asked if my parents were coming to see the play. I hesitated and then said that my mother would be. As soon as I said that, he saw what he'd said, his face changed, the make-up sticks froze in his hands and he asked me to forgive him for forgetting and said "Sorry" about my Dad. It was such a genuine reaction and response and quite unlike anything else I ever saw or heard from or about him. A very genuine bloke. No wonder we remember him so well.

Jim Wilson (1952–59)

New Teachers in the War Years

During the war years, several of the regular teachers joined up, including Messrs Pine, Butler, Phillips and Dunning. Replacements were hard to find, often staying only for a short time before themselves being called up to fight for King and Country. Into this vacuum came the lady teachers, who we will meet later. The few masters who arrived in the war and stayed more than a decade were R. V. S. (Beery) Ward, B. R. (Danny) Burrell, T. G. (Hobo) Cook, L. E. (Lennie) Bratt, and W. (Father) Holmes.

R. V. S. 'Beery' Ward (Economics and History) 1941–1975+

Mr Ronald Victor Seeney Ward arrived as a temporary teacher in 1941 but, unlike his female colleagues, he was made a permanent member of staff by the end of the war. Nobody seemed to know why he was never called up. He claimed that he had sent in his papers, but never heard any more. When Mr Butler and Mr Dunning called in to the school on leave and found him warming his backside by the fire in the staff room, his presence was a topic of conversation. Mr Ward was comfortable at the school. He had his job, he had his regular chair in the staff-room and the *Telegraph* crossword to complete each day. At other times there was always a hand of cards to be played in the break as he relaxed with his faithful pipe.

I remember the morning assembly where Beery Ward put his pipe in his pocket without putting it out properly and his pocket started to smoke.
Adrian Coombes (1967–72)

He taught rugby and cricket and, as all staff were notionally treated as 'Old Boys', he often played for the Wellingborough Old Grammarians, serving as the secretary of their Rugby Club for several years.

His favorite weapon of torture was his slipper called 'Cuthbert', but even this did not give him the temperament to be a really good teacher. He was easily diverted in class to talk about other things, but he cared enough when he got behind in the syllabus to encourage the boys to come and study with him on the field as he umpired at cricket.

Mr Ward, affectionately known as Beery, was side-tracked with ease, You could go into a period and come out without opening the set book. He took six of the sixth form for economics and we didn't finish the set text. In the end he wanted us to go up to the cricket games whilst he was umpiring. We all refused, did the work ourselves and fortunately all passed the Oxford Higher School Certificate Economics subsidiary category. At one time he was near to death with a bad bout of pneumonia. He was a jolly character and I am sure he didn't do any harm; he stayed at the school for many years.
Gerald Neville (1943–50)

During his time in the school, his ways became legendary, and even affected the singing of the morning hymn in assembly. When the Hymn 'Immortal, Invisible' was announced in the sixties, it would be met by a murmur of excited anticipation, particulary among the more rebellious members of the 4th and 5th years.

One of Ron (Beery) Ward's many catchphrases was of course, "Splendid!" As the lines of the first verse of said hymn approached the significant word the tension would mount:

Immortal, invisible, God only wise,
In light inaccessible hid from our eyes,

[OK lads, start winding it up from here.]

Oh Lord we would RENDER, O help us to see,
'Tis only the SPLENDOUR of light hideth thee.

The masters could not have failed to notice it, in fact I'm sure they must have seen the funny side of it, but there was never any visible trace of amusement, or annoyance. Dave Toseland (1959–67)

David Wilson, who was both boy and master at the school, tells a good tale about Mr Ward and a cricket match at King's School Peterborough:

I used to edit the School Magazine and on one occasion, I was given the following result concerning the Under-15 cricket team:

"Wellingborough Grammar School 152, King's School, Peterborough 153. Result: Draw."

I was on the coach that day and knew what happened, so I told him that I wouldn't have it in the Magazine. It happened like this: the two matches finished, we had our tea and got on the coach, all except for Beery Ward, who did not arrive for half an hour. When he stepped onto the coach, he said, "Well chaps, I had a word with their umpire for a little while and we got a draw." David Wilson (1952–60, 1964–75)

He trained the younger school teams in rugby, taking a particular year successively through U-13, U-14 and U-15 and passing them on to the 2nd and 1st XVs:

Beery was responsible for teaching me to play rugby and I am forever grateful. I remember during the training we were not allowed to kick a ball at all and if we did we received a whack with the knotted rope that was attached to his whistle. Even when we started playing we were banned from kicking in the opponents '25' and I wonder what would happen if kids were taught the same way today. Although not the greatest coach he did instill the necessary discipline to provide us with a virtually unbeaten three years from U-13 to U-15 and a lot of the boys from my era went on to play at respectable levels, including Barry Waite who played twice for the USA. Beery also got me through O-Level economics in the sixth form by guessing what the bulk of the questions would consist of. As I needed this for the job I had been offered I was delighted when the forecasted questions came up.

Keith Shurville (1960–67)

R. V. S. Ward (Humph to some, but Beery to most) could always be relied on to digress from the matter in hand to talk about his very limited rugby experience at top level. A well-inserted and very subtle question such as:

"Please sir, is it very hard to play first class rugby?"

would invariably lead to half an hour, ending up with ...

"... so when I broke off the back of the scrum again, they started to call me ITMA. 'It's that man again,' they said. 'Splendid.'"

Richard Oberman (1953–61, 1964–5)

The story goes that Beery earned his Saints socks when he went to watch them play and they found themselves short of a man; Beery played for them because he was carrying his kit with him at the time.

Joe Keep (1933-36), reminiscing as an Old Boy

The truth is more prosaic. R. V. S. Ward did indeed play for the Saints. The official Northampton Saints record of players establishes once and for all that he played 47 times between 1940 and 1943, scoring two tries. He also introduced the young schoolboy Don White to the Saints and they were the two prop forwards in Don's debut game. Yet legend has replaced reality among the boys of Wellingborough Grammar School who see him in a different light:

Who was the boy who, when Beery Ward in an Economics class said: "When I was in the war . . .", asked, "Which war was that, sir?"

John Wittering (1955–62)

B. R. 'Danny' Burrell (French) 1942–1958

Danny Burrell arrived to teach French in 1942 and retired in 1943. But when his replacement struggled and left, he agreed to return to help out in a crisis and stayed for a total of sixteen years.

He was an amiable character, liable to fall asleep by the coke boiler in his classroom during lessons, but also much-loved by the boys.

Danny Burrell used to be in one of the old prefabs. He would get nearer and nearer to the boiler as the winter got colder and on one occasion he set fire to his bat-man's outfit, you know, his cloak [his schoolmaster's gown]. Smoke was rising and he stood there still prattling away in French. We were all ready to dive out the door as we could see him going up in flames, but nobody said a word to him. *Dick Cox (1951–59)*

His solution to corporal punishment was to bring his slipper out on occasion and threaten to use it. Whenever a boy asked him for some ink to fill his inkwell on the desk, he would smile broadly and respond: "Do you want 'smink'?", waving his slipper with the word SMINK written in reverse on the sole. It never failed to raise a laugh and we all willingly got on with our work. Life with Danny was always jovial.

In the first week he asked one nervous boy his name. That admirably polite lad prefaced his every remark by the word 'Sir' but on this luckless occasion the stuttered result of "Sir, sir, — Suspencer, sir" was enough to bring the rest of the form to its knees with laughter and certainly broke the ice.

Over the ensuing year we all got to know each other well and he turned out to be an old master in the grand tradition, often preferring to talk rather than teach. One session was devoted to the objective of cricket which must have had an unconscious effect on me because I turned from a lively tip-and-runner into a cautious player who never seemed to score many runs. Danny's thesis was that the prime objective in cricket was to protect and defend the wicket. If only he had said it was to score more runs than the opposition or to win the match, then as an impressionable lad I might have had a brilliant cricket career like my father.

Chris Talbot (1955–62)

Danny was clearly older than most other teachers in the school:

Mr Burrell started teaching in 1920 and joined Wellingborough Grammar in 1942; he was my form master when I was in class 2AII. My Father was 45 years old when I went to WGS and Burrell was a really old man, much older than my father, had a job to walk and was very gaunt about the face. I could of course be wrong but at the time I was convinced that Mr Burrell came out of retirement to help in school.

Keith Gennis (1943–47)

Danny used to cycle to school on an old touring bike which had a saddlebag capacious enough to carry all his books. It was a machine whose gearing to me was unique – I have never seen its like before or since. It combined a Sturmey-Archer hub with multi-sprocketed derailleur gears with the ability to produce a ratio so low that Danny could cycle up Doddington Road at a pace that would not have made a tortoise hurry. This was essential because, with a slightly gammy leg and advancing years, he was not as sprightly as we young things on our brand-new Raleigh sports bikes, gained from passing the 11-plus.

Looking back I believe that Danny was highly instrumental and effective in facilitating an easier passage for us from primary school into an institution whose senior pupils (to me) seemed to look and sound like (and almost were) fully-grown men. Chris Talbot (1955–62)

T. G. 'Hobo' Cook (History) 1943–1955

Mr Cook arrived in the war and proved willing to turn his hand to almost anything. He took over the role of scoutmaster from Mr Dunning during the war years. He ran a second-hand clothes store and helped cook at the agricultural camp. He was stage manager for the school play for many years. He prepared well for his teaching, and all the notes he gave for School Certificate classes were written out beforehand and dictated to the class.

When the notes were added to our History books he would explain every written paragraph. We made additional notes if we wished on separate pieces of paper, it was not always necessary but it could be done if wanted. Keith Gennis (1943–47)

Fred Nutt remembers his way of keeping control in the classroom:

We all remember Hobo Cook. He came into the classroom and as he walked across the front of the class, he said "Nutt, King-Underwood, out the front." We went to the front, he opened his desk, took out his slipper and said, "Bend over." Bang, bang. "Right," he said, "that's before you start!" I know how Saddam Hussein felt.

Fred Nutt (1952–58)

After leaving the Grammar School to go to King Edward's School, Sheffield, in Summer Term, 1955, he went on to be a Lecturer in History at the Cambridge Institute of Education in 1965. He is remembered on the King Edward's web-site in the following terms:

> *Mr T. G. Cook joined us at the beginning of the Summer Term, 1955, as Senior History Master, having come from Wellingborough Grammar School, Northants, where he had also been in charge of his department.*
>
> *He has taken an active part in all departments of School life. He was Housemaster of Wentworth and Group Scoutmaster of the KES Group (167th Sheffield); for many years he was the announcer at the Swimming Sports, where his powerful rolling Scots voice produced instant silence in the excited competitors and spectators. A keen and enthusiastic player of rugger, he was the coach and referee of the Under 13 Rugby XV (and was also a member of the Staff football team). As master in charge of the Junior History Society he was the original organiser of the famous 'Cook's Tours' to places of historical interest. For many years he was a member of that awe-inspiring group of masters who were in charge of the 'O' and 'A' examinations, and in this capacity he was a tower of strength to us.*
>
> *In all he did he was brisk, vigorous, quick-moving, energetic and efficient. He was cautious in the midst of educational controversies, and as befits a historian, moderate and thoughtful in expression. His unfailing enthusiasm, cheerfulness and courtesy were appreciated by all, not least by his colleagues, who held him in such high regard that for many years he was the Common Room Secretary.*
>
> *http://nlc.oldedwardians.org.uk/mags/66spr.html*

L. E. 'Lennie' Bratt (Modern Languages) 1943–1955

Mr Leo Bratt, known as 'Lennie', was one of the older masters appointed during the war. He was head of languages, teaching Spanish, French and 'German for Scientists', and was responsible for introducing Russian at the end of the war. In his later years he took medication that caused him to fall asleep in class. He used to organise his teaching by getting each boy in turn to translate a paragraph of text in Spanish, and would often fall asleep so soundly that boys did whatever they wanted during the interim and, if he were to awake, they were ready to continue from an appropriate place as if the translation had been going on uninterrupted in the meantime.

He was one of the 'characters'. Some boys believed, from his limp, that he had a wooden leg, probably acquired during WW1. My memory of him is that he would spend the first 5 minutes setting us some work and then nod-off for the remainder of the lesson. We usually woke him up by our noise when leaving the class but this was purely unintentional. He also played the cello in the school orchestra.

Richard Adkins (1950–57)

Dick Cox (1951–59) recalled a time when Lennie woke up unexpectedly one day to be greated by silence. His immediate reaction was, "Who's died on me now?"

John Garley remembers another occasion:

Lennie Bratt's 'Spanish Lessons' normally took place in Mr Tompkins' top prefab room – but one week there was a change of venue due to a play rehearsal. This 'Spanish lesson' took place in Mr Dunning's Geography room – a rare treat to be allowed to get there 10 seconds late and not miss the first 5 questions! Having arrived, Mr Bratt proceeded to go through his usual protocol: "Get out your dung-coloured books – Garley, start reading at page 34," and we began to take turns round the class, translating one paragraph each out loud. By the time we reached the fifth paragraph, Mr Bratt was fast asleep! I suppose it was not only the medication but the repeated monotone voices of successive readers who were by now so practised in the art of 'Bratt hypnotism' that there was a 'book' organised to bet on the time it took us to hypnotise him! On this particular day it was hot and stuffy, so he soon succumbed.

The class consisted of a mixture of boys from all three sets, A, B and C and, suffice it to say, it was a C class boy (whose name escapes me now) who hatched the plot. Towards the end of the lesson he crept to the front of the class where Mr Bratt was sound asleep with his head resting on his hands on Jake's desk, directly below Jake's famous world globe! The boy, who was fairly tall, pulled the pulley to lower the globe to rest about 18 inches above Lennie Bratt's head. The class fell silent – card games stopped, satchels were loaded, ready for a quick getaway!

The bell sounded and the Bratt woke up with the usual start. He raised his head with a jerk and smacked it on the brass knob at the base of the globe that Jake used to lower it to desk level. He shouted blue murder as blood flowed from his wound and the classroom emptied almost instantaneously. He was taken to the Cottage Hospital, returning with a plaster on the offending cut and bruise. He went home and was only seen a week later back in Mr Tompkin's prefab asking us to read from the little dung-coloured books once more. Mr Wrenn interviewed the whole class after the incident but no-one was brought to book. Perhaps he saw the funny side. *John Garley (1952–58)*

W. 'Father' Holmes (Chemistry) 1943–1963

Mr Holmes came to the school at Easter in 1943 to be the senior science master. He had a dry sense of humour and used it to leaven the seriousness that was required when handling dangerous chemicals.

Mr Holmes was good in the way he explained Chemistry as a subject, and he had a humorous way when dictating notes. For example, he started on one occasion thus: "The chemical in this experiment is sulphuretted hydrogen," Mr Holmes started off (spelling out): "t h e c h e m i c a l i n t h i s e x p e r i m e n t i s – spell it yourself!" *Keith Gennis (1943–47)*

Initially his nickname was his first name 'Bill' or 'William', but later it changed to 'Father'. Perhaps it was Lewis Caroll in his line: "you are old Father William, the young man said," or perhaps it was when his son came to the school in the fifties, and called him 'Father' in public; whichever it was, we all adopted the name.

My first experience of Father Holmes was as a first year. To a youngster straight out of junior school he made an imposing sight sitting at the front of the Fleming laboratory, surrounded by impressive glass apparatus, a spectrum of brightly coloured bottles (who remembers Traube and Daggers reagent?) and many thick books. He gave the impression of a mighty monarch on his throne instructing his minions, or a mystic with the tools of his dark arts around him. Or, like the conductor of a large orchestra he directed all from his podium. However, he provided a rock solid basis for chemistry and his notes, dictated word for word each year, were comprehensive and, if learnt, would virtually guarantee Chemistry 'O' or 'A' level.

However, it was only later, when I was a laboratory assistant in the Fleming lab, that I got to know him much better. A fellow pupil, Malcolm Reeves and I lived close to FH (near the Duke of York in Northampton Road) and, for a year or more, travelled with him, his wife and his little white dog (Scottie) to WGS each morning. He was a remarkable individual, every day fighting the pain of progressive arthritis. I developed a great respect for him and the high hopes he had for his students.

Rarely, of course, did he 'walk the laboratory' during lessons although each 'O' and 'A' level practical exam he was known to make his way to each pupil towards the end of the exam to ask what they had decided the unknown substances were. Their answers he wrote on a large pad which he carried with him. This could be seen clearly by anyone. (It was quite possible to see what the others in the class had found.)

He used to tell the story of the annual inspection of the wall-mounted water distillation apparatus. On one occasion, the inspector arrived, entered the lab from the rear and walked past the practical session going on in Fleming to check the still on the wall at the front in order to confirm that it was not being used to distil alcohol. The inspector confirmed all was OK, placed a tick in his book and walked back down the lab and out again. FH would then point out that the practical session was the distillation of alcohol (ethanol) and the inspector had walked past approximately 14 separate alcohol 'stills' all working to full capacity.

Neil Sinclair (1958–64)

Mr Holmes knew the price of everything. There would be a crash and a tinkle and without looking up from his desk he'd say, "that'll be one and threepence lad, bring it in tomorrow." This was for a large thing, if it had been a test-tube it would be sixpence. One day there was an almighty crash and an horrendous noise and he sat there quite still, then got up and walked right to the back — we'd never seen him walk before! A boy had dropped an octagonal flask of sulphuretted hydrogen straight through the sink and it left an octagonal hole in the basin. The lad just burst into tears. You could see the money going round inside Mr Holmes' head, but seeing the distress of the boy, he just put his arm round him and said, "that'll be all right lad, never mind."

Graham Willey (1952–58)

I got to know Father Holmes well in my last year in the sixth. I taught physics and chemistry for a term and WH gave me his lecture notes to use. They were the notes he took at university in the early thirties!

David Tall (1952–60)

After all these years I have a vivid memory of Father Holmes doing these quite elegant experiments in spite of crippling arthritis. Yet all we did was blow air into the gas lines to see the flame collapse .... and us collapse in mirth as well. Quiet, supportive, a great experimentalist and increasingly handicapped. I was an assistant making up standard solutions etc.

The one mistake he would not tolerate was to take off the bottle stopper and put it down. You had to hold it and put it back on so as to be very sure not to cross-contaminate.

He retired when I was still his laboratory monitor and gave me (and Malcolm Reeves) some of his Chemistry textbooks with his signature inside – he knew he would never use these again. I still have them – they show a 'chemistry' which is totally unlike anything that is taught today – only the molecules remain unchanged!

I recall him inviting my parents and me to see him at his home on Northampton Road to talk about university plans. My family had no idea what was involved – they had education up to fifteen or so, that is all. He gave them the confidence to agree to try for Cambridge. It was an incredible leap! At least when I went I felt that I knew how to conduct myself in the lab even if I was very unsure everywhere else.

David Cooper (1951–57)

I think I can just remember being in the Biology lab when Harold came in and said that FH had died from his disease. I wish I had known him much better, especially when he was younger and fitter.

Neil Sinclair (1958–64)

Masters' Miscellany

Although we have chosen to focus on masters who stayed for ten years or more, in the time that an individual attended the school there were others who left an indelible impression.

Of the masters in Mr Lay's time, at least three more individuals stand out. The first is Mr Clayton, who was the Second Master from 1930 to 1939, responsible for a wide array of activities, including First XV rugby, the Scouts and the Old Grammarians as its first elected President. In our review of a wide range of information about the school, he is the only master we have found who commented in public on corporal punishment. Speaking to the Old Grammarians Annual Dinner in 1950, from his perspective as Head of Worksop College Junior School, he said:

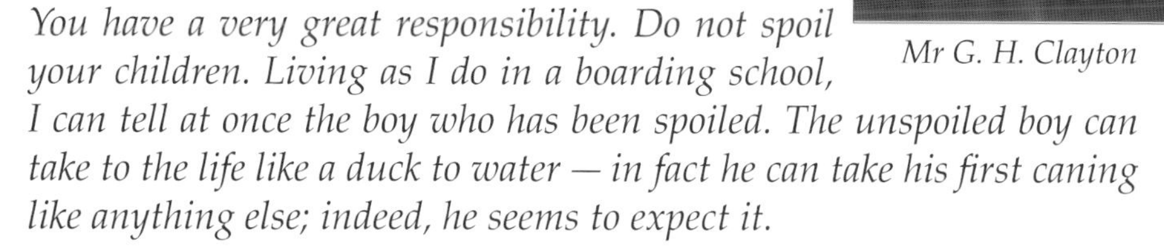

> *You have a very great responsibility. Do not spoil your children. Living as I do in a boarding school, I can tell at once the boy who has been spoiled. The unspoiled boy can take to the life like a duck to water — in fact he can take his first caning like anything else; indeed, he seems to expect it.*

Mr G. H. Clayton

Mr B. W. Appleby

Two other significant teachers from Mr Lay's time were Mr Appleby, who was responsible for developing high standards in music and Dr 'Stinks' Adamson, the chemistry master who came to the fore leading the School Air Training Corps with Mr Nicholas in the war. We will meet both of these in their respective roles later in this book.

Dr A. B. Adamson

Then there was 'Harry' Wintersgill, a hugely talented music master who kept music alive throughout the war:

> *Mr Wintersgill (1939–48) was the music master. The first class with him held the terrors of having to sing a solo song in public, he then decided if you should be in the School Choir. Never having sung solo before, I did not look forward to this but somehow managed to be chosen. The School Choir gave recitals at various times throughout the school*

Mr H. H. Wintersgill

year. Mr Wintersgill was an accomplished musician and played the piano for assemblies and such like, accompanying the choir when they gave public performances. He also arranged for a trio or quartet to perform to the whole school. These people came from Sharnbrook and played 'chamber music'.
Keith Gennis (1943–47)

Mr Albert Richmond

Other individuals arrived to teach in the war who were noted for their special character. We will meet some of them in the main story of the development of the school and others will feature in separate vignettes interspersed between the chapters. These include 'Albert' Richmond who was at the school for seven years and was responsible for starting up the Railway Club, despite being totally unable to control classes of unruly boys who ragged him mercilessly.

In the war we had a succession of odd teachers for sciences, the longest serving I remember was Mr Richmond – who taught physics and maths – who was a little strange in appearance and was given a hard time by the boys.
John Rodhouse (1940–45)

One particular favourite was mathematics master 'Sam' Harris.

Sam Harris *(1942–1947) was one of the best masters, well-known for explaining everything in detail and then asking if everyone was happy about what he had told them. In the first few lessons people were not at ease saying that they did not understand. You could sense he wanted you to ask questions and that became the policy for understanding. I particularly remember we were having an explanation of two angles with an angle between them and he asked the class what was the difference between the two. I shot my hand up and when he pointed at me I replied, "they are the same." He said, "Good boy." I was delighted. I learnt so much from him when he asked these sort of questions. There was very little discipline required in his class and obviously no 'twanking'. He was well-respected by most of the boys.*
Keith Gennis (1943–47)

Mr Sam Harris

Other boys see masters differently. In a later vignette in this book, Noel Pearson remembers Sam Harris using corporal punishment as 'the norm and principal method of achieving discipline'. So it will be in this book of memories: masters are remembered by different boys in different ways depending on their own personal experiences. However, the principal quality that unites all the masters of the Grammar School that differs from the typical teacher today is that they had the right to teach in the way that they thought fit, at a time when rules were rules and physical punishment played its role to ensure order and good conduct as boys were being prepared for responsible citizenship.

Mr and Mrs Tropman

Two other staff who gave long-service to the school in those early years were Mr and Mrs Charles Tropman, the caretaker and cook between 1934 and 1945.

Four hours before we arrived at school, Mr Tropman was stoking the boilers and making sure that everything was ready for another day's work. If any boy – or master – had ventured down into the kitchen at 7 am, he would have found Mrs Tropman busily preparing the day's lunch. She would probably have been making one of her famed jam rolls.

At five minutes to nine Mr Tropman would appear at the top of the playground entrance steps and ring a hand-bell. Woe betide any boys who were seen fighting. Mr Tropman caught them and escorted them to the headmaster's study where their fate awaited them. He was also renowned for his skilled management of the school tuck-shop. Much of Mr Tropman's morning was spent in taking the attendance book around the various classrooms.

Mr and Mrs Charles Tropman

CARETAKER'S DUTIES 1942

Arrive 6.30 am.	Stoke both boilers & kitchen boiler
	Common Rm. & H.M.'s Study fires.
	Dust front corridor
	Put potatoes thro' machine
	Make fires up again.
	Dust Study & Hall platform
	Plates into plate-warmer
after 9.0 am.	Clean out boilers
	Brass-work in Boys' lavatories
	Tea to Common Rm. etc. at 11.5
12.40 pm.	General help at Dinner
	Help clean Dining Room
3.50	Tea to Common Rm. & Study
4.15	Sweeping Corridors & Rooms
5.30	Stoke one boiler.
by 6.0	Shut up School: all clear

In her role as cook/housekeeper Mrs Tropman was busy all day long. When she first came to the school on its opening day she cooked 60 lunches. When she left, 200 hungry boys crowded into the dining hall shortly before one o'clock.

Mrs Tropman still remembers the weekly menu. "On Monday it was roast beef, Tuesday it was salt beef. We called Wednesday's dinner 'resurrection', for obvious reasons. Meat pudding was the main dish on Thursday, and on Friday it was the 'Pass Over'." *Anonymous*

Chapter 3

Previous Grammar Schools in Wellingborough

When Wellingborough Grammar School opened its doors to its first intake of pupils on September 23rd 1930, it had already been preceded by at least three earlier Grammar Schools in the town. The buildings that contained these three institutions still stand: a 'Free School' founded in Tudor times, now the Parochial Hall in Church Street, Wellingborough Public School in Irthlingborough Road, and a Girls' Grammar School in 'The Lindens', Midland Road.

The earliest recorded provision for education in Wellingborough was organized by a Guild set up in honour of the Virgin Mary in 1392, financed by rent from land in the town. When Henry VIIIth severed allegiance with the Church of Rome in 1534, it led not only to the dissolution of the catholic monasteries—including Wellingborough's own Croyland Abbey in 1539—but also to the reorganization of education. The changes continued in the reign of Edward IVth through the foundation of Grammar Schools.

In 1548 an enquiry was held in Wellingborough to decide how to disburse the revenue of the foundation for the Virgin Mary. It reported as follows:

> *Yt is to be consideryd that the townshippe of Wellingbrughe ys a very preti merket towne and the Kinge's towne; and to the intente yt might please the Kinge's maiestie to create there a free schole apoynting the same landes towardes the same, the Vicar there ys contentyd to charge his benefyce for euer with 40 shillings a yere toward the same, and the Towneshipe offerith to purchas as much more lande as shal be conuenyent for the ereccion thereof.*

Permission was forthcoming and gave rise to the foundation of a single Free School combining the teaching of Latin for some and a basic education in English for others.

In the first few years, the school's progress was hampered by the mismanagement of its funds. In 1595, the whole position was reviewed and a new contract of operation agreed by the townsfolk, reinforcing the principle that the school would continue to function with two

The Free School in the grounds of All Hallow's churchyard

teachers, the senior being responsible for the Latin curriculum, and the junior to teach English and simple accounting. By 1619, the Free School building was completed in All Hallow's churchyard, backing on to Church Street, where the building still stands as the Parochial Hall.

The School had two large rooms, one on the upper floor used for the Upper School, the other on the lower floor for the Lower School. Each floor consisted of a single room appropriate to teach twenty or thirty boys. As time passed, the endowment to pay the salaries was eaten away by inflation, and the school relied for its survival on teachers who were able to supplement their salary as curates in the church. Meanwhile, local farmers, with earnings diminished by the changing fortunes of agriculture, were less inclined to pay for the extended education of their children. Matters hit a particular low at the beginning of the nineteenth century. By 1818 there was not a single pupil left studying Latin, with the school reduced to a lone teacher concentrating on reading, writing and arithmetic.

Events took a turn for the better in 1825 with the appointment of Thomas Sanderson MA DD, who introduced boarding and reinvigorated the school. It was again reaffirmed as two separate institutions under his leadership, with him teaching 20 to 30 boys between eight and seventeen in the Upper School while his assistant taught basic English and arithmetic to boys between seven and fifteen in the Lower School.

In his long period as headmaster from 1825 to 1863, Sanderson expanded the curriculum of the Upper School to include Latin, Greek, French, Arithmetic, Algebra, Mensuration & Land Surveying, Geography, History, Religious Instruction, Drawing & Mapping, Mechanics, Philosophy, Book-Keeping, General Knowledge, and Singing.

At the same time, the nation was becoming increasingly prosperous through the development of industry and the widening Empire. The Government became more involved in the life of its citizens, creating new laws to limit child labour and expand education, culminating in the Education Act of 1870, declaring that all children aged 5–13 should receive a basic schooling in reading, writing and arithmetic.

School Boards were set up in each locality to review the provision of voluntary education and, where necessary, to create new schools. This led to new primary schools in Wellingborough, while the Free School continued to provide the only secondary education in the town.

A national Commission of Inquiry in 1868 reviewed the status of grammar schools and proposed three categories: first grade schools for the preparation of pupils for university, second grade for the professions, commerce and farming; all others were to be classified as third grade. In 1872, the Northamptonshire Endowed Schools Committee recommended that Oundle and Peterborough schools should be the only two first grade schools in the county, classifying the Wellingborough Upper School as second grade and the Lower School as grade three.

This stung the Governors of Wellingborough Free School into action and in 1873 they declared their intention to seek to upgrade their establishment:

> *Considering the schools of this charity have the largest endowment of any charity in the county and the central position of Wellingborough in the county with its facilities of railway access, it is desirable that efforts should be made to obtain a first grade school for Wellingborough.*

The Upper School was separated from the Lower School so that it could pursue its desired higher status. It relocated three times in the

Wellingborough Grammar School, at the turn of the century

next eight years, first to the Work House just off the High Street, then to the Drill Hall in Great Park Street (with just 7 boarders and 10 day boys) and finally to the building which is now the School House of Wellingborough Public School in Irthlingborough Road.

On January 27th, 1881, the new Wellingborough Grammar School opened its doors to 41 pupils under its founding headmaster, Henry Edward Platt.

The Grammar School flourished in its new surroundings, growing from the original 41 boys in 1881 to 251 in 1900. In 1904, the Lower School in Church Street was closed and the 54 remaining boys moved to the Grammar School, swelling its numbers to 337.

During the same period, the land owned by the school grew from 2 acres to 30 acres and new buildings were continually under construction. The curriculum emphasised both academic success and excellence in sport (mainly cricket with some soccer).

To monitor the school's academic progress, the boys were entered for the Cambridge Local External Examinations; in the period from 1893 to 1896 they scored more passes than any other school, an outstanding result for such a relatively small institution. Between 1885 and 1907 the school won sixteen open scholarships in mathematics at Cambridge University—a remarkable achievement.

Wellingborough Grammar School for Girls, Midland Road, 1907

The Education Act of 1902 reorganised the provision of education once more, abolishing the School Boards set up in 1870 and passing control to the local councils, which, for Wellingborough, was the Northamptonshire County Council.

The new act called for secondary education for girls to study a range of subjects—including foreign languages, history, geography, science and mathematics—to prepare them for advanced education at teacher training colleges and universities. On January 17th 1907, the Governors of Wellingborough Grammar School opened the Wellingborough Grammar School for Girls in a large house known as 'The Lindens' in Midland Road. There were 28 girls and 7 staff including Miss Anne Rayne Tinkler as Headmistress.

Dr Platt resigned as headmaster in April 1907 and the new headmaster Philip Algernon Fryer was to hold the reins of the school until 1933. In this period the school maintained its academic tradition, teaching Religious Knowledge, Arithmetic, History & Geography, English, Mathematics (Pure and Applied), Natural Science, French, Latin, Greek, Drawing and Vocal Music, with optional lessons in Piano, Violin, Book-keeping and Shorthand. Every year from 1907 to 1917 the school gained the highest number of preliminary, junior and senior certificates of all schools taking the Cambridge Local Examinations.

Wellingborough County High School for Girls, 1912

Achievement in sport, particularly cricket, soared to the highest level. In 1909, 12 old boys and a schoolboy were playing County Cricket, and old boy G. J. Thompson played test cricket for England against Australia. In 1912 the school team was rated alongside Eton as one of the two best school teams in the country. In 1913, three boys – S. T. Askham, G. T. Carter and A. D. Denton – gained county caps while still at school. The cricket dynasty was to continue long into the future with more than thirty old boys eventually playing county cricket for Northamptonshire, six as captain.

In January 1911, the Northamptonshire County Council took over the Girls' Grammar School. It was re-located to new buildings in London Road on January 11th 1912, with 105 pupils and Miss Tinkler as Headmistress. To signal its new County status, and to sever the link with the Grammar School, it was renamed The Wellingborough County High School for Girls.

Wellingborough Grammar School continued to provide secondary education for boys from the town, with a growing number of boarders and up to 150 boys attending on a daily basis.

In 1920, the County Council sought to open a second boys' school in town. Negotiations with the Governors of Wellingborough Grammar School made it clear that the legal power lay with the Council and the

Wellingborough Grammar School, 1930

Governors were in no position to provide such a school. It was agreed that the new Grammar School would be the sole responsibility of the County Council while the current Grammar School would become fully independent. In 1921, Mr Fryer was elected to membership of the Head Masters' Conference (the national association of independent schools), which entitled his school to Public School Status. In 1924 the school was renamed simply 'Wellingborough School' and the title 'Wellingborough Grammar School' passed to the authority of Northamptonshire County Council.

In 1929, construction of the new Wellingborough Grammar School under the auspices of the County Council began in Doddington Road. The main building, seen from the playing fields, looks much as it does today, save for the absence of a second floor of classrooms on the side of the school overlooking the field.

The school was to serve the same dual purpose that was the basis of the Free School of Tudor times, though now fully integrated as a fundamental education for all its boys and an extended sixth form education for the more able to prepare for university, including the teaching of Latin essential for entrance to Oxford and Cambridge. The academic curriculum was to be basically the same as that given by Dr Sanderson in the Upper Free School in the nineteenth century, continued by the original Wellingborough Grammar School, nationally enshrined in law by the 1902 Education Act and formulated by the Board of Education in 1904.

In 1917 the School Certificate Examination was introduced, requiring a pass in five subjects from at least three different areas of the curriculum including English Language and Mathematics.The Higher School Certificate followed in 1921, requiring the study of three main subjects and one subsidiary.

The first school handbook at Wellingborough Grammar School was to prescribe the curriculum as: "Scripture, Writing, English Language, Literature and Composition, History, Geography, Arithmetic, Algebra, Geometry, Advanced Mathematics, French, Latin, Natural Science (including Nature Study), Woodwork, Class Singing, Drawing, Physical Drill, and for those following a commercial career, Shorthand and Typewriting."

The school took its first intake of pupils on September 30th, 1930 and was officially declared open at a formal ceremony on June 11th, 1931. In addition to the new Headmaster, Mr F. C. Lay, the ceremony was attended by two head teachers of previous Wellingborough Grammar Schools: Mr Fryer (Headmaster of the original Grammar School from 1907 to 1924, before it became Wellingborough School) and Miss Tinkler (Headmistress of Wellingborough Girls' Grammar School from 1907 to 1911 before it became the Girls' County High School in 1912). Mr Fryer, in particular, took a deep interest in the new Grammar School as a School Governor and—after his retirement from Wellingborough School in 1933—he served a significant period as Chairman of the Governors of Wellingborough Grammar School from 1940 to 1951.

Wellingborough Grammar School was to be the continuation of a tradition that had grown over the years and was to grow even further to encompass the education of all able boys in Wellingborough and its surrounding district. Its story continues in the chapters that follow.

Chapter 4

The Early Years with Mr F. C. Lay (1930–1937)

Mr F. C. 'Freddie' Lay was specially suited for the task of creating a new Grammar School from scratch. He was educated at the City of Oxford School from 1907 to 1915 in a school conceived as recently as 1877 when the City of Oxford and the University acknowledged that the city had no school capable of preparing local youngsters to become undergraduates. To resolve this situation, The City of Oxford School opened in 1881 with 47 pupils, on a site provided by the corporation between New Inn Hall Street and George Lane. Its sole purpose was to prepare boys resident in the city, who had completed the eighth year of elementary school, to achieve university entrance standards.

Young Freddie Lay won an exhibition to read Science at Jesus College Oxford in 1914, but before taking up this offer, he joined the Inns of Court Officers Training Corps to fight for King and Country in the First World War. He saw service with the Oxford and Bucks Light Infantry, rising to the rank of captain, gaining experience of leading men in a disciplined cause. After the war in 1919, he returned to Oxford to pursue the pure delights of academic study, obtaining an honours degree in natural science and a research degree in chemistry. He also distinguished himself in sport as a rugby player and captain of rowing for his college.

MR. F. C. LAY, M.A., B.Sc.

Having balanced the pragmatism of service with the value of team spirit and the pursuit of pure knowledge, his first employment was as a teacher of science at Liverpool College in 1923. This school shared a number of elements in common with the pattern of development of the Grammar Schools in Wellingborough. It was opened in 1840 as a boy's day school and served more than one purpose, in this case an Upper School was combined with a Middle and Lower (Commercial) School. In 1884, as changes were being made throughout the country, the Upper School moved away to a separate site. In 1907 the Middle and Commercial Schools were sold to the city and the Upper School became an independent public school retaining the name of Liverpool College.

Mr Lay made a highly personal contribution to Liverpool College, which was described by David Wainwright in his book *Liverpool Gentlemen: A History of Liverpool College* in the following terms:

> *Lay joined the college staff as a chemistry master in 1923 — the first full-time science master appointed after the war. Within the school he reconstructed the science side from sordid beginnings — on his arrival, every drawer in the chemistry laboratory was crammed to overflowing with broken glass. He inspired and initiated the Science Exhibitions that attracted wide interest and attention to the school between the wars. On his appointment Lay had gone to live at the University Settlement in Nile Street. There he joined a number of young school masters, social workers and journalists who spent their evenings working in the David Lewis Senior and Junior clubs, in the still squalid and impoverished surroundings of the slums.*
>
> *Soon Lay interested the Principal in the work that was being done, [...] the school came to contribute £100 annually to Nile Street, and College boys went down to take part in club activities. In the autumn of 1925 the Duke of York visited Liverpool and opened a new boys' club (York House) sponsored by the College.*

In addition to his special personal qualities, Mr Lay brought several specific features from Liverpool College that were to help him shape the new Wellingborough Grammar School. The College curriculum balanced individual achievement in academic work with team spirit engendered through sport; it also provided a rich variety of school clubs to support a wide and varied range of extra-curricular interests. It had a school uniform with a black blazer and grey flannel trousers, and encouraged internal competition through a House system with mascots named Stags, Eagles (later Griffyns), Lions and Porcupines — not very far from the names of the houses created at Wellingborough Grammar School as Dragons, Gryphons, Lions and Stags.

The stage was now set for the foundation of the new Grammar School in Wellingborough.

PRINCIPAL, MASTERS AND BOYS FACE THE CAMERA.

The principal, masters, and boys of the Wellingborough Grammar School. The principal, Mr. F. C. Lay, M.A., B.Sc., Jesus College, Oxford, is seated in the middle, and the staff supporting includes Mr. J. F. C. Brown, Mr. A. Perkins, M.A., Downing College, Cambridge, Mr. G. H. Clayton, B.A., Selwyn College, Cambridge, and Mr. E. L. Hole, B.A., Emanuel College, Cambridge.

The School opens its doors

Wellingborough Grammar School opened on September 30th, 1930. In his new challenge, Mr Lay sought a spirit of cooperation in all those he encountered, including his staff, the pupils and their parents. His new staff of four consisted of Mr J. F. C. Brown (1930–32), and three Cambridge graduates: Messrs G. H. Clayton (1930–39), E. L. Hole (1930–43) and A. Perkins (1930–33). The first intake consisted of 64 boys with a minimum age of 8 years, most being 10 or 11 years old, and a few a little older. A test was set on the first day to place them in four forms: I, IIa, IIb and III.

Starting a Grammar School with a staff of only himself and four other teachers required a great deal of flexibility to cover the full range of activities and specialist subjects. Each teacher needed to be willing to take on a broad range of responsibilities.

Mr Clayton, a graduate in English who became the Second Master in 1933, took on responsibility for school rugby, the school scout troop, and later had a prominent interest in the Old Boys' Association as its first President. Mr Hole, a graduate in French, became the coach for school cricket, and used his undoubted musical talents as a pianist and 'a fine tenor voice' to perform in school concerts with Mr Brown, also a pianist, who taught music. Mr Perkins was responsible, among other things, for swimming, which was took place in the River Nene before the opening of the swimming pool in Wilby in 1933. Mr Lay had his expertise in science, and also had other strings to his bow, literally, as an amateur violinist—a talent not revealed until he performed in the school orchestra with the pupils in later school concerts.

To provide suitable facilities for teaching, the school was designed with eight classrooms, with a laboratory for physics and another for chemistry, a library, rooms for art, manual instruction, lectures, preparation, a dark room for photography, an assembly hall that doubled as a gymnasium, and a downstairs dining-room.

There was still much work to be done. The walls had only just been plastered and needed to be left to dry out for some time before they were painted. The laboratories were not yet equipped and other finishing was necessary before the official opening, but at least there was plenty of space available for teaching.

The School welcomes the parents

Mr Lay's first priority after establishing a working atmosphere in school was to have some kind of event to welcome the parents, the governors and others in the town. He chose to put on a school concert using all his available resources, including a group of boys who could be quickly taught to sing in unison and two talented teachers who could perform solo items.

The first School Concert was presented on Monday, December 9th, 1930, with the combined staff and pupils singing choral items, and Mr Hole

PART I

THE NATIONAL ANTHEM

1. INTRODUCTION. SONG–MR E. L. HOLE
   - "Art thou troubled? Music will calm thee" … … *Handel*
2. SONG – MR E. L. HOLE AND CHORUS
   - "Sea Horses" … … … … … … … *Dunhill*
3. DUETS IN CANON – CHORUS AND STAFF
   - "Song of the Shipbuilders" … … … *Gustav Holst*
   - "The Ride of the Witch" … … … *Charles Wood*
4. SONGS – MR E. L. HOLE
   - "Where'er you walk" … … … … … … *Handel*
   - "Cease, O Maiden" … … … … … … *Scarlatti*
5. PART SONGS – MR F. C. LAY, MR J. F. C. BROWN, MR E. L. HOLE, R. P. OLNEY, D. LAWRENCE, C. EDWARDS
   - "O Happy Eyes" … … … … … … *Elgar*
   - "As Torrents in Summer" … … … … … *Elgar*
   - "My Love dwelt in a Northern Land" … … … *Elgar*

PART II

6. PIANOFORTE DUET–MR E. L. HOLE, MR J. F. C. BROWN
   - "Symphony No. 1" … … … … … … *Brahms*
   - "Hungarian Dance No. 3" … … … … … *Brahms*
7. SEA SHANTIES – STAFF
   - "Haul away, Joe" / "Lowlands Low" } Pulling Shanties.
   - "O Johnny, Come to Hilo" – Capstan Shanty.
4. CHRISTMAS CAROLS – CHORUS
   - "In the bleak mid-winter" … … … … … *Handel*
   - "Masters in this Hall" … … … … … … *Scarlatti*
   - "O Happy Eyes" … … … … … … … *Elgar*
   - "Joy shall be yours in the morning" (*Solo* – D. LAWRENCE) *Fraser-Simon*
   - "My Love dwelt in a Northern Land" (*Solo* – R. P. OLNEY) *Geoffrey Shaw*
   - "In the bleak mid-winter" … … / "A Babe is born in Bethlehem" … … } *Traditional xiiith Century*
   - "Come to the Manger" (*Solo* – C. EDWARDS) … … *Traditional*
   - "The First Nowell" (with Descant) / "Good King Wenceslas" (with Descant) } *The audience is requested to sing the air.*

The first School Concert

performing with Mr Brown in duets for piano and for tenor solo with piano accompaniment. Mr Lay made his own contribution, joining forces with Mr Brown, Mr Hole and three of the more musical boys to sing part-songs.

Miss Bavin arrives and the School is officially opened

In April 1931, Miss Bavin, who had recently completed her education at Wellingborough High School, was interviewed and appointed as School Secretary, initially working in the mornings only. The first weeks of her long association with the school were dominated by preparations for the official opening ceremony. The Easter holidays were used to finish painting the school and to make the final touches ready for the big day.

At three o'clock on Thursday June 11th, the boys took their places along the front drive, and the Governors, led by their chairman Mr George Henson, stood at the gate with Mr Lay and Mr Fisher (the Architect), to welcome Sir Michael Sadler, Master of University College, Oxford, who was to declare the school officially open. The Architect presented Sir Michael with the key to the school and, as Sir Michael unlocked the front door, Mr Clayton unfurled the school flag. The procession walked through into the hall for the ceremony.

Sir Michael Sadler is welcomed at the School gates to officially open the School

After a hymn and the reading of the lesson, Mr Lay welcomed Sir Michael, who addressed the assembly and declared the school open. The school was now officially in business.

In September 1931, the second year began with 150 boys in six classes and two new teachers: Mr C. W. F. Laurie (1931–45) from St John's College Oxford to teach mathematics and Mr G. S. D. Page (1931–33), from the Slade School of Fine Arts. Mr Laurie, called 'Uncle' by the boys, was a farmer in his spare time and proved to be a highly eccentric character, given to sleeping through his afternoon lessons, much to the amusement of the boys. Mr Page taught woodwork and on occasion seemed to prefer making frames for his own paintings rather than paying attention to his teaching.

The Christmas concert that year was modified to include a short ceremony to present prizes. Mr Lay explained that the School was still small, and needed to economise in a time of national austerity. By including the Prize Giving as part of the Christmas Concert, it was possible to use the receipts from the sale of tickets to start a fund to purchase curtains and theatrical equipment for the stage in the hall.

Dragons, Gryphons, Lions and Stags

Mr Lay announced two important developments. The first was the establishment of a House system with four houses: Dragons, Gryphons, Lions and Stags. The second was the donation of cups for prizes in House competitions. Mr R. E. Yorke, Chairman of the Wellingborough Urban Council donated a cup for cricket, which had already been the focus of a competition in the summer won by the Stags; Mrs Saxby promised a second cup for rugby.

Dramatic Society and Music Society

The funds from the Christmas Concert were used to furnish the hall with new theatrical facilities and at the end of the Spring Term in April 1932 the newly formed Dramatic Society presented an evening of three plays. One, called 'Dust', was written communally by the boys of 3A and 3B and typed out in several drafts by Miss Bavin. The performance was a huge success, and the reporter from the local paper was amazed to go back stage and find that the boys themselves were in total control of the presentation. In his newspaper review, he reported:

> *To those of us whose education has consisted in acquiring large quantities of book knowledge and the rudiments of our national games, it must come as a revelation to witness the birth and growth of a modern educational unit which has, as a kind of background, the realisation that there is rather more in life than mathematics and football. At last, it can be said that Wellingborough possesses its cradle of the arts, and from the fact that the first performance on Saturday afternoon was played to a packed house, it looks as if the people of Wellingborough are not slow to realise their good fortune.*

A School Musical Society was formed with thirty members intending to put on good quality concerts. Its first performance in the Summer Term featured Mr Hole and Mr Brown performing a piano duet and singing in a newly formed vocal quintet, complemented by chamber music from a string quintet of local players. Two of the singers were Mr and Mrs F. C. Gent who were to make a major contribution to the school as parents. A collection was held for the Appeal on behalf of the Unemployed, made by the Chairman of the Urban District Council, as part of the growing interplay between school and town.

Sports development

The school was making good use of its playing fields, with space for four rugby pitches and a central area between them that was used as a first XI cricket square. In the summer, the grass round the central cricket pitch could be laid out for an athletics track. The school rugby team trained by Mr Clayton began well, winning all but two of its matches in the Autumn Term. In the Summer Term, eight cricket matches were arranged for an 'Under 14' team managed by Mr Hole. It was a learning experience in which no matches were won, three were cancelled, four were lost and one was drawn. However, on June 9th, a match was played against a Parents' XI, in which the school team triumphed. The Parents' Match became a regular fixture in the school cricket calendar and enhanced the growing relationship between the school and the parents.

The arrival of the first long-serving masters

In September 1932, the third year of the school's existence brought new classes and teachers. Mr I. J. Nicholas (1932–73), of Jesus College, Oxford, arrived to teach classics, Mr J. G. Dunning (1932–66) of Peterhouse College, Cambridge, with three years experience teaching in Ireland, was appointed to teach geography and Mr B. W. Appleby (1932–39), a graduate of Wadham College, Oxford, replaced Mr Brown as music teacher.

All three were to make significant contributions to the school. Mr Nicholas had played rugby at a high level at Oxford, narrowly missing a Blue. He was to raise the rugby in Wellingborough Grammar School to unprecedented heights, including two England internationals: Don White, who later became an England selector, and Johnny Hyde, who was the first player to be selected for England while still at school. Always an enigmatic character who would never use two words where one would do, he became the silent power behind the running of the school, planning the time-table during his long years as second master in the forties, fifties and sixties.

John Dunning, known universally as 'Jake', was a different character altogether. A man of great inner warmth—as those who knew him in his dealings with the Scouts or the school Toc H group would attest—he was an unforgiving martinet in his teaching who expected, and attained, high standards in his geography lessons. He devoted his whole life to the school and took on many responsibilities.

Mr Appleby raised music standards to new heights in his seven-year period as music master, before leaving to join Mr Lay at Doncaster Grammar School, and was later to become widely known on the radio as the presenter of BBC music for schools.

The Autumn Term of 1932 saw more new developments in the scope of school activities. Mr Lay continued the spirit of co-operation with parents and town by suggesting that the school would be enhanced by planting trees round the rim of the playing field. Donations were forthcoming from parents, staff and townsfolk and Mr Lay used his botanical knowledge to select a wide range of varieties. He wrote to the local newspaper to announce the choice, including: Red Maple, Norway Maple, Sugar Maple, Allanthus, Common Acacia, Three-thorned Acacia, Alder, Mountain Ash, Common Beech, Purple Beech, Silver Birch, Weeping Birch, Young's Weeping Birch, Horse Chestnut (double red), Horse Chestnut (double white), Sweet Chestnut, American Golden Elm, Cornish Elm, Purple Leaved Elm, Huntingdon Elm, Weeping Elm, Whych Elm, Ginkgo Bilbao, Hornbeam, Turkey Oak, Holm Oak, Scarlet Oak, Golden Poplar, Silver Poplar, Balsam Poplar, Black Italian Poplar, Billeana Poplar, Canadensis Poplar, Prunus Pissarid, Prunus Myrobella, Service Tree, Sophora Japonica, Tulip Tree, White Beam, Catalpa, Douglas Fir, Scarlet Thorn, Scarlet Crab, Atlantic Cedar Weeping Ash, Deodar.

The first edition of the School Magazine appeared in December 1932 edited by the redoubtable Mr Dunning, providing a public account of the school's activities for the first time. One notable entry was the first School Certificate attained in the school in the summer of 1932 by Reg Brown, one of the older boys who entered in 1930.

The Christmas Concert featured a new school choir of boys and masters (Messrs Lay, Hole and Nicholas), directed by Mr Appleby, along with the second School Prize Giving.

Boxing and Swimming

In the Spring Term 1933, the first House Boxing Competition was held with the Gryphons as victors, receiving the Mrs F. C. Lay Boxing Cup. Mr Lay was himself very positive about boxing as a character-building sport that could be continued indoors throughout the whole year.

The Wilby Lido opened in 1933 and the school organised season tickets for the boys whose parents were willing and able to pay. The first Swimming Competition was held at the end of the Summer Term and the W. W. James Swimming Cup was won by Gryphons.

In Autumn 1933 the school had grown from its initial 64 in four forms to 230 in ten forms, with the teaching enhanced by the arrival of Mr C. S. Watkins (1933–6) of Corpus Christi College, Oxford. At the Annual Carol Concert and Prize Giving, Mr Lay recalled that when the school began with only four forms, they had a choice of rooms, but now they had reached the stage where they needed to find seating places for certain forms from period to period, wherever there was a space that was vacant. Despite the depression in the economy, they had built on their own resources and the prizes awarded that night were due to the kindness of donors.

Excursions at home and abroad

During the year, excursions became a regular part of school life. In March a large number of boys and masters travelled to Northampton to see the East Midlands beat the Barbarians. In April, Mr and Mrs Hole took a party to Paris for several days. In June, Mr Dunning and Mr Watkins cycled with a party of 100 boys to explore the battle site at Naseby. Later about 80 boys went to Northampton to see Don Bradman lead the Australian tourists in the first day's play against the county.

The School comes of age

In the summer of 1934, the older boys completed four years at the school and took the Oxford School Certificate. Thirteen were successful. The first cycle of growth at Wellingborough Grammar School was complete.

The Autumn term 1934 saw the school open with 236 boys, the new entrants being balanced by boys leaving to take up jobs in the town.

Three new masters arrived: Dr A. B. 'Stinks' Adamson (1934–43) from Keble College, Oxford, to teach chemistry, Mr J. M. 'Pastel' Goddard (1934–38) from the British Association for Physical Training to teach PT and woodwork in place of Mr Page who left in the summer, and Mr H. C. 'Eddie' Phillips (1934–73) from the Royal College of Art.

Each in his way was to contribute significantly to the school. Mr Adamson stayed in the war years and became an officer leading the School's Air Training Corps with Mr Nicholas. 'Pastel' Goddard revolutionised the teaching of woodwork and, with Mr Phillips, took over the school boxing.

The formation of the Wellingborough Old Grammarians

On October 16th 1934, sixteen boys of the eighty or so who had left the school by that time had a meeting to found an Old Boys' Association, with ten others sending their apologies. Mr Lay was elected as the first President and Mr Clayton became the first Chairman.

Reviewing progress in the light of experience

The school continued to grow with the start of the sixth form to accommodate seven older boys who stayed on to study for the Higher School Certificate.

The age of entrance was raised to a minimum of 10 and to accommodate a four-year course to the School Certificate in the fifth form, the classes were renumbered to begin in the second form. In 1934, the forms were 2A, 2B; 3A, 3B; 4A, 4B, 4C; 5A, 5B.

A worrying cause for concern became apparent as many boys left school as soon as they reached the age of fourteen, despite a legal parental contract to keep them in school until sixteen, with a penalty of £5 in the event of default. It happened often.

Mr Lay reported there were 236 boys at the beginning of the school year 1934–5, but the School Magazine of Summer 1935 listed only 216 at the end. With many working-class families eking out a sparse living in the economic depression of the thirties, boys were leaving school to solve the immediate problem of supplementing the family income. For the first time, Mr Lay was experiencing a serious setback to his long-term vision.

Analysing the data given in the School Magazines in the thirties, it becomes evident that three out of every five boys entering the school in the early years left before moving into a form where they would take the School Certificate. Only one boy in five who started finished with a Certificate. The table given below incorporates all boys from the first two years that were mentioned in the first Magazine of 1932. The A-streams obtained most of the passes and the other forms had high numbers leaving early. Clearly something needed to be done.

1930–31	Total	Leave early						Exam	Passes				
Form	1932	33	34	35	36	37+	Left	Entries	34	35	36	37+	Total
4A	**22**	3	0	0	0	0	**3**	**20**	12	3	0	0	**15**
4B	**22**	11	2	0	0	0	**13**	**9**	2	2	0	0	**4**
3A	**30**	6	7	0	0	0	**13**	**14**	0	8	4	0	**12**
3B	**26**	3	8	3	0	0	**14**	**12**	0	0	2	0	**2**
2A	**5**	0	0	1	0	0	**1**	**4**	0	0	1	1	**2**
2B	**20**	2	4	6	0	0	**16**	**4**	0	0	0	1	**1**
2C	**22**	4	5	6	5	0	**20**	**1**	0	0	0	0	**0**
1	**15**	1	4	3	2	5	**15**	**0**	0	0	0	0	**0**
Totals:	**163**	30	30	16	7	3	**95**	**68**	14	13	7	2	**36**

Boys entering in 1930 and 1931, sorted according to their form in 1932

The First School Speech Day

In the Autumn of 1934, Mr Lay considered the school ready for a full Speech Day, so the Christmas concert at the end of the Autumn Term was changed in format. Mr Appleby conducted the expanding school choir and played the obligatory piano duet with Mr Hole in the first half. After the interval, Mr Lay took up his violin and played alongside seven boys from the school violin group, with Mr Appleby at the keyboard. There followed a play entitled *La Femme Musette* produced by the sixth form, and the evening was rounded off with communal singing of Christmas carols.

The first School Speech Day was celebrated in the Spring Term, on the afternoon of February 7th, 1935. The guest of honour was the Reverend R. W. Howard, Principal of Mr Lay's previous school in Liverpool. It was an opportunity for Mr Lay to make a full report on the development of the school.

He emphasised his commitment to the balance between the academic and the physical, explaining his belief that "development on the academic side of education was dependent on good digestion, good breathing, good circulation and well-exercised limbs." He outlined a graded system of exercises, with standards set at each age-level to be achieved for the award of a standard badge. While this should be within the capacity of every boy, two further badges were available for more advanced performance: a second-class badge (of which two had been awarded in total in the previous term) and a first class badge, "whose standard is so high that it will seldom be attained."

Mr Lay welcomed the emergence of a Sixth Form and the long-term habit of work for its own sake, seeing this as a major cultural and beneficial aspect of school life.

He then turned his attention to encouraging boys to continue their education at school, asking parents not to consider only the earning capacity of their children in the immediate period after leaving school, but to look ahead to their prospects in ten or fifteen years' time.

He commended those boys leaving that year with the School Certificate, and reported an increasing numbers of employers making direct contact with the school to find "the right boy for the right job". He looked forward to a steady stream of boys into commerce and industry, and extolled the virtues of a well-rounded experience of life.

"After all," he concluded, "no manufacturer can run a works from the office, unless he knows the works from bottom to top himself. Industry, therefore, wants the best boys, not to go into the office, but to be prepared to roll up their sleeves and start in the right place, asking for no privileges but a chance to demonstrate a better equipment. Such boys, I hope we shall turn out from this school."

Making refinements in the school system

The consolidation of the school programme continued in the Autumn of 1935, with the same staff and a net increase of just one boy to 237. Details of organisation were steadily refined. The School Magazine specified a 'Head Prefect' for the first time and each House formally named its own Head Boy. The introduction of House colours led to a variety of coloured ties being sported around school.

The problem of preparing boys for the School Certificate was addressed by re-organising the fifth form into a Lower Fifth and Upper Fifth, with only the Upper Fifth taking the certificate examination. Some more able boys (thirteen in 1935) moved from the fourth form to the Upper Fifth to take the Certificate in four years, while the majority took at least five by spending an intervening year in the Lower Fifth.

Mr Lay explained at the Speech Day in February 1936 that, while it may be appropriate for some more gifted pupils to take the Certificate in four years, the majority would benefit from performing well in five rather than poorly in four. He acknowledged that parents would want their boys to be on a faster-moving track, but recommended that a way should be found to organise the curriculum so that a four-year and a five-year course can run in parallel, yet still allow paths for boys to cross from one side to the other to obtain the most personal benefit.

Following a discussion at the School Sports Day, several parents volunteered to form a committee to appeal for funds to build a sports pavilion on the playing field. The committee, chaired by Mr F. C. Gent who was already well-known for his performance in the School Music Society concerts, launched the appeal for £100, organising two whist drives and made good progress towards raising the money.

In the summer of 1936, the school had its first experience of the new regime with the Lower and Upper Fifth. Twenty-six boys in the Upper Fifth took the School Certificate, achieving 15 passes. These consisted of ten out of fourteen boys moving from 4A, and five out of eleven boys repeating a year in the fifth form. Two others who moved from 4B to the Upper Fifth both failed (though they passed the next year).

In the Autumn Term, 1936, the school had stabilised with 220 students in ten classes. Mr J. L. H. ('Johnny') Butler (1936–1975) of St Catherine's, Oxford arrived to teach mathematics, replacing Mr Watkins who had moved to Haberdasher's School, London.

During the term, the school was inspected by a team of His Majesty's Inspectors from the Board of Education, who congratulated the headmaster and his staff on having a thoroughly efficient school.

At the School Speech day in February 1937, Mr Lay reported the details of the recomendations, including support for the extension of the four-year course to five years. He reported that the school activities continued to grow from strength to strength, and the first two boys had been awarded places at University.

On the 10th June in the summer of 1937, at the annual cricket match between the school and the Parents' team, the new sports pavilion was officially opened by Mrs Lay, in the presence of Mr Hedger Edwards, Chairman of the Governors, Mr Gent, the boys of the school, and over two hundred parents and friends.

Mrs Lay declares the new sports pavilion open in the presence of Mr Hedger, Mr Gent, the Headmaster and an audience of boys, parents and friends of the School

This happy occasion uniting governors, staff, pupils, teachers and parents was also tinged with sadness for it became known without any fore-warning that Mr Lay had been appointed Headmaster at Doncaster Grammar School from a large number of applicants. He would leave the school at the end of the Summer Term to start his new appointment in the Autumn.

The legacy of Mr Lay

The first seven years of the school with Mr Lay as headmaster, were a special period of innovation and enthusiastic growth that laid the foundations for the life of the school. Looking back over those times, years later, Miss Bavin recalled:

> *And so the school grew, each new term bringing new faces – boys and staff. It was in 1937 that the originals began to leave, and among them was Mr Lay, whose departure closed the most exciting chapter in the school's life. It had been established, and in many ways has carried on, in the traditions laid by Mr Lay.*

Why did Mr Lay leave at this time when he had built so much? Who can tell? He had set the fundamental framework for the future and everything was in place. The main concern was that boys were leaving before taking the School Certificate. In his final year, though 220 boys were present at the start, only 186 remained at the end. What was needed now was consolidation and continuation rather than innovation.

We believe that Mr Lay left the school to seek another challenge. He found it in Doncaster Grammar School, which was not a new school, but was moving to a completely new location where an energetic head could make a significant difference. He was to stay there for seven years before moving to his last appointment—as head of his old school in Oxford from 1944 to 1962.

He left Wellingborough Grammar School in good heart, as a school that educated mind and body, with a balanced curriculum appropriate to prepare boys for university, while giving a good education for those who went into employment. To accomplish this broad task, he preferred to do selected things well rather than to offer a huge range of less integrated options. The brochure prepared for the school by the County Authority at the time said:

The aim of the School is to prepare boys, from 10 to 19 years of age, for intelligent citizenship. The curriculum is designed to lead to University, Professional and Commercial Careers, to the Civil and Military Services, and to the Teaching Profession. As most professional bodies and many business firms demand the School Certificate as a Certificate of general education it is hoped that all boys will remain at School at least until they have obtained it. As the School Certificate course extends normally over five years (in exceptional cases, four years) it is advisable not to postpone entry to the School later than the beginning of the School year following the eleventh birthday.

The subjects of the ordinary course include Scripture, Writing, English Language, Literature and Composition, History, Geography, Latin, French, Arithmetic, Algebra, Geometry, Advanced Mathematics, Chemistry, Physics, Nature Study, Woodwork, Class and Choral Singing, Drawing, Physical Training. Shorthand and Typewriting may be taken as extra subjects in the upper part of the School. Organised games are part of the Curriculum and exemption from them can be allowed only on medical grounds.

In addition to the basic curriculum, Mr Lay had given the school an internal competitive structure in rugby, cricket, athletics, cross-country running, boxing and swimming through the introduction of the House system. He had extended the boys' wider interest through the establishment of school clubs and travel at home and abroad through school excursions. The Old Boys' Association had been founded and the school had a vigorous Parents' Committee raising funds to support school activities.

This fundamental structure remained for years to come, with the occasional modification, such as the cessation of boxing in 1939, and a vast expansion in school clubs, which at various times also introduced new sports such as tennis, table tennis, golf, badminton, basketball and soccer.

Mr Lay's vision of a four or five year course to the School Certificate with movement between them was catered for by a fifth year which could be taken for one year in the Upper Fifth by the most able and two years in the Lower Fifth and Upper Fifth for others. It was to take a further ten years, in Mr Wrenn's time, to renumber the classes from 1st form to 5th form with A, B, C streams in each, with 4A omitted and the top group going straight into the fifth form.

The remaining teachers from the pioneers who opened the school would leave in the coming years: Mr Clayton in 1939 and Mr Hole in 1943. But there was already a nucleus to carry on the traditions that Mr Lay had built, with Miss Bavin as secretary and a group of masters—Messrs Nicholas, Dunning, Phillips, Butler—who were to maintain the fabric of those early days for most of the life of the school to come.

When Mr Lay left the school in 1937, The School Magazine published the following eulogy:

> *In offering, as sincerely as we can, our congratulations to the Headmaster, on his appointment to the Headship of Doncaster Grammar School, we are for the moment more concerned with a sense of the School's loss. A school always owes the greater part of its achievement to the Headmaster. This is particularly true when that Head is the first, in a new building without atmosphere or tradition.*
>
> *It is just seven years since Mr Lay and four assistants opened the School with sixty boys divided into three forms. We now have some 200 boys divided into ten forms. There was a happy-go-lucky spirit about those early days which it is impossible and perhaps undesirable to recapture. There were no 'Houses' and no rules save those we made as we went along, but there was a very friendly and enthusiastic spirit. It was the days when boys went on training walks before breakfast on Sunday in preparation for the School's first rugger match. This enthusiastic, friendly spirit emanated from the Head and found its climax in the School production of three plays in April, 1932. These were a united School effort. The Head encouraged us to make our own scenery and lighting and to write our own plays; he arranged short talks after prayers on various aspects of dramatic work; he joined us all in a common, community enterprise.*
>
> *It was then we discovered that we had a Headmaster who could willingly go out to buy a box of tacks, if that was the needful thing at the moment. Always has Mr Lay preserved that attitude of being completely free of access to any boy or Master at any time he is in the building. Further he has shown a genuine and fatherly interest in the welfare of each boy, which interest has not been limited to his school days only, as many an Old Boy of the School can bear witness.*

The plays were a turning point. The first Oxford Certificate was drawing near; the School was growing in numbers of boys and staff and the next few years were years of growing pains in which the School was finding itself, adjusting the claims of work and play.

Finally in the last year or so a settled framework has been achieved. Organisation has functioned smoothly so that the School has been free to devote its energies to the varied activities of its life. Rugby, Boxing, Cross-country, Athletic Sports, PT, Cricket, School Certificate and Swimming; the School has found its own yearly rhythm and pattern, and through it all runs the thread of the School Music, gradually taking the lead at School prayers, growing and widening to include a School Orchestra, in which the Head plays the violin, and reaching a peak in the Choir's proposed broadcast.

These things have happened because in Mr Lay we have had a Head who allowed the utmost possible freedom of scope, consistent with balance, to the staff under him. This sounds simple, but it requires qualities of tactful leadership from within the group which, though less showy and blatant than much that passes for leadership, are none the less more difficult of achievement and more lasting in result. These qualities Mr Lay has shown himself to possess. In addition the staff and boys can bear witness to such characteristics as honesty of mind, fairness and kindness, which rudimentary though they may appear, are rare, even in Headmasters.

Nor are all Headmasters as fortunate in their wives. Mrs Lay has always taken a keen interest in the School. It was chiefly at her wish that a move nearer the School was made so that she could feel a sharer in the School life. Medals for the swimming sports and the boxing cup have been a gift from her; while the yearly function she perhaps enjoys best is the giving of tea to all the visitors on the day of the Parents' Match.

Because of what he is and because of the help and encouragement he has received from Mrs Lay, the Headmaster will be leaving a tradition of which he may well be proud. In seven years we have a School that is alive with varied interests; in which each boy has opportunity for continuous initiative and where between big and small boys, between the pupils and staff and between the School and parents, there is a natural, friendly feeling which augers well for the future of the foundations Mr Lay has laid so truly.

Memories of the Thirties

Joe Keep (1933–1936)

I was the tenth of eleven children in my family and it was a surprise to everyone when I won a scholarship to the Grammar School in 1933. My mates in Higham Ferrers accused me of being a traitor to the cause when I left them to take up the scholarship.

Going to school meant catching the train to Wellingborough Station and walking to school. On one occasion it was so cold that my mother lent me one of my sisters' coats although it was too thin to keep me very warm. Walking up to school was perishingly cold in the ice and snow and, even worse, when we arrived we had to wait until the caretaker, Mr Tropman, unlocked the gates to let us in.

Williams, whose father kept a jeweller's shop, arrived at that time, driven in a Lanchester saloon and stepping out from the car wearing a long scarf, fur mittens and a Crombie overcoat. His clothes were very much sought after by those who had the money. The Crombie overcoat cloth was selected by 'gentlemen of taste' who wished to be counted among the best dressed of the age. A Lanchester car was comparable with a Roll's Royce at the time.

There was very much an 'us-and-them' attitude between the scholarship boys like me and the fee-payers like him. We just lived in two different worlds.

When we got into the locker room, Williams began to tease me about my sister's raincoat, boasting that his father was a jeweller while mine only worked in a shoe shop. I just lost it and went for him. If it hadn't have been for my mate pulling me off, I'd have half killed him.

After Prayers, I was told to report to the Headmaster's office. I told him that there hadn't been fighting because, after I had hit Williams, he didn't hit me back. When asked why, I felt I couldn't tell the truth of the rivalry between the boys, so I made up a story that I had taken my school books home to cover them in new brown paper and had put them on the floor where Williams had kicked the pile over. So I hit him.

Mr Lay said that, whatever the reason, he wouldn't tolerate fighting and fetched his cane from the corner of the room. After caning me, as I was leaving the room, he said: "Don't tell anyone, but I would have done the same thing myself."

The best thing that Mr Goddard and Eddie Phillips ever did for us scholarship boys was to introduce the inter-house boxing cup. Mrs Lay donated a silver cup for competition between the houses. Coming from working-class families we had learned how to defend ourselves, and the cup considerably raised our reputations amongst the fee-payers. Whereas before boxing was introduced, the fee-payers and scholarship boys would keep their own company in the playground, after we had shown our prowess in the boxing ring, some of the fee-payers sought us out as friends and would offer us pieces of their chocolate.

If there was a fracas in the playground, the prefects reported the boys concerned to either Mr Goddard or Mr Phillips and they would make them settle things with boxing gloves. They stopped the fight before anyone got really hurt.

Mr Lay himself was very much a gentleman and fundamentally kind to us all, but he maintained a fair sense of discipline. Apart from the incident with Williams there were two other occasions on which I had a 'brush' with Mr Lay's cane. I say 'brush' because that is what it was, a relatively gentle brush of the cane without excessive violence. As headmaster, it was Mr Lay's role to maintain discipline and support his staff; in both these tasks he saw it as his duty to render appropriate punishment.

One day I was told to report to Mr Lay's office. When I was called in, Mr Lay asked why he had not been offered the courtesy of a raised cap when I had seen him that morning. I said in my defence that, apart from prayers, I hadn't seen him before that day and that I dare not pass him without raising my cap. Mr Lay's response was that this could only mean that I was either unobservant, discourteous or a liar, and none of these were acceptable. He walked over to the corner of the room and fetched his cane and told me to bend over. The actual strokes were little more than gentle taps. Afterwards, he told me, "Don't let it happen again."

The third occasion occurred when we were given a spelling test by Mr Appleby. We had a list of words to learn for homework, but the following morning, when he asked us to spell 'vayicul', I had absolutely no idea what he was talking about. When he saw my attempt, he made a damn fool of me, calling me out in front of the class: "Keep, what on earth is that?" I suddenly realized that when he said 'vayicul' he meant 'vehicle', but I had never heard it pronounced like that before.

He sent me to the Headmaster for failing to do my homework. Mr Lay had no option but to support his staff and again he fetched the cane from the corner of his room and 'brushed' my bottom. It didn't hurt. Mr Lay was a gentleman's gentleman; he didn't hit hard, indeed, I'm convinced that each caning hurt him more than it hurt me.

The regular lessons in school included two periods of woodwork a week in addition to the academic subjects. My first woodwork teacher was Mr Page, who was a dead loss as a teacher. He was an amateur artist and spent most of the woodwork lesson making frames for his own paintings and ignoring us lads. He wasn't interested in teaching us how to use the tools properly and took no action as boys used the chisels for all kinds of purposes they were not designed for.

When he left, he was replaced by 'Pastel' Goddard: the difference was amazing. Pastel taught us how to do woodwork. He created a beautiful framework on the wall with racks for the different size chisels and taught everyone how to make a framework in their toolbox lids in which the tools would fit neatly.

Mr Laurie was my Housemaster and I was a dead loss academically in his mathematics class, with the result that he made my life Hell. At meal times Laurie sat at the head of the table. On one occasion, Mrs Tropman, the cook, made a large treacle pudding that looked extremely tasty and put it down in front of Laurie. I sat there staring at it with my mouth watering and Laurie looked at me and said, "Keep, which cut do you want?" I looked at all the treacle and said, "I'll have a piece off the top." Laurie immediately sliced a huge piece off the top and put it on my plate, saying,"Would that do?" I couldn't do anything other than try to eat it all, but there was too much for me and I ate so much that I had to leave the room to be sick. When I came back, Laurie laughed at me. "That will teach you… ."

As I reached my fourteenth birthday in the Spring of 1936, there were hints from my parents that my brothers and sisters all worked in the local shoe factory and although no one told me I should get a job, I felt I had to contribute to the family income. In the Easter holiday on a Friday, I started at one end of Higham and went to thirty-odd firms asking if they wanted an office boy. As I was turned away from each one in succession, I moved further along the road through to Rushden, After having no joy on Friday, later on Saturday morning, I reached Selwood's Company in Harborough Road where I learnt that the girl who worked in the office had just walked out and this left a vacancy for me. I told my parents and my father wrote to the school to say that I wouldn't be going back. He expected a fine, but nothing happened, though Mr Goddard did contact me and said, "My wife would like you to come to tea on Sunday," so we spent the afternoon swimming at Wilby Lido and then went and had tea. I appreciated this very much, but it didn't change my mind. I left school at Easter 1936 before taking the school certificate. I was fourteen years old.

Sometime after I left the school, I worked as a buyer for Whitworth's Agriculture. One day, I received a phone call from Mr Laurie. "I'm Laurie, do you remember me?" I replied that I'd spent the last few years trying to forget him. "I understand that you buy wheat," he said. I confirmed that I did and agreed that I'd go to his farm after I'd been to the nearby Daventry Market.

I drove to Byfield to find his farm. The farm looked like a scrapyard; he kept poultry in an old war-time glider. When I saw him, Laurie was sitting on a mud-splattered old Fordson tractor. He had cut his finger and in rubbing it he had made himself look like an Indian warrior, with red smears of blood on his face.

He offered me a sample of his wheat—it was rubbish—but he asked me what it was worth and I told him, "not much." Despite the poor quality, I agreed to take a sample back for analysis and eventually we came to an agreement that we would pay him a third of the normal price. When the wheat was delivered, I was not popular, the general view that it was a complete lorry load of rubbish.

Don White tells a good story of Laurie. Don went to Northampton to see the County play the West Indies Cricket team. To his amazement, he saw Mr Laurie there. Laurie's view of sport was well known at the school—a total lack of interest. When Don challenged him, Laurie explained that he had been a teacher in Kingston, Jamaica, as a sports master, teaching cricket, rugby, football and swimming. He had become so fed up with it that he had decided that he would have nothing to do with sport in his next school. While they were talking, the captain of the West Indian cricket team came over and warmly greeted Mr Laurie – he told Don that it was Mr Laurie who had taught him how to play cricket!

Masters in the time of Mr Lay, 1930–37

Year	Arrival (term)	Departure (& length of service)
30–31	F. C. Lay (Headmaster), G. H. Clayton, E. L. Hole, A. Perkins, J. F. C. Brown	
31–32	C. F. Laurie, G. S. D. Page	J. F. C. Brown (2)
32–33	I. J. Nicholas, J. G. Dunning, B. W. Appleby, [R. C. Blackie]	A. Perkins (3), G. S. D. Page (2)
33-34	C. S. Watkins, [J. L. Hampson]	
34–35	A. B. Adamson, J. M. Goddard, H. C. Phillips	
35–36		C. S. Watkins (3)
36–37	J. H. Butler	F. C. Lay (Headmaster) (7)

Masters in the time of Mr Woolley, 1937–45

Those present in Autumn 1937

A. R. Woolley (Headmaster), G. H. Clayton (7), E. L. Hole (7). C. F. Laurie (6), I. J. Nicholas (5), J. G. Dunning (5), B. W. Appleby (5), H. C. Phillips (3), A. B. Adamson (3), J. M. Goddard (3), J. H. Butler (1)

Year	Arrival (term)	Departure (& length of service)
37–38	A. R. Woolley (Headmaster)	J. M. Goddard (4)
38–39	C. A. Pine	H. G. Clayton (9), B. W. Appleby (7)
39–40	A. Jackson, H. H. Wintersgill, *D. H. Powell, G. Richardson (Haberdashers')* [P. J. Dark, C. S. Weatherhead, summer]	(C. A. Pine – war service) (J. H. Butler – war service) *D. H. Powell (1), G. Richardson (1)*
40–41	Mrs I. M. E. Ferguson, Miss K. E. Harris, Miss J. M. Harrison *Dr Girley, Mr Brosman, Mrs Gould, Dr O'Connor, Mr Duffy, Mr Crosby, (West Ham Grammar School)* [S P. Sahi, F. Langley, autumn] R. V. S. Ward (spring), [M. B. Jones, March–April], [Mrs K. G. Allen, April–May] [Mrs P. M. Pickard, June–July]	(H. C. Phillips – war service)
41–42	Mrs K. G. Allen, Miss P. Gregory, Miss C. M. Howse, R. W. Sykes, [Mrs K. M. Greening, summer]	*Dr Girley, Mr Brosman, Mrs Gould, Dr O'Connor, Mr Duffy, Mr Crosby, (West Ham, returned home Autumn 1942)* (J. G. Dunning - war service, Dec) Mrs Harrison (2), Miss Harris (2), Mrs Ferguson (2), Miss Howse (1), R. W. Sykes (1)
42–43	B. R. Burrell, G. E. Richmond, S. B. Harris, A. F. Kent, T. W. Findley, Mrs E. P. Colsell	E. L. Hole (13), B. R. Burrell left in the summer, returned in the autumn
43–44	T. G. Cook, L. E. Bratt, D. H. T. Sterry, [I. D. Hughes, autumn], [J. G. Robinson, spring] W. Holmes (summer), G. E. Sharp (summer)	T. W. Findley (2), A. B. Adamson (Dec, 9 years 1 term)
44–45	Miss M. H. Bates, [J. G. Robinson, spring]	Mrs Colsell (Dec, 2 years 1 term), C. F. Laurie (14)

Masters continuing after the war

I. J. Nicholas (14 years), J. G. Dunning (14), H. C. Phillips (12), J. H. Butler (10), C. A. Pine (8), A. Jackson (7), H. H. Wintersgill (7), R.V.S. Ward (4+2 terms), Mrs K. G. Allen (4+1), B. R. Burrell (4), G. E. Richmond (4), S. B. Harris (4), T. G. Cook (3), L. E. Bratt (3), W. Holmes (1+1), G. E. Sharp (1+1), Miss M. H. Bates (1)

Chapter 5

Mr Woolley (1937–1945) and the War Years

When Mr A. R. Woolley arrived at Wellingborough Grammar School in 1937, he joined a small school with a rapidly growing reputation in the local community. Since taking his degree at Wadham College, Oxford, he had taught at three independent public schools: Repton, The Leys (Cambridge), and as Headmaster of Scarborough College.

Mr A. Russell Woolley

In his first year at Wellingborough, his staff were the same teachers who were with Mr Lay the previous year: Messrs Clayton (Second Master, 7 years service), Hole (7), Laurie (6), Nicholas (5), Dunning (5), Appleby (4), Phillips (4), Adamson (4), Goddard (3) and Butler (1). There was a single change in the second year when Mr Goddard was replaced by Mr Pine, who was to become another long-term bastion of the school's organisation. For the first two years therefore, he had the luxury of an experienced team to build for the future.

Mr Woolley's strength lay in his concern for his boys' welfare and his presence, which commanded instant obedience. Where Mr Lay employed enthusiasm and encouragement, Mr Woolley was not afraid to lay matters on the line. The Magazine in Mr Lay's time focused on successes, Mr Woolley revealed both successes and failures. To draw the best out of his pupils, the form lists were now given in order of merit, rather than alphabetic order. In addition a new list appeared in the Magazine stating "the following boys left without having reached the School Certificate form."

In his Editorial in the Autumn 1937 Magazine, Mr Dunning reported:

The first term of our new Headmaster has been eventful but not exciting. There have been no sweeping changes but there has been a tightening up of some rules.

We have a large number of new boys and only a small number left this term. Again this term we are finding some very ill-advised boys leaving before having completed their secondary education and this is certainly to be deplored. Parental cooperation has continued and we are very glad of it; may it not usefully be applied to this problem of boys leaving at the early age of fourteen?

School activities flourish; in fact, unless careful, some of us are in danger of becoming self-satisfied. (School Magazine, Autumn 1937)

In his first public speech at Prize Day in 1938, Mr Woolley continued the theme of Mr Lay and spoke at length about "the evil that hurts the school." "This evil to which I refer is the evil which ensues when parents take their boys away from school as soon as they are entitled to do so. Now that is at 14; next year, thank goodness it will be 15."

He argued that such parents were not only breaking an agreement they had made when the boy entered the school, but were "sacrificing the most profitable years in a boy's school life and maiming him temporarily at least, more probably permanently, intellectually and spiritually for the rest of his earthly existence."

The size of the problem was evident when Mr Woolley reported that 34 boys under 16, about half of the year group, had left that year without taking the School Certificate examination and only six boys stayed on into the sixth form.

A comparison between the cohort who finished just before Mr Woolley arrived and the year in which he left shows that the number of entrants more than doubled in Mr Woolley's time and, although the proportion leaving early decreased (from 61% to 53%), the major change lay in the doubling of the proportion of passes in the Certificate.

1933	**Start**	**Leave early**						**Exam**	**Passes**			
Form	**Total**	34	35	36	37	38	**Left**	**Entries**	37	38	39	**Total**
2A	**33**	0	10	7	3	0	**20**	**13**	3	3	0	**6**
2J	**1**	0	0	1	–	–	**1**	**0**	–	–	–	**0**
Total	**34**	1	10	7	3	0	**21 (61%)**	**13**	3	3	0	**6 (18%)**

The 1933 entry, taking the School Certificate after 4 or 5 years
(Form 2J was filled mainly by junior boys already at the school)

1940	**Start**	**Leave early**						**Exam**	**Passes**			
Form	**Total**	41	42	43	44	45	**Left**	**Entries**	44	45	46	**Total**
2A	**37**	3	6	3	2	0	**14**	**23**	21	2	0	**23**
2B	**40**	11	7	3	4	1	**27**	**13**	1	11	1	**13**
Total	**77**	14	13	6	6	2	**41 (53%)**	**36**	22	13	1	**36 (47%)**

The 1940 entry, taking the School Certificate after 4 or 5 years

In his opening speech of 1938, Mr Woolley also formulated his belief in the parents' part in organising their boys' schedule for bedtime and homework:

> *"There is not a boy in this school – except, possibly a rare sixth former – who ought not to be in bed by 10.00 with the lights out. Boys under 16 should be asleep by 9.30 and those under 13 by 8.30." He added that their homework should be completed within 1 to 2 hours.*

His interest in the boys was evident from the fact that, when he taught classes in Divinity, he always stopped ten minutes from the end for questions, which could be on any topic the boys chose to raise.

> *I remember one boy (name withheld) who was the first to ask a question: "I have only one ball and can anything be done about it?" The Head told him, "Yes, it could," and went on at great lengths about the technicalities. No one ever laughed or was silly about these sessions.*
>
> *Keith Gennis (1943–47)*

Mr Woolley was committed to developing the social/non-academic character of the school and strongly supported school sport, the House structure and regular charitable donations. His level of disciplinary control was excellent, as Keith Gennis remembered:

> *At a concert, one of the lady violinists had the habit of leaving her violin under her chin, just pointing forward whilst she 'rested' her arms. This caused much hilarity amongst the boys and smothered laughs and giggles could be heard breaking out. Once this happened Mr Woolley removed his mortarboard, and brought it down using the edge with a resounding crack – it never failed to quell any further disturbance.*
>
> *I also remember an incident in the quadrangle when a schoolboy went berserk. It was just after school hours as we returned from cross country. I think I am right in saying that we were locked in the changing room by a prefect — it could have been a master. The boy ran towards the art class; he had a piece of wood and he hit the art room window, I think it was broken. Then he used the wood to hit another boy on the back of his head. The Headmaster saw what happened and walked behind the offending boy and just said loudly, "Come with me." The boy followed the Head to his study meekly without any other words being said. The injured boy was from Wollaston and was carried to the hospital across*

the road from the school. The Head walked in front of the offending boy and never turned round; the boy was never seen in school again.

Discipline was maintained not only by the masters, but also by the prefects, who were allowed to give lines for breaches of the School Rules and also to administer physical punishment with a slipper. The tradition of 'initiating' new boys had grown over the years and new entrants faced a first day trial.

I arrived at the WGS on my 'new' second-hand bicycle and, as part of an initiation ceremony, was repeatedly hit on the head with kit bags by older scholars – bending my new bicycle a bit. Every new boy was treated in the same way.

Entering the Grammar School we were given instructions on many items. The one that I remember well is how to raise your cap in the correct manner particularly to members of staff. It was given that the cap was raised up at the front allowing the rear part to reside as it was, say "good morning", or whatever, and then replace the front part of the cap to its original position. We were told that if you lifted the cap too high then there would be difficulty replacing it.

All kit had to have name and number on it, even shoes had to have short bronze nails put in the instep – most local shoe repairers undertook this – Mr Ager in Thomas Street did mine. Both plimsolls had to have the name displayed so that it could be easily read by a prefect.

Keith Gennis (1943–47)

In the summer of 1939, the first significant staff changes occurred, as Mr Clayton married and moved to a new post in Manchester, and music master Mr Appleby left to join Mr Lay at Doncaster Grammar School. Miss Bavin had a soft spot for Mr Appleby and, in later years, when he was in charge of BBC music broadcasts for schools, everyone knew not to interrupt her as she listened to his broadcasts in her office.

The two new appointments were to give great service to the school. Mr Wintersgill, the new music master, was a highly-skilled pianist as well as a good music teacher, and lightened the dark days of the war with a range of excellent concerts involving professional performers as part of the war effort. Dr Jackson, the new English master was to enrich the school with his wit and eccentricity for over thirty years.

The declaration of war in 1939 brought a range of new problems for

Mr Woolley that increased as time passed. His wife was German and they had supported the visit of German boys and girls to the town in 1938, including a concert at the school to raise funds to support their costs. Fortunately, the Woolleys' involvement in the life of the school and the town prevented things getting out of hand. Mrs Woolley visited the school regularly and always came on her 'sit up and beg' ladies cycle, with a zinc bucket on her handlebar that generally contained eggs to share with the staff.

Mr Woolley's many new problems involved coping with the loss of essential members of staff as they were called up to fight in the war, handling staff replacements including a number of young women, keeping the school clean with the shortage of cleaning staff, taking responsibility for the blackouts of the school at night, and generally coping with war-time shortages. He soon had other duties to perform, assisting in the schooling of evacuees who arrived from the Blitz in London. All of this inevitably added an entirely new dimension to the life of the school.

In the first years of the war, four established masters—Messrs Pine, Butler, Phillips, and Dunning—were called up, with their positions at the school guaranteed for their return at the end of hostilities.

Mr Pine was first to go in the first year of the war to join the RAF, to be replaced by Mr Dark, who was himself called up to join the Royal Corps of Signals in the summer of 1940.

With the school expanding and the imminent loss of senior staff, Mr Woolley appointed five new teachers in the autumn of 1940: Mr Langley, a graduate of London University, Mr Sahi, a graduate of the University of Punjab who had just completed a Diploma of Education in London, together with three lady teachers—Miss Harris from Reading, and Mrs Ferguson and Miss Harrison from London. By the end of Autumn Term 1940 Mr Butler left to join REME and in January 1941 Mr Langley was called up to join the RAF and Mr Sahi returned to India. Mr Woolley managed to appoint a local man from Doddington, Mr R. V. S. Ward, who had recently completed his degree in Economics at Nottingham. He found an Oxford graduate, Mr Jones, to fill in during March and April before moving on to Christ's Hospital; Mrs Allen started in April and left in May, to be replaced by Miss Pickard who filled in during June and July. Two new lady masters

Miss Gregory and Miss Howse arrived in the autumn. Meanwhile, Mr Phillips had joined the Army Intelligence Corps over the summer and, by Christmas 1941, Mr Dunning had joined the RAF.

As his parting shot, in his editorial in the Magazine in the autumn of 1941, Mr Dunning left this observation:

> *The continual change of faces upon the staff these last two terms has been, to say the least, somewhat startling. Indeed, instead of a schoolmaster watching his boys change from boys to men and men to ripe old age, nowadays the boy sees the more phenomenal change of master into mistress and then master into soldier.*

On the departure of Mr Dunning, Mr Woolley had just three of his original staff left from 1937: Mr Hole, who had been promoted to Second Master, Mr Laurie, and Mr Nicholas who—despite his great sporting prowess—was declared to have 'flat feet' and had failed his medical. Everyone else had arrived since 1938 and many stayed only a short time. Eight male teachers and four female teachers with no more than two years service in the school left in the war years up to 1943. Of the lady teachers, only two stayed for more than three years: Miss Gregory for four and Mrs Allen for five. It was only in 1942 and 1943 that a number of older male teachers arrived who were to remain and give the school much needed stability. (See table opposite.)

Evacuees

The first evacuees came to Wellingborough soon after the declaration of war and were listed in the School Magazine of Autumn 1939: thirty boys and two masters (Mr Powell-Evans and Mr Richardson) from Haberdashers' Aske's School, Hampstead, and some twenty others. (The link with Haberdashers may be related to Mr Watkins move there from Wellingborough Grammar School in 1935.) The effect on the school was reduced by integrating the evacuees into regular classes with Old Boy Don Stratton remembering, "at least one Londoner was in every form of the school." The evacuees remained locally for some months, returning to London in the summer of 1940.

With the coming of the Blitz in autumn 1940, a new wave of evacuation occurred with the Magazine editorial commenting:

> *Blazers of multitudinous hues mingle freely with the more sombre*

Masters during the War		39–40	40–41	41–42	42–43	43–44	44–45
A. R. Woolley	1937–1945						
E. L. Hole	1930–1943						
C. W. F. Laurie	1931–1945						
I. J. Nicholas	1932–1973						
J. G. Dunning	1932–1966			Sep–Dec			
H. C. Phillips	1934–1973						
A. B. Adamson	1934–1943					Sep–Dec	
J. H. Butler	1936–1975		Sep–Dec				
C. A. Pine	1938–1975	Start					
A. Jackson	1939–1970						
H. H. Wintersgill	1939–1948						
P. J. Dark	Summer 40	End					
C. S. Weatherhead	Summer 40	Summer					
Miss J. M. Harrison	1940–1942						
Miss K. E. Harris	1940–1942			Left in Summer			
Mrs I. M. E. Ferguson	1940–1942						
S. P. Sahi	1940–1941		Sep–Jan				
F. Langley	1940–1941		Sep–Jan				
R.V. S. Ward	1941–1975		Jan–				
M. B. Jones	Spring 41		Mar–Ap				
Mrs K. G. Allen	1941–1946		Ap–May				
Mrs P. M. Pickard	Summer 41		Jun–July				
Miss P. Gregory	1941–1945						Left at Easter
Miss C. M. Howse	1941–1942						
R.W. Sykes	1941–1942						
Mrs K. M. Greening	Summer 42			Summer			
B.R. Burrell	1942–1958					Returned	
G. E. Richmond	1942–1950						
S. B. Harris	1942–1947						
A. F. Kent	1942–1945						
T. W. Findley	1942–1945						
Mrs E. P. Colsell	1942–1944						Sep–Dec
I. D. Hughes	Autumn 43					Sept	
T. G. Cook	1943–1955						
L. E. Bratt	1943–1954						
D. H. T. Sterry	1943–1946						
J. G. Robinson	Spring 1944					Spring	
W. Holmes	1944–1963					Summer	
G. E. Sharp	1944–1949					Summer	
Miss M. H. Bates	1944–1946						

The staff at Wellingborough Grammar School during the Second World War

> *WGS uniform, and we hope that these 'coloured races' will be able to stay here peacefully as long as there are areas more unfortunate than our own. Though sharing the building with the West Ham Grammar and Tottenham Technical Schools we must be considered lucky that we have not been forced to resort to half-time tuition.*

The new evacuees no doubt had stories to tell; the first bombs hit West Ham on the 23rd and 24th August and the Blitz began just before they left on the 7th of September. The evacuees themselves were lucky, two schools were bombed the following month with many children killed.

This second evacuation was more substantial than the first, involving 120 boys, their head teacher (Dr Girley) and five teachers (Mr Brosman – English, Mrs Gould – French, Dr H. O'Connor – Latin, Mr Duffey and Mr Crosby). With such a large group, the evacuees maintained their own separate identity. The boys were billeted with the townspeople and met up daily at Wellingborough School with some lessons in their hall (a class at each end) and in a prefabricated building outside. For the remainder of their lessons they walked to the Grammar School, with art lessons at the High School.

A sharing system was instituted for some of the classes at the Grammar School, as one of the boys remembers:

> *When West Ham School was evacuated to Wellingborough my classmates and I could only attend morning (or afternoon) for several months, because West Ham had the school for the other half of the day.*
>
> *Donald Franklin (1940–44)*

Artin Cornish, one of the evacuees, commented:

> *As a school we seemed to have no association with the Wellingborough schools with which we shared facilities. I expect they regarded us as second-class citizens.*

However, in one instance at least there was close cooperation, as West Ham Grammar School joined with the Grammar School to form the Air Training Corps No. 980 (Wellingborough G.S. and West Ham G.S.) Flight. This was reported in the Summer 1941 Magazine and the co-operation was noted in the thanks proffered to them for the large part they played in "our joint Flight of the ATC" when the school returned to West Ham at the end of the Autumn Term 1942.

On returning to London from Wellingborough, Artin Cornish later recalled his experiences:

> *Back at home, when there was a raid during the night I was not expected at school until 10 o'clock. This was a concession which was made when there was a constant alert and we would go to school regularly at 10 o'clock with lessons being held in the cellars of The Friary next door to the school, which was not very satisfactory. As far as I can recall this situation lasted for two or three months until the Allied Armies captured the flying bomb launching sites in Holland. I recall on one occasion sitting upstairs in the living room hearing one of these flying bombs approaching and tearing downstairs. I just managed to reach the steps of the cellar when the bomb exploded about a quarter of a mile away, near enough to bring down part of the living room ceiling and deposit a great lump of plaster on the seat where I had been sitting.*

Very few bombs were dropped on Wellingborough because it was not an industrial centre and those that fell almost certainly came from planes dropping their load when they couldn't find their intended target. However, air raid shelters were constructed in 1940 in the school grounds, and there is only a single report of them being used by the boys when:

> *... they enjoyed a jovial, if uproarious, half-hour awaiting the all-clear.*

Parade on the field under Commanding Officer Dr Adamson, 1941

Indeed the despairing wail of the sirens is looked upon with joy rather than fear, for it represents either a welcome break from the daily round, or, to some, an extra hour of blissful repose.

Autumn Magazine 1940

To the boys' enjoyment, they were surrounded by American airbases and, according to Don Franklin:

Just about every boy had live ammunition and many a round was pulled apart with attempts to burn the cordite. It burned poorly by the way.

War-Time Activities

In addition to supporting evacuees and running the School ATC, there were many ways in which the school co-operated in the war effort both within the school and also in service to the public.

Within the school it was necessary for the boys to clean the classrooms.

Two boys were required from every form to clean their form room at the close of each day. With about 30 boys in each form, this meant that everyone had to clean the form room once every three weeks.

Keith Gennis (1943–47)

The school had to make preparations in case of fire, and a party of three (staff and senior boys) had to be on duty each night, watching the town for fires at the top of Hardwick reservoir. By summer 1942

... the gallant fire watchers still eagerly await their call to arms and well fortify themselves against its coming with hot, black (usually sugarless) tea, and while away the "still watches of the night" with literature kindly provided by the staff.

At night a blackout was in force and on one occasion a passing policeman noticed a light at the back of the school. The Headmaster, being responsible for the school, was taken to court for failing to maintain the blackout. On the day of the trial, he was "indisposed" and "a member of staff" attended the court in his stead, to be fined 10 shillings with 4 shillings costs.

With the formation of the Air Training Corps in conjunction with the evacuees from West Ham in Spring Term 1941, commissions were awarded to Dr A. B. Adamson, Mr I. J. Nicholas and Mr Crosby from

West Ham. The corps recruited boys over the age of 15 and made visits to RAF stations, prepared the cadets for proficiency certificates and was organised as a military unit, with officers, NCOs (boys) and cadets. The corps met regularly throughout the war and there are regular reports of cadets subsequently joining the RAF and Royal Navy Fleet Air Arm. In the later years of the war, regular visits were made to Sywell for flying Tiger Moths, described in 1945 as "weekly".

A Spotters Club organised by Mr R. V. S. Ward began in June 1941 to identify aircraft flying overhead and was affiliated to the National Association of Spotters Clubs. Of the 50 members, in the following autumn term, 30 had passed the third-class test and 10 the second-class test. Don Stratton remembers that this club was closed down by the Headmaster when there was a clash of priorities between it and the ATC, with the ATC taking precedence.

The 6th Wellingborough Grammar School Scout troop was active throughout the war, had evacuee members and regularly organised camps. On at least one occasion, in 1942, it collected six sacks of waste paper for the National Salvage Effort.

In autumn 1942 the railings protecting the front of the school were removed to melt down for construction of war materials. By summer 1943 clothes rationing was making its difficult to obtain 'ringworm' caps and the design was changed to a black cap with a rose badge. Why, oh why, was it ever changed back?

Forestry and Agricultural Camps

In 1940 a party of 30 senior boys went to the Lake District led by the Headmaster and accompanied by Mr Wintersgill, Mr Hole and Mr Dunning. They worked there for three weeks under the Forestry Commission Scheme making picket posts and pit props. Although there was serious work to do, it was evident that a lot of fun was had. For three weeks the masters had a "beard competition" though none had the courage to return to Wellingborough unshaven.

The Schools Forestry Commission Camp in Monmouthshire in 1941 was led by Mr Wintersgill, ably assisted by Miss Harrison and Miss Bavin, who did the cooking together with Mr Nicholas and Mr and Mrs Mayes. "The well-established morning porridge went down well with the honey supplied by the Government and cold Heinz beans on bread were very tasty after a hard morning's work."

The boys' task was to pile up logs at the side of a bank for a tractor to take away. This involved half the boys directed by Mr Nicholas tossing the logs down a steep hill-slope, leaving the remainder to carry the logs to the tractor. There was also time for local sightseeing, a visit to the cinema and the inevitable horseplay of "the letting down of a certain tent." A planned school forestry camp the following year in Autumn 1942 had to be cancelled because of the greatly extended school term and a shorter holiday of just 4 weeks.

Every July or August the school put forward boys' names of those who wished to go on a school harvesting holiday to camp out for two or three weeks. The School Scouts also camped with them. At this time the boys had taken their exams and were considered to be on holiday.

Potato and Swede Picking

This began in 1941 and involved 4th and 5th form boys helping local farmers. In the following autumn, the Magazine announced: "farm work – mainly beet, swede and potato picking – has almost become an item of the school curriculum, for on occasions, whole forms of boys have been employed by farmers in the district."

Certainly, as far as the boys were concerned, the work commitment was substantial. In the season, classes were released one by one for a week of potato picking. Don Franklin admitted that some of the boys had sidelines that produced rabbits for meat and eggs from chickens. Keith Gennis remembered:

> *I picked on two occasions, the first being at Easton Maudit. We were bussed to the farm and had a day just bending, picking up potatoes and bagging them. We were left on our own. It was all horse and cart work. I was amazed at the number of boys who smoked. Lunchtime was taken and then back to work, the buses came for us and we walked back to the farm to be picked up.*
>
> *The second visit was to Hardwick: this is where the fun started. We got off the bus and looked for the farm; a farm cart came past and we found we had been dropped in the wrong place. We should have been taken to Great Harrowden and to get there we were told to walk across the fields; it was almost 3 miles. The farmer was unpleasant to us for being late and we then had another walk down the road towards Wellingborough to start picking the potatoes.*

Work on farms continued in subsequent years through to the post-war period.

Christmas Post delivery

The request for help delivering mail at Christmas first came in 1941, when thirty boys worked at the post office in the Christmas period. This request continued in successive years. In 1946, Keith Gennis remembers that he was paid £1 and a half penny an hour. Delivering Christmas post was still happening in the late fifties when the present authors remember enjoying mince pies and a few tips delivering the last handful of letters on Christmas Day.

Sport

School sport continued throughout the war years, with the usual programme of House competitions, and inter-school games in rugby and cricket, though matches with other schools were affected by wartime conditions. Distance points for swimming ceased after 1940, with the James Swimming Cup being based solely on the results of the Swimming Competition. The PT competition continued to give light relief with a typical programme from 1945 including a varied range of activities.

PT Competition: Summer Term 1945

Events	Senior	Junior
1.	Turning on bench rib.	Turning on bench rib.
2.	Long astride vault (box).	Astride vault (buck).
3.	Through vault (box).	Forward roll on box.
4.	Dive over benches.	Dive over benches.
5.	Balance on bricks.	Through vault (horse).
6.	Fireman's Lift Relay.	Relay.
7.	Jumping over Stick (Relay).	Jumping over Stick (Relay).
8.	Overhead passing Relay.	Tunnel Ball Relay.
9.	Throwing the Cricket Ball.	Throwing the Cricket Ball.
10.	Tug of War.	

On this occasion, the honours went to Stags who outpointed the Lions and Dragons with Gryphons well behind. Although the boys competed hard to win, in the long run, through the maintenance of their health and fitness, it was not the result that mattered, but the taking part.

Clubs and Societies

Music and drama blossomed in war conditions. Mr Wintersgill continued the school concerts and instituted a further series of concerts in the school hall using local and imported talent under the auspices of the wartime Council for the Encouragement of Music and the Arts (CEMA). The locals included Mrs Woolley playing flute and Mr Hole and Mr Wintersgill performing vocal solos and piano duets. The visiting professionals included string quartets, pianists, vocalists, and instrumentalists, with Mr Wintersgill often featuring as an accompanist, including two particularly memorable concerts with the violinist Louis Godowsky. In 1942, Mr Appleby returned with Mr Lay to present a programme of anthems and songs sung by 33 boys from Doncaster Grammar School.

Drama was re-awakened in 1941 when Dr Jackson and Mr Hole each produced a one-act play. Nora Bavin and Miss Harrison organised the costumes. The same set-up was repeated the next year, but when Mr Hole left in 1943, the school was not yet ready to mount a full production, filling in with short plays produced by individual form masters before Dr Jackson started the regular annual drama production in 1944 with his own adaptation of *Oliver Twist.*

The changing staff

As the war progressed and the lady masters came and went, a number of male teachers were appointed who would stay on a more permanent basis. The young R. V. S. Ward, from Doddington, just returned from Nottingham University had started teaching at the school. No one seems to know why he never joined up: his explanation was that he sent in his papers and nothing happened. Taken on initially as a temporary staff member, he was to stay on permanently until beyond the change from Grammar School to the Wrenn (comprehensive) School.

1942 brought a certain level of stability with the arrival of several staff who were to stay beyond the war years, including 'Danny' Burrell, 'Albert' Richmond and 'Sam' Harris. In 1943 these were augmented by 'Hobo' Cook, 'Lennie' Bratt and Mr G. E. Sharp.

The departure of Mr Hole in the summer of 1943 required the appointment of a new Second Master to replace him. Only two senior masters were left: Mr Laurie who was near retirement and Mr Nicholas.

Any other possible candidates were serving in the war. Mr Nicholas was duly given the job and fulfilled it admirably for the next thirty years, although Mr Dunning, in particular, was disappointed to find that the appointment was a 'done deal' when he returned.

The lady masters

During the War, female teachers continued to arrive and depart as temporary cover for the men who were away at the war.

After the quick turnover of staff in 1940–41, the lady masters reached their maximum of seven in 1941–42. At the end of the year, five moved on and were replaced mainly by older men. Mrs Ferguson left to join her husband who had returned from the war. Miss Howse, who had charmed the boys teaching art for a year, married an American serviceman and moved away.

Mrs Allen and Miss Gregory were joined by Mrs Colsell in Autumn 1942, to give three 'lady masters' in the year 1942–3, and when Miss Bates arrived in 1944, the total increased to four. Mrs Colsell left at Christmas, Miss Gregory at the end of the school year, leaving Mrs Allen and Miss Bates, who remained until the Summer of 1946.

The school had an ambivalent attitude towards its women teachers. As male substitutes, the boys were expected to address them as 'Sir' and to offer them the same respect as other masters. However, the ladies were treated very differently from the men. They were separated from the male staff by turning the sick-room into their staff room. The fronts of their desks were 'filled in' (with the exception of Miss Gregory, whose desk remained 'open' to the delight of the boys).

Lady masters were not expected to administer corporal punishment, and were encouraged to pass on miscreants to a nearby male teacher.

> *In Room 5 Miss Bates tried to teach History and was very patient with us, but, when she had really reached the end of her tether, the culprits were sent through the swing doors to Dr Jackson in Room 3, where pent-up passions were released and 'George' was laid on a bit heavy. In his own lessons, if Jacko was feeling generous, he would offer you the choice of which end of George you preferred, but, when Maggie sent you … no options!*
>
> *Jim Tompkins (1944–49)*

The Staff in Summer 1943

Back Row: *Pat Gregory, Nora Bavin, 'Alfie' Kent, 'Joe' Findley, 'Danny' Burrell, Sam 'Fritz' Harris, Ron 'Beery' Ward, 'Albert' Richmond, Mrs Allen, Mrs Colsell.*

Front row *Miss Harrison, 'Harry' Wintersgill, 'Nick' Nicholas, 'Froggy' Hole (Second Master), Mr A. R. Woolley, 'Uncle' Laurie, Dr 'Stinks' Adamson, Dr 'Alf' Jackson.*

Some of the lady masters were more than capable of controlling mischievous little boys, with Mrs Colsell being acknowledged as a strong teacher who was at least the equal of any of the men. Romance bloomed towards the end of the war as Miss Pat Gregory married Mr Wintersgill and Miss Maggie Bates became Mrs Jackson.

The Fallen

As the war progressed, the school learnt about old boys who lost their lives fighting for their country. Twenty-four old boys died in total, most of them having attended school in Mr Lay's time in the thirties. Their deaths followed the sequence of activities in the war: the air cover to protect the country at first; fighting against Rommel in North Africa in 1942 and 1943; the subsequent drive through Italy in 1943 and 1944; the D-day landings in 1944 and the defeat of Germany in 1945; at the same time, the parallel hostilities in Asia fighting against Japan.

1941

The first deaths came in the RAF. Arthur Abbott (WGS 1933–36) died, aged 19, on May 28th 1941 at the Lancaster isolation hospital and was buried in Doddington Road Cemetery. Richard Mutimer (1932–36) was killed, aged 21, on August 28th serving in Bomber Command over Malta; he was posthumously awarded the DFC the following February. Sergeant Norman Hornsey (1931–35) was posted to Novia Scotia as a wireless instructor where he was killed, aged 23, on 23rd October and was buried in Canada.

1942

Harold Gardiner (1930–34), a 1st XV player and Victor Ludorum of Senior Athletics in school back in 1932, joined the RAF as an apprentice in 1934, becoming a Sergeant Flight Engineer in 218 (Gold Coast) squadron. He was 23 years old when his plane crashed in Holland after a flight over Cologne on 6th August 1942.

Peter Felce (1932–36), of Higham Ferrers, joined the RAF Volunteer Reserve in June 1939 and was called up on 1st September. He was promoted successively to Pilot Officer, then Flying Officer and, as a Flight Lieutenant, he was posted missing after his 37th operational flight on 16th September 1942. His death was confirmed the following month.

Outstanding Air-Crew Member

Higham Ferrers Officer Now Believed Killed

It is now announced that Flight-Lieutenant **Peter Gifford Felce** R.A.F.V.R., the young Higham Ferrers airman who was posted "missing" after an operational flight in September, is believed to have lost his life in the action. The sad news was gathered by the International Red Cross and telegraphed on Wednesday by the Air Ministry.

Fl.-Lieut. Felce.

A volunteer for the flight which ended fatally, Flight-Lieut. Felce had a fine record of war service. He was the younger son of Mr. and Mrs. Fred G. Felce, of 68, Wharf-road, Higham Ferrers.

Douglas Prigmore (1931–35) was the first old boy to die in the army. He enlisted as a regular in the Royal Dragoon Guards in 1937 and died aged 22 from wounds at the Battle of Benghazi on 12th July 1942. He was buried in the El Alamein military cemetery, the scene of Montgomery's famous victory later in 1942 when Rommel and his Italian allies were driven out of Africa.

The next sequence of fatal casualties occurred at sea. Frederick Furr (1930–34), of Bozeat – a member of the school 1st XV and 1st XI – joined the Navy in 1934, and was posted to China in 1935. After returning home in 1938, he was posted to the Mediterranean in 1939 as a telegraphist. His ship, HM Submarine *Unbeaten* was lost on patrol on 11th November 1942 in the Bay of Biscay, where he died aged 24.

Anthony Gillitt (1937–39) left England and transferred to Durban High School in December 1939, joining the Merchant Navy in 1942 as a cadet. On his second voyage his ship, the Dutch vessel S.S. Serooskerk, was sunk by U-boat U-155 on 7th December 1942 en route to Bombay and he was reported missing. He was just 17 years old.

Edwin Hudson (1934–39) played for the school 1st XI and ran for the school cross-country team. He joined the RNVR in April 1941, travelling as an ordinary seaman in the convoys to Murmansk in Northern Russia. After training at HMS King Alfred he was commissioned as Sub-Lieutenant, second-in-command of a motor torpedo boat in 1942. He was killed on 18th December aged 20 when his ship struck a mine. He is commemorated on the Chatham War Memorial.

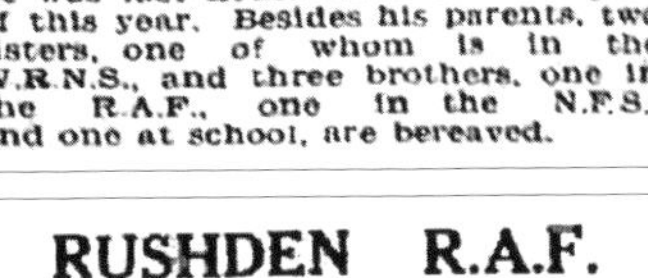

WELLINGBORO' NAVAL OFFICER KILLED

The sad news that their second son, Sub-Lieut. Edwin (Eddie) Hudson, was killed when his ship was recently sunk has been received by Mr and Mrs. E. Hudson, of 26, Alma-st., Wellingborough.

Educated at Wellingborough Grammar School, Sub-Lieut. Hudson was previously employed by Messrs. Weetabix, Ltd., Burton Latimer.

He volunteered for the Royal Navy in April, 1941. Aged 20, he was recently promoted sub-lieutenant, and was second in command of the vessel in which he lost his life. A regular worshipper at St. Barnabas Church, he was last home on leave in August of this year. Besides his parents, two sisters, one of whom is in the W.R.N.S., and three brothers, one in the R.A.F., one in the N.F.S., and one at school, are bereaved.

1943

Harold Cheasman (1932–36), from Higham Ferrers, volunteered for the RAF in 1941, and flew with 102 Squadron as a Sergeant Observer. He was reported missing, later killed, aged 21, on 14 February 1943, and was buried in the Nijmegen (Jonkerbos) British war cemetery in Holland.

RUSHDEN R.A.F. SERGEANT MISSING

News that her husband, Sergeant-Observer Harold A. Cheasman, is missing as a result of air operations has reached his wife, who resides at 14, Upper Queen-street, Rushden. Sergeant Cheasman, whose parents reside at 29 Westfields, Higham Ferrers, is 21 years of age and has one child. He joined the R.A.F. in June, 1941, having been employed in the offices of Weetabix, Ltd., Burton Latimer.

The war against Rommel continued in North Africa. Gordon Elderton (1933–35) had joined the Hampshire Regiment in January 1942 and was posted to serve with Montgomery. On 22nd April 1943 he died of his wounds as the Allies were striking back against Rommel. He was buried in the Medjez El Bab war cemetery in Tunisia.

Raymond Norman (1933–37) volunteered for the RAF and went to Canada to train, becoming a Sergeant Pilot. He was reported missing on 11th March 1943 aged 22; his body was subsequently recovered and buried in St Mary's Churchyard, Wilby.

Robert Howard (1934–39), from Finedon, was a member of the 1st XV and a King's Scout in the Finedon Troop. In February 1942 he joined the RAF, became a Sergeant Navigator, and was posted to North Africa. Once Rommel had been defeated, the Allied Forces under Eisenhower began their attack on Italy via Sicily. Robert was involved in air operations over Italy and was reported missing in August 1943.

Francis Causebrook (1931–34) played for the school 1st XV. He joined the Royal Army Medical Corps when the war began and served in the Far East. He was taken prisoner by the Japanese in 1941 and died in a prison camp on the borders of Thailand (then called Siam) on 31st August 1943, aged 23. His death was not reported until after the war.

HARROWDEN AIRMAN'S VISIT

Sergeant Jack Dunkley, R.A.F., only son of Mr. and Mrs. J George Dunkley of Little Harrowden, recently paid a surprise visit to his home. He volunteered for the R.A.F. in 1941, and received various training in Canada U.S.A., and the Bahamas. Boy Scouts and Wolf Cubs may like to know that he found the training received when he was a boy of great service to him especially in his first few months.

1944

Jack Dunkley (1934–37), of Little Harrowden, was called up for the RAF in 1941 and after training at RAF Cranwell became a Sergeant Air Gunner, seeing considerable service abroad. He was reported missing, presumed killed, on 6th May 1944 at the age of 20, and is remembered on the Singapore War Memorial.

John Loake (1935–38), of Rushden, joined the Royal Lancers in November 1942 and served as a driver in the armoured section until he was killed in the Italian campaign on 28th May 1944 aged 20. He was buried in the Naples military cemetery.

RUSHDEN SOLDIER DIES OF WOUNDS

Mr. and Mrs. Arthur Loake, of 28 Church-street, Rushden, received a letter from the War Office on Saturday which gave the sad news of the death of their youngest son. Trooper John Loake, Royal Lancers. It was stated that Trooper Loake received shrapnel wounds while serving in the Central Mediterranean in April, and died the following day. Just 20 years of age, Trooper Loake had been in the Army 18 months, formerly working in the Rushden Co-operative drapery store. He was educated at the Wellingborough Grammar School and attended the Congregational Sunday School.

One brother is with the R.A.F. in India, and another is in the R.A.C.

Ronald Hales (1935–37), of Higham Ferrers, volunteered for aircrew service in 1942 and served as a rear gunner in Lancasters, reaching the rank of Sergeant. He was killed aged 20 on 8th June 1944 on an operational flight over France, two days after the Normandy landings on D-Day. He was buried in a communal grave at the Viroflay Cemetery at Bonnalles, near Paris.

Norman Sharpe (1933–39), of Irthlingborough, a 1st XV player and school prefect, volunteered as an officer cadet training at Sandhurst in 1942. and was commissioned in the 2nd Northants Yeomanry Royal Army Corps as a Lieutenant. He was one of the first to go to Normandy and was killed on 30th June 1944, aged 21. He was buried at Le-Gaule near Cheux and re-interred at the St Manvieu British cemetery south east of Bayeux, France.

Robert Troath (1932–38) played for the first XV, excelled at PT and boxing, and became a King's Scout in the school troop. He joined the Navy in 1942 and served on HMS *Ledbury*, before being commissioned on HMS *Cottilian*. His last commission was on HMS *Ganilly*, on which he lost his life when it was torpedoed by U-boat 390 off Omaha Beach on the Normandy coast on 5 July 1944. The U-boat was itself sunk by depth charges from the destroyer HMS *Wanderer* and the frigate HMS *Tavy*. The Troath History and Geography Prizes at the school were founded to preserve his memory.

Colin Penness (1935–40), from Rushden, joined the Royal Electrical and Mechanical Engineers (REME) in March 1943. From September 1943 to March 1944 he served in North Africa and then took part in the allied invasion of Italy, where he was killed, aged 20, on 3rd September 1944 in the battle of the Gothic Line. He was buried in the British war cemetery at Montechio in Northern Italy.

RUSHDEN SOLDIER DIES OF WOUNDS

Mr. and Mrs. James Penness, of 71 Newton-road, Rushden, heard on Wednesday that their youngest son Craftsman Colin Roderick Penness, R.E.M.E. attached to a tank regiment in the Central Mediterranean, had died of wounds.

Craftsman Penness was 20. He had been in the Army for 18 months, and abroad for 12, which included eight months in North Africa.

He was educated at Wellingborough Grammar School, and attended the Bible Class and Sunday School of St. Mary's Church. Later he was employed on the staff of the Tecnic Boot Co.

His elder brother is in the R.A.F. Police, and seven cousins are also in the Forces. His father is one of five brothers who served in the last war.

Raymond Osborne (1933–36) joined the RAF in 1941 and trained as a pilot in Canada and the USA, later going to Africa for a course in navigation. Serving with 49th Squadron RAF Volunteer Reserve, he was killed on 27th April 1944 at the age of 21, when his aircraft was brought down returning from operations over Southern Germany. He was buried in the British military cemetery at Bad Toels, Durnbach, near Munich.

1945

Gordon Coe (1932–36) joined the RAF in June 1941 and served nearly three years in Canada as a flying instructor and subsequently pilot of a Mosquito aircraft with the rank of Warrant Officer. On 21st January 1945, aged 23, he was reported missing, later killed, in France. He was buried at Cambrai (Route de Solesmes) Communal Cemetery.

WELLINGBOROUGH AIRMAN MISSING

A Hinwick-born airman, Warrant Officer Gordon Roy Coe, only son of Mr. and Mrs. Gordon Coe, now of 14, Strode-road, Wellingborough, is reported missing as a result of air operations over Germany. Educated at Wellingborough Grammar School, Warrant Officer Coe was formerly employed by the Ideal Clothiers, Ltd., Wellingborough, and at the age of 19 joined the R.A.F. in June, 1941. He was trained in Canada, where he spent nearly three years, and was an instructor there for some time.

Brian Peck (1939–42) joined the Northamptonshire Regiment in June 1944 and transferred to the Royal Scots in 1945. He was killed, aged 18, during the crossing of the Rhine into Germany on 24th March 1945 and buried in the Reichswald Forest British Military Cemetery.

William Berrill (1930–32) joined the Northants Regiment at the outbreak of war in 1939 and served in France, North Africa and Sicily. He was killed, aged 26, on 24 April 1945 in Italy in the last engagement of his battalion at the Argenta Gap and was buried nearby.

KILLED IN ITALY

The sad news has been received by Mr. and Mrs. W. Berrill, of 40, Northampton-road, Wellingborough, that their only son, Pte. William John Berrill, has been killed in action in Italy. He was killed in April, and was probably the last Wellingborough soldier to lose his life there. Aged 26, Pte. Berrill joined up in September, 1939. His wife, Mrs. Mary Berrill, is residing at Bournemouth. He saw service in France, North Africa, and Sicily before landing in Italy. He was formerly employed in his father's dairy in Northampton-road, and was educated at Wellingborough Grammar School.

Mr Woolley kept the boys fully informed of the fate of old boys during the war. The school began each day with a full school assembly including a bible reading and hymn singing. The name of any Old Boy killed in action was read out: a sombre thought for young boys who might very well follow in his footsteps.

Mr Woolley was also totally committed to making social and charitable donations. In Autumn 1944, for example, the Magazine reported the school making donations to the Cottage Hospital, Poppy Day (as usual), and the development of a new fund to send a Christmas present to each of our Old Boys who was a prisoner of war.

ROLL OF HONOUR.

Killed or Died on Active Service :—

A. E. Abbott, R.A.F.V.R.
N. L. Hornsey, Sgt., R.A.F.V.R.
R. S. Mutimer, Sgt., R.A.F.V.R.
D. A. Prigmore, Tpr., R. Dragoon Gds.
P. G. Felce, Flt.-Lt., R.A.F.V.R.
E. Hudson, T. Sub-Lieut., R.N.V.R.
G. G. Elderton.
H. P. Gardiner, Sgt., R.A.F.
R. R. Norman, F/Sgt., R.A.F.V.R.
R. R. E. Howard, Sgt., R.A.F.V.R.
J. A. P. Loake, Tpr., R. Lancers.
J. Dunkley, Sgt., R.A.F.
R. W. H. Troath, Sub-Lieut., R.N.V.R.
C. R. Penness, Craftsman, R.E.M.E.
N. P. Sharpe, Lieut., R.A.C. (Northants. Yeomanry)
C. R. Coe, W.O., R.A.F.
F. W. Furr, Telgr., R.N.
B. T. Peck, Royal Scots Regt.
W. J. Berrill, Northants. Regt.

Missing :—

H. A. Cheaseman, Sgt., R.A.F.
A. R. Gillitt, Cadet, Merchant Navy.

Decorations :—

D.F.C.

Sq. Ldr. F. A. Robinson, R.A.F.
Flt.-Lt. C. Bailey, R.A.F.V.R.
F/Lt. D. E. Braybrook, R.A.F.V.R.
F/Lt. H. W. Catlin, R.A.F.V.R.
F./O. K. Fillingham, R.A.F.V.R.
F./Lt. K. N. Clark, R.A.F.V.R.

M.C.

Capt. T. F. Addis, D.L.I.

D.F.M.

Sgt. R. S. Mutimer, R.A.F.V.R.
F/Lt. F. Langley, R.A.F.V.R.
F./Sgt. V. F. Pitcher, R.A.F.V.R.

D.C.M.

Sq. S.M., R. D. Page, Recce Regt.

Russian Order of Patriotic War, 1st Class.

Sq./Ldr. F. A. Robinson, D.F.C., R.A.F.

Mentioned in Despatches :—

Telegr. F. W. Furr, R.N.
Sq./Ldr. F. A. Robinson, D.F.C., R.A.F.
Cpl. R. Elkington, R.A.F.V.R.
F.Lt. J. G. Dunning, M.A. (Master) R.A.F.V.R.

Prisoners of War.

P. J. Neal, Dvr. (repatriated).
A. Warner, Pte., R.A.O.C. (repatriated).
F. C. Causebrook, L/Cpl., R.A.M.C.
J. R. Upton, F./O., R.A.F.V.R. (repatriated)
F. H. Partridge, L/Sgt., Airbourne Sigs. (repatriated).

The Roll of Honour as known at the end of the War. Subsequently the deaths of the following men were added:

R. D. Hales (1935–37). RAF. Killed in Action, June 1944.
R. G. Osborne (1933–1936). RAF. Pilot. 1944.
J. H. Sharp (1934–1939). Fleet Air Arm. Pilot. June, 1951 Korea.
F. C. Causebrook, (1931–1934). L/Cpl., RAMC, died in Japanese Prisoner of War Camp.

The Departure of Mr Woolley

By the time Mr Woolley was planning to leave the school in 1945, academic success was evident. The number of boys at the school had doubled and the proportion passing the School Certificate had also doubled. The school that year had set a "pretty rigid entrance test" turning down nearly 20 applicants and at the highest level, sixth form boys were gaining entry to university.

By chance, Mr Woolley's departure happened at the most significant point in the development of secondary education in the UK. In 1944 Rab Butler guided the 1944 Education Act through Parliament to provide universal free education for all children from age 5 to 15. The most significant aspects were two-fold: the raising of school-leaving age to 15 with effect from 1947 and the introduction of a new examination to be taken at age 11+ to select children for one of three types of school: Grammar, Technical and Secondary Modern.

Well. News. 29 DEC. 1944

Good Show!

Four 'Varsity scholarships at one sitting from the same school is the proud achievement, noted in our columns recently, of Wellingborough Grammar School. Here are the pictures of the successful scholars and a reminder of their achievements. Top left: E. J. R. Hewitt, 107, Wellingborough-road, Rushden (£100, Nat. Sciences, Christ's College, Cambridge), right, R. D. Stewart, 6, Howard-road, Wollaston (£60, Nat. Sciences, Christ's College, Cambridge). Bottom left: M. M. Woolfson, 11, Cecil House, Southwold-road, Clapton, E.6. (Exhib. of £70 for Physics, Jesus College, Oxford); right, K. R. Spencer, 27, Farndish-road, Irchester (Methuen Scholarship of £100 for Mathematics, Wadham College, Oxford).

The Grammar School was now fully integrated into the system as the most academic of the three types of secondary school. Into the school in future would come a higher percentage of boys from working class families, starting in August 1946.

In his last term in Summer 1945, the school had their first "Day Out" where every boy in the school picked from a large menu of possibilities. Everyone went somewhere, not always to his first choice.

When Mr Woolley left to take up his new appointment as Educational Secretary to the Oxford University Appointments Committee in July 1945, the school's academic prowess was demonstrable. In the words of P. A. Fryer, Chairman of the Governors, Mr Woolley had "left his final triumph to his last year, when the school won five open scholarships at our senior universities – a wonderful record for so young a school; no work in the interests of boys has been too much for him."

Mr Woolley was to serve as Educational Secretary from 1945 to 1962 where he was employed to interview Oxford finalists looking for a position in teaching to help them find appropriate employment. The official history of the Oxford University Appointments Committee described him as having "an astonishing array of contacts and a precise sense of who belongs where," though he also "lacked ebullience and could appear dour and headmasterly." More interestingly it was noted by one candidate that he "seemed only interested in the recruitment of schoolmasters to boarding schools and did not seem to appreciate that one would be happy to settle for a direct grant or LEA Grammar School." Was this a comment on his own predicament steering Wellingborough Grammar School through the war years, appointing 32 teachers in eight years, fourteen of whom stayed two years or less? Whatever his later views, he served Wellingborough Grammar School well, holding a firm rein in changing times and raising the status of the school at a time of adversity.

In 1962 he was ordained and left Oxford to take up a living in Essex as Rector of Gestingthorpe.

Back in Wellingborough in the autumn of 1945, Mr Nicholas took on the role of Acting Head. Mr Pine returned from the forces in time to begin the Autumn Term. Mr Wrenn arrived as Headmaster to begin the Spring Term in January 1946 after serving a final term's notice as Senior Language Master at Birkenhead School. Mr Dunning, Mr Phillips and Mr Butler returned at the same time. The last of the wartime lady masters, Mrs Allen and Miss Bates were to leave in the summer of 1946. The post-war period of further expansion under Mr Wrenn was about to begin.

War and Peace

Noel Pearson (1944–1950)

I entered the school in 1944, having passed the Scholarship (as it was known then) at the age of ten. The war was reaching its final stages, but there were still many restrictions and rationing was in force.

To reach school from Finedon for assembly at 8.50 am, we needed to catch a workers' bus at 7.30 am though there was no guarantee there would be room on it as workers took priority. Instead we caught the 8.20 am and had to walk from Cannon Street through the Lyric and Praed's Brewery yards, reaching school just before 9.00. The powers that be took a dim view, and had periodic grumbles, suggesting that we should walk faster, or even run! Eventually they gave up. School buses were introduced after the war, about two years later.

The school building was still in its original form: the two-storey block facing Doddington Road, with the office and library in the centre flanked by two pairs of classrooms; above were two more classrooms with the Science and Chemistry Laboratories in the middle. The other three sides of the quad were single-storey, with rooms 5, 6 and the Music Room to the left, the Lockers and the Art Room to the right, and the Hall/gym and Staff Room in the centre. Downstairs were the Dining Room and the Boiler House.

School uniform was compulsory, with a black blazer and Tudor rose badge, grey flannels, white shirt and school tie. There were two slightly differing patterns, from the two outfitters, Warwick's in the High Street, or Dixon and Parker's at the top of Midland Road. With clothing rationing in operation, the famous 'ringworm' caps, which gave the school its nickname, were often a problem: if a second-hand 'ringworm' was unobtainable, many wore a plain black cap with a small rose badge. Uniform could not be enforced in the upper school, especially for imminent leavers, but plain grey suits were insisted upon. Many of the first years wore grey flannel shorts.

School Dinners cost 2/6 per week, collected by the form master on Monday morning. Dinners were in two sittings and menus reflected the austere rationing, with little variety—stew, mash and rice were regular items. School milk was always available, distributed at break at the top of the dining-room steps.

Ancillary Staff at the school were down to the barest minimum. One elderly caretaker (Mr Tropman) was responsible for cleaning general areas such as corridors and hall. Classrooms were cleaned by pupils on a rota of about three weeks, working in pairs to sweep out the form room after school.

The teaching staff during the war consisted largely of ageing masters either nearing or past retiring age, together with others who, for some reason, were exempt from military service, and a number of temporary female 'masters'. The Head, Mr A. R. Woolley, was very much a product of the old school and Oxbridge. He always came into assembly in cap and gown and swept off his mortarboard with a flourish on reaching the lectern.

Many of the staff had their own

distinctive way of teaching. Dr A. Jackson, known as 'Alf' or 'Spike', was a Londoner, probably a voluntary evacuee who came to Wellingborough seeking employment after mass evacuations had left him jobless. A chain smoker, he also drank large amounts of tea and was always cadging quarters of tea from members of the class to eke out his own single rations. His drama lessons were always looked forward to, with his legendary call of "Tableau, mime or action!" followed by a smart ring of his bell to set his pupils acting a subject of his choice.

He had a gown that was in a constant state of disrepair. His Cockney accent came to the fore in times of stress, particularly when the waste from the Chemistry Lab above Room 3 overflowed, as it often did with extremely smelly results. "Oh Lor! Groome, go and ask Mr Holmes what he's doing!"

He married Miss Bates – who also taught at WGS during the latter part of the war – and was to stay on after the war as senior English Master until his retirement.

The mathematics master, Mr G. E. Richmond, known as 'Albert' must have had the most chaotic and anarchic experiences in the whole history of WGS. His fate to get 'played up' by even the mildest and well-behaved form was often self-inflicted. His catch phrases, innocently uttered, such as "Watch the board while I go through it," or "Every time I open my mouth some silly fool speaks!" were guaranteed to send any form into a paroxysm of unrestrained glee and anarchy.

His Yorkshire accent made his voice the most imitated in the school and almost every boy for generations has given his own impression of Albert's impassioned tones, usually heard above pandemonium. Looking back at a more sober age one wonders how he survived all those years of anarchy without suffering a complete breakdown, and one reflects sadly on the extreme cruelty if not sadism of the average English schoolboy.

Albert also taught divinity—he was a nonconformist lay preacher outside school—but even these periods contained little that was sacred. Inevitably he would have to resort to corporal punishment, even leading to 'mass executions'. Each stroke of the slipper was greeted with a concerted sneeze by the rest of the class. Legend has it that he once slippered a whole class; some of them had the masochism to go round twice!

Albert's passion for steam trains was revealed after the war, when school extramural activities began to increase. The inaugural meeting of the Railway Club under his chairmanship was standing-room only in Room 2. But even after the 'joy-riders' dropped out, leaving the more serious enthusiasts, the club was probably the most popular of all school clubs. Outings were soon arranged to Blisworth, Roade and Peterborough, and eventually even farther afield to places such as Crewe and other important junctions. Thanks to Albert a whole generation of boys were given the opportunity to enjoy the last years of the Age of Steam, and the Advent of Diesel.

Mr S. B. (Sam) Harris taught maths and turned his hand to PT during 'Chunky' Pine's absence on war service. Sam's PT lessons were on more regimental lines, and did not have the same flair and appeal of Chunky's, but that's not to say they were not appreciated. His form room was Room 15, the top prefab.

Sam, like the majority of staff, looked

on corporal punishment as the norm and principal method of achieving discipline. If you took the wrong book into his class, he would say, "And whose class are you going to interrupt?" and then, with a sadistic leer, "Tell him from me that England expects!", which usually meant two strokes of the slipper, especially if the class interrupted was that of Mr R. V. S. Ward or some other exponent of physical discipline.

Sam's usual mode of transport to school was an aged motor-cycle combination which he rode in a variety of protective clothing, the most remarkable being a huge one piece orange all-weather suit.

Mr C. H. Laurie was probably the most eccentric of all the masters of the war period (and that is certainly something). 'Uncle' Laurie had to be seen to be believed. He was very rotund, with a ruddy complexion. He looked like a farmer out on market day, which was not surprising as he had a pig farm at Byfield near Northampton.

He taught maths with a rural accent, and his normal manner could be described as irascible. There was no why or wherefore with Uncle, whatever the situation it was always, "How much?"

"Please sir, I've brought the wrong book." – "How much?"

He appeared to have a vast appetite; he would go down to First Dinner, have a large meal, then disappear out the front gate, supposedly bound for the Hind Hotel for another dinner or a pint or two. In the afternoon period he would put half a dozen examples on the board, and settle back in his chair with the *Farmer's Weekly* or *Domestic Pig Breeder*. After picking his nose and the wax from his ears, in a few minutes Uncle would drop off for his afternoon nap, which had been known to extend into the next period. Having worked the examples the class, or most of them, would chat quietly or do their other prep. One day a boy came in with a notice from the office,

"Please sir ..."

"QUIET ! don't wake him up."

"But he's got to read this out."

"You read it out."

"But he's got to sign it."

"Give it here."

Tom Groome solemnly read out the notice and duly added a squiggle where Uncle's initials should go.

"Now clear out and shut the door quietly."

At the end of the period we tip-toed out. The next week:

"Well! Have you done your homework?"

"No sir."

"How much? ...You haven't done it!"

"You didn't give us any sir. You must have forgotten."

"In that case you'd better have double this week."

On the last day of term, when Uncle finally retired, instead of walking down the side of the Hall, he passed straight through the massed ranks of boys applauding and cheering on either side like a great guard of honour. He told us all to play up and play the game (we never knew he had any interest in sport!), and promised to use his generous presentation cheque to buy a new pig!

Mr I. J. Nicholas was the longest-serving master of all. 'Nick' was definitely at WGS for most of the life of the school. His main subject was Latin, but he did cover for other subjects. In his capacity as Second Master, if no one else was there, he did it himself. However, a great deal of his time was occupied with administration.

He guided us through a crash two-year course in Latin in the Sixth and, having exhausted the works of Messrs Grey, McEvoy & Jenkins, Moneypenny & Buckle, and others, we wrestled with those of Caesar and Virgil. We soon needed the inestimable aid of a Brodie Classic Translation at 1/10d a time from a secret address in London. This made life much easier and everybody soon had one secreted under the desk. After a few too glib translations, it didn't take Nick long to tumble that we had all invested in a 'bobsworth' as he termed it. However, although he didn't ban them, he was pretty scathing about their merits. But that didn't stop him from occasionally falling back on them as a last resort. "What does your bobsworth say, Furnell? ... Ye-es, I suppose you could say that, but it's not very good."

Nick was in charge of Rugby, and must take much of the credit for the school's excellent record in that field His finest hour came after the war in the season 49/50 when J. P. (Johnny) Hyde, already a regular player for Northampton Saints, left school to do his National Service, very soon to play for the Army against the Navy, and then selected to play for England against France.

Nick is remembered for his dry sense of humour, and the iron under the velvet glove.

In 1945 Mr Woolley left the school to take up a senior post in the University Appointments Board at Oxford. Mr Nicholas became acting head during the summer and autumn terms and ruled with a rod of iron.

Peace came in August 1945. It brought a new sense of renewal to the nation and a significant change to the school. Mr Harold Albert Wrenn was appointed Headmaster and took up his post in January 1946. He soon made his mark and his early innovations and improvements showed his intention of bringing the school into the second half of the twentieth century. The early post-war period itself brought an easing in austerity and restrictions. School buses were introduced and also bus passes. Pupils no longer had to walk to Market Street or the Palace to catch buses home, Broadway soon became a busy bus stop. New caretakers and groundsmen were appointed. The cook retired and Nancy Clark—a new single lady with dietary qualifications—took over the kitchen. The old roster of DIY cleaners became a thing of the past.

Mr Wrenn replaced the system in which the boys entered the school in forms 2A1, 2A2, or 2B, to the more rational 1A, 1B, 1C. The old term names of Michaelmas, Hilary and Trinity became Autumn, Spring and Summer. New textbooks were purchased and better quality exercise books.

The forces 'demob' system began with the return of old teaching staff and several new faces appeared. The school photograph of 1946 shows the following staff line-up:

Nora Bavin (secretary), Mr Atherton (French), Mr C. A. Pine (PE), Mr G. E. Richmond (Mathematics and Divinity), Mr T. J. Cook (History), Mr W. Holmes (Chemistry), Mr H. C. Phillips (Art), Mr J. H. Butler (Mathematics), Mr H. H. Wintersgill (Music), Mr I. J. Nicholas, Second Master (Latin), Mr H. A. Wrenn (Headmaster), Mr J. G. Dunning (Geography), Dr A. Jackson (English), Mr L. E. Bratt (French), Mr S. B. Harris (Mathematics), Mr R. V. S. Ward (Geography and Economics), Mr C. H.

Ward (Mathematics), Mr G. E. Sharp (Physics), Mr W. H. Davies (English), Mr L. J. Jay (Geography), and Mr B. R. Burrell (French).

New faces and increasing numbers brought over-crowding and finally in 1946-47, two new prefab classrooms were built parallel to the hall.

H.A.W. was a great believer in languages. Latin was reintroduced, H.A.W. himself taught Spanish, and also had the foresight to see the coming Cold War. He said, "We either fight them or trade with them," and the Sixth Form began to learn Russian under Mr Bratt and the newly-arrived Mr Cheale, who had spent the closing months of the War and after in the Slav countries.

Not all innovations met with Harold's approval. One of his memorable speeches went, "I wouldn't advise you bise to biy a beero!" Biro pens had been recently invented by a Czech of that name, and the early models were pretty awful. Harold considered them a curse and an abomination, a passing fad that would never last! He tried to get them banned: they were banned in public examinations, as he said, they faded within a few weeks, and of course they did not improve one's handwriting. It was a battle he eventually lost.

Another battle was 'The Great Kitbag Mystery'. "What kind of boy has the mentality to hang a kitbag out of the locker window," he railed. After games and a shower, one had to leave looking one's best, especially with the High School waiting at the bus stop. The only way to see to comb your hair, was in the reflection made by a kitbag hung outside the window, used by a succession of boys and invariably left there after the last one. [Some-one else's bag of course.] Harold threatened dire reprisals if the practice did not cease, which it didn't, and he continued to lose his reputed wig. Finally somebody explained – probably a prefect. "Why doesn't someone tell me things," he groaned at the next assembly. "Mirrors will be provided." And they were. By the state of them, Harold must have sent Nora down to Wilfords.

Nora Bavin 'Duke' Atherton 'Chunky' Pine 'Albert' Richmond 'Hobo' Cook 'Father' Holmes 'Eddie' Phillips

'Johnny' Butler 'Harry' Wintersgill 'Nick' Nicholas 'Harold' Wrenn 'Jake' Dunning 'Spike' Jackson 'Lennie' Bratt

'Sam' Harris 'Beery' Ward 'Charlie' Ward G. E. Sharp 'Trigger' Davis 'Laddie' Jay 'Danny' Burrell

The masters on the 1946 school photo

Thoughts on WGS

Peter Wilson (1942–1949)

In the main the male members of staff in the 40s were either too old or too incompetent to be of use in HM forces. Certainly the most effective teachers were the women. I remember in particular Mrs. Colsell who taught us French, largely by the direct method. She was quite an inspiration and coped admirably with little boys who baited her. I suppose it was she who first awakened my passion for foreign languages.

Mr Nicholas, Deputy Head in my first year, was an essentially kind and even-tempered man whose clear aim was to instil in us the disciplines of Latin grammar. But even he resorted to the slipper to drive home some important truths. A careless grammatical error could incur a reminder delivered on the seat of one's trousers to punctuate the stressed syllables of ***object*** of verb, ac-***cus***-ative case. It seemed to work. During the interregnum he would leave classes unattended for long periods, sometimes the whole lesson, as he went about administrative duties.

Other masters were much less sparing of the rod, which was generally part of a broken desk, but in Mr Laurie's case, a knotted rope. The administering of corporal punishment was seen as the normal state of affairs and necessary for our good. The weapons used were often given friendly names like 'George' or 'Arthur'.

Mr Wintersgill invented a whole new vocabulary for the treatment. He would twank anyone who projected missiles while he was at the keyboard, singing his favourite songs from Gilbert and Sullivan.

In a few instances when a baited master lost control of his temper it was clearly brutal and offensive, not to say dangerous. This frequently happened in the case of Mr Richmond whose odd appearance and northern accent invited ridicule from unruly boys. "Watch the board while I go through it", "every time I open my mouth some fool speaks" were two commonly heard utterances of his, but he never saw the joke.

Other disconnected incidents fly into my mind: we were once gathered round the front bench in a science lab when Mr Sharp was explaining that sodium and water are not a friendly mixture. He cut a lump of sodium off a larger chunk and dropped it into a glass tank filled with water. We enjoyed watching the sodium fizzing round until it suddenly exploded, shattering the glass tank and showering the most inquisitive pupils with caustic soda. Risk assessment was unheard of in those far-off days.

Fear ruled among the younger pupils but, by the fifth form, masters seemed more reasonable (maybe it was we pupils who had changed). Though I was no great shakes at maths, Mr Butler always had a friendly word for me, showing an interest in my musical activities – he, of course, was a keen clarinet player and performed on a number of occasions in school concerts.

As little ones we were terrified of the Welshman Sterry, but in later years he turned out to be quite affable. As Sixth Formers and Prefects we still had a healthy respect for Mr Dunning's tongue. I remember he once caught Brian

Toms (who went up to Christchurch and gained a first in Modern Languages, Russian and Polish) carving his name under the long table in the library. We were all made to feel very small.

I was certainly not inspired by Lennie Bratt, whose heart was clearly not in his job. He never marked written work, and, as the end of each term loomed and marks were a pre-requisite, he conducted a moving-up session. A question would be fired at each pupil in turn, starting on the left of the front row (to the right of the teacher's desk). If he answered satisfactorily he stayed put, if not the question was passed down the line until the pupil who answered correctly moved to the position of the failed pupil and the rest moved down a place. It was a complete lottery, rather like snakes and ladders and no more informative. But when the bell went to end the session positions were noted and (presumably) marks invented to justify the positions.

The Headmaster himself always saw to it that he took the Second Form (i.e. first year) for RE (in those days called Scripture). And he was always eager to digress on various social and ethical subjects.

I remember on one occasion as we read from the Old Testament the vale of Shittim had us all tittering with embarrassment. Woolley confronted the situation, explaining that the place name had absolutely nothing to do with the perfectly good Anglo-Saxon word 'shit'.

Thoughts on WGS

Under A. R. Woolley the school was run on the lines of an old public school. It seems to me now that bullying was accepted as normal: the new boys on the first day had to run the gauntlet of a volley of swinging kitbags wielded by much bigger boys as we entered the lower gate in Doddington Road.

I'm quite surprised that no one was seriously hurt, as far as I know. Force ruled.

The prefects were for the most part brutal in their doling out of corporal punishment. On occasion a whole form would be lined up outside the prefects study in morning break, entering one by one for the dreaded six of the best. The prefects seemed to take it in turn to deliver the blows with a gym shoe, specially chosen for its weight and flexibility, while the others watched with evident glee.

The prefects' rule continued through Nick's interregnum; no doubt he did not see his role as a policy-maker. But their rule ended abruptly on the arrival of Harry Wrenn, who instituted a much more pupil-friendly régime.

One thing for which I am immensely grateful was Mr Wrenn's great drive to get all worthy pupils into university, and he helped me in another way: when he discovered I was to visit my pen-friend over the Easter holidays he took advantage of the fact that John Hyde, my contemporary, was in the English team, and arranged for me to pick up two tickets for the match from the *Daily Mail*'s Paris office. It was a memorable day at Stade Colombe. But we lost.

Masters after the War
I. J. Nicholas (14 years), J. G. Dunning (14), H. C. Phillips (12), J. H. Butler (10), C. A. Pine (8), A. Jackson (7), H. H. Wintersgill (7), R. V. S. Ward (4+2 terms), Mrs K. G. Allen, (4+1), B. R. Burrell (4), G. E. Richmond (4) S. B. Harris (4), T. G. Cook (3), L. E. Bratt (3), W. Holmes (1+1), G. E. Sharp (1+1), Miss M. H. Bates (1)

Year	**Arrival** (term)	**Departure** (& length of service)
45–46	H. A. Wrenn (term 2), C. J. H. Ward, J. W. Davies, L. J. Jay, H. N. Atherton, [E. Essex]	Mrs K. G. Allen (5 years +1 term), Miss M. H. Bates (2 years + 1 term), S. B. Harris (5), D. H. T. Sterry (3)
46–47	A. W. Leftwich, H. F. Christopherson	H. F. Christopherson (1)
47–48	W. Henderson, M. S. Cheale	H. H. Wintersgill (9), H. N. Atherton (2)
48–49	R. H. Temple, Mrs M. Fisk	G. E. Sharp (5), Mrs M. Fisk (1)
49–50	A. E. Sparrow, E. J. Pfaff, [C. Feldman from USA], [J. L. Hewland, on exchange for Mr Dunning in NZ]	G. E. Richmond (7 years 1 term)
50–51	W. J. Jessup, D. J. Hoskin	D. J. Hoskin (1)
51–52	S. J. Branson, J. Butterfield	W. Henderson (5), Jessup (2)
52–53	J. W. Huddart, R. C. F. Parish	L. J. Jay (7)
53–54	D. J. Riach, G. W. Cooksey, D. C. Clutterbuck	L. E. Bratt (11), J. Butterfield (3), R. C. F. Parish (2)
54–55	J. P. Hyde, M. J. Gray, P. A. Goodman	T. J. Cook (12), J. W. Davies (9), E. J. Pfaff (6), S. J. Branson (4), D. C. Clutterbuck (2)
55–56	T. J. Sulch, R. E. Knight, G. B. Stanley, E. P. Butcher, B. J. P. Tompkins, T. B. J. Mardell	
56–57	J. A. Stratfold, J. R. Hollister, [A. A. Jackson]	G. W. Cooksey (4)
57–58	C. McCall, L. Greenwood, J. E. Barker (2) [D. N. Hall]	B. R. Burrell (16), P. A. Gooodman (4), T. B. J. Mardell (3), J, R. Hollister (2)
58–59	E. A. Pritchard, P. A. J. Pettit, J. K. Halliwell, P. J. Delmon (2), [M. Currie, 2 terms] [C. B . Johnson]	M. J. Gray (4 years + 1 term), D. J. Riach (6), J. A. Stratfold (2 years + 2 terms)
59–60	A. J. B. Tussler, C. F. Taylor, G. T. Ridge, P. D. J. Johnson, [D. O. Tall]	C. McCall (3 years + 2 terms), J. L. Greenwood (3), P. J. Delmon (1+2)
60–61	A. Bantoft, R. Bentley, S. W. Brown, P. Gillibrand, R. Miles, R. H. Templar, A. R. Chesters (2), R. J. Shaw (2)	G. B. Stanley (5 years + 1 term), E. P. Butcher (5+1) P. D. J. Johnson (2+2)
61–62	A. J. L. Alden, [S. C. Norsworthy], [H. S . D. Cole]	C. J. H. Ward (16), B. J. P. Tompkins (7+2), R. E. Knight (7+2)
62–63	C. J. Cox, M. J. Parkin, T. D. Norman, P. J. Warren	W. Holmes (19+1), J. K. Halliwell (5), G. T. Ridge (4), S. W. Brown (3), R. Miles (3)
63–64	C. H. Stevenson, R. D. Beacham, C. W. Andreae	R. H. Templar (4), R. J. Shaw (3+2), P. J. Warren (2), C. W. Andreae (1)
64–65	A. R. Kingston, R. J. Lane, R. E. Oberman, D. F. Sturman, R. B. Taylor, T. G. Tomlinson, D. S. Wilson [W. R. Orton]	C. F. Taylor (5 years + 1 term) , R. E. Oberman (1)
65–66	M. F. Hendley, C. R. Isted, N. M. C. Anderson	P. A. J. Pettit, (7 years+ 1 term), J. G. Dunning (34), A. J. L. Alden (5)
66–67	W. J. Walker, L. C. Harding, A. P. G. MacDonald, P. J. Warren	E. A. Pritchard (9), A. Bantoft (7), T. D. Norman (5), R. J. Lane (3), C. R. Isted (2), N. M. C. Anderson (2), P. J. Warren (1)
67–68	M. K. Wright, N. S. F. Wills, T. A. J. Rowe, I. L. MacDougall, T. C. Goodman, R. P. Turville, L. J. Alvis	M. J. Parkin (6), A. R. Kingston (4)
68–69	–	A. W. Leftwich (22), P. Gillibrand (9), C. J. Cox (7), R. D. Beacham (8), D. F. Sturman (5), M. F. Hendley (4), L. J. Alvis (2)
69–70	D. H. Buchanan, P. F. Cameron, R. A. Farey, K. Parkinson, R. Pope, M. S. Vann, I. Rawlins (2)	A. Jackson (31), A. P. G. MacDonald (4), R. Pope (1)
70–71	G. B. Dean, T. W. Lewis, R. D. Till, [K. P. Ash]	W. J. Walker (5), L. C. Harding (5),
71–72	P. Buckby, R. Armstrong, P. C. Hayes	R. D. Till (3), I. Rawlins (2+2)
72–73	W. A. Bates	C. H. Stevenson (9 years, 1 term), I. J. Nicholas (41), H. C. Phillips (39), M. S. Vann (4), W. A. Bates (1)
73–74	M. D. Webster, B. L. Gilbert, B. Emerson, N. P. J. Way, [P. P. York]	T. W. Lewis (4 years + 1 term), J. E. Barker (16+2), R. P. Turville (7), P. C. Hayes (3)
74–75	R. P. Yorke, P. M. Layton, E. J. Holt, M. F. Hager	J. H. Butler (39), H. A. Wrenn (29+2), R. B. Taylor (11)

Masters continuing in the Wrenn School
C. A. Pine (37), R.V. S. Ward (34), M. S. Cheale (28), R. H. Temple (27), A. E. Sparrow (26), J. W. Huddart (23), J. P. Hyde (21), T. J. C. Sulch (20), A. J. B. Tussler (16), R. Bentley (15), A. R. Chesters (14+2), D. S. Wilson (11), T. G. Tomlinson (11), M. K. Wright (8), N. S. F. Wills (8), T. A. J. Rowe (8), I. L. MacDougall (8), T. C. Goodman (8), K. Parkinson (6), R. A. Farey (6), P. F. Cameron (6), D. H. Buchanan (6), G. B. Dean (5), P. Buckby (4), R. Armstrong (4), M. D. Webster (2), N. P. J. Way (2), B. L. Gilbert (2), B. Emerson (2), R. P. Yorke (1), P. M. Layton (1), E. J. Holt (1), M. F. Hager (1).

Chapter 6

Long-Serving Staff Post-War

The immediate years following the war saw an influx of new teachers, many of whom were to stay for a decade or more, including Mr Wrenn, the school's longest serving headmaster for a period just one term short of thirty years. Over the years there was a subtle change in the style of teaching. Mr Wrenn himself instituted a more humane environment, leading autocratically yet fairly, while at the same time wielding his cane with appropriate vigour when required. The old stalwarts remained, true to their earlier character, and new masters arrived with their own idiosyncracies, including an increasing number of career teachers who were distinguished mainly by their straightforward manner in class.

H. A. Wrenn (Headmaster) January 1946–75

It is worth saying, just in case an Old Grammarian's grandchild reads this book, that the headmaster actually *taught* the boys, in most cases he taught Religious Education to the first year to get to know their names, and gave a range of other lessons such as 'German for Scientists' to sixth-formers needing some German for reading scientific papers at university. He was a firm disciplinarian, leading the school and taking care of the discipline while his second master Mr Nicholas organised the curriculum.

When he first arrived, his interest in sport was self-evident:

Mr Wrenn liked sport. He had an interest in cricket and regularly ran with the boys on cross country. Shortly after his arrival, I was running cross country and taking an unauthorised short cut when I heard the sounds of someone running behind me; glancing round I discovered that I had the new Head close on my tail – he was following me for the correct route! He was obviously not aware of this as I heard nothing further of the event – a close shave! — *Keith Gennis (1943–47)*

School in those days was a very happy place, more so in the Sixth Form form. I. J. Nicholas and H. A. Wrenn were very influential, the former for rugby the latter for pushing our years to try for places at Oxford and Cambridge. It's not supposed to mean so much these days. However, for a Grammar School started in 1930, it was exceptional.

Gerald Neville (1943–50)

I had the cane from Harold Wrenn. He took about six strides back and whacked me with his stick and hit me half way up my back. So he had another go. I don't remember what I did wrong. But I was never his favourite because I didn't like to call him "Sir".

Ray King-Underwood (1952–58)

Harold Wrenn – I suffered so many strokes from his cane I lost count but he made an impression on me in a more positive way.

Roland Sewell (1956–63)

I was a proud victim of Mr Wrenn's scissors on speech day, when he cut off my sideburns. *Paul 'Squatter' Scroxton (1965–72)*

Mr Wrenn was in absolute control of the school. He wielded his power with a dry wit and humour in his announcements at assembly:

I see the paper dart season has begun again. I now officially end it.

A ten-shilling note has been handed in to Miss Bavin. Will those boys who claim it kindly form a queue outside my room.

He was also remarkably fair in making and reconsidering decisions, focusing on the issues themselves and taking a logical decision based on the evidence, as we found through personal experience:

My brother Graham had a serious accident at Wicksteed Park just before going to Wellingborough Grammar School which affected his memory. When he was asked to choose Spanish or Biology at the end of his first year, he was too confused to specify a preference, and ended up with Spanish. I went to Mr Wrenn to explain his difficulty: he was already seriously failing French, so this would make two subjects to fail instead of one. Mr Wrenn changed him to Biology. Graham never passed French, even after sitting O-level seven times, but he obtained a good honours degree in Biology.

On another occasion, my mother, who was a formidable woman, complained to Mr Wrenn that I had been awarded the Prize for Biology rather than Mathematics after O-level when I had the top mark in both subjects and intended to study mathematics at university. Mr Wrenn saw the rationality of the argument and had the strength of character to agree.

David Tall (1952–60)

It takes a secure and special personality to listen to the evidence and take a fair decision regardless of any personal vanity. Mr Wrenn had this wisdom and would always listen carefully to other viewpoints and then make a firm and instant decision on his own authority without fear or favour.

C. J. H. 'Charlie' Ward (Mathematics) 1946–1963

Charlie Ward was one of those special teachers who taught through his eminent reasonableness and feeling for his subject, mathematics. He did not require to operate any system of punishment; working for him was just the natural way of things.

In 1948 he was an official timekeeper at the Olympic Games and brought a natural authority to athletics which he led at the school in his early days.

He was also the beloved teacher of 5B – not the natural choice of form for anyone wanting an easy life but it was something he enjoyed with a sense of fun and unflappability.

Charlie Ward taught me algebra in the first, third and lower sixth forms. He was infinitely patient, never got ruffled, and really helped me when I struggled. To my knowledge he never used corporal punishment. He was, quite simply, one of the nicest of the masters.

David Pope (1956–64)

The general lack of comment about him in retrospect, compared with the more colourful masters, is a testament to his quiet excellence as a teacher without any obvious personality quirks and no need to threaten any pupil with physical punishment. An appropriate view of him is that given by his friend and colleague 'Ivor' Cheale when writing his obituary:

I got to know Clem most of all when, in 1952, with his wife Ethel he joined my wife and myself in organising and accompanying the school foreign tours until he left us in 1962. Some hundreds of boys went on the tours in this period and their willingness to reminisce on their enjoyment of their experiences is itself a fine tribute to Clem's ability to plan, to forsee snags in good time and to present total good humour and cheerfulness whatever might occur.

Such little incidents as returning to Wellingborough at 11.30 pm with one party and leaving the next day at 4 am with the next; turning aside the wrath of rail staff finding boys stretched out asleep in first-class compartments; illness of almost epidemic proportions with 36 running high temperatures out of a party of 60 and, perhaps finest of all, getting a whole party's packed meals by rushing, with Ethel, through the passport control at Basel, without passports, of course! Clem coped with them all.

Martin Cheale

M. S. 'Ivor' Cheale (Mathematics/Technical Drawing) 1947–1975

Martin Cheale was a mathematics teacher who also covered Technical Drawing and Russian. Legend has it that he came in once with a stinking cold and said "I've a chill" – henceforth to be known universally as Ivor Cheale. He arrived in the school after the war, having spent the post war years in Eastern Europe, so it was natural for him to be roped in to help in the teaching of Russian.

He was fully committed to the school, not only in term-time, but after school on Friday evenings and Saturday mornings, building the model railway with the Railway Club. This 'band of brothers' also provided a source of stage staff every year for the school play. In the summer he would organise school trips to the continent, first with Mr Ward, and later with Mr Wrenn.

He was a good teacher, but easily distracted. All that was required during a lesson, was a question about his knowledge of – or his experiences in – the war. Whatever had been planned was then either forgotten or subsequently taught in much more restricted form.

Are there more than two hundred ways of saying, "What did you do in *the war Mr Cheale?" to avoid having to learn how to speak Russian. After two years of Russian education, I learnt like a parrot, "*Один день мы пошли для езды поездом в страну.*" That was the opposite of what was required for the GCE exam. That means, "One day we went for a ride by train into the country". The trouble was it should be "One day we went for a ride in the town." ... I failed Russian.*

Roy Tomlin (1952–59)

The worrying thing about learning Russian was that Jock Reid was using the same 'Teach Yourself Russian' book as Mr Cheale, but Jock was ahead of him. *Graham Willey (1952–58)*

What Ivor is really remembered for is not his teaching, but the Railway Club and the trips he organized abroad.

I recall that at certain times of the year his maths lessons began with telling us to work through all the examples on pages X to Y, while he sat there working on the details of the next foreign holiday.

Paul Robinson (1955–62)

A. W. 'Gus' Leftwich (Biology) 1947–1969

'Gus' Leftwich was a soft, gentle man who had no desire for corporal punishment; as a result he suffered more than most from minor misbehaviours. In Miss Bavin's scrapbooks, two highlights are recorded to his academic ability. The first is in 1950 when he with some of the older boys carried out a mosquito survey in the area, the results of which were reported to Northamptonshire Health Department. The second is his publication in the late fifties of his *Dictionary of Zoology*.

My recollection of Gus is far more prosaic: he was an adequate but not an enthusing teacher. He was extremely proud of the new biology lab (the Cockcroft Laboratory) when it opened in 1958. He was so proud that he hated to see the wall marked in any way. As a result, he dabbed paint on any pencil mark/scuff etc. The result, by the end of the year was that the lab looked as if it had chicken pox — because his can of paint was a different shade from the original. *Graham Tall (1955–63)*

Dear old Gus, bless him. Can you remember the times when the lab stools would be piled up at the back of the room while he was teaching, and everyone clinging to the benches to make it look as though we were still sitting? I also remember when we had a lesson in one of the prefabs and he stood at the door marking us in. He was rather confused when we arrived at the door again having gone out of the window and around the side. *Norman Keech (1963–70)*

Richard H. ' Buzz' Temple (French) 1948–1975+

Although the origins of the nickname 'Buzz' were seemingly lost in the mists of time, the man himself explained that it arose from his way of pronouncing the plural of a French noun that starts with a vowel, for instance, *l'arbre* (singular), *les arbres* (plural). The exaggerated z-sound in *lezzz arbre* was the origin of the name that stuck to him throughout his life as a teacher.

He was a consummate professional who got on with his job with the minimum of fuss and absence of eccentricity. When the Grammar School transmuted into the Wrenn School, he saw it as a new challenge and made it his business to learn how to operate in the new environment.

He had a wry and undemonstrative sense of humour, though his patience was tried when boys simply were unable to pronounce French words properly. In one class, John Hobbs (1952–59) remembers a fellow pupil making a mistake with the word 'allumette' and Buzz was given to say, "You have just confused matchboxes with matchsticks," to which the voice of Fred Nutt muttered in goonish terms from the back, "You can't get the wood you know!"

He had his own jokes:

"I hope you know why all Frenchmen ride old bicycles." As the class rumbles with various answers, Buzz responds: "B. C. Clettes."

He flew a swordfish biplane with the Navy in the Pacific during the war and it was therefore highly appropriate that, as a new master, he helped with the Model Aircraft Club flying planes on the field, and took a party to visit the Royal Navy at Portsmouth, staying on the

Royal Yacht *Victoria & Albert*. He also taught evening classes in French and is remembered for the wider qualities of his teaching:

> *Buzz not only gave most of his students a good grounding in French, he also provided an insight into a new culture.*
>
> *Chris Talbot (1955–62)*

> *I realise now that he must have drummed a fair bit of French into me, since I recently took an evening class in French. I was amazed at how much vocab and grammar had lain dormant in the brain for 45–50 years. But he upset me a little bit by awarding me the nickname of 'Les Phares' (the headlights) because I wore glasses. He upset me a lot more by catching me and ANO sneaking round the streets along the back of the school as a shortcut to avoid the dreaded 5 mile run. We ended up doing 5 miles round the playing field after school. At the time he was out driving his new car, a Citroen DS (a lovely car); what else would you expect from the French master?* *Paul Robinson (1955–62)*

A. E. 'Tony' (aka 'Spadge') Sparrow (Spanish) 1949–1975+

Mr Sparrow was head of Spanish, but he is best known for his coaching of the first XV, which he took over from Mr Nicholas in 1954.

> *Apart from his rugby influence Tony Sparrow also had a big influence in my decision to take Spanish and French at A-level. He was a real 'wordsmith'. His reports on every 1st XV game would be pinned to the notice board on a Monday morning, the players gathering eagerly in the quad to read what gems he had come up with this time – Benoist making 'labyrinthine sorties' from the wing into the opposition, McIlroy cutting through the defence like a 'dirk through haggis'.*
>
> *In lessons he would have Dick Iliffe and the rest of us racing to the dictionary to find the meaning of long, 'posh' words with lots of syllables, like pragmatic, erudite, analytical, incongruous, gregarious, big words for a muppet from the council estate whose vocabulary extended to knowing unwittingly how to use the 'f' word as a noun, verb, adjective, exclamation and imperative, but not much else.*
>
> *Dave Toseland (1959–67)*

In rugby, he had a simple philosophy: the forwards won the ball and passed it to the backs to score tries. Because our boys tended to be small compared with those of other strong rugby-playing schools, he concentrated on having a mobile pack who were fit and were first to the breakdown, so that over the length of the match, the fitter WGS pack would last longer and the school would score heavily towards the end. Mr Sparrow taught us that the time to work hardest was when you had your backs to the wall when it became possible to turn a set-back into a victory. He gave us a vision of how to succeed in a way that would serve us well as much in life as on the field of play.

He was enthusiastic and supportive in his praise, but honest and forthright in his criticism, a quality which endeared him to those who learned to succeed when facing difficulty.

> *Thoroughly enjoyed my time at WGS, my most enjoyable rugby memories are also of that era. Tony Sparrow remains my hero I'm only sad that he is not around for me to tell him. In my fifties I am proud to say I am still playing, although only on soft ground!*
>
> *Dave Toseland (1959–67)*

> *Tony Sparrow was my hero too. He told me I was too small to play in the County XV as a prop (only 10 stone 7 then, but twice that now!) but I had a flukey final trial in which I broke from the tight-head of the scrum and tackled the fly half in possession in the opening minutes, fell on the ball in a terrifying forward rush, was carried off with bleeding head, and got in the county team on the strength of this brief show of glory. It was my greatest achievement, because, frankly, I was useless at sport. But I played with Andy Johnson hooking and Bob Taylor as captain to reach a level way beyond my natural capacity. That was what WGS was about.*
>
> *David Tall (1952–60)*

> *Beery Ward taught us to play rugby and then Tony Sparrow gave us the special coaching that made the 1st XV of '66 and '67 what it was–brilliant! I still remember the pre-sixth form interview with Harry Wrenn when he uttered those immortal words, "Shurville, I am only letting you into the sixth form because Mr Sparrow wants you for the first fifteen," to which I could only reply, "Thank you sir." Considering what I have done since it was a pity I never got round to telling Tony what he had done for me.*
>
> *Keith Shurville (1960–67)*

Barry Waite (1960–67) remembered the two great years of 1965/66 and 1966/67 and the most difficult match in 1967, which was perhaps Tony Sparrow's finest hour.

It was to be my last academic year at WGS. We congregated in September 1966, with great hopes for our 1st XV performances on the rugby field. After all we were coming from a 14 wins–3 losses the season before and had retained many players.

First match, at home, against juggernaught Northampton Grammar School. Disaster: a 22–0 loss. Tony told us we had not played well, but without emotion set the expectation for much better to come.

The season began to move well, win after win, multiple games in sequence without points being scored against us. It included an almighty hard-worked victory against a much more powerful Old Grammarians XV on their playing field.

In January we came to the hardest game of the season: at Northampton Grammar school against the team that had well-beaten us in our opening match – a fine team with well-known players.

Tony Sparrow was calm; he had said he thought we would win. I need not worry about making tackles, he told me he knew I would. He knew Alfie Allen would be explosive in the centre, that Dave Toseland would put his silky touches into the game. Bill Drew would be unmoveable. He told us how we would win, in his calm quiet way.

A game it was – nothing given on either side. With little time left, WGS one score ahead, Bernie Cotton, the Northampton centre, a great athlete and England hockey player, burst through. Oh no, Bernie and one man outside him against E. R. Nevett, our full back. The world went in slow motion. Why was I not back there; where was the support?

Bernie threw a dummy: Rex Nevett nailed the tackle. Within microseconds we were 15 men behind the ball. Rex had one tackle to make that season and he made the season with that one tackle.

Dave Hill our scrum half played the time out wonderfully on the touch line. The final whistle sounded. We were there. The most important victory in what was to be 18 consecutive victories.

Tony Sparrow would not have visible celebrations, he was a decent man, respectful to opponents, and our play was to do our talking. How the world of sport needs more Tony Sparrows today.

As we sat in the changing room, Tony walked in, and a spontaneous outburst of "He's a jolly good fellow" rang out from all. Tony stood there, a blink of the eye and a short slight wry smile. It said it all. We will never know if we won it for him, we won it for ourselves or he made us think we were winning it for him, but he really wanted it for us. And we did it. Was this his finest hour or ours? What a legacy he has left!

The Fifties

John W. 'Ernie' Huddart (Physics) 1952–1975+

Ernie was a physics teacher with strong opinions who was able to terrify us in class. On one occasion he handed out a set of text-books to a sixth-form group and ceremoniously instructed them to cut out six pages on centrifugal and centripetal force, claiming that the theory of centripetal force was conceptually wrong and therefore should be removed.

It was all for effect to create an atmosphere of dedication to learning. He was totally committed to boys giving of their best.

As a physicist, he was a natural choice as the lighting expert for the school play and served over the years as stage electrician with his team of boys, alongside 'Ivor' Cheale as stage director and 'Cloddy' Barker on props. He also had a large van that he used to transport anything that required moving for his colleagues or the school clubs.

Many of his qualities emerged amongst the staff, as we shall hear towards the end of the book in the tales David Wilson tells of his time as a school master.

John Huddart scared the pants off me as a boy, and yet, when I got to know him as a master, was an absolutely lovely man who sent me plants every year, One year, he rang me up and I duly went and collected my plants. "These are pepper plants," said John, and I grew them on in the greenhouse. About two months later I had to ring him up and say, "that pepper plant you gave me John … is actually deadly nightshade."

David Wilson (1952–60)

J. P. 'Johnny' Hyde (Sport) 1954–1975+

Johnny Hyde was Wellingborough Grammar School and rugby entwined as man and boy. As a schoolboy in the forties, he was the outstanding athlete in the school, an aggressive short-leg fielder for the First IX and a dashing winger for the First XV, playing for the Saints, the East Midlands, the English Schoolboys, and selected as a full England International while still at school.

On returning to school as a teacher, he was a hero and a legend. Essentially quiet and mild-mannered, he became a whirlwind when he played sport. As a result, he was respected and admired by the boys without needing any other way of maintaining discipline. In keeping with the policy of the school, masters in charge of sports teams remained with them for a long period, so he initially coached the second XV while Tony Sparrow remained in total charge of the first XV from 1955 to 1969.

Johnny Hyde brought various alternative interests into games. When the weather was unsuitable for play on the field or for the 'three-mile run' down London Road, along the country lane and back along Doddington Road, he would bring out huge padded boxing gloves, set up a ring with four benches and ask for volunteers to decide who to fight for two one-minute rounds. It was an activity that might fill an idle hour but it never rose to the heights it aspired to in the thirties.

Another activity was 'Pirates' at the end of term gym lesson.

> *Johnny would set out all the fun apparatus in the hall – beams, wall bars, ropes, vaulting horse etc. and then strategically place the gym mats on the floor, or rather in the 'shark-infested' waters. Two boys were selected as 'pirates' to hunt down their quarry, while the latter ran, jumped and swung chaotically around the apparatus trying to avoid capture. Hugely enjoyable, but sadly not for the modern generation of schoolkids, since the 'powers that be' decided sometime in the 70s that the activity was not only dangerous but, God forbid, even worse … un-educational! That was probably the point when Johnny finally decided it was time to stop teaching PE and to concentrate his teaching career on biology.*
>
> *Dave Toseland (1959–67)*

T. J. C. 'Herbie' (aka 'Terry') Sulch (Mathematics) 1955–1975+

'Herbie' Sulch (aka 'Sludge', or 'Terry' was one of the most organised masters one could ever expect to meet. For his A-level applied mathematics lessons, he had written out a complete solution of every question in the book, so if a boy had a problem and Herbie had forgotten how to solve it, he simply gave the boy his book. He was also a good cricketer and a runner for the Kettering Harriers. When boys were out on the 'three-mile run', he would often run with them, and he was good at it too. When Mr Nicholas retired, he was promoted to Second Master and became Senior Deputy Head of the new Wrenn School.

His seriousness of purpose involved teaching the principles of mathematics with full meaning, so that every solution to a problem began with deriving the required equations from first principles. We would often write half a page or more to derive an equation before using it to solve the problem. As a pupil of Herbie Sulch, David Tall later became an A-level examiner and had on occasion to mark the work of WGS. There were all these beautiful lengthy solutions written out in full. The only problem was that there were no marks to give for deriving the equations, only for using them to solve the problem. So WGS boys were spending time on every question writing out detail that cost them time without gaining any credit. Given the delicacy of the situation—an old boy marking his old school's exams—this information was never made public … until now.

Herbie's seriousness of purpose had a double-edge to it. If a boy finished a piece of work, Herbie would give him more of the same for additional practice. As a result, we soon learned to work at the same speed – slow. The resulting boredom led to all kinds of pranks. On one occasion, the whole class hummed a low tone, each breathing at will so that the sound was continuous. Poor Herbie looked confused, not knowing where the sound came from. He stuck out the rest of the period without making a comment and it didn't happen again because the class tired of doing it too. Having said all this, we had a great deal of respect for him: he gave his all to us and always maintained the same high level of preparation and service.

J. E. 'Cloddy' Barker (Mathematics) 1958–1974

Cloddy taught mathematics and smoked a pipe which he often put into his pocket, with the result that the pocket itself continued 'smoking' during the lesson. He was a good maths teacher, one of the old school, but with no distinguishing characteristics. He was very droll. *Dick Smart (1960–68)*

I particularly remember Cloddy Barker (maths, ex-Japanese POW) and the way he spat his teeth out if you got him in a big enough rage.
Nick Tompkins (1969–75)

A. J. B. 'Brett' (or 'Cheyenne') Tussler (Geography) 1959–1975+

Brett Tussler came to the school in 1959 to join the Geography Department under Jake Dunning, becoming Head of Department when Jake retired in 1966. He had an incredible energy for life, playing rugby for the old boys with the vigorous intention of 'making the game-line', as coach of the 2nd XV, as a constant support to the scout troop in working for their badges, and as a 'Christian gentleman' working at All Saints' Church. With another member of staff, A. J. L. Alden, he produced a series of commercial map-books, including, France, the Benelux Countries and West Germany. His colleague Mr Ian MacDougall remembered:

> *As a schoolmaster he was inspiring to his pupils both young and old, asking for and getting the highest standards. As a colleague he was equally inspiring and an honour to work with. A pungent sense of humour, coupled with a great depth of comradeship, helped to create in the common room an atmosphere of bonhomie, scholarship and true professionalism.*

On the changeover to the new Wrenn School, he was appointed a Deputy Headmaster and was responsible for planning the timetable for the new school. He became Headmaster of Moulton School in 1978.

The boys had no doubt about him:

*Tussler was built like a brick s**t house, with very wide shoulders, so the name came from the cowboy TV programme of the time 'Cheyenne (Bodie)' played by Clint Walker, a man of similar build. Why the nickname changed to 'Brett' I have no idea. You will have to get that from a younger generation chappie.* *Keith Brealey (1959–64)*

(Of course, the reason Brett was called Brett was because that was his name! You can't win 'em all! [Ed.])

Brett Tussler taught geography and ran the school 2nd XV. Before our first match of the season 1964/5, we 15 year olds were offered a packet of 20 fags if we managed to break an opponent's leg by tackling him.
Keith Shurville (1960–67)

Brett was still also known as Cheyenne in the sixties. He was a strong character and he and Jake made a strong team, obtaining excellent examination results. Brett didn't need to use a weapon, his discipline, like Jake's, depended purely on force of character.

One of Brett Tussler's favourite stories related to his National Service in the Black Watch: "I had just embarked to go to Korea when the little yellow men surrendered. They clearly knew I was coming."
Dick Smart (1960–68)

The Sixties

R. 'Ron' (or Dick) Bentley 1960–1975+

'Ron' Bentley taught chemistry and mathematics. In 1962 he was one of the moving initiators of the School Modern Jazz Club to listen to Jazz LPs on Monday lunchtimes and encouraged boys to play Modern Jazz.

His true talent emerged when he retired early at 51 and subsequently took to playing piano in hotel lounges, including *The Tudor Gate Restaurant* in Finedon on Saturday nights. He may also be heard playing the grand piano in the foyer at the Derngate Theatre in Northampton to provide a pleasant background for the audience having a relaxing drink before going in to the concert.

A. R. 'Charlie' Chesters (Music) 1961–1975+

Alan 'Charlie' Chesters was the music master in the latter years of the school. He benefited from the build-up of the teaching of musical instruments and began the school's first wind band, combining woodwind, brass and percussion.

He was also a composer who wrote music for the school choir and orchestra and composed original music for the school plays. He was conductor of the Wellingborough Orpheus Choir from June 1979 until April 2002.

Still running choirs in Northampton until recently.
Dick Smart (1960–68)

R. B. 'Bob' Taylor (PE/Sport) 1964–1975

Bob Taylor was an old boy of Northampton Grammar School who captained the County Schoolboys in 1959–60. After training as a Physical Education teacher at St Alfred's College Winchester, he came as a sports master to Wellingborough Grammar School, later becoming captain of the England rugby team and a member of the Lions.

As a PE teacher, he introduced several new sports. In 1966, he started a five-a-side soccer competition for sixth-formers after they had taken exams. He emphasised field sports in athletics, including discus, javelin and the shot. His major gift to the school was his personal organisation of the School Basketball Club that leapt from nothing to a major sport within two years. At its height in 1969, there were six school teams (Seniors, Seconds, Under 16 sixths, Under 16 fifths, Under 15 and Under 14). To cater for the additional interest among the boys, he organised a House Competition and competitions between the forms at each age level.

As a Saints and England Rugby player, you didn't dare give Bob Taylor a nickname! Rugby player for the Saints, England and British Lions, he introduced basketball into the school. He was also a magistrate and the President of the Saints Rugby Club. *Dick Smart (1960–68)*

T. G. Tomlinson (Sport, Technical Drawing) 1964–1975+

'Tim' Tomlinson taught sport, technical drawing and metalwork, thus widening the curriculum to involve practical applications.

Tim Tomlinson came in 1964 (the same year as I started) to teach metalwork. We had had technical drawing before then (Martin Cheale began that) but Tim set the practical workshop up from 1964 and he also taught technical drawing. *David Wilson*

He taught engineering drawing in the old dining room which was opened as an Engineering Room by Douglas Bader. He was a keen sailor. *Dick Smart (1960–68)*

D. S. 'Dave' Wilson (English) 1964–1975+

David Wilson was an old boy who was head boy of the school in his time, but a boy with character who had spent some of his schooling in the B-stream. He knew from experience what it meant to be a lad. He had the gift of getting on well with everybody, including Jock the caretaker who used to share his carrot wine with him and Ernie the groundsman who used to let the boys "have a fag" in his hut on the field during morning break and lunchtime. When a group of boys were reported for smoking on the school bus by a girl from the High School, Mr Wrenn saw them one by one and told each to run round the field as a punishment, until head prefect David Wilson was also named. Mr Wrenn looked at him and railed, "How can I send them all round the field when you've been smoking? Get out, Get out."

After his study at Leeds, he was welcomed back as a teacher, taking over as Head of English when Dr Jackson retired. He had a good relationship with the boys:

Old Boy — a Good Teacher. *Dick Smart (1960–68)*

David Wilson, like Johnny Butler, always saw the good in us, so he could get the best out of boys who few other masters could control.
Tony Beadsworth (1961–66)

As an all-round sportsman and a fine batsman he became master in charge of the first eleven and after one exasperating season when there seemed to be little success in a limited time, he exhorted the boys to go out and enjoy their cricket the next year, with great results.

Master's Miscellany

In addition to the masters discussed individually with at least ten years service, there were 87 others appointed after the war who stayed at least a year and less than ten. With a stable set of senior masters who remained in the school for many years, ambitious young teachers would be likely to arrive, stay for few years experience and move on to a more senior position elsewhere. It was the natural order of things.

Geoff Cooksey, the master remembered by Sir David Frost in the foreword, did just that, becoming an executive with the Schools Council and then the headmaster of a large comprehensive in Milton Keynes.

G. W. 'Geoff' Cooksey

The twenty-nine staff members who served ten years or more did the lion's share of the teaching overall (around 58% of the total) even allowing for the increase in teacher numbers, from the four starting with Mr Lay, ten beginning with Mr Woolley, 20 in Mr Wrenn's first year and 36 in 1974/5. As the staff numbers grew, individual boys could pass through the school without being taught by an increasing number of them. There were post-war masters who were unknown to some pupils, perhaps remembered by others for their good teaching with few distinguishing characteristics, while a few had such highly individual personalities that they made a strong impression on many boys whether they taught them or not.

B. J. P. 'Tonk' Tompkins

Who, for example, can have been in the school in the late fifties and not know of 'Tonk' Tompkins? David Frost's immortal mimicry gave us the famous Tonkism: "Wotcher got there, a pork pie?" It was spoken by Brian Tompkins to Robert

Deacon in a 5Aii history lesson. It caused great hilarity at the time and has lived on as one of the memorable sayings of our masters.

Tonk, a very good cricketer, made several big scores against the 1st XI, and once ran Don Riach out on his third run. Tonk smote the ball to the boundary; Don called for the run and ran. He saw that there were two or three runs so continued running the second. Tonk, convinced that he had hit a boundary, did not budge from his crease. Don called for the third run and ran but Tonk was still rooted. Don turned back but the ball had been returned and Don was run out. He was not best pleased and mumbled for some time afterwards. Tonk went on to get 70 odd.

He was a most untidy man in the staff room. He sprawled into a chair, almost the same as he sprawled at his desk in the classroom. He would read the Telegraph with his arms out-stretched and when the bell went for the next lesson, he would simply throw the newspaper over his head onto the floor. In the classroom he would sometimes sit with his feet in the open drawer of his desk. He could achieve some fantastic positions too. I have seen him dictating notes while being almost horizontal in his chair and writing a spelling on the board behind while maintaining a forward-looking perspective on the class. He commonly scratched his left ear with his right hand over the top of his head – another movement we all copied. *David Wilson (1952–61, 64–75)*

Another master who left his mark was G. T. 'Doddy' Ridge (1959–63); a fine athlete while a boy at the school, he went on to be a parliamentary Labour candidate, afterwards becoming a local Labour councillor.

'Doddy' was my form master in 1B, Room 16, the prefab, when I arrived at the school in September '59; teaching first year French, he was the first to encourage and develop what became a lifelong love of languages. He was also my first rugby coach, taking the Under 13 team the following year for the 1960/61 season. I played my last game of rugby 44 years later, so you would have to say he had quite an influence on two significant pleasures in my life. I had the pleasure of meeting him at least 25 years later when he was the Head of Huxlow School, Irthlingborough. I was trying to sell a skiing holiday to the school, no luck

G. T. 'Doddy' Ridge

there, but I took with me a photograph of the above U-13 team for him to look at, and was both surprised and impressed by how many of the lads he was still able to name. *Dave Toseland (1959–67)*

As an old boy, he was familiar with the system of punishment in the school and took instant action when he considered it necessary, as we will read in one of the later vignettes written by individual boys.

Mr Halliwell was a master remembered for his highly idiosyncratic way of dealing with inattentive pupils:

J. K. Halliwell

His home classroom was in the first prefab closest to the bike sheds (right-hand side as you entered the prefab). His speciality, besides teaching languages, was throwing the board rubber (no doubt up with the best on masters' sports day). Inattentive pupils were the sudden recipients of a high velocity missile aimed at some part of their upper body. On one occasion the dozing pupil was seated by the window, dreaming on the aspect of the Elysian Fields just outside the classroom (actually the school vegetable garden). It was a tricky shot given the angle and distance but not unduly difficult for an experienced hand. The aim was a little high but would have successfully impacted the cranium had not the intended recipient slumped forward even further. The missile passed through the glass with considerable terminal velocity into the Elysian Fields leaving a large hole, a suddenly awake pupil, and a class trying very hard not to laugh out loud.

The window was replaced by the next day and nothing was said, though it would have been of interest to have heard Jock's comments as he mended it. Subsequently JKH's missile serves were more down the centre than to the side lines so perhaps there had been a mention of the cost of window repairs. We will never know.

JKH's class room also contained the sports kit second hand store which he was stuck with operating. Cricket and rugby boots were stocked and I remember obtaining a fine pair of cricket boots on which I lavished loving attention. No fake leather in those days. It was all the more a pity that I could not play cricket for toffee and got a bad attack of hay fever from seeing grass even at a distance from spring onwards. But the boots were magnificent! *Michael Eakins (1957–65)*

Ernie the Groundsman and Jock the Caretaker

Wellingborough Grammar School valued all its staff and considered them an integral part of the community. Ernie Bryan the groundsman and Jock Walker the caretaker gave their loyal support to the school for many years. David Wilson remembers:

I first met Ernie as an 11 year old schoolboy at the Grammar School, Wellingborough in 1952. He was considered a genuinely decent chap who could be relied on to ask no questions if he caught you smoking behind his groundsman's shed. Equally, he would have no truck with boys who were rude (nor with staff who were rude either; Brian Tompkins (aka 'Tonk') certainly rubbed him up the wrong way). Over the years I came to know him well and to respect him for his many other qualities.

He was one of the 'Staff' taking a party of 30-odd boys to Switzerland in 1953, with his wife, showing the esteem in which he was held by the School and its teachers. In those days society thought of caretakers and groundsmen as belonging to an under-privileged class, but the Grammar School valued Ernie for his qualities as a man and a skilled worker who worked hard for his money. Mr Wrenn always included him and the other domestic staff on the School photographs because he saw them as integral to the ethos and management of the School.

As I went on through the school and played for the School's teams, I came to realise the lengths Ernie went to, to ensure that we had cricket pitches good enough (and safe enough) to play the best teams around, including all the local public schools who had dedicated cricket fields and several groundsmen to look after them. To create the best pitches, he used cow manure that he carried to the school on the bus. It produced flat wickets without awkward or vicious bounces.

I was fortunate enough to go back to the Grammar School as a teacher in 1964 after taking my degree and was soon put in charge of School cricket. This involved working with Ernie to get pitches and equipment prepared for six games every day and two special pitches ready for Saturday home matches. Ernie made it easy for me because he knew just what we needed – all he asked in return was a few minutes' conversation every day to discuss the weather, work to be done and perhaps to ask advice about little problems. He did not like to be taken for granted and I hope I never failed in this regard.

When the County Council introduced a time and motion study and later a 'gang' system of maintaining school fields, we all suffered. We lost Ernie and he lost his pride and joy – the playing field he had tended as if it were the County Ground. Ernie never had the same ownership of his work in a 'gang' and left to care for Scott-Bader's gardens in Wollaston. I ended up having to work on the squares myself to prevent the pitches deteriorating to such an extent that we could not play prestige matches against public schools like Oundle, Rugby and Bedford. In the end it became a lost cause.

I met Ernie many times as he walked around Wollaston after he retired. He always thought of me as one of his boys and always held Mr Wrenn and the Grammar School in high regard. In many ways, it must have been one of the happiest periods of his life and he looked back on it and on the hundreds of friendships that came out of it as a proof of his success as a human being.

Ernie never had the opportunities that I and many others of a later generation had. If he had had the chance to go to a Grammar School, he would have become a success in any field he chose, but certainly in Botany, or Horticulture. (He discovered a previously unknown flower in Wollaston and it was named "Bryan's Bittercress" in his honour.) As it was, his 'field' was the school playing field, human relationships, local history and nature study – not a bad series of subjects in the University of Life! And all this was made more remarkable by his incredible memory which served him faithfully to the very end.

Ernie Bryan passed away in May 2005. He was 97 years old and had lived in Wollaston all his life. At his funeral we heard his qualities and personality remembered with genuine affection both in church and in private conversations. He would have been very proud that his life was remembered so fondly by so many. There must have been 250 present.

Jock Walker, the caretaker also made his mark on the school, as David Wilson remembers:

"Jock … … Jock…" I can hear Mr. Wrenn's voice now, echoing along the front corridor, the pitch rising with each successive shriek of Mr Walker's name.

Jock became an institution, certainly to us boys and especially to those in the elite group that was welcomed into his house at lunchtime and in the evenings during the School Play week.

Jock was a canny Scot who did his work around the school in his own time. He was rarely where Mr Wrenn expected him, or wanted him, to be – hence the shouting for him down the echoing corridors. But Jock and his wife Gladys were 100% supporters of the School. They prepared the teams' teas in winter and summer but went further and supported the teams on the field too, especially cricket. Their voices were loud and strong on the boundary, sometimes making comments that were not strictly "sporting" in their content. On at least one occasion Mr Wrenn had to have words with Mrs Jock to get her to restrain her enthusiasm.

Jock made good use of his stoke hole. It had a pleasantly warm atmosphere, winter and summer, ideal for three things in particular.

Home brewing needs a consistently warm temperature to achieve successful and speedy fermentation. Jock brewed both beer and wine there, and was very generous with his libations among the senior boys who visited him at lunchtimes for a quick smoke and somewhere homely to eat their sandwiches. Those of us who came from outlying towns and villages had to stay at School when School Plays were on in the evening, so Jock and his wife kindly entertained us and allowed us to have "just a wee taste" of the latest carrot wine or marrow rum.

The stoke hole was also of an appropriate temperature for the curing of tobacco. When Jock came across an advertisement for "tobacco plants complete with instructions on how to cure your own tobacco", he leapt at the opportunity and produced his own smoke for several years. St Bruno went out of the window and in came a potent (and to be honest, foul-smelling) product. The flavour never appealed to the Head, which was surprising because in the seventies he turned to his own "bonfire mixture" which was Gold Block mixed with one of the tax-free Natural Herbal tobaccos.

And of course the stoke hole was warm and sleep-inducing (and not just for caretakers either).

WGS seemed to produce memorable characters without really trying.

Chapter 7

The 1944 Education Act and Mr Wrenn (1946–1975)

Mr Wrenn arrived at Wellingborough Grammar School in January 1946 in a world recovering from a devastating war and looking to the future. The school vibrated with renewed life as its masters returned from service in the war and new staff were appointed. Mr Wrenn's first task was to prepare the school for the new eleven-plus entry in Autumn 1946 and also to renew other aspects of school life, including the school clubs and societies.

The 1944 Education Act

The new Education Act formulated a nationwide system of free, compulsory education from 5 to 15 (to be eventually raised to 16), with a range of support services including transport, free medical and dental treatment.

The major change was the new eleven-plus examination to separate secondary children into three distinct kinds of school (grammar/technical/secondary-modern) with the grammar school at the apex of the system. This operated for the first time in 1946, providing free grammar school education for all boys and girls who passed.

The two classes of boys at Wellingborough Grammar School – a majority of fee-payers with well-to-do parents and a minority of scholarship boys whose parents had insufficient money to pay – was a thing of the past. Now there was a level playing field in the school, though the wider problems of selection were yet to be resolved in society at large.

The 1944 Education Act formulated three levels of responsibility:

- Central government set national policies and allocated resources to Local Education Authorities (LEAs),
- Local Education Authorities set local policies and allocated resources to schools,
- Head teachers and school governors set school policies and allocated resources within the school.

This act had several consequences: it confirmed the headmaster as the sole arbiter of everything within his school, subject only to a formal report to the school governors every year, which at Wellingborough Grammar School was presented also to the parents on Parents' Day. There were no new requirements for the curriculum, which had been broadly the same for many years, except for the requirement for a daily act of worship. This left what was taught in the control of head teachers which Mr Wrenn delegated to his masters. They in turn would need to respond to the examination system offered by the Examination Boards which set the School Certificate.

A new broom

Mr Wrenn arrived at Wellingborough Grammar School in January 1946 intent on bringing the school into the second half of the twentieth century. As if to declare the subtlety of this change, the Magazine replaced the traditional Latin headings 'Salvete' and 'Valete' by the English equivalents, welcoming 'Entrants' and saying goodbye to 'Leavers'. Latin was still taught to the most able because it was a pre-requisite to enter Oxford or Cambridge, but the major focus remained the wider liberal education to educate the whole person seeking excellence in academic and personal qualtities.

Mr Wrenn faced two major challenges: to develop the school academically for its new role after the 1944 Education Act and to invigorate its liberal curriculum in terms of its clubs and societies. As he did this, the school continued with its rich activities in sport, drama, music, together with a number of on-going activities from the war.

War-time activities continue

The Air Training Corps continued to operate after the war, but interest waned and it closed down in 1946.

Work in summer helping the farmers bring in the harvest continued for some years. In the summer of 1946 a large party of boys picked apples and plums at Haselor Farm near Evesham, organised through the Ministry of Agriculture by the Worcestershire War Executive Agricultural Committee. They were led by Mr Dunning, Mr Wintersgill, and Mr and Mrs Pine, with a visit from Mr Nicholas and Mr Wrenn, who, according to Mr Dunning, "stayed over Monday – saw us work

– and hastily departed on Tuesday (but he did come and join us again for our last week)."

The winter of 1946/47 was the longest for many years, with the coldest February in the Midlands since records began in 1659 and strong blizzards and the deepest snow until mid-March, when the thaw led to widespread flooding around the country.

In Wellingborough, the School Magazine recorded that:

> *A member of staff dug (with assistance) a train out of the snow and then decided that was a day's work done. Another fought his way to and from Wollaston for two days and then he, too, gave up the struggle. ... Wells walked from Finedon; Goodbody came in from Earls Barton with a spade and a bicycle; Coles came in over the fields from Harrowden – stout efforts all.*
>
> *At the height of the blizzards only 80 boys appeared at school, who were regaled with lectures and hand-ball, whilst the staff, not occupied thus, kept their minds whole and their tempers frayed with bridge and badminton. Rugger was completely out for weeks and many were the snowballs hurled in place of the ovoid.* School Magazine 1947

In contrast, the summer of 1947 was one of the hottest since records began, exceeded only twice before in 1826 and 1846; it also had more than its share of heavy rain.

The school repeated the trip to Evesham to pick fruit and a second group went to Wallingford near Oxford to do general farm work.

> *On the Friday night prescribed we boys were told to take our bikes down to London Road Station and load them into a railways van. They were due to travel later in the evening and would be at Wallingford ready for us to ride our bikes to the campsite just south east of Wallingford. The next move was to be at London Road Station early the next morning. We had to change trains at Northampton, Blisworth, Bletchley, Oxford, Cholsey and then finally to Wallingford. When we arrived, the bikes had not and we had to walk to the camp which was a good way; the bikes arrived the following Wednesday.*
>
> *Mr Cook and Mr Dunning were in charge and did all the cooking. We had to fetch tents and fill palliases with hay: once finished we were hungry. The cooking was excellent and we hoped that it would be maintained. It was.*

We had lots of rainy days and nights and, instead of working for either 12 or 19 days, I worked for only 4 days, limited to weeding. The harvest was late so, instead of picking up a nice quantity of cash, the return was poor. I came home after two weeks taking my bike with me on the reverse route and, fundamentally, that was the end of my Wellingborough Grammar School days. *Keith Gennis (1943–47)*

The headmaster was responsible for distributing the money earned:

At Evesham 41 boys earned £228 by picking over 50 tons of plums and apples. At Wallingford 26 boys earned approximately £100 by clearing 40 acres of weed and lifting 70 tons of hay.

In the following years there was more potato picking and a new task, harvesting flax:

I can remember in my later school years going out on organised paid summer work pulling and tying flax by hand. It was organised by the school and we were paid by the acre, transported in buses from the school gates and goodness was it hard work! Both the flax and the sisal string used for tying the sheaves cut into the soft fleshy skin on every joint of the hand. *Pedro Howes (1947–52)*

Two types of summer work prevailed around 1949/50, potato picking and flax pulling as mentioned by Pedro. Flax pulling reminds me of the final pay day, when we were paid by HAW in his office. He kindly informed us that he had deducted the first year's subs to the WOGS from our wages. We were not amused! *Roy Catling (1945–50)*

Re-organising the forms

In the initial years of his headmastership, Mr Wrenn rationalised the numbering system of forms since 1934 whereby boys had entered into the second form and spent one or two years in the fifth form,

In Mr Woolley's last year, the school had a three-form entry into year two with three forms a year to year five, and a single sixth form:

- IIA1 (30 pupils), IIA2 (30), IIB (26), [aged 12+, total 86];
- IIIA1 (33), IIIA2 (32), IIIB (31), [13+, 95];
- IVA1 (32), IVA2 (33), IVB (26), [14+, 92];
- VA (25), VB (20), Remove (26), [15+/16+, 71];
- VI (27), [16+/17+/18+, 27] [Total 13 forms, 371 pupils].

In this system, the more able took a four-year course to the School Certificate with selected boys moving from IVA1 to VA, while the others spent an extra year in the Fifth Form 'Remove' class before moving into VB to give them a further year to prepare for the exam. Along the way, around half the boys left before taking the Certificate.

Mr Wrenn arrived part way through his first year and the system was maintained with a second 'Remove' class in the fifth form and a subdivision of the 31 sixth-formers into four: VIB Arts and Science, VIA Arts and Science.

- IIA1 (34), IIA2 (34), IIB (26), [aged 12+, total 94];
- IIIA1 (33), IIIA2 (32), IIIB (31), [13+, 96];
- IVA1 (32), IVA2 (33), IVB (26), [14+, 91];
- VA (23), VB (28), Remove I (26), Remove II (17), [15+/16+, 94];
- VIB Arts (9), VIB Science (6), [15/16+, 15];
- VIA Arts (9), VIA Science (7) [16/17+, 16],
  [17 forms, 406 pupils].

These changes were possible because, for the very first time, the school had a new, if temporary, prefab building with two classrooms, built on part of the school vegetable garden adjoining the playground. The School Magazine reported that it was soon occupied by an "alarming number of Sixth Formers who avail themselves of the comfort of the heating stoves in each of these new rooms."

In 1946/7, Forms II to V were renamed A, B, C, with an extra fifth form called the Lower Vth, and the sixth form reverting to two classes VI arts and VI science, each containing two school years. (The precise number of sixth-form classes was a moveable feast as different groups came together for various subject options.)

- IIA (31), IIB (30), IIC (28) [aged 12+, 89];
- IIIA (32), IIIB (29), IIIC (31), [13+, 92];
- IVA (27), IVB (28), IVC (24), [14+, 79];
- VA (28), VB (29),VC (29), LV (32), [15/16+, 118];
- VI Arts (17) ,VI Science (22), [16+/17+/18+, 39].
  [15 forms, 417 pupils].

The major change occurred in 1947/8, with the first five forms renumbered from I to V, with no IVA, and the A-stream moving from IIIA to VA. At the beginning of the year, the Autumn Term Magazine mentioned a "VIth General Form" containing "those unfortunate beings who have not yet reached the maturity of the normal VIth form, or who are still searching for remunerative employment." Presumably all the boys found suitable employment during the year as the General VIth did not figure in the class list in the Summer Magazine:

- IA (30), IB (30), IC (27) [aged 12+, 87];
- IIA (29), IIB (31), IIC (26) [aged 13+, 86];
- IIIA (30), IIIB (32), IIIC (29), [aged 14+, 91];
- – IVB (25), IVC (19) [aged 15+, 44];
- VA (31) [15+], VB (32), [15+/16+, 63];
- VI Arts (17) & Science (27), [16+/17+/18+, 44], [15 forms, 415 pupils].

The school was now in a settled fundamental shape ready for the future. Increasing flexibilty in housing the classes became possible in 1948 with another prefab that added two classrooms, and by the early fifties, a total of three prefabs with six classrooms were available.

However, even the best schemes of mice and men can be easily dashed by bureaucracy. At this point, the Ministry of Education announced a new General Certificate of Education to give a certificate to all who passed at least one subject. To maintain standards the pass mark would be raised from 30% to 45%, but that was not all. On Parents' Day 1949, Mr Wrenn commented wryly:

The Ministry of Education had laid down that in future no boy may sit for the School Certificate before the age of 16. This meant that next year only the B and C forms in the fifth would be able to enter. In 1951 the standard of the examination would be raised, but the minimum requirement for the award of a certificate would be a pass in any one subject.

The raising of the minimum age caused havoc in the school:

The minimum age limit of 16 for O-levels was overcome by our being set into Arts or Science before O-levels and starting on the A-level syllabus before we had taken O-levels. This was all very well but we tended to concentrate on the science at the expense of the other subjects. The first year having proved the rule to be counter-productive, it was quickly abandoned. However, it illustrated only too well how disruptive changes to the education system can be, especially if not well thought out and adequately piloted. Richard Hall (1946–54)

The boys who fell foul of the system were those under sixteen who were due to take the last School Certificate in 1950; instead they took the first O-level in 1951 at the end of the first year sixth.

This led to the following sequence of results:

1949: (62 pupils) 44 School Certificate with at least 5 subjects;

1950: (54 pupils (excluding 19 under age)) 36 School Certificate with at least 5 subjects;

1951: (74 5th form, 19 lower sixth) 32 GCE O-level passed with at least 5 subjects, 33 others passed with at least one.

The 19 boys in the lower sixth took only subjects considered necessary, with the result that no 'arts' boy passed in a single science subject, and no 'science' student passed in Spanish, history or geography!

The science stream had a particular disaster in French, due in part to a rapid succession of changing teachers in earlier terms who did not take them much beyond the first book before O-level:

Except for one clever soul, the whole group, by then streamed as Science, failed the French exam. Needless to say all hell let loose, especially when the same thing happened with retakes, and we were finally crammed through the exam by the Boss himself. Richard Hall (1946–54)

Liberal developments

The post-war years saw a distinct lightening up of the atmosphere in the school. After years of austerity and focus on significant academic and sporting excellence, the School Magazine, edited now by Johnny Butler, encouraged boys to have their say, including a page of sixth-form notes where the author 'told it how he saw it', as follows:

... the prefects, wishing to sweeten the atmosphere of the school let off DDT cartridges in the prefects' room and sent themselves coughing to the other side of the school building for a while.

One most interesting feature of the term has been the commencement of dancing lessons at the High School. Lessons have been given on

Monday evenings and the Library has subsequently been misused for dancing demonstrations and practices during Tuesday dinner hour. The small fry of the school should note that any senior seen doing an about turn at the corners of the quadrangle is not devoid of intelligence but is merely practising a reverse turn, a forward change or a backward passing change for the next lesson.

A further contact between the Girls' School and our own has been in the physics laboratories where the High School science sixth form now studies physics with our science sixth. However it has been noticed that since the biologists of the sixth have heen dissecting rabbits and dogfish the number of girls attending has dropped. Some feel that biology should be purely theoretical.

In spite of numerous hints the prefects have not been given the old mistresses'common room which has now become a sixth form class room. However, since the prefects have overflowed into the sick room, the feeling is that the Head would prefer to keep the sick room as such.

School Magazine, Autumn 1946

One of the jewels in Mr Wrenn's crown was his expansion of the school's clubs and societies. A fuller story will be given in a later chapter; it is sufficient at this point to say that Mr Wrenn was the first headmaster to broaden the curriculum to give boys full vent to any activity they desired to follow. Mr Lay had been visionary in starting school societies mainly of a worthy academic nature such as music, drama, debating, and these continued throughout the life of the school. But it was Mr Wrenn, after the limitations of the war years, who re-introduced old clubs and societies, and encouraged the creation of new ones.

He also widened the extent of internal competition between the Houses, reintroducing athletic standards for boys to gain house points to add to their scores in the inter-house athletics match for the Martin Athletic Cup and distance points in swimming to contribute to the James Swimming Cup.

His enterprise also extended to caring for the inner boy in a profitable way, restarting the School Tuck Shop and using the profits to good advantage to buy sports equipment. Mr Holmes balanced the books while a select team of boys ran the shop to sell a range of snacks including Smith's Crisps with the blue packet of salt, Wagon Wheels, Mars Bars and other goodies.

I was very disappointed for about thirty seconds when I wasn't appointed a prefect because I thought that was a position of power. Then I found the real position of power when Mick Coles, Martin Spriggs and myself got the tuck shop. Holding people to ransom for Jammy Dodgers! They'd come up in front and say "got any Jammy Dodgers?" and you'd say "nahhh", then somebody you liked came past and you'd say "surrre".

John Hobbs (1952–59)

'Father' Holmes asked me to take over running the tuck shop. He felt that the profits weren't great enough taking into account the size of the turnover. So I went in, but I don't think the profits increased. In my view the habit of eating some of the 'profits' was strongly linked to the fact that the tuck shop boys were paid just 10/- a term for the task, whereas the lab boys were paid 10/- a week. I certainly ate my share.

Dave 'Tufty' Pope (1956–64)

Reading Prizes

Mr Wrenn also had a desire to widen the horizons of his pupils through more extensive leisure reading. Dr Jackson drew up a reading list of about twenty-five books suitable for each age group, chosen for their interest as well as for their literary value, and during the winter months each boy was expected to read up to eight of them. The School Library, through the generosity of the Parents' Committee, and the Public Libraries of the district helped to ensure that sufficient books of the right kind were available.

The Old Grammarians provided prizes to be awarded to the highest-scoring boy in each form in a test held in the summer term.

For some of us these lists created a life-time hobby of reading. Without them, would I have ever read the C. S. Forester's 'Hornblower' series, John Buchan's '39 Steps', Leslie Charteris's 'Saint' or H. Rider Haggard's 'King Solomon's Mines'? The book lists opened up for me a whole new world; without them my reading was limited to comics — good comics (The Eagle, Adventure, Hotspur, Rover and Wizard) but just comics. Now my parents bought me books and I started using the library. It even gave me, a B-stream boy, the opportunity to win one of the annual form reading prizes. To me, the reading lists remain the most valuable part of my education at Wellingborough Grammar School!

Graham Tall (1955–63)

School Extensions

As the fifties progressed, the first permanent extension to the school buildings occurred in the shape of the Fleming Laboratory and the new Art Room above the original ground floor of the school overlooking the field.

This led to a master-stroke played by Mr Wrenn, who invited Sir Alexander Fleming to present the prizes at the next Parents' Day and to officially open and name the new Fleming Lab. It might seem as if the school was fighting well above its weight by having the bare-faced cheek to ask a Nobel Prize winning scientist of international repute to come and name a room in a provincial county grammar school. The truth was that no-one had asked Sir Alexander to present school prizes before and he was absolutely delighted to do so.

He was to be the first of a long line of famous guests at Parents' Day in future years to present prizes and to give their names to rooms throughout the school. It took Mr Wrenn a year or two to really get going, but in the late fifties and throughout the sixties, the eminent guests constitute a list without parallel. They will be considered in detail in a later chapter.

Boys playing rugby on the field in 1953, with the Fleming Laboratory shell finished and the Art Room being built

The School continues to expand

Throughout the late fifties and sixties, the school continued to expand without ever increasing the first form intake; this remained as a three-form entry with just over 30 or more boys per class for the life of the school. The major expansion was through keeping almost all boys in school to take their O-level and to greatly expand the sixth form.

With the rise in perceived importance of academic qualifications, and the steady economic improvement, it became the norm for almost all boys to stay on to take their O-level and an increasing number desired to stay on to take advantage of the expanding university system.

In 1956 Mr Wrenn was able to thank the parents for their support and say:

> *The fact that the premature leaver is now a very rare bird in this school, that boys are invariably properly equipped for all games and activities, the determination that boys shall get the utmost out of their school career, all of these mean a great deal of self-sacrifice from parents and I assure you that it is appreciated here.*
>
> *Newspaper cutting Evening Telegraph, 1956.*

Ask Me Another on the BBC

Boys were encouraged to operate on their own initiative and it was no surprise when three sixth-formers, Max Wyman, Roger Allen and David Lee wrote to the BBC in the summer of 1958 and challenged the 'Brains of Britain' team to a contest on the *Ask Me Another* quiz programme. What was a surprise was the comprehensive way in which the boys resoundingly defeated the team of nationally-known experts by 34–23, one of the greatest margins ever recorded on the programme.

In 1958 a further extension was added to the front of the school on the right as we look at it, including a new biology laboratory upstairs and a new music room downstairs. The architecture is so perfect that when we look at it today, we can no longer see the distinction between old and new.

Extension on the right in its newly-built, unweathered condition in 1958

The photograph above, taken in 1958 by Mr Colin McCall, then a master at the school, shows the unweathered roof and frontage on the right contrasting against the rest of the building. It is a perfect example of extending an original so that it looks as if it was always the way we see it now.

Once again there was a new Laboratory to open and Mr Wrenn scored again with his second Nobel Prize Winner, Sir John Cockcroft in 1958, following this immediately with his third, Sir Lawrence Bragg, in 1959.

By this time the prefabs were showing their age and the school was applying for completely new buildings with more classrooms, a modern sports centre and a larger assembly hall to double as a dining room. This was becoming essential to relieve the pressure on the tiny original dining room with its double sitting for dinner. (In those days 'dinner' was our midday meal followed by 'tea' in the early evening.)

In the following academic year, Mr Wrenn was unwell and Mr Nicholas took over as acting headmaster. During Mr Wrenn's absence, Parents' Day 1960 eschewed its taste for Nobel Prize Winners and invited Mr Penn, the Chairman of the Northamptonshire Education Authority, who reported that the extension would probably materialise in 1964. It was duly built in the years 1964–5 over the original school vegetable garden.

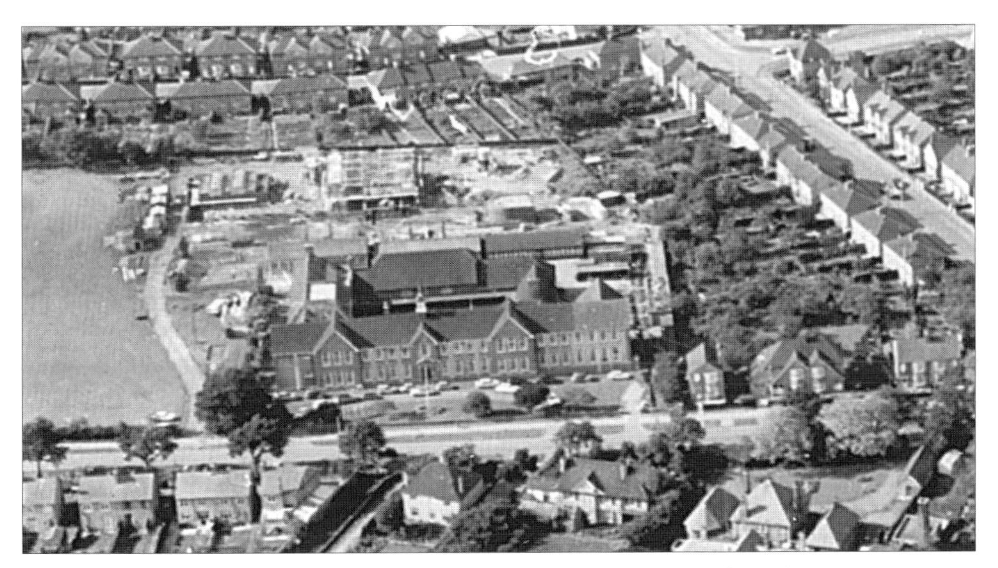

The building of the school extensions in 1964–5, seen from the air

The new extensions were opened on March 5th 1965 by distinguished historian and broadcaster Mr (later Sir) Alan Bullock, Master of St Catherine's College, Oxford, who contrasted the society of the day with the depression and unemployment in the thirties when the original school was opened.

The changes greatly increased the size and completely revolutionised the available facilities. The original building was modified by transforming the old school hall into a library with a study gallery above. The dining room became a metal craft room with lathes, machines, tools and a forge. The old kitchen became a technical drawing room. Other rooms were modified into a language laboratory and a sixth form common room.

The new buildings were interconnected with the old by a raised walk-way with brick and glass walls to allow easy movement throughout the school, even in inclement weather. There was a ten-classroom block with designated rooms for geography, history and English. All classrooms were fitted with an internal communications system and many had cine-screens for visual instruction. New changing rooms (now re-named 'dressing rooms') had individual lockers for the students and sprinkler showers. On the one side they led directly on to the playing fields, on the other to a centrally situated 70 foot by 40 foot gymnasium with a spring floor. The whole building was heated

Mr Wrenn explains the new facilities to his guests, Mrs Jill Carter, Chairman of Wellingborough Urban Council, Alderman Steele and Mr and Mrs Allan Bullock.

by warm air flow from a new oil-fired boilerhouse. Nearby the new school hall doubled for assembly and dining, with a 25 foot stage, dressing rooms, and full theatrical fittings.

Ever mindful of the history of the school, Mr Wrenn took the opportunity of inviting the first headmaster, Mr Lay, to attend the ceremony. Afterwards Mr Lay told the *Evening Telegraph* reporter, "I think the extensions are a wonderful addition to the amenities of the school and I think they fit extraordinarily well." He went on to make a nostalgic journey through the corridors of the old school to the spot where the original opening took place. Then he and Mr Wrenn shared a moment of contemplation at the *Book of the Fallen* who died in the war, many of whom would have been known personally to Mr Lay.

With the new buildings up and running all now seemed complete. But Mr Wrenn had yet another card up his sleeve. Although the new buildings had been opened, the new hall remained unnamed. On this occasion, he hit the jackpot by persuading Lord Mountbatten to officially dedicate the new school hall in 1966, a coup which opened up new avenues to attract yet more eminent visitors in the future. All that was necessary was to intimate to each prospective guest the list of those who had come before.

Mr Wrenn and Mr Lay contemplate the Book of the Fallen in 1965

The School maximises its potential

The expansion of the school allowed greater freedom for planning the timetable. The three-form entry was retained throughout the sixties and seventies, but more classrooms allowed smaller classes. In the mid-fifties, the fifth form was expanded to four classes (5Ai, 5Aii, 5B and 5C). This, in essence, only exchanged the missing 4A for the corresponding 5th form group.

During the sixties the second to fourth forms were also expanded to four smaller classes. Meanwhile the sixth-form expanded to take on the greater number of boys desiring to go to university, including a distinct third year sixth for those requiring a further year to reach the standards required to go to Oxford and Cambridge.

The curriculum changed little, although craft skills returned in 1965 with the appointment of Mr Tomlinson to teach metalwork in the engineering laboratory in the old converted dining room, officially named by ace pilot Douglas Bader in 1967.

The school continued to follow its time-honoured tradition of long-term stability of responsibilities. In 1969, when the Head of Spanish, Mr Tony Sparrow, retired from coaching the first XV, Mr Wrenn noted in his Headmaster's Report on Parents' Day:

For the past 15 years Mr Sparrow has been in charge of the first XV. In that time he has produced some excellent results. … Before Mr Sparrow took charge of School Rugby, Mr Nicholas had coached the 1st XV, also for 15 years.

What he did not add was that Mr Nicholas's predecessor had held that post since the school was opened in the 1930s. In 39 years from 1930 to 1969, there were just three masters in charge of first XV rugby. He also failed to state that an English international, 'Johnny' Hyde, had been appointed to teach games in 1954 and had stood on the sidelines for 15 years before he was given the honour. Hardly the best news for R. B. (Bob) Taylor, another English International and a British Lion who had already been at the school for five years, although it should be said that those playing regular rugby for the Saints and England would have other priorities on a Saturday than coaching a school team.

In any case, Bob had other strings to his bow as he turned his attention first to five-a-side football in a summer competition in 1965, then introduced basketball throughout the school in 1966. Mr Wrenn allowed and encouraged innovation, even in terms of changes that went against the traditions of a rugby-playing school.

Bob's greatest triumph was in introducing the round ball game to the school. Admittedly it was only the five-a-side version and only in the summer for the seniors as a new venture in the, by now, fairly anachronistic PE competition day, but it was a start and something we all thought we would never see. I think he had a great ally in Trevor Norman, a young cricketer, in charge of the 1st XI, who used to play for Essex and was a big football fan. I also have him to thank for teaching us to play bridge in a general studies lesson, free periods in the new library were great from then on. Although it didn't do much for my A-level grades!

The two reports in the Magazines of Autumn '65 and Autumn '67 (strangely not in '66, the World Cup winning year, although I'm sure it took place) show how popular it became. We simply made up our own teams and names, as you may see, by '67 the names had become a lot more daring than the '65 efforts – the fairly tame 'Arveyesses' and 'The Five Faces of Cyril' had become 'The Many Splendoured Chins '67' and 'The Greasian Erns'. I'm sure the younger members of staff must have loved seeing all the piss-taking. *Dave Toseland*

The five-a-side football tournament extended into the seventies, expanding into a six-a-side format. Soccer became an eleven-a-side game in 1971 when Mr Dean responded to the desire of soccer-mad teenagers to start a Soccer Club that played in the local Rushden and District Soccer League. Although it never rose to the level of a full school sport (all its activity was out of school time), it satisfied a need at the time and Mr Wrenn organised the use of a soccer pitch behind the houses on the other side of Doddington Rd.

Basketball went further. While it may have been introduced in PE lessons, it too was mainly an out-of-school activity, with matches organised so that they did not clash with established school sports. Indeed, many of the 'stars' of the basketball sides were often also the stars of first XV rugby and the first IX cricket.

The sports of the sixties and seventies will figure in greater detail in a later chapter.

The final years

Despite government policy to turn all schools comprehensive, and the Northamptonshire Local Education Authority being controlled by the ruling Labour Party, Wellingborough Grammar School was little affected. To cope with the diversity of the full school population in a single comprehensive school was seen to require a large entry of 8 to 10 classes and so there were technical details to be overcome to integrate a system with the 3-form entry of the Grammar School.

Even in the late sixties, there was no evidence of any change in direction. When Jake Dunning retired in 1966, the School Magazine rightly applauded all he had done unstintingly for the school.

> *[He would be] remembered above everything else for his brilliant work in the Geography Department, which soon reached and always maintained an extremely high level through his forceful teaching and insistence on high standards of work and behaviour.*
>
> *He gave unceasingly of his energies to his work with the School Magazine, with the Athletic Sports, with the Sixth Form General Course, with the School Excursions, with Toc H and above all with the Scouts, who for nearly twenty years profited from his wise guidance and unbounded enthusiasm. His remarkable gifts of leadership and organization combined to make a great success of all these activities.*

The school continued after he left without there being a 'hole' that had to be filled. The Geography department remained successful under Brett Tussler, the School Scouts and Toc H went from strength to strength. Indeed the latter's greatest success was demonstrably after Jake had retired. It not only continued to take books round hospitals and have its usual money-raising activities, it created a unique 'concert' in the form of "a mammoth extravaganza with few concessions to culture, a mixture of *Opportunity Knocks* and *It's a Knockout* which would have made Carol Levis turn in his grave," (1969 Autumn Magazine). It paid for an annual trip taking a bus-load of senior citizens to Hunstanton.

The only task that Jake fulfilled which was less easy to maintain was the School Excursion Day, and even that continued annually until it ran out of steam in 1971.

Sports, clubs and societies continued to the end with rugby, cricket, basketball, soccer and badminton figuring in the final years. The Scouts, Toc H and the Railway Club remained strong, with the Railway Club under the indefatigable Ivor Cheale not only continuing to build on their huge model railway, but also providing stage hands for all school plays over the years.

The Railway Club inherited a huge quantity of track through the good offices of Mr Chesters, so that "the whole layout will only just fit into the hall, and no more than a third in the music room at any one time." After measuring many rooms in the school someone suggested that the majority of the boards that are almost complete would fit into the physics lab. After some adjustments all but three of the boards were fitted in and, on Speech Day 1969, a better layout than ever before was exhibited – and it worked.

Mr Cheale continued to organise annual trips abroad. For instance, in 1968 he organized a trip to Switzerland with 76 boys divided into two groups, one led by himself, the other by Mr Wrenn.

The clubs and societies continued and diversified with a Radio Club for those interested in amateur radio transmission in 1971 and an Ornithological Society in 1972.

In 1973, 'Nick' Nicholas, 'Eddie' Phillips and Miss Bavin all retired and the School Magazine intimated the changes in the air:

> *It was with a deep sense of loss that the school said goodbye to Mr I. J. Nicholas, Mr H. C. Phillips and Miss N. Bavin. This is definitely the*

> *end of an era, the retirement of three members of the small group who some forty years ago started a Grammar School from scratch, then made it into a fine school and kept it that way. Whatever changes may be impending the school will for many years retain the character and sense of purpose which its founders stamped on it from its outset.*

The final denoument was not long in coming. In the autumn of 1975, Mr Wrenn asked permission of the Masters to include his wife Barbara on the final school photograph. As the stalwart Chairman of the Parents' Committee supporting the school for the previous 29 years, it was a fitting tribute. Always a stickler for protocol, Mr Wrenn also asked permission to bring Mrs Wrenn into the staff room for the final photocall.

The last two years of the school were focused on the impending changes of structure and new requirements for teaching the wider population. When Rushden School expanded to include a Sixth Form, its headmaster, Bert Catlin sought advice from Wellingborough Grammar School. Now the boot was on the other foot and the school consulted with Bert to get some ideas as to how to proceed. So it happened in the end that a Grammar School boy gave the school advice on how to turn comprehensive.

The Final Panorama October, 1974 (Masters Overleaf)

Martin Layton Michael Hagar Michael Webster Nigel *Bert* Way Richard Buckby Geoffrey Dean Kenneth Parkinson

Roderick Farey Nick Wills Terry Rowe Bob Taylor David Wilson Ronald Bentley John Hyde Tony Sparrow

Ivor Cheale *Chunky* Pine Tony Sulch Harold Wrenn Mrs Barbara Wrenn John Butler Ron *Beery* Ward

Richard *Buzz* Temple John *Ernie* Huddart *Brett* Tussler Alan *Charlie* Chesters Tim Tomlinson Michael Wright Ian MacDougall Terry Goodman

Peter Cameron Howard Buchanan Richard Armstrong Brian Emerson Brian Gilbert Philip York Edward *Ted* Holt

OCT  1974

The final team of Masters 1974–1975

Caramba! Is that the only Spanish I learnt?

Graham Sharp (1958–1964)

As I reflect on my time at WGS (1958–64) my emotional state is as it must have been for those plucky chaps who, in the 'fifties', wrote all those books about their time at Colditz – "we absolutely hated the place but, by jove, we love looking back at it all from a distance with a certain fondness." Frankly, I think some of the chaps at Colditz probably had it relatively easy.

I graduated to the Grammar School via an 11+ success from Victoria Junior School, Wellingborough. I loved Junior School and I was expected to pass the 11+, which was, essentially, a basic intelligence test coupled with a bit of story writing.

Like most of my peers, I spent the summer of 1958 getting used to the new bike I got for passing the 11+ and looking forward to coming to terms with life in Doddington Road. This was certainly the high point of my full-time academic career. For in September 1958, I was captured by the enemy, Northamptonshire Education Authority, and sentenced to a six-year imprisonment with no possibility of remission.

On day one, just as I was reflecting on the fact that I was, apparently, one of the most "intelligent" eleven-year olds in quite a big geographical area (there were people with me in 1B from Rushden, Irthlingborough, Earls Barton, Ecton and places in between I'd never heard of), everything that could be done to bring us down to earth with a bang was done.

It was made clear that we would be taught not by 'teachers', as we had been hitherto, but by 'masters' – a professional nomenclature deliberately chosen, no doubt, to clarify incontrovertibly the institutional pecking order. While we were known only by our surname or, more usually, a derogatory version of it; masters were known as "Sir". This, it seemed, was to be no equitable educational partnership!

Our introduction to the Grammar School life came at Morning Assembly where some five hundred boys, of which we were by far the smallest (and the only ones in short trousers), crowded into a hall that doubled as a gymnasium.

We listened intently to the headmaster reading out a few notices (one of which, on my first day, was that an old boy – David Frost – was to make his first television performance that evening on ITV – "but don't waste your time watching!") and a prayer; a prefect offered a Bible reading and another man (who we later learned was Mr Nicholas – aka 'Tinbum') merely stood there mum-chance on the platform, with the other two, undertaking no apparent role. In fact, he stood there with no evident purpose every school morning for six years.

We were then expected to join in the singing of a hymn without the benefit of having been provided with a hymn book. We were instructed to stay behind in the gym "to be streamed" and we followed our new classmates in a crocodile line to our Form Room – a wooden construction that had clearly been salvaged from the nearby Doddington Road allotments.

A few seconds of acclimatisation followed, during which burgundy coloured calendars on which one had to write the timetable were handed out, then we launched straight into French.

I'd never heard anyone speak French and I had no reason to believe I ever would. Our Form Master and French master were one and the same Mr Stratfold – known, for some reason[†], as 'Jasper'. He was the first teacher I had ever seen in a black gown – Junior School teachers all wore those brown tweedy jackets with leather elbows. Jasper's gown was so badly ripped that the hem line was a mass of knotted material.

It seems that the way of teaching French in 1958 was to speak to small boys in French and then hit them over the head with one of the knots in one's gown when they didn't understand and reply in a language they couldn't speak. The less they understood, the bigger the knot that was selected from the array at the hem. Needless to say, this strategy worked so well in my case that, in Year 2, I dropped French and was put onto Spanish instead.

After break – during which I was put in 'detention' three times by less than empathetic second formers – I made my way, without the aid of maps, compasses or any other help, to the chemistry lab for my first taste of science. Since my dad worked for Boots, I instinctively thought I should be rather good at chemistry. How wrong I was.

The chemistry master was a kindly looking man by the name of Mr Holmes – nicknamed 'Father', presumably in deference to his advancing years. To this eleven-year old, 'Father' appeared to be at least ninety. 'Father' was disabled and confined to a wheelchair.

Having no secure knowledge of where the science labs were, I arrived at the Fleming lab later than most of my cohort, I found myself on the back bench, what seemed like a hundred yards from the action at the front – the 'action', of course, being the head and just the top of shoulders view of 'Father'. Consequently, there was next to no engagement with either 'Father' who, for self-evident reasons could not come and visit us at the back, and even less engagement with the subject of chemistry.

Following several weeks of trying to learn a series of 'Laboratory Rules' and copying them down in our exercise books, we got down to some proper chemistry – making copper sulphate crystals. I recall vividly pouring some liquid or other into a vessel, putting it on a tripod and setting fire to a Bunsen burner. The liquid began to bubble and from a hundred yards away, through the roar of thirty other Bunsen burners, came the faintest of instructions to dip a glass rod into the mixture. If crystals formed, we were then told to "pour off the mother liquor." Obviously, I hadn't the slightest idea what a 'mother liquor' was and, frankly, I still don't.

Six years of hard scientific graft and that's all the chemistry I remember! As far as I know, I haven't poured off any 'mother liquor' since 1958.

The last period before lunch was another eye-opener. The timetable said 'English' with Dr Jackson back inside the garden shed form room. Outside surgery hours, I'd never seen a 'doctor'– and I've never, ever, seen another like Dr 'Spike' Jackson. I was anticipating a serious looking 'doctor', perhaps tall, elegant and well turned out.

What we got, few of us were prepared for — a small, shambolic-looking individual with wiry national health glasses perched on a hooked nose

[†] His initials were JAS (Ed.)

beneath which sprang a moustache that seemed to have its own eco-system. He ambled along as if none of us had a care in the world. As he greeted us cheerily, it became all too apparent that his eccentric looks were matched by a pronounced lisp (pronounced 'lishp').

English, it transpired, at Grammar School level consisted of pushing all the furniture to one side, dividing up into four teams, dressing up in smelly, tattered clothes and unsavoury headgear and taking it in turns to act out a scenario in the available six-foot square until Spike had had enough and rang a bell (known as the 'tocsin', er ... 'tocshin').

In this precursor to *Whose line is it anyway?*, Spike would award a number of points known as 'goods' (goodsh) with a top mark of six goods (shix goodsh) being greeted with a combination of delight and anxiety for the amount of spittle heading in one's direction from the adjudication point.

The real objective – and the way to clinch victory for your team – was to get your column of desks back in place in a straighter line than those of your competitors. The teams, of course, had to undertake this task by eye, but Spike umpired this most crucial of deciders with the help of the pole that had originally been designed to open windows. He would close one eye and, pretentiously peering down the pole through his closed eye, would bark out "four goodsh thish row"; "three goodsh for you"; "very good – shix goodsh".

Now why can't FIFA come up with a tie breaker like that? In the event of a draw, it's not the lottery of the penalty shoot out competition – it's the team that can line up straightest for the national anthems.

Home for lunch, where I implied to my anxious parents that the morning had "gone OK" – a strategy I used every day for years; they never challenged this analysis despite a succession of abysmal school reports. After lunch, mathematics was going to be fine – I'd always been good at sums at Victoria. But this wasn't just sums.

Mr C. J. H. Ward (Charlie, not to be confused with the easily identified 'Beery' Ward) was a very well-meaning teacher although he made his mind up very quickly that every one of us would end up in Bedford Jail. He soon got down to introducing us to the delights of algebra, trigonometry, geometry and arithmetic with logarithms and, astonishingly, made it all fairly interesting – and, best of all, his teaching methods did not incorporate any gratuitous violence of any kind.

The first day concluded with geography with Mr Dunning – held in the next room to Mr C. J. H. Ward's except for the Headmaster's office. I set out for Mr Dunning's room only to be apprehended by a stocky lady (the only one in the entire school) we came to know as 'Nora', who explained quite forcibly that I was not allowed to go down the front corridor. To go the fifteen yards from Mr Ward's room to Mr Dunning's involved what would, nowadays, involve hiring a fleet of mini-buses for the kids to make the circuitous journey around the other three sides of a grass quadrangle – it was, it transpired, an even greater transgression to set foot on the quadrangle.

Mr Dunning, we got to appreciate, always started his lessons bang on time, irrespective of the number of pupils present. My confrontation with Nora meant that I arrived part way through his explanation that the earth was divided into 24 time zones and each time zone occupied 15 degrees of the earth's circumference. He proceeded to tear up a couple of sheets of an exercise book into scraps of paper about two inches square and told us that it was 5pm in San Francisco, 120 degrees west and asked us to calculate the time in Cairo, 30 degrees east.

Whilst this seems like a doddle all these years later, the crucial missing part of the explanation and a certain pressure to get this right completely overwhelmed me. Noting that a minority of us had not entirely covered ourselves with glory in this basic piece of geographic calculation, Mr Dunning explained that he would scatter the scraps of paper at us at the beginning of each lesson until all of us got the correct answer every time.

The fact that we were still being thrown scraps of 2x2 well into the second year was testimony to his perspicacity and our (er…my) abject failure to grasp the basic idea. Obviously, Jake never tried a further explanation or coming at the problem from a different direction to help the educational process; I just had to get it right.

This first day was a microcosm of my entire WGS career which lurched from crisis to bigger crisis. The far from impressive performance in Year 1 resulted in relegation, in Year 2, to 2C. WGS was renowned for fast-tracking its brightest boys in the A-stream through to Oxbridge – and the A-stream kids earned the school a truly impressive academic record. However, life in the C-stream was an altogether different experience – in hindsight, if the A stream was probably where the staff got their professional gratification; the C-stream was certainly where they got their target practice.

The back of the head was, it seemed, the only place through which staff felt knowledge could be imparted at C-stream level. I suppose it worked to a point; I can still remember, courtesy of Mr Nicholas's left hand, the five relative pronouns: 'who' [crack], 'whom' [slap], 'whose' [biff], 'which' [bang], 'that, meaning which' [thud]. Although I can't remember the relevance of having to learn them.

Mr 'Chunky' Pine had a predilection for deploying the Bunsen burner pipe to 'encourage' a love of physics. Question: "Definition of 'work'?" – all hands shot heavenward immediately (anyone not raising hand slapped with pipe as punishment for visible ignorance). Answer: "load divided by effort, sir?" "Correct." [Thwack.]

Chunky's triple-psycho approach to education was, at least, entertaining when one's form colleagues were on the receiving end. A rare treat unfolded before our eyes when, in order to demonstrate Newton's Laws of something or other, Chunky proceeded to line up about 15 boys and stood them shoulder to shoulder across the front of the lab. After opening the door, he walked to the other end of the line, took a run up and shoulder charged the boy at his end of the line. To universal acclaim (except from the boys at either end of the line) the boy at the other end of the experiment flew forcibly off the end of the line, out of the open door into the wall on the other side of the corridor.

In 2001, I attended the funeral of Jake Dunning (expecting, of course, to find the service sheets on 2x2 scraps of notebook) and Chunky gave the eulogy. Over the cuppa and ham sandwiches, I reminded him (still calling him 'Sir', of course) of the Newton experiment which he feigned to know nothing of

– and, having Bunsen burner piped me several times a week for many years said, to our mutual relief, that he had no recollection of who I was, either! Chunky's biggest disappointment was that, as I described it, it appeared that he had only injured two of the 15 boys – 13 missed opportunities.

However, Chunky apart, science was, of all faculties, the one used as some form of light relief from the punishment blocks of languages and humanities. It was here we encountered Mr Leftwich (Gus). Now I'm sure he was a brilliant biologist; the walls of his room boasted the usual Rolls of Honour – boys who had gone on to study biology at Oxbridge – and these achievements bore testimony to his professional talent. But for 2C, Gus was the ideal antidote to work and flying board rubbers.

On one memorable occasion, by making a hissing sound at the back of the room and suggesting that there was a smell of gas (and when he went to investigate, the 'gas leak' had mysteriously moved to the front bench) Gus spent over twenty of the forty minutes allocated to his lesson chasing a hiss around the Cockcroft lab (known, of course, as the Cock-up lab).

You can imagine our delight the day Gus locked the Cockcroft door, nervously drew down the blind and proceeded surreptitiously to unroll a diagram of the reproductive organs of the rabbit; Gus provided the only formal sex lesson I ever had – about ten minutes in total including some impudent questions which Gus just about managed to fend off.

Science faculty time-tabling for C-stream boys seemed to throw up a disproportionately high number of student teachers, adding to the air of light relief.

One student meticulously set up an experiment called, I think, Fletcher's trolley. This basic piece of kit had a trolley, a couple of feet long and about three inches wide, onto which a piece of paper was pinned. The trolley ran the length of the teacher's bench on glass to minimise friction and was pulled by weights which were set up on a pulley overhanging the end of the bench. By dipping a paintbrush in ink, putting the inky brush on the paper, plucking the brush assembly and letting the trolley go, the weights were meant to make the trolley accelerate and the wavy line produced by the paintbrush could be analysed to demonstrate that the trolley got faster.

Fine in theory, except that the student teacher, from his viewpoint at one end of the bench (so maintaining, understandably, full responsibility for the inky paintbrush) didn't pick up on the fact that one of our colleagues at the other end of the bench could reach the weights with his foot, unseen, and interrupt their descent.

The series of outcomes included the theory that falling weights can slow down as well as speed up or, alternatively, slow down and then speed up alarmingly again – "probably an atmospheric thing, sir?" Clearly, it's a good thing that 3C were not assisting Sir Isaac.

If science was the most entertaining time I could contrive (not, of course, because I learned any science other than the names of the experiments we cocked up or apparatus that could be used to generate an awful stink – Kipps was an all-time favourite), Spanish was definitely the very least appealing way to pass the day.

Acknowledging the usual norms of recalling memories of our youth – to the effect that all comments are intended as affectionate and shouldn't be taken seriously, and writing in that spirit, it would be best to draw a suitably lacy veil over Spanish and my relationship with the [allegedly] charmless Mr Graham Ridge. In all honesty, even 40+ years on, I couldn't think of anything at all I could say about this individual that would come even close to 'affection'. We absolutely detested one another with a passion.

Last time I looked, Mr Ridge could be viewed on www.wellingborough.gov.uk in his role as a Councillor in the Borough Council of Wellingborough. Since my former adversary gives a passable impression on the site that he is still alive, and, hence, remains in a position to sue I'll restrict my memories to the irrefutable facts – he failed to teach me any discernible Spanish in five years and, to his further credit, spurned all the usual instruments of torture that were readily available – books, knotted gowns, sports equipment, slippers, *et al.*, preferring just to use his bare hands on me. Gratifyingly, I long ago discovered that it is not impossible to enjoy a visit to Spain without speaking any Spanish.

On the other hand, I quite liked Art. Eddie Phillips taught us a few things that have since proved useful and encouraged me to take an interest in architecture. It turned out that I could draw and paint reasonably well although, when the matter of the subjective assessment of our efforts in art examinations reared its head, it always seemed remarkable that those who were members of his puppet club did just that bit better than those of us who weren't.

Despite Mr 'Beery' Ward's best efforts, I also liked history. In Year 2, my two best exam results by a long way were in art and history. Consequently, it came as no surprise that at the end of Year 2, it was announced that a decision on future options had to be made that involved dropping either art or history. There was no possibility of dropping Spanish or any of the sciences at which I was pathologically incapable – I had just two reasonably good subjects and had to drop one of them and persevere with Spanish.

Further up the school, similar options needed to be made but, as I was just about bottom in everything but Art, the impact of the choices was far less damaging on what passed for my academic career.

There were some inexplicable consequences of various choices that can only be explained by the fact that there were 'x' teachers, 'y' subjects and 'n' kids and, so, the number of lesson options was probably something like n/(x:y) with the remainder doing what was left. Consequently, for example, if you chose to do geography, you were, inadvertently, also choosing engineering drawing and, hence, dropping music and English literature. Alas, nothing you could choose would make Spanish drop out of the bottom of the equation's discard pile.

At the end of five agonising years, I gained one O-level with a top grade in Art – obviously the examiner was misled into assuming I belonged to a puppet club. My attempt at the Spanish paper had clearly not taken the examiner too long to mark and could still be the lowest mark ever achieved in a language O-level. To no one's great surprise, I failed every one of the science papers – presumably unable to concentrate on the questions without the encouragement of a Bunsen burner pipe between the shoulder blades.

The final rendition of "Lord, dismiss us with thy blessing" and the last end of term service navigated, it was off home for the ceremonial burning of the school cap and to hand over the last-ever school report to bewildered parents. That, I thought, was almost certainly that. One last trip round the perimeter wire with Billet and Perkins, under the vaulting horse and out through the escape tunnel under Doddington Road and thence the freedom of the workplace.

What the escape committee hadn't counted on was the school's practice of making the last school report especially rosy – even with the most unsuccessful boy. This was, of course, the report that prospective employers would get to see and the usual "He's completely useless" battery of comments would not exactly reflect well on the school. So my summer 1963 report was not recognisable as one of mine. Any poor grades were described as 'unusual' and, despite setbacks, I showed 'great promise' and, with the 'application we all know he's capable of' success was said to be 'assured'.

Astonishingly, my parents were also convinced that the appalling set of O-level examination results were inconsistent with what they perceived as my true ability and they wondered if I should be given another year to see if I could prove everyone right.

Even more astonishingly, Harold Wrenn agreed with them and signed the order paper that extended my sentence for another year in the Fifth Form. There was no Board of Appeal – could I not have the decision overturned by Graham Ridge?

The thought of being returned each year to the Fifth Form until I was in my thirties apparently did the trick. Head down, nose clean, I managed six O-levels – no sciences, of course, and still rock bottom at Spanish.

Thanks to the wonderful Open University, I later managed to astound John Dunning by gaining a geography-based degree and now can even calculate the time in any part of the globe.

I've managed to do without algebra, trigonometry and logarithms since 1964 and, having developed a serious aversion to Bunsen burner tubing, leave the sciences in the hands of others. And I still have absolutely no plans to see whether, even with a decent teacher, I could improve my Spanish.

III : WHAT MADE OUR SCHOOL SPECIAL?

APRIL		
W. 15	Term begins 8-50 a.m.	
	On Duty : Mr. P. J. DELMON.	
M. 20	HOUSE MEETINGS 12 noon.	
	On Duty : Mr. M. CURRIE.	
M. 27	On Duty : Mr. J. G. DUNNING.	
Th. 30	HOUSE MATCHES : Senior First Round.	
MAY		
M. 4	On Duty : Mr. H. C. PHILLIPS.	
Tu. 5	HOUSE MATCHES. Junior First Round.	
	Parents' Whist Drive 7-15 p.m.*	
Th. 7	Athletic Sports 2-15 p.m.*	
	Presentation of Cups by H. C. L. Warwick, Esq.	
M. 11	On Duty : Mr. J. H. BUTLER.	
Tu. 12	U-15 XI v. Northampton G.S. U-15 XI	Home
	U-14 XI v. Northampton G.S. U-14 XI	Away
W. 13	1st XI v. Kettering G.S. 1st XI	Away
Th. 14	Athletic Match v. King's School v. Deacon's School, at Peterborough.	
F. 15	Commemoration Service 3 p.m.	
	Address by the Vicar of Finedon.	
S. 16	1st XI v. Old Cytringanians	Home
M. 18	WHIT WEEK HOLIDAY.	
M. 25	On Duty : Mr. C. A. PINE.	
Tu. 26	U-15 XI v. Wellingborough Sch. U-15 XI	Home
	U-14 XI v. Bedford Harpur U-14 XI	Away
W. 27	1st XI v. Deacon's School 1st XI	Away
	2nd XI v. Deacon's School 2nd XI	Home
	U-15 XI v. Deacon's School U-15 XI	Home
	U-14 XI v. Deacon's School U-14 XI	Away
Th. 28	HOUSE MATCHES : Senior Second Round.	
S. 30	1st XI v. Oundle School 2nd XI	Home
	2nd XI v. Oundle School 3rd XI	Away
	U-15 XI v. Oundle School U-15 XI	Away
	U-14 XI v. Towcester G.S. U-14 XI	Away
JUNE		
M. 1	On Duty : Dr. A. JACKSON.	
W. 3	1st XI v. Bedford Modern 2nd XI	Away
	2nd XI v. Bedford Modern Colts XI	Home
	U-15 XI v. Bedford Modern U-15 XI	Home
	U-14 XI v. Bedford Modern U-14 XI	Away
Th. 4	PRIZE GIVING.*	
	Chief Guest : Sir Lawrence Bragg.	
S. 6	2nd XI v. Towcester G.S. 1st XI	Away
	Scouts : Silverwood Cup.	
M. 8	On Duty : Mr. R. V. S. WARD.	
Tu. 9	HOUSE MATCHES : Junior Second Round.	
W. 10	U-15 XI v. Corby G.S. U-15 XI	Away
Th. 11	1st XI v. Bedford School 2nd XI	Away
	2nd XI v. Corby G.S. 1st XI	Home
S. 13	2nd XI v. Kettering G.S. 2nd XI	Home
M. 15	On Duty : Mr. A. W. LEFTWICH.	
Tu. 16	U-15 XI v. Northampton G.S. U-15 XI	Away
	U-14 XI v. Northampton G.S. U-14 XI	Home
Th. 18	1st XI v. Wellingborough Thursday C.C.	Home
	2nd XI v. Laxton G.S. 1st XI	Away
	U-14 XI v. Laxton G.S. U-14 XI	Away
S. 20	1st XI v. Kettering G.S. 1st XI	Home
	2nd XI v. Kettering G.S. 2nd XI	Away
	U-14 XI v. Kettering G.S. U-14 XI	Home
M. 22	G.C.E. Examinations begin.	
	On Duty : Mr. C. J. H. WARD.	
Th. 25	2nd XI v. Daventry G.S. 1st XI	Home
	U-14 XI v. Bedford School U-14 XI	Home
F. 26	Scouts : Gilbey Cup.	
S. 27	1st XI v. Northampton G.S. 1st XI	Away
	2nd XI v. Northampton G.S. 2nd XI	Home
	U-14 XI v. Corby G.S. U-14 XI	Home
M. 29	On Duty : Mr. M. S. CHEALE.	
Tu. 30	HOUSE MATCHES : Junior Third Round.	
JULY		
F. 3	FINAL MARKS.	
S. 4	1st XI v. King's School 1st XI	Home
	2nd XI v. King's School 2nd XI	Away
	U-15 XI v. King's School U-15 XI	Home
	U-14 XI v. King's School U-14 XI	Away
M. 6	On Duty : Mr. R. H. TEMPLE.	
W. 8	School Examinations begin.	
Th. 9	U-14 XI v. Kettering G.S. U-14 XI	Away
F. 10	U-15 XI v. Kettering G.S. U-15 XI	Away
S. 11	1st XI v. Lawrence Sheriff School 1st XI	Home
	2nd XI v. Lawrence Sheriff School 2nd XI	Away
	U-15 XI v. Lawrence Sheriff Sch. U-15 XI	Away
	U-14 XI v. Lawrence Sheriff Sch. U-14 XI	Home
M. 13	On Duty : Mr. A. E. SPARROW.	
W. 15	School Excursions.	
Th. 16	HOUSE MATCHES : Senior Third Round.	
	G.C.E. Examinations end.	
S. 18	'A' XI v. Old Grammarians	Home
	U-15 XI v. Kettering G.S. U-15 XI	Home
M. 20	Athletic Match v. Northampton G.S. v. Kettering G.S., at Northampton.	
	On Duty : Mr. J. W. HUDDART.	
Tu. 21	Swimming Sports 10-30 a.m., at Wilby.*	
	School Music Recital 7-15 p.m.*	
W. 22	House P.T. Competition 11-20 a.m.*	
Th. 23	1st XI v. The Masters	Home
F. 24	End of Term Service.	

August 19th—School Party to Italy.

Autumn Term begins Thursday, 10th September, and ends Friday, 18th December.

Half-Term : October 30th, November 2nd and 3rd.

Parents are welcome at these events and at all School Matches.

Summer Term time-table 1959, typical of the fifties and sixties

Period	Monday	Tuesday	Wednesday	Thursday	Friday
1	Eng 20	Geog 3	Eng 6	Hist 13	Fren 1
2	Geog 3	Alg 2	Fren 1		Geog 3
3	Arith 1	Music M	Geog 3	Alg 2	Eng 6
Break	B	R	E	A	K
4	Biol C	Chem 13	Geom 2	Fren 17	Phy 6
5	Fren 15		PT	PHY 12	
Afternoon	L	U	N	C	H
6	Hist 20	Div 19	T.D 3	Geom 2	Trig 2
7	Games	Shake 6		Biol C	PT
8		Fren 1	Chem 13		TD 7
Preps	Eng, Fren, Biol, arith	Chem, Eng, Geog	Math, Geog	Fren, Alg	Hist, TD, Phy

Assembly
9.10 Period 1
9.50 Period 2
10.30 Period 3
11.10 Break
11.30 Period 4
12.10 Period 5
12.50 Lunch
2.10 Period 6
2.50 Period 7
3.30 Period 8
4.10 School ends

A typical academic time-table of forty periods, each of forty minutes

Chapter 8
The Liberal Curriculum

The School's belief in the liberal curriculum was to 'create a healthy mind in a healthy body', with a desire for boys to learn about cultural aspects not present in the lives of many of their parents. On the one hand it meant offering a high quality academic education, but on the other it involved not only sporting activities, but also experiences from a range of other clubs and societies, and opportunities to visit places of interest at home and abroad.

Every boy was given a fold-over school calendar containing the calendar of events inside and a blank weekly time-table on the back to fill in their own programme of lessons.

On the page opposite is the calendar of activities in a typical summer term in the fifties and sixties. Each week a master was on duty to supervise the school. There was a full range of school competitive cricket matches and two inter-school triangular athletic matches. Within the school itself, there were House competitions in the House Cricket Matches, Athletic Sports, Swimming Sports and House PT Competition. Parents were welcome to all these events, in addition to a Parents' Whist Drive to raise funds, the School Music Recital, and the School Prize Day when their sons were presented with their prizes. While the main prizes were awarded for the best performances in examinations, reading, and other competitive activities, from the fifties onwards – when the GCE was awarded to every boy who passed at least one subject – virtually all parents had the opportunity to see their son presented with his certificate.

Also featured in the summer programme are the School Excursion Day and the departure of the School Party to Italy. Conspicuously absent are the wide range of School Clubs and Societies which work to their own separate schedules.

Below, opposite, is a typical timetable, with eight forty-minute periods every day, a break of twenty minutes in the morning and an hour and forty minutes for two sittings for dinner at mid-day. Every boy has his own schedule, but in a three-form entry school with limited classroom space, the possibility of making personal choices were few.

The table opposite collates the structure of a full year's activities in the fifties, and is typical of the stable post-war activities in the school. In organisation, it represents the fulfilment of the original vision of the first headmaster, Mr Lay, in the manner of the longest-serving headmaster, Mr Wrenn.

School teams played on virtually every Saturday, with rugby in the autumn and spring, and cricket in the summer.

House competitions occurred throughout the year, with the House Meetings held every term on the first day to make plans for the term. The emphasis was on a range of sporting activities including rugby, cricket, athletics, PT and swimming. In the team sports, pupils of the appropriate years would be shouting for their House, but with athletics and swimming, the whole school was the audience. House Music and House Play Competitions inevitably encouraged the involvement of far more pupils than the prestigious whole school events.

In the first year, examinations were every term as boys were moved up and down according to their overall examination performance. After that, class tests occurred as required to provide marks for the end of term reports, with an annual school examination at the end of each year.

The public face of the school is evident in the 'Other' column, with two music recitals, the School Play and the best House Plays presented to parents and friends of the school. On Parents' Day the Headmaster reported on the academic achievements of the school and an eminent guest presented prizes to the boys.

The School Excursions Day was devised as an annual trip out for all pupils after the external Certificate examinations. The boys were offered the choice of a wide range of excursions and Mr Dunning reviewed their preferences to give every boy the best available choice.

Finally, while Junior and Senior Reading Competitions are specified in the timetable, boys were encouraged to read at least eight novels during the year to compete for a general reading prize in each form, with assessment by a simple test (testing knowledge, say, of a major character in the book).

The discipline of the School was based on the School Rules which changed over the years. Teachers and prefects set the copying of the rules as a punishment for minor misdemeanors. (See overleaf.)

School	House	Academic	Other
	Autumn Term		
Rugby 5 teams: 1st XV, 2nd XV, U-15, U-14, U-13 often with 4 or 5 matches every Saturday	**House meeting** 12 noon first day **House Rugby** 2 rounds played during normal games lessons	**Examinations** 1st Form	Sixth Form visit to Stewarts & Lloyds October 2nd **School Play** every evening second week in December **Christmas Music Recital** – evening **End of Term Service** 2 pm
	Spring Term		
Rugby 5 teams: 1st XV, 2nd XV, U-15, U-14, U-13 often with 4 or 5 matches every Saturday 1st & 2nd XV v Old Boys XVs **Athletics Standards** begin Feb 17th	**House meeting** 12 noon first day **House Rugby** Last round **House Music Competition** March 13th, 2 pm **House Plays** March 20th, 2 pm	**Mock GCE Examinations** Advanced & Ordinary January **Examinations** 1st Form	French Play: Palace Theatre, February 19th **House Plays & Parents' Bazaar** March 23rd, 7 pm **Junior and Senior Reading Competitions** March 24th **End of Term Service** 2 pm
	Summer Term		
Athletics Competition May 14th Thursday, July 20th Monday **Cricket** 4 Teams: 1st XI, 2nd XI, U-15 XI, U-14 XI play most Saturdays A XI v Old Boys 1st XI v The Masters	**House meeting** 12 noon first day **House Cricket** 3 rounds Junior & Senior in school time **House Athletics** May 7th **House Swimming** July 21st, 10.30 am **House PT** July 22nd, 11.20 am	**GCE Examinations** June 22nd–July 16th **School Examinations** July 8th	**Commmemoration Service** May 15th, Friday **Parents' Day** June 4th **Scouts** Silverwood Cup June 6th Gilbey Cup June 26th **School Excursions** July 15th **Music Recital** July 21st, 7.15 pm **End of Term Service** 2 pm July 24th

Typical Events during the School Year (here 1958/59)

The School Rules

Earlier School Rules	Later School Rules
1 School uniform must on all occasions be worn to and from school.	1 School uniform must on all occasions be worn to and from school.
2 At other times, either complete school uniform or complete mufti must be worn.	2 At other times, either complete school uniform or complete mufti must be worn.
3 Boys will never walk more than three abreast on a footpath.	
4 Boys will always raise their caps to masters, except when cycling.	
5 Boys will not stand with their hands in their pockets while talking to a master.	
6 Boys will dismount at the school gates and will not cycle in the playground.	3 Boys must dismount at the school gates and must not cycle in the playground.
7 Balls are for use on the field only and there is to be no throwing of stones or other missiles.	4 Balls are to be used on the field only: not in the playground.
8 Fireworks, peashooters, catapults, water-pistols, smoking materials are not to be brought to school.	
9 All boys bringing a note after the absence or of excuse from games or P.T. will come in at the front door and leave their notes at the office.	8 All boys must bring a note after absence or an excuse from games or P.E. and must come in at the Front Door and leave their notes at the office BEFORE PRAYERS.
10 Gym shoes are worn for prayers in the Hall.	5 Gymn. shoes or house shoes must be worn for Prayers in Hall, and boys must not walk in studded boots on corridors or class room floors.
	6 The Front Corridor is out of bounds except for those going to the Library, the Headmaster or the Office.
27 Boys may change from gym shoes to out-door wear either in the break or before lunch. Prefects are responsible for seeing they do not dawdle in the changing rooms.	7 Boys may change from gymn. shoes to out-door wear either after Prayers or before lunch. The changing-rooms are out-of-bounds except for P.E. during the rest of morning school.
	9 Boys who arrive at school too late for Prayers must report at the Office or the Headmaster's study immediately.
11 There will be complete quiet before prayers when the prefect mounts the platform.	10 There must be complete quiet before Prayers in the Hall as soon as the Prefect has mounted the Platform.
12 In corridors and on the stairs, boys keep to the left and there is to be no running.	11 In corridors and on the stairs, boys must keep to the left. There is to be no running within the school buildings.
13 No boy may go to another's form-room or desk without permission from a master.	

14 After lunch a boy may either go into prep., into the library, or onto the field except on wet days when all boys must remain in the building.	12 Before or after lunch a boy may go either into prep. or on to the field except on wet days when all boys must remain in prep.
15 Prep rooms are as follows:– VIth in their own room (1) Va & Vb in Va room (2) 4a & 4b in Vb room (5) 3a & 3b) 2a & 2b) in 3b room (4)	
16 All boys will go outside at 1.45 on fine days until the bell.	13 Boys must return from the field at 1.40 p.m.
	14 During the winter terms Rubber boots must be worn on the field and the door by Room 6 must not be used.
17 No dinner boy may leave the school grounds during the dinner hour without his housemaster's permission.	15 No dinner boy may leave the school grounds during the dinner hour without his house-master's permission.
18 Boys who take balls or cricket gear on the field are responsible for their return.	
19 Boys may not borrow each other's kit.	16 Boy's must not borrow each other's kit.
20 After games and P.T. all kit must be put away, gym shoes unless wet in bag, and boots hung on peg.	17 After games and P.E. all kit must be put away (gymn. shoes unless wet, in bag, and boots hung on peg). Towels and wet clothing must be dried at home.
21 All kit must clearly marked with name and number.	18 All kit must be clearly marked with name.
22 Lost property should be reported to a master immediately.	19 Lost property must be reported immediately.
23 Property found should be handed in at the office.	20 Property found must be handed in at the Office.
	21 Boys may keep private property in their desks. Lost keys or any interference with locks should be reported to the Form Masters. At the end of each term desks must be left unlocked.
24 Boys should hand money, watches spectacles and other valuables to a master and not carry them about or leave them in the cloakroom or form-rooms.	22 Boys must leave money, watches, spectacles and other valuables with a master in the Common Room or lock them in their desks. They must not leave them in the cloakroom. The School is not responsible for any loss. Watches should not be brought to School.
25 Form-rooms will be locked at 4.10 p.m.	
26 Damage to school property or balls lost over the fence must be reported immediately. Boys are not to climb fences to recover balls or to trespass on other property. Failure to report damage will cause it to be treated as wilful.	23 Damage to school property or school balls lost over the fence must be reported immediately. Boys must not climb fences to recover balls or trespass on other property.
27 [*see previous page*]	24 Food, sweets, etc. must not be taken on to the School field.

Overview of the following chapters

The chapters which follow cover various strands of the liberal curriculum, beginning in chapter 9 with the development of the academic curriculum, where we shall find substantially the same framework throughout the school's existence. It was soon built up in the early nineteen thirties, settling down when the school reached a viable size and remaining largely unchanged except for the introduction of additional languages including Russian, German and Italian, and specialist subjects such as Technical Drawing and Metalwork.

Sport will be considered in chapter 10, with its focus on rugby and its successful links with the England rugby team, together with school cricket, athletics, PT, swimming and later developments in basketball, cycling, soccer, badminton and other sports.

The major opportunities for the boys to widen their experience through the many clubs and societies are reviewed in chapter 11, as they grow from the worthiness of music, drama, debating, the leisure of the Cinema Society and the ever-present Scouts in the thirties, through the trials of the war to a full panoply of clubs and societies in the late forties, fifties, sixties and seventies.

The trips home and abroad are reviewed in Chapter 12, from the annual Excursion Day from 1947 to 1971, when everyone went somewhere to relax after the summer exams, trips to stay with the Navy in Portsmouth, field trips under the auspices of the Field Survey Society for geography and biology, and the annual school trip abroad for those whose parents could afford to pay.

Chapter 13 features the eminent guests who came to the annual Parents' Day & Prize Giving, to present the prizes and, in later years, to name a laboratory, specialist room or department in the school. This reveals a County Grammar School with ambition to achieve excellence in its academic and liberal curriculum and to underline its successes through visits from great scientists, authors, war heroes and royalty.

Chapter 9

The Academic Curriculum

The fundamental underlying plan of the academic curriculum in Wellingborough Grammar School remained stable throughout the school's life. With minor changes it followed the pattern of earlier Grammar Schools in Wellingborough, outlined in chapter 3:

Dr Sanderson's curriculum for the Upper School in Church Street in mid-Victorian times:

> *Latin, Greek, French, Arithmetic, Algebra, Mensuration & Land Surveying, Geography, History, Religious Instruction, Drawing & Mapping, Mechanics, Philosophy, Book-Keeping, General Knowledge, and Singing.*

Wellingborough (Grammar) School under Mr Fryer at the turn of the century:

> *Religious Knowledge, Arithmetic, History & Geography, English, Mathematics (pure and applied), Natural Science, French, Latin, Greek, Drawing and Vocal Music, with optional lessons in piano, violin, book-keeping and shorthand.*

The Board of Education—set up by the Government following the 1902 Education Act—made specific recommendations for the nature of the subjects to be studied, even down to the time required for each, though the content remained in the control of the School:

> *The Course should provide instruction in the English Language and Literature, at least one Language other than English, Geography, History, Mathematics and Drawing, with due provision for Manual Work and Physical Exercises ... Not less that 4 hours per week must be allotted for English, Geography and History; not less than 3½ hours to the Language where only one is taken or less than 6 hours where two are taken; and not less than 7½ hours to Science and Mathematics of which at least 3 must be for Science. The instruction in Science must be both theoretical and practical. When two languages other than English are taken, and Latin is not one of them, the Board will be required to be*

satisfied that the omission of Latin is for the advantage of the School.
Regulations for Secondary Schools, 1904

The detailed number of hours was soon relaxed, nevertheless, the outline curriculum remained a template for secondary education into the time of the Grammar School, within a framework broadly familiar to boys in the 1930s and throughout the life of the school:

Secondary School ... offers to each of its scholars, up to and beyond the age of 16, a general education, physical, mental and moral, given through a completely graded course of instruction of wider scope and more advanced degree than that in Elementary Schools.

a) The instruction must be general; i.e. must be such as gives a reasonable degree of exercise and development to the whole of the faculties, and does not confine this development to a particular channel, whether that of pure and applied science, of literary and linguistic study, or, of that kind of acquirement which is directed simply at fitting a boy or girl to enter business in a subordinate capacity.

b) The course of instruction must be complete; i.e. must be so planned as to lead up to a definite standard in the various branches of instruction indicated above, and not stop short at a merely superficial introduction to any one of them. *Regulations for Secondary Schools, 1904*

Passing in Five Subjects

The Board of Education went on to specify the number of subjects that was to be considered the minimum requirement for a School Certificate to be awarded. They arrived at the magic number five, which has remained to this day in the current requirements for students to have "five good passes at grades A–C" in the modern General Certificate of Secondary Education.

The key aspects of the original School Certificate were:

... to assist and emphasize the principle that every secondary school should provide, for pupils up to the average age of 16, a sound basis of liberal education which ... would serve as a foundation upon which varieties of further education could be based.

Report of the Consultative Committee of the Board of Education on Examinations in Secondary Schools, 1911

The School Certificate was finally agreed in 1917. Pupils had to pass at least five subjects from at least three different areas of the curriculum including English Language and Mathematics. The pass mark was 30%, a credit was 50%. The *raison d'être* of the curriculum was to keep broad areas of learning open for longer-term development. The inevitable problem was that children with a strong bias in some subjects, but not in others, might never pass the School Certificate. It was common for students to take up to eight subjects with the intention of achieving the required standards in at least five.

To obtain exemption to the London Matriculation Examinations as a pre-requisite to going to university, five passes were required at credit level, including: English Language, Mathematics, a foreign language, and a science. This was to lead to candidates re-taking subjects at successive examinations in order to reach the required standard.

In 1921 the Higher School Certificate was introduced as an examination at the age of around 18, requiring a minimum of three main subjects and one subsidiary.

The School Certificate in Wellingborough Grammar School

Wellingborough Grammar School opened in 1930 with five staff and 64 boys, beginning with the required spread of subjects, though it took time to get 'up to speed' with a full array of options.

> *In September 1932 there were eight assistant masters. Gradually various departments of the school have been put into commission. The lecture room has been earmarked in particular for geography, the laboratories have received an initial amount of equipment, and the woodwork room now receives six double period classes each week.*
>
> *Mr Lay, School Magazine 1932*

Apart from a single older boy taking the School Certificate in 1932, the first full School Certificate was taken in 1934, with the range of subjects limited by the small number of pupils and teachers. At this time only English Language was offered, not English Literature, the only science was Chemistry, the languages were Latin and French, and the humanities, History, Geography and Religious Knowledge. Thirteen boys obtained the necessary five subjects (listed overleaf) and another four added the necessary passes at Christmas.

	English	Maths		Science	Languages		Humanities			Total
Bean	E	m			f		h	G		5
Boswell	E	m			F(o)		h		r	5
Bradshaw		M		ch	F(o)		H		r	5
Crowther-Green		M			F		h	G	r	5
Drage	e	M		ch	F(o)		H			5
Ferry	e	M		ch	F(o)		h		r	6
Gowen	e	M			F(o)		h	G		7
Langley	E	M		Ch	F(o)		H		r	6
Lansberry	E	M	am	ch	F(o)		h			6
Pack	e	M	AM	Ch	F(o)	l	H		r	8
Sears	E	M*	AM	Ch	F(o)		H		r	7
Sheppard	e	M		Ch	F		H	g	r	7
Stock	E	m			F(o)		H		R	5

School Certificate 1934
E–English, M–Mathematics (=distinction), AM–Additional Mathematics, Ch–Chemistry, F–French, O–Oral French, L–Latin, H–History, G–Geography.*
A capital letter indicates a credit (50%) rather than a pass (30%) in that subject.

In 1935, Physics was added and more boys took Additional Mathematics to broaden the choice of subjects to nine. This continued as the available choice for the remainder of Mr Lay's headship at the school.

In Mr Woolley's time, English became two subjects in 1939 ('Essay' and 'Selected Literature', renamed as 'English Language' and 'English Literature' in 1942). One boy passed 'Manual Training' in 1939—the only time the subject figured in the examinations. Biology and Art were introduced in 1943, making a total of thirteen subjects: English Language, English Literature, Mathematics, Additional Mathematics, Physics, Chemistry, Biology, French, Latin, History, Geography, Religious Knowledge and Art.

By this time, Additional Mathematics was taken as an exception rather than the rule. All boys studied English Language, English Literature, Geography, French, Mathematics, Chemistry and Art. Boys in 5A studied the more academic subjects of Latin, Physics and possibly Additional Mathematics, while boys in 5B studied History, Religious Knowledge and Biology. All students studied nine academic subjects drawn from every curriculum area, and in addition would have lessons devoted to games, PT, religious knowledge and music.

The table of results for 1944, opposite, is of particular interest as the only one in which a Magazine lists failures as well as passes. It gives a broader picture of the nature of the School Certificate.

	English		Maths		Science			Languages		Humanities			Art	Total
J. A. Abbott	E	E	M		ph				F					5
E. W. Barber	e	E	M		ph						g		A	6
R. Berry	e	E	M					L			g		A	6
R. E. Bridgeford	e	e	M			Ch	Bio			H	G	rk		8
M. D. Britton	E	E	m		Ph						g		a	6
D. E. Burridge	E	E	M		Ph				f		G			6
A. J. Carter	E	E	M		Ph			L	F(o)		G			7
A. S. Cohen	E	E	M			Ch			F(o)	h	G			7
K. W. Collins	E	e	M		Ph			l	F(o)					6
E. Cross	E	E	M		Ph			L	F(o)		G			7
J. C. Desborough	E	E	M		Ph				F		g			6
D. A. Franklin	E	E	M			ch	Bio					rk		6
J. T. Hardwick	E	E	M						F(o)	h	g			6
M. Hight	e	E	M		Ph	Ch					g			6
G. J. Howard	e	E	M		Ph	Ch		l			G			7
J. R. Hudson	e		m			Ch	Bio		F(o)		g			6
A. J. W. James	E	E	m				Bio		F	H	G	RK		7
F. R. C. James	E	E	m		Ph				f(o)		g			6
R. L. Jellis	E		M		Ph	Ch		l	F		g			7
J. R. Jones	E	E	M			Ch	Bio		f	h	g	rk		9
D. Knight	e	E	m			ch			f(o)	h	g	rk		8
P. Leach	e	e	m		ph			l			g			6
H. K. Maddams	E		M	am	Ph						g			5
M. H. Martin	E		M		ph			L	F(o)		G			6
R. D. Patenall	e	e	M		ph			l	f(o)		g			7
W. P. Patenall	E	E	M		ph			l	F		g			7
P. R. Redley	E	E	M				bio		f		G		A	7
A. W. Reed	E	e	M						F	H	g		A	7
M. W. Richardson	E	e	M		Ph			L	F(o)		g			7
J. C. Rodhouse	E	E	M		Ph			L	F(o)		G			7
F. Taylor	e	e	M				bio		f		G	rk		7
K. G. Tompkins	E	E	M		Ph				F(o)		G		A	6
D. A. J. Turner	E	e	M		ph				f		g		A	7
R. Wallis	E	E	M			Ch	Bio		F(o)	h		rk		8
W. A. Warner	E	E	M		ph			L	F(o)					6
R. G. Weed	e	e	M			ch	bio		F(o)	h	G	rk		9
H. R. White	E	E	M			ch	bio		F(o)	H	g	RK		9

The following failed to obtain a certificate but passed in the subjects indicated:

A. G. Bartlett†	e	e	M									rk	A	4
G. Brown†	e	e			Ph	Ch		l			g			5
C. H. Clarke†	E	e	M			Ch					g			4
J. B. Hanger†	E	E				Ch					G			4
Lucas	E	E								H	G	RK	a	6
R. C. Sturgess†			M		ph						G			3
Summerlin	e	e							f					3
D. S. Taylor	e	e	m										A	4
K. E. White†	e	e					bio					rk		4

School Certificate 1944. Key to subjects: E–English Language, E–English Literature; M–Mathematics, AM–Additional Mathematics; Ph–Physics, Ch–Chemistry, Bio–Biology; L–Latin, F–French, (o)–Oral French; H–History, G–Geography, RK–Religious Knowledge; A–Art.

[Those marked † completed the certificate the following year.]

All those who failed were successful in at least three subjects, with five students passing in four and two obtaining five or more. At the time it was the practice to limit entry to the Certificate only to boys who had a good chance of passing. Those considered unlikely to pass either continued to study to take the examination at a later date, or left early. Two candidates who passed in five or six subjects failed the Certificate because they failed to obtain passes in Mathematics and English.

Fortunately:

School Certificate regulations certainly did not involve taking the whole lot again if you failed one subject. I know this because English Language was my bête noir and I took it five or six times before getting through. It may have been that I also needed a credit to matriculate.

Brian Horn (1945–52)

In the autumn of 1944, five of the boys who had just missed the requirements for a Certificate took papers again and upgraded to a pass; a further boy completed his certificate the following summer. Three others left without a certificate, including one who had passed six subjects, five at credit level but had failed in Mathematics. This illustrates the fatal weakness of the original School Certificate: it fails to give any credit to high quality work if there are weaknesses in other areas. A survey of the 77 boys who started in 1940 (see page 80) revealed that 41 left school without taking the Certificate examination. The glass was nearly half full, but it was also more than half empty.

Other subjects

In the first year (Form 2) in 1940, we were taught Esperanto and started French in the 3rd Form. When I went into the Sixth Form in September 1944, I started Russian for the Higher School Certificate but could not continue when I moved back to Suffolk in January 1945. Esperanto was taught by Froggy Hole and, as I recall, we did it for a full year, then started French – again with Mr Hole. This meant that we had to reach School Certificate standard in three years – so he was a good teacher.

John Rodhouse (1940–45)

I remember my Oxford School Certificate 1946 included Eng Lang, Eng Lit, French, Latin, Geog, Art, Phys, Chem, Maths. There must have been more than one paper for the maths as we did Arith, Alg, Geom, Trig, and Calculus (as part of Additional Mathematics). I think that there was an option for Art as opposed to Additional Mathematics. In those days Latin at 'credit' level was needed for Oxbridge for either Arts or Science degrees. I failed Latin in 1946 and Charlie Wrenn had some misguided notion that I should go there and kept wittering on about it. To shut him up I re-sat and got the credit but never went to Oxbridge, or to any other university. Apart from Art, I cannot think there was much choice allowed in the School Certificate. The Higher School Certificate of course split into Arts or Sciences. I do recall doing Divinity in the earlier years but dropped it at some stage.

Michael King (1942–49)

Other areas that were studied but not examined included woodwork, PT, games, and religious knowledge.

Woodwork was taught in the 1930s first by Mr Page and then Mr Goddard who was also responsible for PT and boxing. The 1938 Autumn School Magazine welcomed Mr Pine as a replacement for Mr Goddard, so he could be expected to carry on with woodwork in addition to PT. (In the forties he demonstrated his considerable talent for woodwork by building the wooden stage for the Puppet Club.)

I have a memory of 'Chunky' Pine telling me long after he retired that he originally taught woodwork. My memory could be playing tricks, but it stuck because, at the time, I did not know woodwork was ever a subject at the school. *Brian Corn (1948–53)*

Woodwork was abandoned at the beginning of the war.

I was at the WGS from 1939 to 1944 and during this period there was no woodwork or metalwork as the materials were needed for the war effort. The practical work would have been done in the music room and I think the benches and vices were still there in 1939. Mr Wintersgill had a piano in there and a radiogram which, in later years, we used to tune in to 'The American Forces Network' at lunchtime.

Frank Taylor (1939–44)

In addition to the shortage of wood and an appropriate teacher, the ever-growing number of pupils fitting into the original school buildings required every inch of space.

Woodwork has, perforce, had to be abandoned and the room used as a music and form room … due to the doubling of the school's numbers in the war years.

After the war, woodwork did not return, the nearest thing to craft was the Puppet Club organised by Eddie Phillips in the late forties. The workbenches were kept in his art room and the puppeteers learned their techniques under his guidance. It was the only 'practical' activity that the school offered.

In my time at WGS the Education Authorities seemed to have a definite split in which the Grammar School was for those of us who were 'academics' whilst those skilled in 'hand-working' (bricks and mortar, wood, metal, etc) received a very comprehensive education at Wellingborough Technical College. Having spent all my working life in the building materials industry, albeit not as a hand worker (although I did start as a labourer in a concrete factory), I often wonder if I went to the correct school. It was not all disaster if one failed the 11-plus as is exemplified by a very good friend of mine, Arthur Handscombe (his father and mother managed the Horseshoe Hotel in Sheep St, Wellingborough) who went to Technical College and became an eminent gynaecologist in Edinburgh. Pedro Howes (1947–52)

Other aspects of the wider curriculum suffered during the war years:

The perpetual excuse (the war) came up for the lack of teachers available, for example, to teach swimming. I was fortunate to go all the way through in the A-stream, emerging with 5 credits, and when I started work at Rolls Royce, it was just enough for me to start on a part-time Engineering Degree course. I do recall quite a few boys leaving 'early' without any qualifications. It has always been a bone of contention for me that, in those days, there was nobody to offer advice about careers. I fancied RR because I was brought up with a Meccano set – but what a way to choose a job for life! Arthur Warner (1940–45)

At the end of the war, the rise of Russia on the international stage prompted a perceived need to learn the language. The Senior Language Master, Mr Bratt, already fluent in French, Spanish and German, set about polishing up his Russian:

Six members of the VIth Form, accompanied by Mr Bratt, spent a very profitable month at Oxford on a Russian Course and now go about muttering Russian words which, to the less learned members of the school, sound most alarming. School Magazine, Autumn 1945

In 1947 'Ivor' Cheale arrived to teach mathematics but also contributed to the teaching of Russian based on his recent service in Eastern Europe where he had experience with languages. 'Buzz' Temple arrived in 1948 to teach French and 'Tony' Sparrow in 1949 to teach Spanish. At this time, a number of changes occurred in language teaching:

> *At the end of the war, the languages studied were French and Latin, with German and Russian as VIth Form options, then Latin was demoted and Spanish came in.* *Jim Tompkins (1944–49)*

> *I started WGS in September 1945 in the A-stream and took Latin in the 1st year, but then Latin ceased to be taught. I started Spanish and managed to pass it in the two years leading up to taking the Oxford School Certificate in 1949. In September 1949, the School re-introduced Latin for sixth formers, because it realized that without Latin no one would get into Oxford or Cambridge. I proved to be so good at this I was asked to leave the class at the end of one year. For my remaining 2 years in the 6th form, Latin was replaced by Scientific German with Lennie Bratt. This was most enjoyable as it was almost on a one-to-one basis. In good weather classes were either in the quad or on the sports field.*
> *Brian Horn (1945–52)*

Higher School Certificate

The school struggled in its early years to build a sixth form, with only a handful of exceptional boys staying on to take the Higher School Certificate. The choice was always between an Arts course based on English taken with Languages or Humanities and a Science course including Physics and Chemistry and either Mathematics or Biology.

> *There was a two-year course to take you to the Oxford Higher School Certificate exam. You passed through the Lower Sixth to the Upper Sixth. The Sixth form was divided between Arts and Science and never the twain shall meet.* ARTS: *English, French, Russian, Latin, Greek, History, Geography, Economics.* SCIENCE: *Chemistry, Physics and either Maths (Pure and Applied), or Biology (Botany and Zoology).*
> *Gerald Neville (1943–50)*

The Higher School Certificate results in 1950 given overleaf reflect the pattern of subjects described above. The boys on the 'Arts side' studied History, English and Geography, as their principal subjects, with two

OXFORD HIGHER SCHOOL CERTIFICATE.

B. Cross	Prin. :	History, English, Geography (Good).
	Subsid. :	Economics, Russian.
J. P. Edwards	Prin. :	History, English, Geography.
	Subsid. :	Russian.
P. W. Furnell	Prin. :	History (Good), English (Good), Geography (Good).
	Subsid. :	Economics (Very Good), Russian (Very Good).
M. A. Goodband	Prin. :	Art, History, Geography.
B. A. Groome	Prin. :	History, English, Geography.
	Subsid. :	Economics.
N. F. Pearson	Prin. :	Art, History, English, Geography (Good).
R. Shawley	Prin. :	French (Good), History, English.
	Subsid. :	Economics (Good), Russian.
P. A. Wills	Prin. :	History, English, Geography (Good).
J. H. Anderson	Prin. :	Pure Mathematics, Applied Mathematics, Physics (Good).
B. Bazeley	Prin. :	Chemistry (Good), Botany, Zoology.
	Subsid. :	Physics.
K. M. Bradshaw	Prin. :	Pure Mathematics, Applied Mathematics, Physics, Chemistry (Good).
N. F. Elmore	Prin. :	Pure Mathematics, Physics, Chemistry (Good).
	Subsid. :	Applied Mathematics.
D. M. Fidler	Prin. :	Pure Mathematics, Applied Mathematics, Physics (Good), Chemistry (Good).
J. W. Gramshaw	Prin. :	Physics (Good), Chemistry (Good).
	Subsid. :	Applied Mathematics, French.
P. H. Hunt	Prin. :	Pure Mathematics, Applied Mathematics, Physics (Good), Chemistry.
R. Lawrence	Prin. :	Pure Mathematics, Applied Mathematics, Physics, Chemistry.
E. R. Tilley	Prin. :	Pure Mathematics, Applied Mathematics, Physics, Chemistry.
S. T. Wells	Prin. :	Pure Mathematics, Physics, Chemistry (Good).
P. Wix	Prin. :	Chemistry, Botany, Zoology.
R. L. Goodbody	Prin. :	Physics.

Higher School Certificate Results, 1950

boys passing in Art and one in French, with subsidiary subjects in economics and/or Russian. On the 'Science side' the predominant principal subjects chosen are Pure Maths, Applied Maths, Physics and Chemistry, with two boys passing in Chemistry, Botany and Zoology. Gramshaw† is the exception who proves the rule by taking subsidiary French in a predominantly science-based selection of subjects. The following year taking A-level, he concentrated on the standard double Mathematics, Physics and Chemistry to win a State Scholarship.

† Gramshaw J. W. is the same as Gramshaw J. M. There is an error in the Magazine.

GENERAL CERTIFICATE OF EDUCATION RESULTS.

Capital Letters indicate passed at Advanced Standard.
Small Letters indicate passed at Ordinary Standard.
* Indicates Qualification for County Major Award.

Name	Results
*B. Bazeley	PH CH B Z
D. C. Buckey	pm ph
*M. A. Crawley	ph CH B Z
H. G. Fitch	pm PH ch
*J. W. Gilbert	PH CH B Z
J. M. Gramshaw	PM AM PH CH (State Scholarship)
*B. Horn	PM AM PH ch e
*M. G. Horne	PM AM PH CH
*A. M. Jessop	PM AM PH CH
K. B. Jones	ch B Z
*R. E. Knight	PH CH B Z
*J. A. Norris	PM AM PH CH
*M. Wells	PM AM PH CH
*R. Clarke	E F(o) SP(o) ec
*J. P. Edwards	E H G ec
*P. J. Frogley	E H G
*P. W. Furnell	E H G l f
*B. A. Groome	E H G l f
*C. B. Johnson	E F(o) SP(o)
*P. F. Jones	E H G ec
*J. L. Robson	E F(o) H ec
*R. Shawley	E F(o) H
B. D. Stokes	H G e
D. Tear	E H f(o) ec
B. H. Warren	F(o) H e ec

General Certificate of Education, A-level Results, 1951

PH–Physics, CH–Chemistry, B–Botany, Z–Zoology,
PM–Pure Mathematics, AM–Applied Mathematics,
E–English, H–History, G–Geography, EC–Economics, F(o)–French (oral) SP(o)–Spanish (oral),

The transition from the Higher School Certificate to GCE A-level was relatively smooth, with principal subjects becoming full A-levels and subsidiary subjects in Economics and Russian becoming O-levels taken in the sixth form. Russian remained at O-level while Economics progressed to become an A-level in its own right in 1957. On the Science side, the situation was simplified with everyone taking four subjects: Physics, Chemistry and a choice of Mathematics (Pure and Applied) or Biology (Botany and Zoology).

Period	Monday	Tuesday	Wednesday	Thursday	Friday
1	Geog 9	French 16	French 16	Music 8	Biol 14
2	French 16.	PT	Geom 15	His 19	Chem 13
3	His 19	Biol 18	Div 10	Eng 16	
Break	B	R	E	A	K
4	PT	Arith F	Physics	Geom 4	French 16
5	Eng 3	His 19	11.	Arith 19	Geog 9
Afternoon	L	U	N	C	H
6	Alg 17	Alg F	Drama 3	French 16	Music 8
7	Biol 9	Games	Art	Eng 16	Geom 15 10
8	Eng 3		Art	Eng 3	Geog 9
Preps					

Subject	Periods
Arithmetic	2
Algebra	2
Geometry	3
English	5
Drama	1
French	5
Biology	3
Physics	2
Chemistry	2
Geography	3
History	3
PT	2
Games	2
Divinity	1
Art	2
Music	2

The Timetable for 2B in Summer Term 1957

The School Timetable in the Fifties

Every Grammar School boy for the major part of the school's history will recognise the timetable we wrote on the back of a school calendar each term. Above is a timetable for 2B in 1957, as filled in by Peter Clark (1955–60).

The curriculum is heavily weighted towards English, mathematics, a language (French), sciences (biology, physics and chemistry), the humanities (geography, history) and divinity, together with art and music, PT and games. The timetable above already includes one choice of options: choosing biology instead of Spanish as a second foreign language. The timetable is pragmatically balanced, allowing double periods for subjects that profited from them (practical experiments in science, creative work in art, and time to play a full game of rugby or cricket in the afternoon). French, on the other hand is taught by a drip-feed approach, little and often, with a period a day.

Biology has three periods: one more than physics and chemistry. The alternative option, Spanish, would probably benefit from the same five periods as French, so three periods is almost certainly a practical choice to allow biology and Spanish to be taught at the same time.

The parallel A-stream would have its own particular choices suitable for a more academic career, including the introduction of Latin in the second form. The timetable changed as the boys move through successive years to give more time for subjects to be studied for the GCE examination.

In 4B, the student with the timetable opposite took English, mathematics, the three separate sciences, French, geography, history and a new subject, Technical Drawing (introduced in the late fifties by 'Ivor' Cheale). Games and PT continued to have four periods a week (10% of the time available) and music and divinity were still taught.

His timetable in the fifth form was similar to the fourth, though the number of periods for the sciences and geography increased at the expense of English and PT.

The main differences in the A-stream timetable involved the introduction of Latin in the second form and the shortened four-year course to O-level in the top stream. To provide a full four-year course in Latin, pupils took the GCE examination at the end of the Lower VI.

At the end of the third form all pupils had to choose between history and art. In the fifth form, while 5Aii, 5B and 5C took geography, the top group 5Ai—who had one year less to study the subject—had to choose between taking geography with combined physics & chemistry or studying physics and chemistry as separate subjects. Depending on the circumstances, other subjects might be made available, such as music as an O-level in place of geography.

The number of passes obtained in GCE in 1953 and 1960 are shown in the bar-charts overleaf. There are several significant pieces of information in these results. First, the boys in the top class (5A in 1953 and 5Ai in 1960) achieve far better results than the others, even though they studied for a year less. Second, the class sizes for the C-stream are much smaller than the A-stream, but they still get much lower results. By 1960, 27 out of 29 boys in 5Ai and 24 out of 26 boys in 5Aii achieved five or more O-levels, while only *one* out of 16 achieved this level in the C-stream. Third, there is a huge overall improvement between 1953 and 1960. Thirty-one boys obtained five or more O-levels in 1953 (35%); sixty-four boys obtained five or more in 1960 (67%): a doubling of the pass rate for O-levels with five or more passes.

At this time, GCE results were 'norm-referenced' meaning that the percentage of passes were the same each year to provide an assurance that standards were being maintained. If *all* schools improved, the standards would remain the same! If other schools maintained their

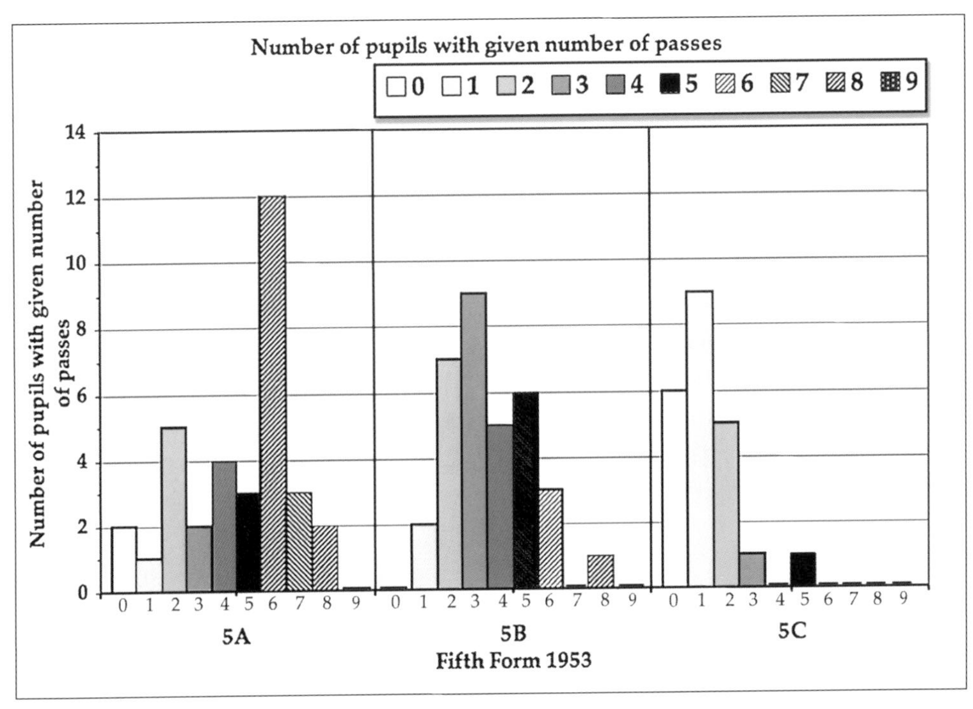

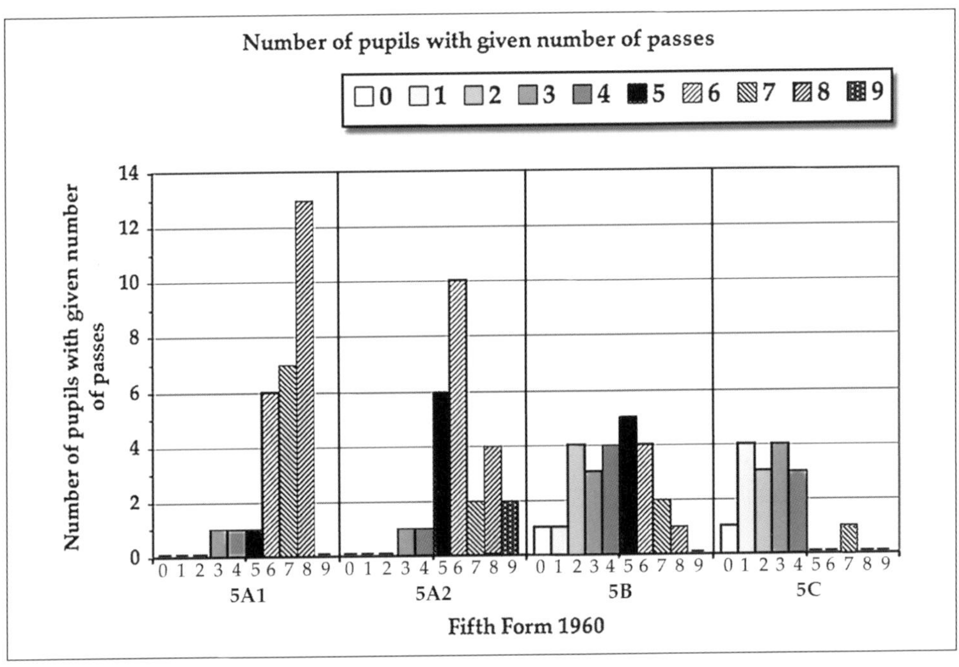

Number of passes achieved by boys taking GCE in 1953 and 1960

strategy of entering most students for the examination, a school could improve its pass rate in comparison by restricting entry only to those likely to pass. At Wellingborough Grammar School under Mr Wrenn, the opposite was true: boys were entered for examinations even when the chance of passing was low, especially when a subject was essential for a particular purpose:

A pass in French was believed to be essential for university entrance. I failed French seven times: the pass mark was 45%, and in successive summer and winter sittings I obtained 15%, 20%, 20%, 25%, 30%, 35% and finally 40% in the last year. I was the sole student left and ended up with one-to-one tuition! Fortunately, by 1963 three universities had regulations that allowed entrants to Biological Science without French. As a result, Hobson's choice meant that I studied Biology at Hull University. *(Graham Tall 1955–63)*

In this light, the improvement of the level of performance in the fifties is immense. It compares directly with the corresponding improvement in the war years when the school's percentage of School Certificate passes also more than doubled.

A bizarre side-effect of the single-subject pass for the GCE is that it focused on the few who fail everything as much as those who pass. Each year Mr Wrenn constantly bemoaned the ones that got away. In 1959, he announced that yet again just one boy had failed O-level, saying that, had he known which boy was due to fail this year, that boy would have been hard at work during the prize-giving ceremony.

In 1964 Mr Wrenn was able to report at Prize Day that the failure rate had finally hit zero and all 103 candidates had been successful in obtaining a GCE O-level certificate. This was a school record!

Many schools only enter the candidates who are likely to pass and then only in their best subjects. Here everyone is entered for the full range of subjects. On three occasions we have only had a single failure and now at last everyone has obtained a certificate.

Mr Wrenn, Parents' Day, 1964

Of course, while encouraging boys to enter a full range of subjects, Mr Wrenn was not beyond providing advice to help the likely failures to consider their position. While not insisting that boys should leave, he had his own way of presenting the various alternatives.

Mr Wrenn took me on one side in the spring term before O-levels and said "What do you plan to do then?" The result was that I got myself a job and told the Head that I was leaving school. It was the best piece of advice Harold could have given me. *Roy Pettit (1959–60)*

1964 was a significant year from another point of view. Mr T. G. Tomlinson was appointed to teach metalwork and engineering. In 1965, Mr Allan Bullock, Master of Mr Butler's *alma mater*, St Catherine's, Oxford, opened the new block with the new dining room which released the old dining room to be kitted out for metalwork.

The school re-introduced craftwork, including not only woodwork as prescribed in the school curriculum at its opening, but now expanded to include metalwork and engineering design.

Intentionally, or not, the move was being made towards a wider curriculum as envisaged by the new Labour government and its circular 10/65 that paved the way to comprehensive schooling.

However, apart from the introduction of O-level and A-level in metalwork, A-level engineering drawing, and the addition of Italian as a language, the basic format remained the same.

During the sixties and seventies, the school ran like a well-oiled machine with a three-form entry to the school, re-grouped into four forms by the time they reached O-level GCE. The names of the forms changed from Ai, Aii, B, C to A, alpha, B, beta, but the results remained essentially consistent over that time, apart from the usual minor variations as the boys changed from year to year. The last year published in the 1974 Magazine showed a similar overall level of performance in O-level to that in 1960. The percentage of boys obtaining 5 or more O-level varies marginally from 67% in 1960 to 65% in 1974 with the level of success spread a little more in the lower forms:

1960	5Ai	5Aii	5B	5C	Total
Five or more O-levels (percentage)	27 of 29 (93%)	24/26 (92%)	12/25 (48%)	1/16 (6%)	64/96 (67%)
1974	**5A**	**5 alpha**	**5B**	**5 beta**	**Total**
Five or more O-levels (percentage)	24/24 (100%)	16/26 (62%)	16/27 (59%)	5/17 (29%)	61/94 (65%)

Number of pupils with five or more O-levels in each form

The foundational five continue today

To be able to understand the quality of the Grammar School's results from today's perspective, it is necessary to look at the changes in examinations that have occurred in the meantime. The General Certificate of Education (GCE) that we have just reviewed was introduced in 1951 for the top 20% of the ability range; in the sixties came the Certificate of Secondary Education (CSE) for the next 40% with grades 1–5 where the top grade 1 was required to be equivalent to a pass in GCE. In 1986, these were brought together in the single General Certificate of Secondary Education (GCSE) graded A to F, where Grades A, B and C were to be equivalent to O-level passes and grades C down to G corresponded to levels 1 to 5 of GCSE. In particular, a GCSE pass at grade C was equivalent to an O-level pass or a Grade 1 CSE. The first GCSE examinations were held in 1988.

The methods of awarding certificates also changed from being norm-referenced (the same percentage passes each year) to criterion-referenced (marked according to the student's ability to accomplish specific levels of tasks). The major national statistic used continued to be the percentage of pupils obtaining 5 GCEs or 5 GCSEs at grade A to C. The percentage of students reaching this level is given below.

It increased from 23% to 27% between 1975 and 1982, then held steady until 1987—a consequence of normed-referencing. During this period, the marks were adjusted so that the same percentage passed

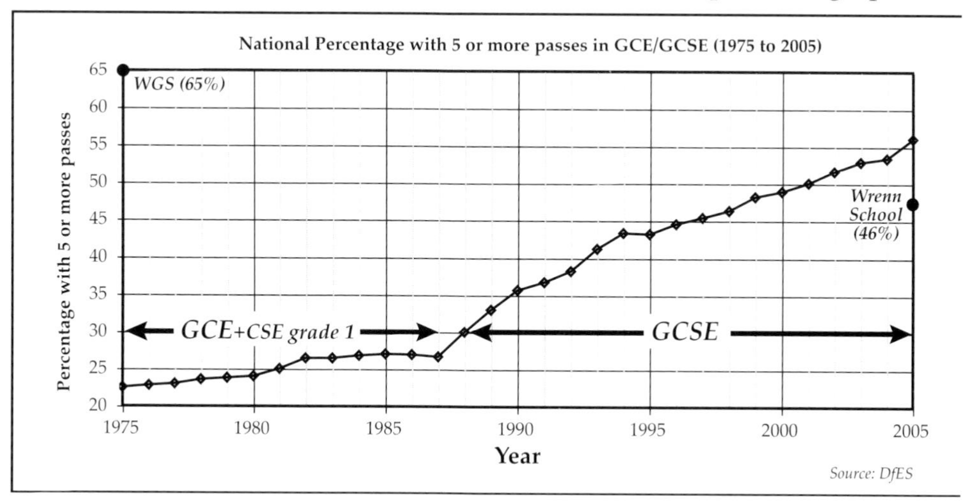

National percentages of pupils with five or more O-level GCE or GCSE passes 1975–2005

each year. Once the system became criterion-referenced, the number of passes doubled from 27% in the 1987 GCE to 56% in the 2005 GCSE.

In 1974, 65% of the high-attainers in Wellingborough Grammar School, achieved 5 O-level passes. In 2005, 46% of the Wrenn School achieved 5 GCSEs at grades A to C.

Direct comparisons are not in any way possible as the Grammar School included only the most able boys while the Wrenn School covers the full population, including those with learning difficulties.

The Grammar School's pass rate was high in 1974 and, had the School remained, the pass rate would almost certainly have increased to the near 100% achieved by comparable grammar schools in the few areas that maintain the eleven plus to this day.

The main question-mark on the 1974 performance concerns the low pass-rate in the lowest form, 5 beta. Had the school remained intact after the switch to the criterion-referenced GCSE, the pass rate would have almost certainly have shifted up as teachers and pupils developed techniques to pass the required criteria over the years.

The Wrenn School's pass rate in 2005, with 46% achieving 5 or more GCSEs at grades A to C, is below the national average of 56%. In the list of Northamptonshire schools, these results place it 25th out of 43.

At A-level the situation is different, as the focus shifts to the higher attainers who may benefit from university education. In the twenty four years from 1992 to 2006, the national pass-rate has increased year on year, again achieved in criterion-referenced examinations where teachers have focused on the techniques required to pass them. A better measure of performance is to compare the school with other schools who have been part of the same upward trend.

The Wrenn School in 2005 was placed 7th in Northamptonshire, exceeded only by selective schools and (marginally) by Bishop Stopford School in Kettering. Sixty-eight students averaged 317 points (where A-levels are graded as follows:– A: 120, B: 100, C: 80, D: 60, E: 20, with half scores for 1-year AS-levels). This is equivalent to an average performance of an A and two Bs. The Wrenn School serves the higher attainers at A-level well, broadly maintaining a tradition in keeping with the Grammar School and the High School.

Chapter 10
Sport

Wellingborough Grammar School sought not only excellence in sport through endeavouring to create winning teams in rugby and cricket, but also to encourage physical achievement across the board with internal House competitions in rugby, cricket, swimming, athletics and PT. (For any youngsters reading this, PT stood for Physical Training, or as it was regularly described 'Physical Torture', later to be renamed PE for Physical Education.)

The major school sports were rugby in the autumn and spring terms and cricket in the summer, with a regular schedule of school matches around the county and beyond. Physical training was mainly an internal matter to maintain fitness, but manifested itself more widely in House and inter-school athletics and cross-country running. Boys were taught to swim in the summer and a few went on to further levels of competition. Before and after the war, all boys were able to contribute points to the scores in House competitions in athletics and swimming by surpassing standards set for each event in athletics and distances covered in swimming.

Boxing was introduced in 1932 and was taken up by a few boys, sufficient to run a House competition for a cup donated by Mrs Lay. The boxing competition continued annually until 1939 but ceased with the arrival of the war and was never revived. (The gloves were taken out on occasions later, for example, in the fifties, one of us remembers Mr Pine getting out the gloves in a PT lesson and a few boys had a go, but most of us had no interest.)

Other sports, such as lawn tennis, table tennis, badminton, golf, fencing, basketball, and even association football, were catered for by clubs which appeared from time to time, lasting for as long as they held the interests of the boys.

House competitions occurred throughout the year including rugby, cricket, athletics, PT and swimming. In the team sports, pupils of the appropriate years would be shouting for their House, but with athletics and swimming, the whole School was the audience.

Rugby

The school's major sport was rugby union. Two of its boys later played for England (Don White and Johnny Hyde) and one (Barry Waite) played for the USA. Three of its masters (Jeff Butterfield, John Hyde and Bob Taylor) were England rugby internationals. Both Don White and Bob Taylor captained the English team and both continued to play a major role on the national rugby scene.

For the first nine years, rugby blossomed under the guidance of the Second Master, Mr Clayton. With only 64 boys of a younger age group when the school opened in 1930, it took several years for the older boys to reach an age where a full First XV could operate. By 1933 the school had three representative teams, settling down in subsequent years to an Under 14, Under 15 and First XV. By 1937 it was reported that 71 boys represented the school in the autumn term. In 1938 a young Don White in the Under 14 XV was "developing into a very useful hooker whose other play and knowledge of the game is improving."

In 1939 Mr Nicholas took over the Eirst XV on the departure of Mr Clayton to a new appointment in Manchester. The beginning of the war proved to be a difficult time. Bad weather and war-time conditions caused many games to be cancelled. There were no international rugby matches for the duration of the war. Wellingborough Grammar School managed to continue to field three school teams, but the shortage of clothing meant that the school black and white outfits were replaced by a variegated collection of jerseys.

In 1943, R. V. S. Ward introduced the 16-year old Don White to the Northampton Saints and the two of them played as props in Don's Saints debut against Coventry. Don White joined the army in 1945, playing for the national army team, and then for England in 1947, the first of 14 international caps. Meanwhile, school rugby prospered even more. In the 1947/8 season, Mr Nicholas declared in the School Magazine that the First XV was "probably the strongest in the history of the School", going on to win 12 of its 13 matches. In the year 1948/9, a Northamptonshire Grammar School Union was formed and four boys from the team played in the first County Schoolboys team: John Hyde as captain, together with Bob Leslie, Gerald Neville and David Law.

Hyde played for England Schoolboys against Wales in April 1949, then against Scotland Schoolboys in January 1950. He was chosen for a full England trial a few days later and became the first schoolboy since 1903 to be awarded a full England cap, playing against France and Scotland. He was a speedy runner and a fearless tackler: speed off the ground is essential for the kind of flying tackle he achieved to catch Cliff Morgan around the ankles when playing for the East Midlands against the Barbarians in 1949. However, his vigorous commitment came at a cost and made him injury prone. A few days after beginning his studies at Loughborough College in 1951, he broke his leg in a trial match and had a steel plate inserted, leaving him slower than before. He never played again for England, but had a long and successful career for the Northampton Saints from 1947 to 1963, converting sheer speed into a deceptive jinking run to outwit his opponents. In 1954 after completing a three-year course, he returned to the Grammar School as a sports master.

Johnny Hyde tackling Barbarian Cliff Morgan in 1949
and handing off a French player when playing for England in 1950

His comrades in the 1947/8 school team also played at higher levels: in 1950, Bob Leslie was selected for the English Schoolboys against Wales, Gerald Neville reached the Final Trial for the same team, and David Law played again for the Northamptonshire County Schoolboys. In 1951, John Whiffing followed him into the English Schoolboys team.

The Grammar School was now part of a huge network, building from individual schools and local teams through the Saints and onwards and upwards through the East Midlands team and on to the international game. In this network, Don White played a central role, linking the junior teams in the county into the Saints to feed the better players into the club.

Jeff Butterfield taught at Wellingborough from 1951 to 1954, playing alongside White and Hyde for the Saints, being selected for England in 1953 and winning 18 England caps in all. His experience as a student at Loughborough brought a new approach to fitness at a time when rugby was changing from a game played for fun to a game played to win with style. His training regime at the Saints brought new fitness to the club, producing players who outlasted their opponents and were able to run riot, scoring tries in the last twenty minutes as their opponents tired. It was a great time in the fifties to see the Saints play on a Saturday afternoon at Franklin's Gardens, with White, Butterfield and Hyde prominent in a side that on at least one occasion contained fourteen internationals. At that time, the Saints were the best team in the country (or so we could believe as there were no league tables); they just kept winning most of their matches and in that success, Wellingborough Grammar School played its part.

As White retired from club rugby in 1961, followed by Butterfield and Hyde in 1963, a new hero arrived in 1964: Bob Taylor—an old boy of Northampton Grammar School—was capped 16 times for England while he was a teacher at Wellingborough.

All four had extensive rugby careers with the Saints; three of the 21 players having more than 300 games with the club had WGS connections: Don White with 448 (second only to Ron Jacobs with 470); Bob Taylor played 313, John Hyde 308, and Jeff Butterfield 223. Don White remains the only Saints player who is in the top ten for number of games played (448), tries scored (116), and points scored (930).

A fifth WGS player became an international. Barry Waite (1960–67) played for the School First XV in 1965/6 and 1966/7, rising through the ranks, playing 63 times for the Saints between 1966 and 1972 before moving to the United States in 1973. He qualified to play for the American national team by residency and played twice for the USA in 1976.

Don White ***John Hyde*** ***Jeff Butterfield*** ***Bob Taylor***

Wellingborough Grammar School's England Rugby Internationals

This remarkable continuity of internationals linked to the Grammar School meant that every boy during the last thirty years of the school from the mid-forties to the mid-seventies had the potential of knowing or being taught by one or more of them.

Throughout this time the school resolutely went its own way with the masters running the First XV having a lengthy period building their teams. Mr Clayton was the First XV coach for 9 years and continued to remain in position when Mr Nicholas arrived from Oxford.

When Mr Nicholas took over in 1939, he continued in charge until 1955, despite the arrival of Jeff Butterfield and John Hyde, who took their turn with younger boys' teams. Indeed, John Hyde did not coach the first fifteen until the retirement of Tony Sparrow in 1969.

Meanwhile, Bob Taylor used his wide sporting prowess to take the sport in the school in new directions, with five-a-side football, basketball and badminton, at the same time expanding athletics to include the javelin, shot and discus and to increase general fitness through circuit-training.

In the early fifties under Mr Nicholas, several boys played for the County Schoolboys each year: John Whiffing, Peter Jones, John Gilbert and Clive Daniels in 1951; John Whiffing, Jim Hyde, Clive Daniels, Alan Towers and Peter Coles in 1952; Bill Priest in 1953; Bill Priest, Michael Beeby and Graham Ridge in 1954.

When Mr Nicholas handed over the reins of the First XV to Mr Sparrow in 1955, the system of five school teams had been established for several years. The Under-13, Under-14 and Under-15, had a rotating sequence where a single master took a team through successive years, before moving on to the Second XV with the First XV being trained each year by Mr Sparrow.

Boys continued to play at County level, with Tony Bean in 1956; Richard Attley, Ray King-Underwood, Sellick Norsworthy, 1957; John Greenhalf and John Poyner, 1958; David Tall in 1959 (playing under the captaincy of Bob Taylor, then a schoolboy at Northampton Grammar); Graham Drage played in 1960; Peter Tomkins, 1962; Robert Mason, Clive Dobbs, M. Parker, 1962; Neil Palmer, Brian Bellamy, 1963. A major climax was to occur in the years to come, with the 1965 team featuring five players: Bob Benoist, Bill Drew, Steve Grant, David Toseland, Barry Waite.

At the Under-15 County level, the success was even greater; in 1963, no less than *nine* of the County XV were from Wellingborough: Peter Betts, Kevin Crossley, Roy Gayton, Brian Gilbert, Martin Layton, Paul Marriage, Keith Shurville, K. L. Tymkov and Barry Waite.

In 1969 the First XV finally passed to Johnny Hyde. In 1972, Ian Lutter, Peter Mankiewicz, and Keith Manning played for the County Schools Seniors. Ian Lutter was also selected for the Midland Schools XV and the England Schools XV with whom he toured Australia.

Other successes over the years included Blues for Bob Leslie (Oxford, 1954), David Stevens (Oxford, 1959) and Austin Jessop (Cambridge, 1972).

The school was fortunate in its outstanding characters in rugby, both boys and masters. But what made the school special was the way it always strove to punch above its weight with its teams in school matches. We were taught the value of team spirit, working together for a common victory, and, in particular, how to bounce back if we had a reverse. It taught us not just about rugby, but about life.

After the peak in the year of 1946/7 with its future England international in a team with several other high-quality individuals, the second peak came in 1966/7 with a team that also included a future international. Barrie Waite, who played for the USA in later years, recalled:

> *The 1st XV of 1965/6 and 1966/7 years did more for me than all the A-levels combined. It kept me off the streets of Irthlingborough, set values and team spirit which I have appreciated since and took me to*

a sporting life which I later found to be a great recipe for success in business leadership.

I remember my father bringing out a crate of beer from his car after we had beaten the Old Grammarians on the original OG's field. Tony Sparrow smiled and turned his head. That could never happen nowadays! So many memories.

I later played for the USA against France in Chicago in 1976 — took the week off from my work to do so, with some made-up excuse, only to have my boss see the game live in France — what an embarrassment! I was a replacement against Australia the same year.

Barry Waite (1960–67)

Wellingborough Grammar School 1st XV 1966-1967

R. J. Benoist T. M. McIlroy D. J. Hill S. Huddart P. Toombs J. D. Hall P. Warburton E. R. Nevett

P. M. Layton B. Waite D. Toseland (Vice-Captain) S. W. Grant (Captain) W. Drew (Hon. Secretary) K. L. Allen K. Shurville

	Played	Won	Drawn	Lost	Points For	Points Against
Playing Record:	19	18	0	1	438	73

Cricket

Just as rugby was the school sport in the autumn and spring terms, so cricket was the main sport in the summer. For the first thirteen years of the school, cricket was under the guidance of Mr 'Froggy' Hole. Cricket is a team game, as is rugby, but it also thrives more on individual performances: a striking innings with the bat, a burst of wickets with the ball. It therefore is even more prone to the changes of individual talent over successive seasons.

At first the teams struggled but around 1940, the standards began to rise, with the 1st XI captained by Bert Catlin losing only a single match, against the Old Boys. John Fielder scored 204 runs and took 53 wickets at an average of 5.41. The following year he again took over 50 wickets as the team won seven games. In 1942 the 1st XI under captain Alan Hall was undefeated in 11 matches. Only two matches were lost in 1943: captain Roy Cross topped the batting with 249 runs and John Hardwick took 31 wickets. In 1944, Hardwick broke the school record by taking 62 wickets at an average of 5.2; Don Knight scored 304 runs. In the last season of the war, captain Ken Bond scored 332 runs averaging 33.2.

Several of the successful players during the war years were to remain on the local scene in the years to come, including Ken Bond, Bob Chapman, John Fielder, John Hardwick, Don Knight, John Minney and Derrick Pearce. However, compared with rugby where players such as Alan Hall and Don White were by this time playing for the Saints, the school had yet to produce a county cricketer.

This was in direct contrast to Wellingborough School, where long before in 1909 there were ten old boys playing cricket for various counties and, over the years, thirty old Wellingburians played for Northamptonshire, six as captain.

Wellingborough School had several built-in advantages. As a boarding school, its boarders had long weekends to practice technique, with a cricket field good enough to be used annually for a three-day county match from 1946 onwards. Schoolboy cricket took place as a single-innings for each side in an afternoon and the gap between this form of club cricket to three-day county cricket was one which was easier to bridge with those who had time to build up the necessary technique. Until 1962, players in county cricket were of two kinds: 'gentlemen' of private means who played for pleasure, and 'players' who were paid as professionals. A public school would have more 'gentlemen' than a grammar school, with grammar school cricket more attuned to the amateur club game.

In 1946, the school captain John Hardwick led a successful side, scoring 299 runs and taking 55 wickets in the season. He became the first Wellingborough Grammar School boy to have a county trial and played a game with the County 2nd XI. This was as far as it went.

In the same year, the Magazine reported that a young John Hyde "occasionally scored runs, but was unreliable owing to his impatience and a partiality for the crossed bat; his failures were redeemed by his excellent fielding, which gave a lesson in mobility to a safe but rather stolid team of fielders."

After the war, a one-time Glamorgan county cricketer, Wyn 'Trigger' Davies (1945–55) arrived as a master. Standards continued to rise through to a high in the early fifties. Mr Davies was good with bat and ball, taking seven for 27 in the 1947 Masters match, with Mr Wrenn holding up the other end taking three for 21.

In 1948 the school team under Jack Hodgkins won eight of 11 matches with David Roberts emerging as a specialist leg spinner, taking 40 wickets at 4.9. There was a particularly pleasing 47 run victory over Northampton Grammar School with Keith Lawrence batting through the innings for 49 not out and taking six wickets for 32 runs.

By 1949 the system of school teams had expanded to include a 2nd XI to bridge the gap between Under 13, Under 14 and Under 15 teams and the first XI: cricket was now a prominent part of the liberal curriculum.

The 1950s started on an even higher note as the 1st XI completed an unbeaten season captained by David Law. This time the team was inspired by the pace bowling of Paul Wills, Ian Wills and Pat Hunt, with no spinner at all. The unbeaten record continued under John Whiffing in 1951 with Ron Holmes spinning the ball both ways to take 39 wickets. Brian Warren scored the school's first recorded century.

The peak passed in 1952 as the team became 'draw' specialists, drawing 10 out of 13 games with the pattern repeated in subsequent years.

In 1955, Mike Dilley took 58 wickets in 12 matches bowling fast medium. He later became the only old boy to play for the county with a career from 1957 to 1963, taking 80 wickets at an average of 30.88, including two hat-tricks, and scoring 247 runs at an average of 10.88 in just 33 first class matches. In the school team alongside him was a certain David Frost who scored 45 not out against King's School.

First XI 1956, including our only future county player and future TV star
Standing: Alfred Young, Trevor Field, Gerald Rose, D. G. Hodson, David Frost, Tony Bean
Seated: Brian Rigby, Bill Priest, David Stevens (captain), Mike Dilley, Julian Wills

The year 1957 saw only three wins, although David Wilson batted well, scoring 70 against the Masters XI while Mr Wrenn scored 69 in return. In 1958, the school commended the groundsman, Ernie Bryan, who made a special effort to prepare the wickets. David Wilson remembers:

> *Ernie Bryan was a groundsman of some considerable repute and he took his work very seriously. So seriously that he enquired of a county player how he could improve the wicket at the Grammar School and he was told that the best thing on our poor soil was to put cow muck on the pitches with plenty of water and roll them out. So Ernest duly went over the Wollaston fields, collected a large sackful of cowpats, brought them on the bus, mixed them with water and laid them on the pitch. Those of us who played in the staff matches against the boys will bear me out; we had some very, very good wickets. And during the winter, Ernie's cowpats grew some superb cabbages.*

Cricket is a beautiful game in which one can enjoy the performances of individuals, even if the match is lost. During the sixties and seventies the school won fewer matches than the heydays of the forties and early fifties, but there were performances to savour. In 1962, Jackson scored a century against the Masters in a continuous drizzle on a damp wicket. In one match in 1964, "Barron split his trousers, the score-book was lost and extras 34 was our top score"; in another, Barron took a hat-trick. In 1968, Richard Hobbs also took a hat-trick in an otherwise unremarkable year with 3 matches won, 3 lost and 4 drawn. Commenting in the Magazine, Mr Wilson wrote with a touch of irritation:

> *One continually hears criticism of the game of cricket and occasionally one wonders what the future holds in store. With GCE examinations beginning in May and term ending early in July, unless our English weather is uncharacteristically clement, school cricket barely stands a chance of reaching a moderate standard before the season is over. This year the weather has taken its toll of matches and also severely curbed net and other practices.*

At the beginning of the 1969 season, with a change of resolve, he wrote:

> *Let it never be forgotten that cricket is a sport and a game. It has the ability to be the most boring or the most entertaining of games and it was decided at the beginning of this season to treat our matches as contests to be enjoyed and won. The policy paid dividends, and even the matches that were drawn were played in this spirit.*

1969 proved to be a fine season with 5 wins, 4 draws and only one loss. The results continued to be creditable in 1970, with 3 wins, 5 draws and 2 losses, but the season that followed yielded only a single victory, rising to two wins in each of 1972 and 1973. The last School Magazine in 1974 recorded simply a list of results and statistics:

Played 10: Won 3, Lost 4, Drawn 3.

As in all good cricket stories, the tail wagged in the closing overs. In 1973, five boys were chosen to play for the County Under-15 XI against Bedfordshire, Hampshire, Buckinghamshire and Leicestershire: D. G. Sharrock, P. B. Nightingale, A. B. Gregory, S. G. Hamilton and J. Lambert.

In 1974, five more boys played for the Under-15 County Team: J. Desborough, S. E. York, T. A. Gray, M. P. Rush and M. Bond, with Desborough as County Captain.

In cricket, as in rugby, when the full range of boys were available in the fifth form before some left at 16, Wellingborough Grammar School often performed exceptionally well.

Athletics

The third major sport at the school was athletics. Within the school the major athletics focus was on the annual School Sports Day which doubled as a House competition. For the ordinary boy who was not able to excel at the highest level, Mr Lay introduced a system of standards to encourage every boy to aim at an appropriate level of success. Mr Woolley, however, expressed strong personal opinions on physical training in his first speech on Prize Day:

> *Discussing the educational value of physical training Mr Woolley said "In my opinion there is far more educative value in games of rugger, cricket or tennis than in any amount of physical jerks performed merely as a duty; but athleticism can be overdone, exercise can be the cause of nervous strain when what is aimed at is restful recreation; exercise and recreation should not be confused."* *Speech Day, 1938*

Athletics standards ceased until Mr Wrenn restored them in 1948 with the additional incentive of scoring House points:

> *This year a system of standards for all events was introduced and those who reached this standard in an event gained one House point. Judging by the number of boys seen out training prior to the standard tests a keen interest has been developed and it is hoped that this will continue. Every boy now has an opportunity of assisting his House to the best of his ability and he can gain valuable House points. The success of the Stags was largely due to the number of points gained in this way.*
> School Magazine, Summer 1948

While encouraging many boys to do their best, the standards were a 'one-size-fits-all' which also excluded others. Neither of us 'Tall' brothers were especially athletic, so it largely passed us by until, one year, one of us attained the mile standard and high jump standard, giving a huge boost to personal morale.

The School Athletics Competition was a great afternoon for all the boys cheering on their own House athletes. Those who were talented in athletics might win two or more events. Every so often, a particular individual came to the fore who swept away all opposition and went on to live in the memory of those who were there.

In 1942, Gordon Shipman won the full set of over-15 running events: the mile, half mile, quarter mile, 220 yards and 100 yards. In the same year, Don White cleared 4 feet 11 inches in the over-15 high jump.

In 1946, John Hyde, won four senior events in the 440 yards, 200 yards, 100 yards and the long jump. He repeated the victories in 1947 and 1948, adding the half-mile in 1947 to give a total of five. In 1949, as other athletes came forward, he retained the 100 yards, 200 yards and long jump.

In 1950, Graham Ridge (later to return to the school as a master) won all the junior events and broke two school records: the half mile, 220 yards, 100 yards, high jump (a record 4 feet 5 inches) and the long jump (a record 17 feet 6 inches).

Later in 1969, Graham Phillip won five events in the over-15 category: the (now metric) 100, 200, 400 and 1500 metres, plus the long jump.

As part of the renaissance after the war, three new inter-school athletics events were instituted: a match against Bedford Modern School and two triangular matches, one against Northampton and Kettering, and the other against King's School and Deacon's School in Peterborough. In the inaugural matches, Bedford won by 45 points to 39, and the triangular matches finished: Wellingborough 127, Northampton 88, Kettering 57, and King's 91, Wellingborough 86, Deacon's 21. The three matches were repeated in 1948 with the Bedford match divided into senior and junior. The Bedford event ceased after this, but the two triangular matches were an annual event for several years to come.

In 1948 the school began to enter competitors in the Public Schools Athletics Championships at the White City stadium. Three boys — John Hyde, Ian Simmons and Graham Surridge performed creditably — with Surridge securing a championship standard in the mile in a time of 4 minutes 43.2 seconds.

In the coming years, the school regularly entered their best athletes in the Northants County AAA Championships and the Northants Schools Athletics Association Championships.

In 1954 the captain of athletics David Barber, won the Midland Counties AAA one mile junior championship at Birmingham. In 1956

John Sharman was chosen to represent the county in the 880 yards at the schools inter-county championships in Plymouth.

Neil Palmer, the most successful athlete at WGS, first came to notice in 1959 when he won both the junior 100 yards and 220 yards in the triangular match against Kettering and Northampton. He went on to represent the county in the 220 yards race at the 1960 schools inter-county championships in Shrewsbury, along with Tony Bayes in the long-jump. By 1962 Neil was captain of athletics and ran 440 yards in 50.6 seconds at the Midland Counties Youth Championships at Duston – a new school record only seven-tenths of a second ouside the English schools record. In 1964, he went on to become the All-England Schools 440 yards champion in a time of 48.4 seconds. His achievement inspired others and Peter Lindsell, Robert Ball, Graham Walden and Robert Pine also came to the fore. Matches with other schools were won through the overwhelming superiority of the seniors, combined with steady performances by the middle and juniors.

Neil Palmer

After this peak, the years that followed returned to the ebb and flow of individual talent as some athletes did well in moderate seasons while the school continued to be well-represented at district and county level.

Swimming

Swimming was the fourth regular sporting activity at the school, first in the River Nene and, from 1933 onwards, at Wilby Lido. House competitions began at Wilby in 1933, based on points earned for boys who swam distances from 40 yards up to a mile and three competitive races. The following year, the School Swimming Club had 52 members (a quarter of the school) and over the years, the numbers increased and the Swimming Competition became more extended.

Distance swimming points were suspended in the years 1941–1945 to be re-introduced after the war. In 1947 Mr Pine declared in the

Magazine that "this was the first year in the history of the school that boys have been given the opportunity of learning or improving their swimming in school time." Boys were requested to bring cycles to school to ride to Wilby, or walk and miss most of the swimming time if there was no room in the sidecar of Mr Pine's motor-bike. He added "Many boys have already learnt to swim and nearly all swimmers can dive, or to be more precise, can enter the water approximately head first." Ninety-nine boys achieved house points for swimming the maximum distance of a quarter of a mile, and nearly half the school could swim.

Swimming had its lighter side, as reported in the Summer Magazine of 1950:

> *Form 2C's first trip left Northampton Road strewn with broken-down bicycles. Two had punctures, two had broken chains and one had a pedal fall off. Reasons given to be excused swimming are varied, but to suggest that one cannot attend as one's costume is still damp from the day before is hardly satisfactory.*

Water Sports

EXCITEMENT was at its height in an inter-form relay race, when this picture was taken at Wellingborough Grammar School's annual swimming sports at Wilby Lido yesterday.

Boys sit on the banks at the side of the Wilby Pool watching the Swimming Sports

Graham Tall dives in at the start of the 1958 100 yards open freestyle race

> *Swimming at Wilby Lido, what was that all about? I remember biking up there – it must have been a lesson that included break or it wouldn't have been worth it. It was always freezing cold and we always got a bollocking for being late for our next lesson. Can you imagine a bunch of 11 and 12 year olds being told to bike a couple of miles along a main road unsupervised to learn to swim in an outdoor unheated pool. I don't remember a single parental complaint!* *Dave Toseland (1959–67)*

Over the years, the focus continued on teaching boys how to swim, with the year's highlight being the Swimming Sports, attended by the whole school. On occasion, some of the more talented swimmers were entered to take part in the Northamptonshire Schools Annual Gala.

Other Sports

Over the years, new sports waxed and waned as enthusiasts became interested in games such as tennis, table tennis, badminton, cycling and golf. Two stand out for their vigour and extent in the late sixties and seventies: basketball and football (soccer, rather than rugger).

The Basketball Club owed its existence to the enthusiasm and organisation of England rugby international 'Bob' Taylor, who arrived to teach PE and mathematics in autumn 1964. By autumn 1965, the school officially had four basket ball teams: Seniors, U-16s, U-15s and U-14s playing a total of 57 matches. By summer 1967, five teams (including a Senior Second team) played a massive total of 77 fixtures.

> *As far as I can remember Bob looked after all the basketball teams on his own with very little help from other staff. Mrs Jock was a big fan, coming to watch most of the games. I think there was some initial scoffing by the more traditional 'sporting' members of staff when the sport was introduced but we loved it; the mocking stopped when they realised how much our rugby handling skills were improving as a result. Bob of course was not allowed to coach any rugby teams; presumably as Captain of England and a member of the British Lions he didn't have enough experience!*
>
> *I remember him taking us on two basketball tours at the end of the spring term, one to his old stamping ground in Hampshire, where we stayed at King Alfred's College in Winchester and played games in Portsmouth and Southsea. The second was to North Yorkshire where we stayed in a village pub near Reeth, out on the Moors. On the last evening after the locals who had been playing dominoes by the open fire left to go home, the landlord went to bed and left Bob in charge behind the bar. Eventually Bob decided it was time for bed and handed over the keys to Steve Grant, the captain, trusting us to pay for our beer and not get too pissed. As far as I remember we never betrayed that trust and we hero-worshipped the guy, so different from any of the other staff.*
>
> *Dave Toseland (1959–67)*

The sport spread like wildfire through the school. At its peak in 1969, there were six school teams (Seniors, Seconds, U-16 sixths, U-16 fifths, U-15 and U-14) all playing local league matches, with Inter-form competitions and a fully-fledged House Competition. The Easter tour with three teams going to Sussex in 1968 and a combined Senior/U-16 team to Bournemouth in 1968. In 1969 the Senior and U-15 teams were selected en-bloc to represent Northamptonshire Schools in the East Midlands League, the U-15 team winning its section and the Seniors coming second in theirs.

Standards of play in successive years fluctuated as established teams moved on and new teams were rebuilt. School Basketball reached its climax in 1973 when the annual basketball tour took the Seniors and U-15s to Quebec, Canada.

Bob Taylor was also responsible for introducing a Badminton Club—for which he organised fixtures—and a range of field sports, including javelin, discus and shot, which became part of the annual Sports Day. He had played soccer as a boy and had been invited to sign for the Cobblers. As a Rugby international, his most interesting feat was to introduce soccer into a rugby-playing school as a five-a-side competition for the sixth form after the summer exams in 1965.

Soccer as a full team sport made its appearance in 1971/72.

> *Soccer started with Geoff Dean. I seem to recall him asking Mr Wrenn several times before he was allowed to form a team. It began as an after-school activity which Geoff organized for fun (and maybe because there were enough rebellious anti-rugby boys around). It took off well, I seem to remember, and attracted a strong following. Geoff became an accredited referee and officiated at games.* David Wilson

Soccer was never a school sport in the sense that it was part of the normal games curriculum, unlike basketball, which was on occasion called *School* Basketball. Nor did it have its own House competition, as did other sports, including basketball, tennis and badminton. But it did have teams that played in the local leagues. Under-13, Under-15 and Under-16 teams played in 1971/72. Despite the large number of boys pressing for a place in the Under-13 team the following year, only the Under-16 team played in the league and reached the final of the league cup for the second year running, losing at the last hurdle to Wollaston School. The U-13 and U-15 teams played friendly matches, though conflicting calls of duty to basketball made it difficult to maintain a consistent U-13 team.

Mr Wrenn supported the boys in forming their club, even though it did not fit the pattern of a rugby-playing school. He regularly asked how well the team had played in a match and organised the use of a pitch for games in Roseacre field behind the houses on the other side of Doddington Road to give soccer its own home close to the school.

A range of other sports had their own clubs at various times. In the final School Magazine the results of House competitions in the school year 1973/74 were reported in Rugby, Basketball, Drama, Music, Tennis, Chess, Swimming and Cricket, revealing the range of sporting and competitive activity in the closing years of the school.

Chapter 11

Clubs and Societies

Clubs and Societies were part of Wellingborough Grammar School from its founding. The longest lasting clubs and societies were the Dramatic Society, Musical Society and Scout Troop, all three of which are referred to by Mr Lay in the first School Magazine in autumn 1932.

> *With the growth of the School, several Societies have been found practicable, and further reference to these will be found elsewhere in this issue. Beside this routine expansion, other activities have taken shape. ... The Dramatic Society made a most promising beginning in April, 1932, with three one act plays, having previously made all the scenery and fittings. The Scout Troop has, from small beginnings, become a valuable force for good in the school, and the Musical Society has a regular programme of meetings.*

However, two out of three of these rarely functioned as a club or society at all. Music had a dual role: concerts produced with external performers which occurred in the time of Mr Lay and during the War, and concerts given by the boys, masters, and others, under the direction of the music teacher of the time. As time passed, the name 'Music Society' was replaced in the School Magazine by the generic term 'Music Notes' to cover the range of musical activities. The Dramatic Society began as a society run by the boys in 1932 but only blossomed fully when it was organised by Dr Jackson during the war. From then on, its sole function was the annual school play with boys auditioned or chosen for the parts and a large supporting group including make-up, stage-staff, electricians, and front-of-house organisation. The single club that 'belonged' to its members was the School Scout Troop, organised initially by Mr Clayton in the thirties, continuing throughout the war under Mr Cook and being led for most of its existence by Mr Dunning.

Nobody can know how many clubs and societies existed at the school: they varied from the ephemeral (a single year) to the virtually permanent. Some were reported regularly in the School Magazine, others were announced when they were formed, or re-formed, others continued without making a written report.

The difference between the terms 'club' and 'society' is not absolutely clear. Indeed names sometimes changed, with the Photographic Society formed in 1946 becoming the Camera Club in 1947 before reverting to its original name. Essentially the difference relates to the status of the organisation in the school. The major societies were teacher-organized cultural, academic organizations; some of which, like the Scientific Society, were *de rigeur*, in which each science sixth-former was invited to give a scientific talk on a topic of his own choice. Others, such as the Music Society or Dramatic Society, had their programmes chosen by the master-in-charge and boys were essentially 'volunteers' to take part in a particular event. Those with special talents would feel a stronger allegiance to these societies, as a musician or actor, but they rarely had any controlling part in advance planning other than perhaps a talented musician suggesting a piece of music to play as a soloist or as part of a chamber group.

Clubs, on the other hand were usually more pupil-oriented, with a nominated teacher to take responsibility and participate as appropriate, though the teacher was rarely named in the School Magazine. Foremost among these was the Railway Club, led by the enthusiastic Mr Cheale, building a grand railway layout over the years. The Puppet Club, led by Mr Phillips, involved boys making string puppets to give shows outside the school using a wooden puppet theatre made by Mr Pine.

All clubs and societies, whether supported by staff or not, relied on the commitment and enthusiasm of boys at the school at the time. When enthusiasts left the school, the continuation of the club depended on younger boys carrying the torch. Long-term clubs such as the Chess Club and the Debating Society had their natural cycles of rise and fall. Both began in 1933 and had varying periods of success only to fall into abeyance and to be relaunched when new enthusiasts arrived.

It is only when one looks at the clubs and societies over the years that a distinct pattern begins to appear. Mr Lay began by setting up the Scout Troop, a Musical Society, a Dramatic Society, a 'Literary and Scientific' Debating Society, a Chess Club and a Cinema Society. These include worthy academic and cultural organisations to extend the work of the school in educating 'mind and body'.

The one 'leisure' club – the Cinema Society run by Mr Page – mixed Charlie Chaplin Films and Errol Flynn in *Captain Blood* with factual material on topics such as the Post Office, the LMS Railway and the Yorkshire Fishing Fleet.

Although there was no Photographic Society in the early days of the school, the innovative inclusion of a dark room in the original design led to regular competitions for the best photographs.

The Musical Society initially incorporated teachers, parents and local musicians to add their talents to the growing prowess of the school choir of treble voices.

The Dramatic Society, on the other hand, blossomed for a single year in spring 1932 with the boys writing their own plays, and, while there were occasional dramatic presentations in concerts, there were no full-length play evenings until 1941.

In Mr Woolley's time, several new clubs were formed in 1938 and 1939: a Play Reading Society, a Second Form Lecture Society, and a Tennis Club. Other more interesting innovations involved 'Chunky' Pine starting a Scandinavian Dancing Club, 'Eddie' Phillips initiating a Model Aircraft Club, and the first incarnation of the Model Railway Club with boys putting their personal model railways together on Friday evenings and Saturday mornings.

The onset of the war brought new priorities: getting boys home for the blackout, cleaning the rooms, coping with the deprivations of the war. Musical concerts were arranged as part of the war effort and were often accompanied by Mr Wintersgill at the piano, including visiting professionals such as the violinist Louis Godowsky.

A successful attempt was made to reintroduce evenings of drama, with Dr Jackson and Mr Hole producing a one-act play each in 1941 and 1942, followed by several form teachers producing short productions in 1943 and 1944. The producers in these 'form plays' included Dr Jackson himself together with Mrs Colsell, Mr Findley, Mr Wintersgill, Mr R. V. S. Ward and Mr Bratt.

During the war, the Scouts continued their activities and contributed to the war effort. The Air Training Corps led by Mr Nicholas and Mr Adamson was formed, followed by the Aircraft Spotters' Club organised by R. V. S. Ward. But there was a dispute about priorities and (we learn from Don Stratton, a schoolboy at the time) the headmaster, in his wisdom, closed down the Spotters' Club. Mr Woolley, under the *force majeure* of the war, has the distinction of being probably the only headmaster to close down a school club.

The Scientific and Literary Debating Society continued operating in the war and a new Table Tennis Club was formed in 1944. But the great explosion in clubs and societies took place after the end of the war, enouraged with great enthusiasm by Mr Wrenn. He expected his staff to take responsibilities for clubs and societies: new clubs were begun while older ones that had lapsed were re-launched. The Summer Magazine of 1946 reported the ongoing activities of the Scouts, Air Training Corps, Dramatic Society, School Music, the Second Form Lecture Society, the Railway Club, and the formation of the Scientific Society to replace the defunct Literary and Scientific Debating Society. Autumn 1946 saw the return of the Table Tennis Club, the Chess Club and the Model Aircraft Club. By Parents' Day in 1948 Mr Wrenn was able to declare that the school had fifteen societies, including the renewal of an earlier Violin Class to provide class lessons for a group of boys in years one and two who paid a small fee.

In the coming years the school organised a richer environment for the wider education of its pupils, through the development of

- *specialist sports clubs* when the need arose in lawn tennis, table tennis, cycling, golf, fencing, badminton, with basketball and association football being added to the regular diet of rugby, cricket, athletics and swimming;
- *musical and artistic clubs* to suit varied tastes, such as the Recorder Club, Record Society, Modern Jazz Club, Folk Club;
- *extensions to the science curriculum*, including the Natural History Society, Microscope Club, Astronomical Society, Field Survey Society, Junior Chemistry Club, Entomological Society, Geology Club, Ornithological Society;
- *extensions to the arts curriculum*: Modern Language Society, Historical Society, Arts Club;
- *hobbies* such as the Railway Club, Puppet Club, Stamp Club, Photographic Society, Tape Recording Club, Numismatic Club, Radio Club;
- *service clubs* such as the Scouts, Toc H, Christian Fellowship.

Society/Club	Approximate Activity	Approximate length
6th Wellingborough Scout Troop	1930–75	45
Musical Society / Musical Notes / Concerts	1930–75	45
Dramatic Society / School Play	1931/2, Summer 1941–1973	34
Photographic Society (Camera Club 1947/48)	[1932–4], 1946–48+, 1952–68	20+
Cinema Society / Film Society	1933–38, 1946–48	7
Gymnastic Club (later Physical Training)	1933–37, 1952–54+, 1958+	8+
Chess Club	1933, 37, 47, 54–62, 70–74+	15+
Literary and Scientific Debating Society *Literary and Debating Society* *Debating Society*	1933–38, 1942–45, 1947/48, 1955–1960	8+ 1+ } 14+ 5+
Play Reading (and Acting) Society	1936–38, 1957+	3+
Railway Club	1937+, 1944–75	31+
Tennis Club	1938, 1947+	2+
Scandinavian Dancing Club	1939/40	1
Model Aeroplane (Aircraft) Club	1939/40, 1946–48+, 1950–52	6+
IIA Lecture Society (1A in 1947/8)	1939–48	9
Air Training Corps	Spring 1941–46	6
Spotters Club	Summer 1941– 42	2
Table Tennis Club	1944–48, 1956–58	6+
Scientific Society	Summer 1946 – 1970+	24+
Puppet Club	Spring 1947 – 1964	18
Stamp Club	1947–75	28
Natural History Society	1947–51+, 1957–60	8+
Microscope Club	1949/50	1
Square Dancing Club	1950–52+	2+
Cycle Club	1952+, 1965–68+	6+
Toc H	1954–74	21
Historical Society	1954–56, 1958?	2
Recorder Club	1957+, 1961–66	6+
Record Society	1957/8, 1962–64, 1968	4+
Modern Languages Society	1959–65+, 1968	7+
Golf Club	1960/61+, 1963/64	2+
Field Survey Society	1960–69	10
Junior Chemistry Club	1962–70	8
Christian Fellowship	1959–74+	15
Modern Jazz Club	1962–64	2
Arts Club	1962–70	9+
Fencing Club	1964–69	5
Astronomical Society	1964–69	5
Badminton Club	1965–75	10
Basketball Club	1965–73+	8+
Entomological Society	1967–69	2
Tape Recording Club	1967–69	2
Folk Club	1968–75	7
Numismatic Society	1969/70	1
Radio Club	1971–74	3
Soccer Club	1971–73+	2+
Geology Club	1971–73	2
Ornithological Society	Summer 1972	1+

Societies and Clubs in approximate order of creation
bold italic for clubs over 20 years, *italic* for over 10;
+ indicates a club that may have operated longer than suggested

It is the diversity and availability of these clubs according to interest at the time that made the school so special.

The approximate duration of these clubs is listed in the table on the previous page, where the '+' symbol suggests that the club may have operated for longer but is not mentioned in the School Magazine. Where additional dates are added, they signify a new entry to the Magazine, though there may also be other times when the club waxed and waned.

The long-lived clubs and societies

Dramatic Society

The Dramatic Society was first highlighted in Spring 1932 when Mr Lay used the proceeds from the Christmas concert to set up the hall for dramatic productions. The first production (reported in the earlier chapter on Mr Lay) was organized by the boys, supported by Mr Brown, who was to leave the school shortly afterwards. In the years that followed, while there were occasional productions as part of other activities, there were no full evening performances until the summer of 1941 when two one-act plays were presented: a farce called *The Crimson Cocoanut* produced by Dr Jackson and a pirate play called *Scuttleboom's Treasure* produced by Mr Hole. The event was repeated the following year with Mr Hole producing a story of kidnap and adventure called *At The Mermaid's Tale* and Dr Jackson a comedy entitled *Queer Street.*

With the departure of Mr Hole in 1943, there was no production that summer and the School Play shifted to the autumn term with a group of short plays acted by different forms, produced by the various form teachers. The same format occurred again in the summer of 1944.

In the autumn of 1944, Dr Jackson produced the first of a sequence of major School Plays. He had a talent for writing a good story (with a side-line writing short adventure stories for boys' magazines such as *Wizard* and *Hotspur* which he would sometimes read out in his lessons). His first two full play productions were his own adaptations of *A Christmas Carol* (autumn 1944) and *Oliver Twist* (autumn 1945).

He went on to produce most of the plays annually until the late fifties. On his retirement, he commented, "I used to put on modern stuff, especially Agatha Christie. It gave the youngsters something to bite on as a contrast to Shakespeare." He never produced a Shakespeare

Date	Title	Author	Producer
1932 Spring	Three Plays: *Dust*, *X=0*, *The Man in the Bowler Hat*	Forms IIIA and IIIB A. A. Milne John Drinkwater	The boys
1941 Summer	Two one act plays: *Crimson Cocoanut* and *Scuttleboom's Treasure*	Ian Hay Ronald Gow	Dr A. Jackson, Mr E. L. Hole
1942 Summer	Two one act plays: *At the Mermaid's Tale*, *Queer Street*	Oscar Turner J. D. Kelly	Mr E. L. Hole, Dr A. Jackson
1943 Autumn	Form Plays		Mrs Colsell, Mr Findley, Dr Jackson, Mr Wintersgill, Mr R. Ward, Mr Bratt
1944 Summer	Form Plays		Mr Findley, Dr Jackson, Mr Wintersgill
1944	*A Christmas Carol*	Dickens ed Jackson	Dr A. Jackson
1945	*Oliver Twist*	Dickens ed Jackson	Dr A. Jackson
1946	*Vice Versa*	F. Anstey	Dr A. Jackson
1947	*Badger's Green*	R. C. Sherriff	Dr A. Jackson
1948	*The Private Secretary*	Charles Hawtrey	Mr J. W. Davies
1949	*Treasure Island*	Stevenson ed Jackson	Dr A. Jackson
1950	*Ten Little Niggers*	Agatha Christie	Dr A. Jackson
1951	*Arsenic and Old Lace*	Joseph Kesselring	Dr A. Jackson
1952	*Libel*	Agatha Christie	Dr A. Jackson
1953	*Morning Departure*	K. Woollard	Mr J. W. Davies
1954	*Busman's Honeymoon*	Dorothy L. Sayers	Dr A. Jackson
1955	*Macbeth*	Shakespeare	Mr G. Cooksey
1956	*Alibi*	Agatha Christie	Dr A. Jackson
1957	*The Party Spirit*	Peter Jones, John Jowett	Dr A. Jackson
1958	*Twelfth Night*	Shakespeare	Mr J. Greenwood
1959	*Lifeline*	Norman Armstrong	Dr A. Jackson
1960	*Bird in Hand*	John Drinkwater	Mr E. P. Butcher
1961	*The Caine Mutiny*	Herman Wouk	Mr S. Brown
1962	*The Tempest*	Shakespeare	Mr R. J. Shaw
1963	*Arsenic and Old Lace*	Joseph Kesselring	Mr C. W. Andreae
1965 March	*The Clue of the Stone* *Sweeping Reductions*	H. A. Wrenn	Mr D. F. Sturman Mr D. S. Wilson
1965	*Julius Caesar*	Shakespeare	Mr D. F. Sturman
1966	*Not in the Book*	Arthur Watkin	Mr D. S. Wilson
1967	*Rope*	Patrick Hamilton	Mr D. F. Sturman
1968	*Sweeney Todd the Barber*	Brian J. Burton	Mr M. K. Wright
1969 Summer	*The Long and the Short and The Tall*	Willis Hall	Mr D. S. Wilson [Cast of 8 staff]
1969	*One Way Pendulum*	N. F. Simpson	Mr D. S. Wilson
1970	*Zigger Zagger*	Peter Terson	Mr M. K. Wright & Mr G. B. Dean
1971	*The Murder of Maria Marten*	Brian Burton	Wright & Dean
1972	*The Royal Hunt of the Sun*	Peter Shaffer	Wright & Dean
1973	*The Alchemist*	Ben Johnson	Wright & Dean

The Plays produced by the Wellingborough Grammar School Dramatic Society play. *Macbeth* was produced in 1955 by his number two, Mr Cooksey (with Spike dropping in for the odd bit of support), *Twelfth Night* (1958) by Mr Greenwood, *The Tempest* (1962) by Mr Shaw, and *Julius Caesar* (1965) by Mr Sturman.

Spike, of course, knew his limitations. He *did* assist in the production of Shakespeare, but how could a man with a lisp and a cockney accent inspire his charges by declaiming the lines? In the case of *Macbeth*, he spent time helping the actors with some of the scenes. For instance, he worked with Banquo (David Frost) and the three murderers, at one time removing the phrase "What, you egg!" from the dialogue as he didn't think it worked. He also helped with the make-up, though his idea of stage make-up was bizarre: a foundation of Leichner greasepaint numbers 5 and 8, with coloured lines that often made the actors look like red indians on the war-path.

6 **Wellingborough News, Fri. Dec. 18, 1948**

Enjoyed School Dramatic Society's Play

HERE is a section of the audience which on Tuesday evening enjoyed the Wellingboro' Grammar School Dramatic Society's presentation of "The Private Secretary." There were further performances on Wednesday and last night.

Boys Present "The Private Secretary"

WELLINGBORO' Grammar School Dramatic Society has enhanced its reputation this week with some fine performances of the farcical comedy, "The Private Secretary." Here are the members of the cast photographed at the opening production on Tuesday evening. Mr. J. W. Davies, a member of the school staff, was the producer.

The Private Secretary (1948) produced by 'Trigger' Davies, with a young Syd Brown, bottom left.

In the earlier plays, my brother Peter remembers that 'Christmas Carol' and 'Oliver Twist' were both Spike's own adaptations. Spike was the only producer in his time at the school. Peter remembers playing the part of a girl at a dance in 'A Christmas Carol'. The music was 'Roger de Coverley' played by a pupil on the violin and he remembers a barrel organ in another scene and his best mate Bob Leslie (they went up to Oxford together) playing the part of a monkey! Peter prompted 'Badger's Green' (he still has a copy) and 'Vice Versa'. The aforesaid Bob Leslie, he thinks, played the lead in 'Badger's Green'. I also realise now that I saw 'Treasure Island' – I distinctly remember the brown stage curtains and that at one point the pirates came up through the audience.

I remember the moment in 'Libel' when the defendant has to lift up his hand to show he has a finger missing. I went home and practised that for days!

I can still hear the sound of a chain being dragged on the offstage radiator as the submarine went down in 'Morning Departure'.

'Macbeth' was the first school play I took part in as Lady Macbeth (I frightened my mother in the sleepwalking scene). Geoff Cooksey produced it because Spike didn't think 'shchoolsh should do Shakeshpeare'. It was the O-level set work. David Frost, who played Banquo, brought tinned haggis for the banqueting scene and arrived somewhat late one evening, climbing in through the dressing room window!

In the following years, Spike produced 'Alibi' and 'The Party Spirit'. On one occasion, I know we were short of scripts and my mother volunteered to type some out.

I was Malvolio in 'Twelfth Night'. I made a late entrance at the dress rehearsal as I was talking to Jock the caretaker at the other end of the quad when I suddenly heard Ivor Cheale calling my name. I cracked my head on the doorway as I hurtled onstage and spent the rest of the play with stars and a splitting head. I remember the next day's inquest on the dress rehearsal when Mr Greenwood the producer just looked at me and asked what happened. Before I had a chance to say much, he said, "It won't happen again, will it?" *Jim Wilson (1952–59)*

'Alibi' (1956) with Jim Wilson, Geoff Martin, Michael Bolton, Roger Allen, Barry Clarke, David Tall, David Frost, P. A. Tear (hidden), Martin Spriggs, David Cooper, and (sitting), Brian Whitney, Brian Clayton, D. Roberts

The forties and fifties were vintage Spike; they will be celebrated in more detail in a vignette following this chapter. He occasionally took a year off, handing over twice to Mr Wyn 'Trigger' Davis—a cricket-playing Welshman who could hit a boy in the back row with a deft throw of a board-rubber—and once each to Mr Cooksey and Mr Greenwood to take over the production of the obligatory O-level Shakespeare.

After the Jackson dynasty, the early sixties saw a succession of one-year producers: Mr Butcher (1960), Mr Brown (1961), Mr Shaw (1962), Mr Andreae (1963). Mr Butcher left at Christmas 1960, immediately after producing the play, Mr Brown and Mr Shaw left in 1963, and Mr Andreae left in 1964, making continuity problematic.

The school extensions were built starting in the summer of 1964 and Mr Wrenn turned to two new English teachers, Mr Sturman and Mr Wilson, to christen the new hall by producing two plays that he had written himself—*The Clue of the Stone* telling the Easter Story and a radio comedy, *Sweeping Reductions*. The hall proved to have magnificent facilities, but an unforgiving accoustic. Nevertheless, the production in March 1965 was a triumph for all concerned.

Julius Caesar (March 1965)

Mr Sturman and Mr Wilson alternated productions in the next three years, starting with a mighty performance of *Julius Caesar* with a cast of sixty directed by Mr Sturman in autumn 1965.

Mr Wilson's production of *Not in the Book* in autumn 1966 was a comedy thriller for a small cast. The ever-present Mr Cheale and the Railway Club had to design a small box set on the large stage, which the director generously described as "the best set we have ever had."

Mr Sturman returned with the murder thriller *Rope* in the autumn of 1967.

Another new teacher, Mr Wright, arrived in 1967, and produced *Sweeney Todd* in 1968. It was the first joint production with the girls of the High School. It put huge demands on the stage staff to cope with 15 scenes with 10 different sets that took all of 20 minutes to change during the three-hour show. Played as a melodrama with audience participation encouraged, it was a huge success.

Kris Misselbrook as 'Sweeney Todd' threatens his assistant played by Andrew Bailey

A scene from The Long and the Short and the Tall, with Mike Wright, Brett Tussler, Nick Wills, David Wilson, Ian MacDougall (standing) Howard Buchanan, Martin Vann, Sandy MacDonald.

David Wilson returned in summer 1969 to produce *The Long and the Short and the Tall* with a cast entirely of teachers in honour of Dr Jackson and followed this up in the autumn with the regular annual production, this time of the zany play *One Way Pendulum*.

From 1970 to the final production in autumn 1973, the plays were co-produced by Mick Wright and Geoff Dean. It was a time of transition as the girls from the High School took the female parts and of renewal as the society continued to produce a wide range of plays: from the National Theatre's football play *Zigger Zagger*, the melodrama *Murder of Maria Marten*, Peter Shaffer's modern classic *Royal Hunt of the Sun*, closing with *The Alchemist* by Shakespeare's contemporary, Ben Johnson. After the long life of the Dramatic Society where Shakespeare plays were given in their original form with young boys playing the parts of women, it was a telling conclusion to the Grammar School Dramatic Society that a performance of Shakespeare's contemporary was given with the women's roles played by girls.

Musical Activities

Over the years, the school was a centre of musical activity for two kinds of public performance, one by groups of boys singing and playing under the direction of the music master of the day, the other as concerts given by the masters, friends of the school and the occasional professional performer. As the years passed, successive music masters gave of their talents: Mr Brown (1930–32), Mr Appleby (1932–39), Mr Wintersgill (1939–48), Mrs Fisk (a visitor from the USA, 1948–49), Mr Pfaff (1949–55), Mr Stanley (1955–60), and Mr Bentley (1961–75+).

Each of these brought their own talents to the music of the school. Mr Appleby developed highly effective music using mainly unbroken boys' voices, augmented by three teachers and later by a small number of senior boys to sing tenor and bass. His orchestral forces were limited to eight violins, two clarinets and a piano. In 1936 his school choir was invited to sing on the BBC, the start of a long career in broadcast music which blossomed when he transferred to Doncaster Grammar School in 1939, and performed regularly on the BBC with Miss Bavin an avid listener in her office. In a distinguished career he produced practical singing collections for schools which are still on sale from Oxford University Press today, including 100 unison songs in *Singing Together* and a collection of rounds and canons to begin to sing in two parts entitled *Firsts and Seconds.* His legacy is enshrined in the William Appleby Music Centre in Doncaster, which currently has 2,000 singers and instrumentalists from local schools attending each week. Our loss was definitely Doncaster's gain.

Mr Wintersgill, who took over in 1939, proved an inspiring leader to take the school music through the war years. Not only did he continue the school concerts, but organised a regular sequence of war-time concerts with visiting singers and instrumentalists, often featuring himself on the piano as soloist or accompanist. When he left in 1948, after an interregnum filled by a visiting American teacher, Mrs Fisk, 'Sparky' Pfaff arrived in 1949. (The name probably comes from his penchant for playing the record 'Sparky's magic piano' ad infinitum in his music classes.)

At this point, the Violin Class had been restarted as a handful of first and second formers paid for lessons on the violin with Mr Harding (known to his pupils as 'Uncle Ron') who travelled weekly from Northampton. Initially the occasional pupil learned to play the recently purchased school viola and school cello (starting with N. J. Bonham and R. M. Hall). Later, a few of the boys in the Violin Class graduated to private lessons with Mr Harding in Northampton to continue their studies (Nickerson, Spriggs, Tall and Jolley in the fifties).

'Sparky' Phaff

Mr Pfaff combined with Miss Thomas from the High School to build a School Orchestra, incorporating the said instruments and anyone else who could perform appropriately. This included Mr Butler on clarinet and various other passing wind-players over the years, such as boys playing brass instruments in local brass bands and the Salvation Army and – in the late fifties and early sixties – other wind players such as flautists Bradshaw and Baxter and clarinettist Williams. A welcome addition to the unison Junior Choir and the part-singing Senior Choir was a Male Voice Choir organised for several years in the early fifties by R. O. Knight and his successors.

Apart from learning the violin and graduating to viola or cello with Mr Harding, the only other instruments explicitly taught in school were the recorder and piano. The recorder group continued over the years initially led by Mr Butler, continued by Mr C. F. Taylor in 1962, with Mr Cox taking over when Mr Taylor moved to a new appointment at Christmas 1964. Piano lessons were available and some had private lessons outside school, with the stars in the mid-fifties and early sixties being R. B. Wilkinson and Michael Lambert.

Mr G. B. Stanley arrived in 1955 to replace Mr Pfaff and continued the good work with choirs and orchestra, making some of his own arrangements of music for orchestra to fit our peculiar list of available instruments, including a rather splendid arrangement of pieces from Bartok's *Music for Children*. He was known simply as 'Geoff' (though not to his face) by the musical boys, but the main body of boys who had their one period a week with him knew him as 'Stan' ('Stan, Stan, the music man').

'Stan' Stanley

Mr Chesters arrived in January 1961, bringing not only an energy to continue the work with the Junior and Senior Choir, but also to compose original music for his musicians and for a succession of school plays. He developed a wind ensemble that played in varying combinations over the years, working with the players at his disposal:

> *Vaughan Williams' 'English Folk Song Suite' is an original piece for military band, and, though it lost something in tonal contrast in this performance through lack of oboes, saxophones and bassoons, it lost nothing through lack of enthusiasm on the part of the players.*
> *School Magazine, Autumn 1963*

The exciting prospect of moving to the new Mountbatten Hall proved satisfactory for drama, but was a disaster for music.

> *The room has a lack of resonance which has a disturbing effect on singers and instrumentalists alike, though speech seems to suffer much less. There is a total lack of warmth in the musical sound produced which must surely be due to an excessive use of sound-absorbent materials in the hall's construction.* *Summer Term Magazine 1965*

The following year the accoustics were enhanced by amplification with some improvement and, by autumn 1967, a permanent amplification system was installed.

As the years passed, the staple diet of Senior and Junior Choirs continued with the Orchestra and Wind Ensemble building on the available talent, including the emergence of a brass ensemble on some occasions. Cooperation between the Grammar School and High School continued in the orchestra and the final School Magazine in 1974 reported a huge concert with the District Youth Concert Band and combined choirs and orchestra from the Grammar School, High School and Wellingborough School.

Scouting at WGS

Scouting at Wellingborough Grammar School was the one club that lasted continuously for the full life of the school, initially under the leadership of Mr Clayton (1930–39). The war years saw many changes of masters in charge: Mr Pine took it over for a time before going off to war, was replaced by Mr Dark who soon followed into the forces, and then by Mr Weatherall who left in Summer 1940. Entering and occupying centre stage in the autumn of 1940 was the 'main man', Jake Dunning. He too was called up at the end of 1941 and the remaining war years fell to Mr 'Hobo' Cook, before Jake returned and led the Scout Group through to his retirement in 1966, with strong support from Mr Stanley in the second half of the fifties.

Every summer the Scouts competed for the Silverwood and Gilbey cups which were given for camping competitions.

> *Mr Silverwood was the local chief scout and the cup was awarded for points scored on camp cleanliness, cooking, a camp fire act, and being quiet at night. In our time the camp fire act was usually musical and choreographed by Stan.*
>
> *The Gilbey cup competition took place in the grounds of Harrowden Hall where Baroness Vaux of Harrowden had married William Gordon Gilbey, the owner of the wine and spirits group that made Gilbey's Gin. I remember it was a 'rough' camping event where we had to build our own shelters for the weekend — I recall experiments at roofing with large wild rhubarb leaves.* Terry Stratton (1955–61)

Jake Dunning was succeeded (but never replaced) by the newly-arrived Mr MacDonald.

> *Jake was a scoutmaster who had clear ideas of what should and should not be done. We couldn't use camp or air beds, we had to sleep on the ground. Unless it rained for a considerable period of time, cooking had to be done on a real fire, not using a cooking stove. In the evening we had to dig a hole and create a hay box into which we placed a cast iron pot – a witches cauldron full of porridge – and covered it with a tray. There it stayed over night, slowly cooking away. In the morning we relit the fire. By that time the top two inches of the porridge had set hard. After we had broken it up and mixed it in again, we'd warm it up once more. Two days later, we had to have prunes for dessert to get the bowels working properly again; if one didn't like prunes the medicine was a large spoon of liquid paraffin. Incidentally, I've never met anyone who ever appears to have heard the first question in Jake's tests.*
>
> Dick Smart (1960–68)

More stories about the scouts in general and Mr Dunning in particular are given in *Scouting at WGS* by Peter Godfrey which follows this chapter.

Puppet Club

Under the auspices of Mr Phillips, several boys, in particular Newnham (LV), Cunnington (3C) and Taylor (IIA), began experimenting on how to make string puppets in 1947 and put on a small performance for Parents' Day. Mr Pine built the club a collapsible stage and a year later, confidence had grown so much that the club produced and presented 'Aladdin' at Rushden, Hinwick, Great Doddington and Wellingborough, and subsequently presented a play called 'Blood Money' and a variety show with individual acts. Presenting several puppet shows every year outside the school became a regular activity: a good example of a school club reaching out to the community, as well as providing its own members with considerable enjoyment.

In 1951 the club prepared a new pantomime 'Cinderella', followed in 1952/3 by repeated performances of Aladdin, and a new show:

> *The projected show for the Coronation Day Celebrations was found impractical on the Castle Fields and was transferred to the Drill Hall for the benefit of the old folks. To be ready in time, a good deal of work was necessary in the Whitsun holiday, but the puppets were of a good standard and the set proved colourful, particularly for 'Britannia'.*
>
> *School Magazine, Summer 1953*

In 1954/5 the School Magazine reported:

> *'The Enchanted Horse', duly presented at several shows last season, was appreciated by our various audiences. The play also provided plenty of opportunity for the members of the club, who once more produced an interesting show. The brightly dressed puppets against the backcloth of the palace courtyard, together with the changing lighting effects, gave an atmosphere well suited to a story from the Arabian Nights. The supporting items included some old and some new puppets, all very creditably made and manipulated and all helped to make up a varied and successful programme.*
>
> *We are continually making alterations and additions to our stage and equipment, with the object of achieving smoother and more effective presentation of our shows. Our curtain rail has been extended and we are constructing some portable side screens. Now we are glad of the opportunity presented by the issue of the Magazine to express our pleasure and thanks to the Parents' Committee, who have generously*

offered to replace our record player. This has stood up to some very hard wear for several years but is beginning to show signs of wearing out.

School Magazine, Summer 1955

The puppet skeleton [below] *brings back memories, as it was cleverly made so that its arms, legs, and head separated from the body to the tune of 'dem bones, dem bones, dem dry bones,' played on the old 78 rpm gramophone. Happy days!* *Ian Richardson (1951–57)*

Maintaining the club over the years was subject to the coming and going of enthusiastic and talented puppeteers, together with experienced operators to look after the stage, the lights and the music. The Puppet Club passed into oblivion around 1964 when the School Magazine reported that the members were all juniors and the more experienced boys were too busy to come. However, those golden days in the late forties, fifties and early sixties continue to glow in the memories of those of us who were there.

The Puppet Club in 1954, left to right, Ron Sherwood (standing), David Tall, Ricky Wrenn, Ian Richardson, Trevor Parker, Martin Spriggs, Michael Beswick.

Railway Club

The Railway Club can trace its origins back to Mr Lay's time when boys laid out their personal model railway tracks together in the physics laboratory on Friday nights and Saturday mornings.

> *You run your engine more or less when you like or when the signalmen let you, but if you are caught passing a signal at danger you are shunted into a lie-by siding for five minutes or so. All the same you enjoy yourself!* School Magazine, Summer 1937

According to Miss Bavin, one of her causes of pride in the school's life was that she founded the railway club. It was re-formed in 1944 by 'Albert' Richmond, primarily as a club to learn about the railway system of the district by having talks and discussions during the winter and visiting important junctions, such as Blisworth, Sharnbrook summit and Market Harborough in the summer.

In 1948 it was taken over by 'Ivor' Cheale, who continued the visits and talks but returned to the modelling aspect by putting on an exhibition of a model railway using models loaned by various members of the club.

In 1949, thirty boys made a trip to London in February where the club visited several main line stations before splitting up into three groups for visits to places like the Waterloo Signalling Box.

> *This excursion was so successful that another trip to London was organised during the Easter Holiday, the main focus of attraction being a display of model railway stock at the Central Hall, Westminster.*

The focus changed to model making:

> *The model section has learned to make gauge 0 track and points, and has also begun to make gauge 00. They are grateful to the Parents' Committee for an allowance of £25 with which they have bought an electric engine. On Parents' Day an exhibition of gauge 00 outfit was given by Priestley, and the Club's engine was on view.*
>
> School Magazine Summer 1949

> *The Railway Club was valuable to me. Ivor decided that we needed to build a model railway but none of your Hornby Dublo. He decided to go for Bassett Lowke 0 gauge and that was real modelling. The track had to be constructed in the same way as the real thing with sleepers, chairs,*

A demonstration by the Railway Club in 1949

rails and keys. The difficult part came with the points which also had to be constructed from scratch. The experience I had with soldering and the other metal work has been invaluable to me all my life since leaving WGS. The other skill learnt from the club was with the electrical work for the layout. Ivor managed to come by some ex-GPO telephone relays which we spent hours adapting to operate a sophisticated automatic signalling system which we also designed. I remember Ivor covering the board in the physics lab with circuit diagrams which we all criticised, altered and added to in order to get a workable system.

Every half term or school holiday we visited railway works, engine sheds, carriage works, signal boxes, etc., all over the country, travelling by train, of course. What an experience! We saw steam engines being built from scratch at Derby and, ominously, the first two diesel electric locomotives 10,000 and 10,001 hauling experimental passenger trains between St Pancras and Leicester via Wellingborough. This was the beginning of the end of steam traction in the country and we saw it happen. We also visited York when it had railway workshops. What a pale reminder the engine shed is now, converted into a museum. We saw it with real steam engines when it was alive with smoke and steam and the smell of hot oil. Little did we know then that within our lifetime virtually all of this would be gone. Richard Hall (1946–54)

I spent two years in the Railway Club but never seemed to graduate from tearing newspapers into one inch squares to produce papier mâché. It seemed that slave labour in the third world would not attempt this soul-destroying task. I never got to applying the papier mâché, which seemed to be the preserve of the more senior boys. The only relief seemed to be when Ivor opened the tuck shop – that was if John Bridgeford had not bought up the entire stock before it was your turn. Once again seniority seemed to hold sway. *Terry Gotch (1954–61)*

The Railway Club became more than just a bunch of lads obsessed with steam and model trains, it also became the major force behind the creation of stage sets. The story is told by Neil Sinclair:

It's a long story that began before I entered WGS. The drama master Spike Jackson was complaining in the staff room one day about lack of support for the stage sets. Ivor was listening and volunteered that his Railway Club members would do something for him and so it all began. From then forward, the Autumn Term Railway Club was always devoted to preparing the stage for the Christmas production. We did some model

Railway Club as stage hands

Back Row: Peter Clark, Michael Payne, Richard Nobes, David Hill, Mr M. S. (Ivor) Cheale, Richard Sherwood, Mrs (Poppet) Cheale, David Pope, Dave Hanger, Richard Blunt, Middle Row: Michael Leach, Terry Wood, Paul Coleman, Robert Buckler, Neil Sinclair, Front Row: Chris Norman, D. A. Powis, P. P. Jones, Michael Prior, Alan Robinson, Ralph Baxter.

railway building in September and October but progressively became more 'stage-work oriented' as the term progressed. For the final two weekends before the play began we would spend all of Friday evening, all of Saturday until late in the evening and often Sunday afternoon preparing the set. We would also be on duty as stage-hands during the productions themselves – hence the photos were probably taken after the final performance on the last night. We were very proud of the sets which did take a vast amount of time. It is only now, looking back, that I realise the incredible team management skills that Ivor had. Each year, he would take a bunch of unskilled lads and produce some fine sets on time. Although I cannot remember fully, I think we did the same for the house drama competition – giving each house equal attention! The stage units were stored in the bunker behind prefab 19 (Beery Ward's room).

Neil Sinclair (1958–64)

I was a member of the Railway Club and enlisted to help with School Plays. On approaching the Sixth Form I assisted John 'Ernie' Huddart with the lighting. The bug started to bite and I shifted scenery, worked in the 'flies', and helped lighting at other local productions at the Palace and Lyric in Wellingborough and also at Rushden and Kettering. Instead of staying on to go to university from the 3rd year 6th in 1964, I 'jumped ship' and joined the BBC as a Technical Operator in 1963. Not very popular with 'Harold' Wrenn! After nearly 40 years working in TV Sound, Studios then Outside Broadcasts, I took early retirement in 2001. I still work part time, having just finished Wimbledon and looking forward to a few Proms. *Bob Buckler (1957–63)*

The Railway Club and the Stage Staff, continued through the life of the school, with the Stage Staff scoring a particular triumph when the play shifted from the original school hall to the much larger Mountbatten Hall. It finally lost steam after the change to the Wrenn School.

I joined the school in 72, and left in 77, and it was still just running, although its popularity had waned by then. It was still led by 'Ivor' and the club had taken over half of 'Jock's Hole' – the old boiler room under the 6th form cloak room, where we built an operational 00 gauge layout. The club disbanded shortly after I left. I never did find out what happened to all the equipment, nobody knew, or at least, nobody let on.

Regarding the connection between the Railway Club and the Stage

Staff, as they were known in my day. There may have been some pupils involved with both, I was for a while, but the two were completely separate entities, the link being that 'Ivor' was in charge of both.

As for the model railway layouts, I believe that before my time (1970s), they used to set up an 0 gauge layout in the Penney Lab. This would be started on Friday evening, and run on Saturday mornings. All the parts were stored in the loft above the labs. There was still some remaining when I started there in 72. I believe all the 0 gauge stuff was sold off to buy 00 gauge. *Martin Percy (1972–77)*

Chess Club

The Chess Club was first mentioned in the School Magazine in 1933, rising and falling throughout the life of the school, with a strong presence in the final years. It was typical of the waxing and waning of certain clubs that rose in popularity, then struggled and died only to be started again when new enthusiasts arrived. The first Chess Club began under the guidance of Mr Hole who offered to instruct any learners who wished to become members. The meetings were well-attended and it was hoped that the club would soon be taking part in representative matches. If this ever happened, it is not recorded in the School Magazine. The club was "revived" with about 15 members in 1937, and again in autumn 1947 when "the dead and buried Chess Club was reincarnated by a few enthusiasts, led by Mr Leftwich."

On this occasion, Dr Jackson, who had played for Middlesex in the Inter-County Championships, played simultaneous games against the whole club, defeating all the members one by one.

The club again fell silent and was re-formed in 1954, but waned again until "a desire to renew the Chess Club" occurred in 1957 with a new club of forty members, mainly younger pupils.

The seventies saw a major resurgence with the objective of 1933—to take part in representative matches—finally being achieved in 1971. Chess blossomed with a school knockout competition of up to sixty players a year, and the school participated in the Wellingborough Chess League and the Sunday Times Schools' Competition. Performance was sound rather than spectacular, coming second or third in the Chess League to Wollaston or Wellingborough School and being knocked out in the first or second round of the national Schools' Competition.

Photographic Society

The inspired inclusion of a dark room in the original plans of the school led to photography featuring in the early years of the school, in terms of a photography exhibition in summer 1932. The boys were encouraged to use the dark room and Mr Page was on-hand to give assistance. Entries improved in 1933 with boys using the dark room for special effects in developing their photographs. Mr Page left in Summer 1933, the dark-room was re-organised for other teaching duties and mention of photography ceased until a Photographic Society was featured in the Autumn Magazine of 1946. Mr Burrell talked about different kinds of cameras and Mr Sharp demonstrated the process of enlargement. A mention of Skells – "the former secretary" – speaking on the development of roll films and contact printing intimates that the society may have been active before that date.

In 1947 the name changed to 'The Camera Club' and again featured talks on enlargement, development and contact printing. The Society went silent, though not necessarily inactive, until the Summer Magazine of 1952 noted: "The Photographic Society, although almost completely unexposed throughout the year, managed to produce a display on Parents' Day", demonstrating printing and colouring photographs.

As each new generation arrived and the technology advanced, the Society moved with the times, from printing and enlarging photographs to using a 16 mm movie camera for sporting and other school events in the sixties. Enthusiasms were high in some years but waned in others as new generations moved through the school. The last report in the Magazine occurred in 1968.

The Scientific Society

The giving of lectures of various kinds was part of the school from the very beginning. The Literary and Scientific Debating Society was in existence at various levels of participation from 1933 to 1946 when it split into two: the Scientific Society beginning in Summer 1946 and the Literary and Debating Society starting in 1947 later reverting to a Debating Society in the late forties and fifties. The Scientific Society was made of sterner stuff. It was organised by Mr Holmes assisted by Mr Huddart, Mr Leftwich and other science teachers. Every science sixth former in the Lower Sixth was encouraged to give a lecture on a subject of his choice. The best lecture was awarded the Senior Science Prize.

Recalling the Scientific Society at a reunion in 2002, the 1952 first form was entertained by John Garley reading the report from the School Magazine of 1957. What was interesting was the quick response and wit from the audience—very typical of the atmosphere in the school in the old days. It went something like this:

[The Scene: A WGS 50th Reunion Dinner in 2002.]

John Garley: I have an old Magazine here, and of the persons concerned, there are six out of nine assembled in this room. So I wondered if each of those six would repeat their performances. It's the Scientific Society. [Loud laughter.] Exactly. [Oh God!]

I don't know whether you all know, but "lectures were delivered". [Giggles.] Yes they were delivered. I don't know what year this was. [Various voices call out "fifty seven", "nineteen fifty seven".] The first one to stand up and give a lecture is Mr J. S. Hobbs. He gave a lecture on 'Radiation and its Uses'. "The utilisation of atomic power was discussed in this lecture." Would you like to stand up and ... [Laughter.]

Right, the next one was 'Fuel Elements in an Atomic Reactor'. I think those two must have got together. That was Peter Bird. Would you like to .... [more laughter. Peter Bird says: "Pass".] "The purification and canning of uranium was discussed." Remember this was in the fifties. [Looking at Peter Bird.] I don't know where you got your information from.

The funny one who is not here, as Fred has pointed out when we got this list together, was Gerry Bermingham. [Laughter."Hooray" "Good Old Gerry."] He gave a lecture on 'Space Travel'. "The principles of space travel were *interestingly* expounded to a rather amused audience." Again, remember the 1950s, space travel! It's a bit way out, ... rather like Gerry Bermingham. [Uproar.]

Then we have Mr Ray King-Underwood. He gave a lecture on 'The Efficiency of the Internal Combustion Engine'. [Laughter.] "In this *interesting* lecture [more laughter], the speaker described the various factors that affect the efficiency of an engine." Now, I bet that went down a bomb. [Spriggs: "We could tune our motorbikes after that."]

Now the last two are probably the most interesting of the lot. There's a guy here called G. Willey, he gave a lecture on 'Glass'. And it says, "the manufacture and uses of glass were explained ..." [voice quips: "interestingly"] "and the art of the glass blower interestingly [uproar] explained."

And then last but not least, somebody called J. F. Nutt … Now we must have this one, he's gotta stand up and do this one … 'Sugar!' By J. F. Nutt. [Spriggs sings from the side: "Sugar in the mornin', sugar in the evenin' …"] "The principles of sugar refining were interestingly ...". [More laughter.] Honest, it says here, "... *interestingly* expounded in this detailed lecture."

Fred Nutt: I got every detail from Arthur Mee's *Children's Encyclopaedia* … of 1901.

John Garley: That was very interesting! [Applause.]

Nick Butler: Have you got Keith Bailey's?

John Garley: Keith Bailey didn't do one, but Keith Bailey was on the committee.

Fred Nutt: He wrote the notes, the *interesting* notes.

Nick Butler: Somebody did a lecture. I think it was on atomic structure and the apparatus was ping-pong balls, sand, and wire netting. [Aside: "and sugar."] And all that I can remember is that sand goes through wire netting and ping-pong balls don't. [Prolonged laughter.] And it's the only one of all those lectures I remember.

[Curtain]

Toc H

Toc H seemed to be the unlikeliest club to succeed in a school, being linked to an organisation formed by soldiers from the First World War and yet it became a leading light among the school's societies in its later years. The name comes from the signalling language for the letters T H, the initials of Talbot House in Poperinghe, which was a recreational retreat for soldiers of all ranks. On 19th September 1946, its founder, the Reverend P. B. (Tubby) Clayton visited the Senior School to give "a lively and interesting talk" on the Toc H movement. Much later, in 1954, the school formed its own Toc H group in consultation with the local Broadways Branch. It was the only school group in the country. It was first mentioned in the School Magazine in Autumn 1955:

Before giving an account of our activities it would be as well first to say something about Toc H itself. Founded in the First World War and re-created in 1920, Toc H seeks to bring together groups of men from every walk of life to share in a common fellowship. 'To love widely, to build bravely, to think fairly and to witness humbly' are headings contained in the Main Resolution.

Shortly before Christmas of last year, Mr F. G. Chesworth, editor of the Toc H. Journal, talked to us about Toc H. Since then we have had many other speakers, the last of which, Mr A. S. Greenacre, Toc H Area Secretary for Southern England, presented us with a rushlight. We are thus officially recognised as a Toc H group, the first of its kind in the country, an example which it is hoped other schools will follow.

How much have we achieved?

***'To love widely'** – As a group we have attempted to form a fellowship between boys in the school — the more differences they have the better, in this we have been fairly successful, many firm friends have been made through the group.*

***'To build bravely'** – Our services to the public are extensive. We run weekly library services in two of the Wellingborough hospitals. No other regular jobs are done at present, but at Christmas we are to help a local Toc H branch run a party for underprivileged children and we are also organising visits by the School Choir to the hospitals shortly before Christmas.*

***'To think fairly'** and **'To witness humbly'** – We try not to be prejudiced – to see the other person's point of view as well as our own. Thus, although at our meetings (held once a week) we may have violent*

Taken from a photograph in the Toc H Magazine:
Back Row: Graham Tall, Richard Orton, Alan Randall, Ian Prior, Robert Fish.
Front row: Paul Manton, Michael Weekley, Jake Dunning, Brian Westcott, Paul Neville.

arguments, at the end we consolidate our feelings in mutual friendship, realising that we are all equal in the eyes of God.

To be the servants of others is at times hard, but we strive as it is put in the Royal Charter for Toc H, "to spread the Gospel without preaching it."

Autumn Magazine 1955

In the Autumn Term 1955 the group received its rushlight and in the Summer of 1956, the first committee consisted of: G. S. Regis (secretary), W. W. Stevenson, (treasurer), S. J. Green (jobmaster), with S. H. Fox and D. O. Tall as District Representatives. Regis, for a period of time subsequently became a member of the national Toc H staff.

The number of members varied through the years. In 1960 there were just 13 members. Delivering books at the Cottage Hospital and Highfields Hospital continued well into the sixties. Money was raised initially by collecting and selling jam jars at a penny a piece. David Frost was one of those who did his stint of jam-jar collecting in the early days.

In the late fifties, early sixties, jumble sales were organised highly efficiently by Jake Dunning. He would get pupils in a class to write out information on slips of paper stating when Toc H boys would collect the jumble. The slips were delivered and a day or two later Jake would drive round the area where teams of boys were collecting jumble. He would fill his car to the roof and drive back to WGS where it was unloaded and then return to collect more. Gardens were dug and parcels containing 5/– worth of groceries distributed (value circa £3.50–£4.00 in 2006).

Both my brother and I were members and, on one occasion, we were invited to dinner with Tubby Clayton in London. Tubby recalled his visit to the school and his admiration of the photograph of Johnny Hyde's flying tackle he saw in the Headmaster's study. He had asked his friend Cecil Thomas (the designer of the Queen's head on the sixpenny coin) to turn the photo into a small statue. Years later, that statue was given to the school and became a rugby trophy.

Graham Tall (1955–63)

'The Tackle' by Cecil Thomas

The national Toc H Magazine sent a representative to the school, who reported on the Toc H meeting in the following terms:

I visited what is a most unusual unit of Toc H, whose members are, with one exception, schoolboys at Wellingborough Grammar School, most of whom are sixteen or under. I was met at the school gates by the group's fifteen-year old secretary Anthony Jones, who showed me to the School Library and introduced me to each member of the group in turn. After tea and chocolate biscuits, the meeting got off to a prompt start. I was immediately impressed with the efficient handling of the meeting by the chairman who, reading from a short agenda, asked each of the groups officers to make their report. This they did with commendable brevity. To hear the treasurer talking easily about No.1 and No.2 banking accounts was quite an experience. It was obvious from their reports that they were most knowledgeable about Toc H and quite familiar with its procedure.

Their Rushlight was then produced and the Ceremony of Light taken. I have seldom been so deeply impressed. *Toc H Magazine Feb. 1963*

In 1965 the group had grown to 19 members and organized a dance and concert to celebrate the fiftieth anniversary of Toc H. Interestingly, a comment made in a newspaper cutting in Miss Bavin's scrap album states that *it is run without any assistance from the staff.* However,

By the time I had joined the Toc H group (about 1970/71), HAW had little involvement and one of the masters interested was the late Mick Wright. *Arend Hoogervorst (1966–74)*

One of the last pages in the Nora's scrap album (around 1973) includes a large newspaper cutting in which Mr Wrenn refers to the importance of clubs and societies in the life of the school and to Toc H in particular:

These activities range from the radio and folk clubs to the Christian Fellowship and the geology club, but towering above the other activities in the school is Toc H, which every year provides a day trip for some of the senior citizens of the town. Last year's trip took them to Woburn, a departure from the traditional trip to Hunstanton.

Arend Hoogervorst (1966–74) commented:

The Hunstanton trips were paid for from funds raised by the annual 'Toc H Concert' (a cross between Monty Python, drag extraordinaire and Oxford Footlights) – I was involved in organising and acting in a

couple and I even recall doing a skit on Prize Giving where I imitated HAW in my head boy year. Tin Bum sat in the front row and was not amused, but nevertheless just as appreciated by the senior citizens.

Christian Fellowship

The Christian Fellowship was formed in Spring Term 1959 by Mr McCall, Dr Pettit and Mr Phillips to encourage older boys of different denominations to talk about aspects of their faith. There was a regular programme of meetings with outside speakers of various denominations, the showing of films, and discussion of Christian topics, including Christian unity. In 1962 the fellowship separated into two groups, one for senior boys in the fourth form and above and the other for juniors. The senior fellowship flourished through the sixties and seventies, but a drop in attendance in the late sixties caused the society to carry out a survey in 1967 which had 260 responses from the third form and above. It revealed interesting details of the boys activities, including their beliefs in religion, and attitudes to smoking, drinking and drugs, represented in the table below.

Membership built up again in the seventies as the club met with the girls of the Wellingborough High School in a joint fellowship from 1972 onwards.

		Age				
Question	**Answer**	**14**	**15**	**16**	**17**	**18**
Do you attend church every week?	Yes	39%	24%	40%	29%	20%
Do you attend church at all?	Never	54%	58%	56%	54%	65%
Do you drink alcohol?	Yes	46%	83%	84%	86%	91%
Do you smoke?	Yes	18%	48%	32%	34%	43%
Have you thought a lot about Christianity?	Yes	28%	34%	44%	58%	50%
Does God exist?	No	58%	50%	40%	52%	40%
Would you take LSD under supervision?	Yes	35%	31%	30%	51%	41%
Is there life after death?	No	45%	37%	65%	45%	50%
Do you do more than the minimum at school?	Yes	60%	50%	70%	65%	75%

Percentage of responses to selected questions from a Christian Fellowship Survey of 260 senior boys aged 14–18 in the summer of 1967

Other Clubs

Many other clubs will be dear to those who participated in them. The Field Survey Society will feature in the next chapter on 'school trips', organised by masters in geography and biology to cooperate in projects over the Easter and summer holidays.

Music Clubs ranged from passive listening of the Record Society (1957) to active participation in Modern Jazz (1962) and Folk Song (1968). They appeared and lasted as long as there were enthusiasts who wished to pursue their interests, then they passed into oblivion as new clubs arose and old clubs were reconstituted. They were supplemented by many other musical activities (the School Orchestra, Senior Choir, Junior Choir, Madrigal Group, Male Voice Choir, together with chamber music, the Wind Band and so on).

Dancing Clubs emerged on several occasions in the history of the school, invariably under the enthusiastic lead of Mr Pine. His first venture was a Scandinavian Dancing Club in 1939 as a joint activity with the High School, involving about a dozen from each institution.

After the war, Mr Pine initiated a square dancing club with about fifty boys and fifty High School girls meeting once a week after school. It hit a high-spot with a radio broadcast from Birmingham in 1951. (Think about it, *dancing* demonstrated on the radio!) In 1952 a team took part in a demonstration at the Royal Albert Hall in London.

Folk-Dancing in the Albert Hall

> *Two years ago, a headmaster started a club for schoolboys who were too shy to ask girls to dance with them. A mixed team of 64 will be giving a display at the Albert Hall this weekend.*
>
> *Evening Telegraph, January 4th, 1952*

Clubs arose to satisfy a need, that was the beauty of the system at Wellingborough Grammar School. So you want to learn about tape recorders? Form a Tape Recording Club. What about Ham Radios? Form a Radio Club. In need of spiritual sustenance? Form a Christian Fellowship. Want to play Soccer or Table Tennis or Chess? The answer is always the same: form a club.

Mr Wrenn in particular was always willing to provide support from the school and one or more of the masters with an interest would help support the club's activities. It would last as long as it was needed and it would die when it was no longer of interest.

A good example was the cycling club which arose in the fifties and again in the sixties, only to subside as the local cycling club provided the facilities desired for boys interested in competitive racing.

The provision of clubs and societies satisfied the needs of successive generations of boys as they passed through the school. It was one of the major features that made Wellingborough Grammar School special.

Grammar School riders, Terry Stratton in the lead (right), Hugh Cole (front left), and the Roche brothers in the pack, take part in the Regional Cycling Championships

'The Play's The Thing ...'

Geoff Hodgkins (1955–1962)

The thing that stands out for me in my memories of WGS is taking part in the annual school plays. These usually took place in December, normally in the last but one week of term. Monday afternoon was a dress rehearsal for the school, and then the play was performed on four evenings, Tuesday to Friday. Tradition has it that Tuesday had its fair share of mistakes, Wednesday was the best, as by Thursday we were getting a mite complacent and by Friday we were all knackered. That was certainly true for those of us who didn't live in Wellingborough and so had to stay at school, and then face a long bus journey home afterwards. (It was actually a good laugh to be in the school for a couple of hours when there was hardly anyone around. I seem to recall that we never did anything too outrageous: legend has it that Bob Leslie once peed into Jakey's rain gauge, but it was never proved).

The first play I was in was in 1957, my third-form year, a farce called *The Party Spirit*. I was chosen for one of the women's parts, for although my voice had recently broken, I could still get away with it. The other 'women' – Richard Oberman, Roy York and Martin Spriggs – and myself had to go to Nora to be fitted up with wigs and padded bras.

The Party Spirit (1957)
Back row: Richard Oberman, Roy York, Barry Clarke, Michael Bolton, Keith Bailey, David Carrington, Geoffrey Martin, Sam Harris,
Front row: David Tall, Geoff Hodgkins, James Wilson, Martin Spriggs.

The play was set in the House of Commons at a time when the government had a tiny majority, and a small party, the Free Whigs, had just won a by-election, increasing their strength to two MPs. This gave them clout and they were courted by both the main parties as an important vote was coming up.

The new member was a bit of a wide boy, on the make, and elected with more than a hint of rigged ballot papers, etc – a total contrast to the other older man. This 'new boy' was played by David Tall and I was his girl, Chloe (nature of relationship unspecified).

I can see now that my lines were full of double meanings and other references, but in those far-off innocent days, most of them were lost on me: for instance, I was supposed to be a singer in a nightclub called 'The Bag O' Nuts'!

David Tall was superb in the part: he was a total extrovert and completely confident. But acting with him certainly kept you on your toes.

One night (one of the earlier ones as I remember) he skipped about a page of dialogue. For someone like me with a photographic memory, that was nightmarish: I had to 'turn pages' in my head till I caught up with him.

Another night he made an extravagant gesture, and knocked a glass over which was on the bar. It smashed on the stage, and David ad-libbed, telling the barmaid to come and clear up the mess.

What he had forgotten (if he ever knew) was that Roy York had persuaded Spike to allow him to wear his trousers and plimsolls (you remember plimsolls, the ancestor of trainers?). This was because Act 1 was set in the bar of the Commons and Roy played Mabel the barmaid who stayed behind the bar all the time, which meant that she (he) could only be seen by the audience from the waist up.

The ad-lib went something like this:

> David: Oh, how clumsy of me! Mabel, come and clear that up for me, would you?
>
> Roy: Not likely.
>
> David: What you mean, Mabel? It's a terrible mess.
>
> Roy: Oh, that'll be OK. Leave it. I'll clear it up later.

So that was quite a baptism, but really enjoyable.

I suppose the air of innocence helped in my portrayal of Chloe as an airhead (the School Magazine described me as "a vapid blonde", and I had to look the word up in the dictionary to see what it meant!).

Unfortunately, I did not appear in the 1958 play as I missed most of the latter part of the autumn term having a cartilage removed. Mr Greenwood directed *Twelfth Night*, and several of the 1955 intake made their debuts then – Bob Scott, Richard Bradshaw, Ian Prior, Brian Westcott, and others.

Spike was back again for the 1959 play. This was called *Lifeline*, a 'drama' about a merchant ship during the Battle of the Atlantic. I played Casey, the Irish cook. Brian Westcott (being small) was the cabin boy, and I was supposed to bully him something rotten.

I remember that one of my lines referred to him as 'a snotty-nosed little bastard', but Shpike decided it was a little too much for the audience so it was changed (I think the illegitimacy was changed to 'devil' as I recall).

Much of the drama centred around the animosity between the captain (Bob Scott) and the chief engineer – Scottish, of course: all engineers in plays and films seem to be Scottish, don't they? – played by John 'Moose' Bayes.

The play opened with me laying the table for the officers and singing along to an Irish song. The late lamented Albert Fenner (whose family came from Northern Ireland) lent us a 78 (remember those?) of The All-Lammas Fair in Ballycastle. I had to sing along with this, and what with all the rehearsals became heartily sick of it before the end.

The stage crew were, of course, the ubiquitous Railway Club, led by the redoubtable Ivor Cheale, by now supported by 'Cloddy' Barker, who was chiefly responsible for the props.

The first act took place in port, and Cloddy tried to add some authenticity by standing behind the scenery dropping chains and such like, and saying naval type things like "Lower away there: easy aft!" in his impeccable Oxbridge accent. Sometimes I think our best acting was keeping a straight face at such times. The other two acts took place at sea, when we came under fire, and managed to sink a submarine. (Could a merchantman do that?)

However, Cloddy by this time was carried away and while we were in the middle of the Atlantic during a dramatic argument between the officers and captain, came the familiar bleat of 'Lower away there – easy aft' which as you can imagine was most disconcerting and hugely funny (to us, anyway). More of Cheale and Barker later.

Another memory of *Lifeline* is of poor Phil Bratby. He played a seaman (unnamed) and had one line to say. He had to come on and report to the captain during the scene when the ship was on fire. The line was – we heard it so many times it is branded for ever on my memory – "Sir, the forward hatch covers have just caught and all the men are aft," and then he would exit. Phil would walk up and down saying this wretched sentence to himself. The last run-through before the dress rehearsal Phil got so nervous he came on, said it at triple speed and ran off. Spike went ballistic. "No, no, no, Bratby. We never heard a thing. Much too fassht. Come back and sshay it again."

More authenticity came in the shape of Malcolm Billing's smoke machine (his family did beekeeping, apparently). This was to accompany the end of the second act, when the ship was on fire. Dear old Billing took to his task with such enthusiasm that the smoke drifted out into the audience, causing Harold to storm backstage at the interval: "What the hell's going on? We're all coughing in the first four rows!" You couldn't make this stuff up, could you?

In 1960 we did a 1920s comedy by John Drinkwater called *Bird in Hand*. It was set in a country pub, and focused on the change and tension going on in attitudes to social class at the time.

The landlord's daughter (Chris 'Babyface' Norman) was loved by the hunky son of the local squire (the dashing Richard Bradshaw), but her father objected as he was out of her class. The guests at the 'Bird in Hand' decide to support the young lovers by pleading their case with her father. "Why does he disapprove? Is she not 'good enough' for him?" "My daughter is good enough for any man alive," he answers. "So what's the problem?" they say.

Ultimately he faces his own prejudices and they all live happily ever after. At one point when things come to a head, and the landlord ('Moose' again) realises she has gone to her boyfriend, he loses his temper and calls out in a loud voice, "Time, gentlemen, if you please!" This is

'Bird in Hand' actors, Brian Westcott and Bob Scott, look on as John Bayes, playing Thomas Greenleaf, vents his anger on Richard Bradshaw as the squire who loves Greenleaf's daughter.

followed by a long pause; but one night out of the tense silence came two voices we knew and loved:

"Eh? Er, that clock must be wrong, George!"

"Yeth, it theemth fatht to me, Welph."

The thing was, we never knew this was going to happen: we had not rehearsed it, and again it was an absolute miracle that we managed to keep straight faces. It also totally ruined the dramatic silence. I wonder if the director knew!

Bird in Hand was directed by Ted Butcher. I liked him: he was a good sort, and I got my love of Shakespeare from him, when we read through *The Merchant of Venice* in class (the third form, I think it was).

The intellectuals among you will recall that the story revolves around Shylock and 'the pound of flesh', but the key sub-plot concerns the choosing of the correct one of three caskets for the hand of the beautiful Portia.

One of the suitors was the Prince of Arragon, and Ted asked me to read the part. He said the character was rather affected—I don't think he would have used the word 'effeminate', but we all knew that a limp wrist or two would not be out of place. He suggested that every 'r' should be pronounced as a 'w' (a bit like Cloddy, in fact).

This worked well until the line, "And rank me with the barbarous multitudes", which caused the extreme embarrassment of the reader, and the total collapse of the rest of the class. (I think Ted hid a smile as well).

Ted Butcher left WGS at Christmas, after the play, to become Head of Department at a school in Nuneaton. On the final night Brian Westcott, who played a miserable old man seeing down side of everything, changed one of his lines, which went something like: "My brother-in-law is one of the unluckiest blokes you could ever meet. He got knocked down by a car and broke his leg. He got over that, but then he had to go and live in Wolverhampton." On the

Friday, Brian changed the name of the town to 'Nuneaton', to huge laughter and acclaim.

I made a bit of WGS history in this play. There was a scene where quite a lot of dialogue centred around the subject of cigarettes, and my character (a young 'man-about-town' called Cyril Beverly) had to light up. I talked this over with Ted and he agreed that it would be difficult to play the scene without lighting up. He got permission from Tin Bum (this was the time when Harold had a breakdown of some kind and T. B. was acting head) and actually bought me a packet of fags! So I became the first (and last?) to smoke in a WGS school play! It was said at the time that Harold would never have given permission.

In my final year, 1961, Sshpike's protegé and former pupil, Syd Brown, directed us in *The Caine Mutiny Court Martial*. It was a dramatisation of Herman Wouk's novel of the Second World War, which was made into a successful film in the 1950s starring Humphrey Bogart, Fred MacMurray, and Jose Ferrer. Military plays were popular in boys' schools as they did not call for female roles.

The Railway Club broke new ground during this play. The two long acts in the courtroom are followed by a short denouement in a bar somewhere as the acquitted sailors celebrate the verdict.

In order to change the scene as quickly as possible, Ivor got the poor little beggars to sit in Room 6 with the lights out wearing dark glasses for about half an hour so they could rush on at the end of Act 2 and change the scenery in the dark! I kid you not!

It was a difficult play in many ways, all but the last ten minutes set in a court room, with a minimum of stage movement, except by the two briefs, and the various characters taking the witness stand. Many characters were on stage virtually the whole time (some saying absolutely nothing, like the members of the court martial panel).

I played Maryk, the mutineer first mate, who had taken over command of the Caine from Captain Queeg (the inimitable 'Moose') during a storm, when the captain panicked. What made it difficult was that, even when you weren't speaking (which may have been a long time), you still had to act by responding to all that was going on – especially in my case, as my future was on the line.

Bob Scott was outstanding as Greenwald, the defence counsel, who has to destroy Queeg on the stand – much against his better judgment – in order to get his client off. Likewise Moose's disintegration on the stand was brilliant. A great last play of my WGS career.

I never acted in plays again, although the first two schools I taught in in London in the late sixties both had amateur operatic societies and we did Gilbert & Sullivan, so that I could combine acting with my other great love, singing (I played the Major-General in *The Pirates of Penzance* and the Duke in *Patience*).

I moved on from there via suburban choral societies to sing for ten years in the London Philharmonic Choir, under such great conductors as Sir Adrian Boult, Sir Georg Solti and Bernard Haitink. We did proms, recordings, and loads of concerts, mostly at the Festival Hall or the Albert Hall.

I suppose these things are special to me because of a sense of achievement; preparing a work and performing it before a large and (hopefully!) appreciative audience; plus the camaraderie and working together in a common purpose.

Scouting at WGS

Peter Godfrey (1955–1960)

Yes, I was a member of the glorious 6th Wellingborough at the time when Jake Dunning and Stan Stanley were the Scoutmasters.

I am not really sure, why I joined the troop. It may have been because my father had been a Scout when Baden Powell was the Chief Scout, and he recounted stories of his troop's camping trips and the songs around the campfires. The stories were perhaps told with a slightly rose-coloured hue, because I discovered that he had omitted the fact, that on cold nights only the parts of a person facing the fire actually stayed warm and on warm nights the midges and mosquitos were a constant menace and seem to delight in my blood.

In order to avoid those plagues it was necessary to sit closer to the smoke which tended to keep them away, but also had the tendency, to turn Boy Scouts into kippers, or at least something that smelled very much like one all through the night curled up on solid ground in our sleeping bags.

Anyway, the romance of the campfire, the thought of the open road, service to God and Country instilled in me by my father must have had their effect, because without telling my parents, I stayed behind at school on the evening of the Scout Meeting and offered my meagre services.

The first consequence of my action was that – since I had not told my parents of my intentions – they became rather worried when I did not appear at home for several hours. Not a good start for a person joining an organisation which prides itself in its sense of responsibility and care for others.

I suppose today a nation-wide search would have been instigated and I would have appeared on the local news, with a by-line, about the fear of a kidnap. When I turned up at home feeling rather proud of myself, my father's grim visage told me that my joy would be short-lived, only to be saved by blurting out where I had been and what I had done, so seeing grimness turn to pride at a son following in a father's footsteps.

The down-side was, that I had to listen to all those old Scouting stories again and I am sure that they were even more embellished. Perhaps a bond had grown between us, based on joining the same 'club' and being ready to learn the secrets that any specialised group must have in order to separate it from the herd.

Over the years, we shared many stories of Scouting, but none of mine could top his, perhaps because he knew if I was indulging in embellishment and of course I could never know if he was.

The strange thing about it is that I joined the Scout Troop when it was in the charge of Jake Dunning. Jake was my Geography master and he terrified me to the core. I feel quite able to say this, because I know that many others felt the same, including perhaps some of the staff.

There were some occasions, when if Geography was on that day's timetable, that I complained bitterly to my parents, of some awful illness, which had to keep me in bed. If I had been more informed or inventive I could have conjured up symptoms of beri beri, yaws, malaria or even plague, but my pleas never worked and I was packed off to school, with comments such as, "You'll be alright dear," from my mother, and, "Be a man," from my father. I suppose we 12-year olds were made of sterner stuff then.

The strange thing about the whole initial experience was that I found Jake to be an entirely different man as a Scout leader, than as a teacher of geography, or at least I thought that I did.

Gradually I was awakened to the fact that a person can seem to be two different individuals in different circumstances, but in reality Jake was applying the same principles to his teaching as he was to leading boys in the Scouts. It is just that different circumstances demanded that the same principles be applied in different ways.

Perhaps I should say virtues more than principles. He gave all of us the understanding, that we should always act honestly and openly. That there was no place for skulking behind an excuse when you were to blame and that everyone is responsible for his own actions.

He also showed us what it means to work hard and expected us to follow his example. In saying that, he never ever created a divide between the leader and the led and shared our triumphs, failures and discomforts. Jake was actually a real leader of boys and one who was able to fashion them into decent, honest men. If some failed to achieve that, it was not Jake's fault; no person can succeed in everything.

From memory, every single meeting was interesting. We were always offered new challenges or presented with information which taxed our memories or fortitude. The acquisition of various badges came high on our agenda and this was encouraged by both Stan and Jake.

I believe there were several reasons for this. Firstly we were learning useful information, often information which would last a lifetime. Secondly, we were productively employed, and thirdly we had to face the challenge of the work and place ourselves in a position where we might fail.

A major factor in our thinking was, that when we passed a badge and were presented with it at a small ceremony in the school hall – where we often had our meetings – the badge looked really great when sewed on to our uniforms. Every other Scout in the world could tell what you had achieved, just by looking at the badges which festooned a uniform.

Some of our greatest times of fun were when we had what were known as 'wide games'. This meant, games played over a wide area, and in reality meant a sophisticated form of hide and seek. The games were played in woodland near Wollaston and we would scatter in various directions and one of us or perhaps a pair or even a whole patrol, would have to seek the others.

Those who had scattered had to leave clues, but they were clues known only to Scouts, or at least we thought so. Once again we were members of a worldwide community which had its own jargon, language, code, ceremonies and signals. Scouts even shook hands using the left instead of the right. I wonder how many Scouts became Freemasons, because there was certainly an element of secrecy, yet commitment to all things good, within the Scouts' Movement.

Stones and sticks pointing in various directions meant something to us. A bent twig or blade of grass gave added clues and our young and sharp eyes searched the ground and bushes for such clues. A rabbit which has passed in the night and scratched for food could lead an unsuspecting Scout on a merry dance, so perhaps we were not that good at reading signs. We would leave scratches in the earth, a mark on a tree, stones arranged in certain ways and all of these were meant to be picked up by our fellow scouts so that they could track our path.

Imagine the superiority of feeling, to know that mere mortals who lacked our training could never have followed our companions and would be isolated in the wild wood, no doubt to be attacked by weasels, ferrets and stoats. What Baden-Powell must have picked up on the African veldt to pass onto us, although we never ever saw a lion in the woods of Wollaston! No matter, it made us all far more observant and far more attuned to the natural world.

I certainly remember one of these occasions when Stephen Dobney was searching for us and we were trying to avoid him. We had passed the point when young boys concentrate on the job in hand and now we wanted fun. We gave false clues and made odd noises so that he followed us, only to find that we had gone.

We of course knew exactly where he was, not because of special skill, but because it was the height of spring, blossoms were everywhere, and poor Stephen suffered from hay fever.

This combination meant that he advanced through the woods accompanied by explosive sneezes which could be heard for miles. He did not stand a chance. He was not particularly pleased with us when he did catch up, although we did not understand what he said, as his voice was muffled by a handkerchief and interrupted by his sneezes. His eyes streamed with water and his handkerchief was a sodden mess.

The highlight of the Scout year was the annual camp. One which particularly stands out was a camp at Boars Hill near Oxford. I remember that one of our past Scouts, Graham Willey, who had become a Queen's Scout, was up at Oxford and he came to visit us at the camp. We had a camp fire with him I think and he taught us a comic song, about *My old lavender trousers*.

On the first day at another annual camp, we established camp and Jake went off to inspect the whole site and to meet the Warden. He returned to tell us that we had volunteered to do a job which would benefit all.

It seems, that during his inspection he had checked the latrines, only to find them in a disgusting state. He sprang into action, and we were detailed as latrine cleaners. They really were disgusting, no other word can describe their condition. We were many yards away when we smelt them and we held back from even approaching the door. Jake led the way and all of us except Jake gagged when we entered. It made me wonder even then what life experiences he might have had in order to be able to face such a repulsive atmosphere. But, Jake wearing large industrial rubber gloves led the way and to be honest did the lion's share of the work. I can see him now, pouring a highly caustic liquid into the large latrine cans, dragging them to a septic pit and pouring the contents into it.

At one time the indescribable mess splashed so much that some of the mixture spotted his brow. The effect was an instant sting from the caustic liquid and Jake threw off one glove, pulled out a handkerchief, passed it to me and told me to wipe the mess off his brow, while he still kept a firm grip on the can.

This was the man who, was so dominant in the classroom, whose knowledge was encyclopaedic, a man of culture and experience, a man before whom everyone trembled and there he was doing the meanest of jobs and asking me to wipe his brow.

To me, it was one of those boyhood learning moments, when I realised what it really meant to be a human being and stand on your actions, not on what others may say about you. Perhaps, at that moment, I could see for the first time, what service meant and I knew that what ever he did, it would never demean him and that all service gave dignity.

There were many more pleasant memories of the camp. The games, meeting Scouts from other parts of the country, the great camp-fire, when every troop had to put on a 'skit' for the entertainment. I remember that we did one where Terry Stratton ended it by pretending to stab himself, although I cannot remember the details. No Oscars were awarded, I do remember that.

Camp-fire sites seemed to have particularly significance to me, because during one of our annual camps north west of London (I cannot remember the place), I had chased someone across the area, tripped, fallen and skidded, only to crash my knee against the corner of the brick fireplace.

The result was that Jake took me to hospital in Chalfont St Giles, where I had stitches in the knee, a sorry disposition and eventually, a scar, which I carry with me to this day. Ah! Happy memories.

I think that camp was one of those fairly wet ones. Rain followed by fine weather followed by rain. It made life difficult, because we cooked all of our meals over an open fire, but like good Scouts we did not have any old fire.

Peter Godfrey and fellow scouts see Graham Willey receive the Queen's Scout Award. Looking on: Mr Stanley, Martin Gray, Ted Taylor, R. Darvil (hidden), Ron Palmer, Peter Godfrey (behind certificate), Alan Kitto, Stephen Dobney, Chris Talbot, Terry Stratton (The certificate on the right is held by David Wignell, who also became a Queen's Scout.)

We had been taught how to build an altar fire, which consisted of gathering rocks and other hard debris and building a structure about two meters long and about one meter high and perhaps half a meter wide. The top was recessed and had mud packed into it, which became rock hard with the heat from the fire. On top of this we placed iron grills on which the cooking pots were placed.

It looked as though we had constructed an altar, suitable for the priests of Baal to dance around and make sacrifice, but it was very efficient and it meant that we could stand up while cooking. Each patrol had to take a turn as cooks, and on one particular evening meal it was the turn of we of the Otter patrol.

Perhaps we were aptly named, because it rained incessantly, but in true 6th Wellingborough style, the challenge was on! It was a particularly important meal, because it was the occasion of Jake's famous currant duff. It was a tradition, that we had this fantastic meal as a dessert once on every annual camp. It was heavy enough to moor a ship, but succulent with currants and sugar, steamed for what seemed to be hours in our camp steamers and served, if I remember, with custard. It was famous and it was a favourite, and woe betide those who spoiled it.

Eventually the rain was so heavy, that only three of us were outside at the fire: myself, Terry Stratton and Ron Palmer. We had wet-weather gear and between us one large old-fashioned wide-brimmed Scout hat, which we passed around when water leaked down into our shirts from our collars. It was the best of headwear and was fully water proof, much better that the berets we normally wore.

We would not let anyone else near the meal, we wanted to make it special despite the circumstances. It was a great moment, keeping the fire going, water dripping off our clothing and knowing that the rest of our troop were counting on us to have a good meal.

Jake and Stan gave us a pat on the back when the meal was over and perhaps that meant more to us than anything else.

In hindsight, I now know that we did it because we had been given the example of service and that we were doing it not only as schoolboys, but also as members of a special group, who had been given, without knowing it, the gift of companionship, friendship and, above all, a will to serve others no matter how unpleasant the task.

Although I have the physical reminders of Scouting in the form of belt, knives and of course a scar, it is really the spirit and lessons of scouting which remain with me. They were wonderful times, led by men who understood what the Scout Movement really meant and who had the integrity, skill, knowledge and leadership to actually make it work.

After I left WGS, I took no further part in scouting, yet the influence on me was great. I have applied many of the principles of the Movement to my everyday life and can still do sheepshanks, half hitches and square lashing when needed. Two of my daughters were Guides and if I had had a son, no doubt I would have encouraged him to join, with stories about my times, much embellished of course.

Now I think back to my time in the 6th Wellingborough and remember those wonderful experiences, perhaps I would not need to embellish my stories, and come to think of it I do not think my father did either.

Mmm ...

Chapter 12

School Trips at Home and Abroad

School trips began early in the life of the school, with five outings in 1934: a large contingent travelling to Northampton to see the Barbarians play East Midlands, an Easter trip for a small party of boys to France, a group of over a hundred boys cycling to Naseby with Messrs Dunning and Watkins, eighty boys travelling to the county ground to see Don Bradman play for Australia against Northamptonshire.

During the war, trips involved practical activities: picking fruit, gathering the harvest, logging in the woods. In Mr Woolley's last term, in 1945, the School had its first 'Day Out' where every boy went on a day-trip to somewhere selected from a range of possibilities.

After the war, there were several different kinds of school trip: the annual excursion day where everyone selected from twenty or so possible choices; the annual summer trip abroad for a small party led by Ivor Cheale and Charlie Ward (or later by the headmaster); several three-day trips to the Royal Navy at Plymouth; annual field trips to different parts of Britain; and a range of other regular outings to scout camps, the Royal Society's educational talks in London, and so on.

School Excursion Day

After the day excursion in Mr Woolley's time, Mr Wrenn instituted regular annual excursions in 1948, organised, as ever, by the indefatigable Jake Dunning. Boys were given a list of planned visits and asked to tick/rank those they preferred. Mr Dunning did his best to provide everyone with their desired trip and put up a list with the cost of each trip displayed. Theoretically, anyone not wishing to pay could stay at the school with a volunteer teacher; when Mr Temple was asked about this many years later, he had no recollection of anyone not going, which is hardly surprising, given the following descriptions.

> *I was in the 1947 intake, which was the first year of the 1st Form. I can remember going to Dovedale the next summer. It must have made an impression on me because the following year I went to Matlock! Now there is the exploratory spirit for you!* *Pedro Howes (1947–52)*

A varied number of educational trips have been arranged for the boys of Wellingborough Grammar School who will be dispersed next Wednesday while the school is used for the annual scholarship examination. Coaches will take 360 boys by road to places as varied as Windsor, The Imperial Institute, Kensington, Whipsnade Zoo, Raleigh and Boots works at Nottingham, W. H. Allen's Engineering Works and the London Brick Company. The railway club are going by rail to Crewe, botanists to the Natural History Museum, Kensington and Kew and the architecturally minded to Hampton Court Palace. In all 100 boys will travel by train.

Newspaper Cutting circa 1950 in Miss Bavin's Scrap Book

I remember going down a coal mine at Coalville one Saturday when it was only open for maintenance and visiting Stoke on Trent when the bottle kilns were still in use and the city was covered by smoke. I only live about 20 minutes away from there now and it is almost unrecognisable as the place we saw in the early fifties. We also saw Stewarts and Lloyds at Corby in full swing with their Bessemer converters and the big rolling mill. One of 'Father's' college friends was in management there so he was able to get us good conducted visits.

Richard Hall (1946–54)

Mr Wrenn and a group of schoolboys down a coalmine.
The boys include Brian Whitney (second left), John Pettifer, Roger Miles, David Cooper, 'Perce' Long, kneeling: John Sharman, David Britton.

David Spencer, Richard Buchta and Colin Bingham on a School Trip to Matlock as second formers in 1957. [Chris Talbot behind the camera]

These trips were thoroughly enjoyed by the boys but, as shown in the photograph above, most of the boys did not consider them educational! Everyone went in school uniform and if the masters had seen the paddling, they may not have been impressed, though they must have become used to the raucous singing in the coach on the way home:

> *Where else did I learn 'Old Uncle Tom Cobleigh and all', 'Where have all the flowers gone?', 'Ten green bottles' and highly personalised versions of 'The Quarter-Master's Store'.* *Graham Tall (1955–63)*

One of the last boys to go on a trip wrote:

> *I lived opposite the Grammar School from the age of two. One day each year Doddington Road was lined with coaches from in front of the school to half way up the playing field. A party atmosphere and absolute chaos prevailed as the whole school loaded up for the annual school excursions. Eventually I started at the school and went on an outing in 1970 to the Grand Union Canal, Blisworth Tunnel. AND THAT WAS THAT. They stopped the next year, money reasons I suppose. So I watched the days happen for ten years and only got to go on one.*
> *Nick Tompkins (1969–75)*

Trips Abroad

At least one trip abroad was made to Paris in 1934 before the annual trip abroad was started by Mr Cheale in 1951. The *raison d'être* of these trips was explained by Mr Cheale as:

> *The idea is to give the boys as wide an experience of the world as possible, while enjoying a holiday at the same time.*

He then added:

> *Before they go they will be given this advice: "Don't spend all your pocket money in the first three days." … "We are going to give the boys this special advice about money because last year some boys spent most of the cash on presents in the first few days. Then they had to resell the presents to get some money." Mr Cheale explained that he could take charge of the boys' money but he felt that part of the educational side of the trip was learning how to spend considerable sums of money. The boys will spend an average of seven pounds each.*
>
> *Newspaper report, 1954*

In 1958 the numbers wishing to go was so high that two separate parties went to Norway. In the photograph on the left, the boys just arrived are in school uniform, which was compulsory whilst travelling. At other times, casual wear was the norm, as worn by Barrie Tall, Robert Gibson, Roger Brown and John Wittering in the photo on the right.

The cost of the trips, advertised in the School Magazine, was substantial for working-class parents. (£29 was equivalent to £490 in 2006 according to the Retail Price Index.)

Photographs on the Norway Trip in 1958 with Mr Cheale and 'Charlie' Ward

SCHOOL PARTY TO

ITALY

FLORENCE AND VENICE

AUGUST 20th — AUGUST 31st, 1956

COST : £29 (approximately)

including travel, accommodation, meals *en route*, and sightseeing in

VENICE • FLORENCE • SIENA • PISA

The reports of the boys to their parents must, however, have been so positive that, not withstanding the cost, many boys went repeatedly. The positive response was almost certainly because the trips were both well-organized and yet provided considerable freedom.

Personally, I found that sticking close to the CHEALE/WARD *collaboration seemed to provide numerous opportunities to escape to the continent, a pre-occupation that lives on to this day!*

Richard Nobes (1955–60)

Ernie Bryan was very popular with both pupils and staff and, accompanied by his charming wife, went on the fabulous foreign holidays organised by Martin Cheale (and wife Poppet). During the long rail journeys, I remember Ernie's spell-binding accounts of his war service with the Baltic Fleet: the stories were horrendous.

Richard Adkins (1950–57)

Ernie was always considered to be a 'teacher' on the school trips abroad.

Barrie Tall (1955–62)

I went on two school trips to Norway and to Switzerland/Paris.

The sea crossing to Norway was really memorable as we were hit by a really strong storm. The crew had battened the hatches (or whatever they do) but a crowd of us found an unlocked door; we were caught running around the decks in heaving seas, soaked to the skin … and loving it.

I remember we all bought toy pistols that fired a cork impregnated with gunpowder as a jet of flame poured out from the barrel. Ivor became quite frantic and we all had to hand them in for destruction.

I remember that Barrie Tall scored with the chalet maid at the Vinje Hotel and we found him necking with her in various hotel rooms as she cleaned them. I think he must have been a little more advanced in that way than us as we were all only about 14 years old.

In Paris, our hotel rooms all had balconies. Being lazy I decided to enter another room by climbing across the balconies, I guess we were eight or ten floors up and this resulted in some French 'busybody' phoning the police who rushed to the hotel looking for a suicide candidate. Needless to say someone grassed me up and I received the usual nasal scream from Ivor. *Roger Brown (1954–61)*

Mr Cheale provided the boys with detailed booklets of information on the places visited. The boys were given the times of all journeys and when and where they had to be at particular times, allowing them considerable freedom as long as they acted responsibility. His planning and organization of the trips abroad were highly successful and many boys went repeatedly. To them the trips were valued holidays. Casual wear was the norm and there was a level of freedom that could not be offered in a trip organized in the 21st century.

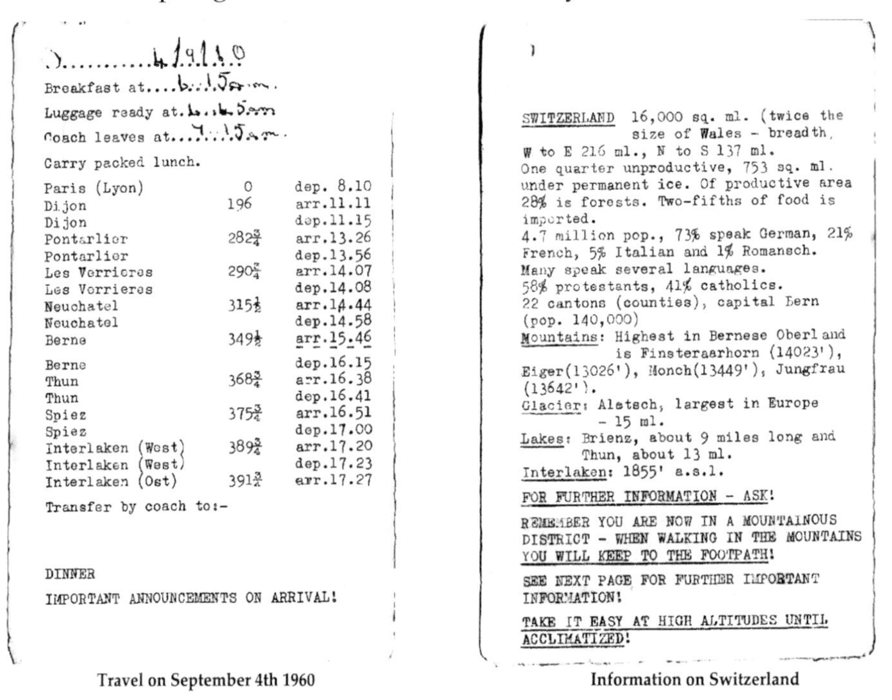

D..........4/9/60

Breakfast at....6.15a.m.

Luggage ready at.6.45am

Coach leaves at....7.15a.m.

Carry packed lunch.

Paris (Lyon)	0	dep. 8.10
Dijon	196	arr.11.11
Dijon		dep.11.15
Pontarlier	282¾	arr.13.26
Pontarlier		dep.13.56
Les Verrieres	290¾	arr.14.07
Les Verrieres		dep.14.08
Neuchatel	315½	arr.14.44
Neuchatel		dep.14.58
Berne	349½	arr.15.46
Berne		dep.16.15
Thun	368¾	arr.16.38
Thun		dep.16.41
Spiez	375¾	arr.16.51
Spiez		dep.17.00
Interlaken (West)	389¾	arr.17.20
Interlaken (West)		dep.17.23
Interlaken (Ost)	391¾	arr.17.27

Transfer by coach to:-

DINNER

IMPORTANT ANNOUNCEMENTS ON ARRIVAL!

SWITZERLAND 16,000 sq. ml. (twice the size of Wales - breadth, W to E 216 ml., N to S 137 ml.
One quarter unproductive, 753 sq. ml. under permanent ice. Of productive area 28% is forests. Two-fifths of food is imported.
4.7 million pop., 73% speak German, 21% French, 5% Italian and 1% Romansch.
Many speak several languages.
58% protestants, 41% catholics.
22 cantons (counties), capital Bern (pop. 140,000)
Mountains: Highest in Bernese Oberland is Finsteraarhorn (14023'), Eiger(13026'), Monch(13449'), Jungfrau (13642').
Glacier: Aletsch, largest in Europe - 15 ml.
Lakes: Brienz, about 9 miles long and Thun, about 13 ml.
Interlaken: 1855' a.s.l.

FOR FURTHER INFORMATION - ASK!

REMEMBER YOU ARE NOW IN A MOUNTAINOUS DISTRICT - WHEN WALKING IN THE MOUNTAINS YOU WILL KEEP TO THE FOOTPATH!

SEE NEXT PAGE FOR FURTHER IMPORTANT INFORMATION!

TAKE IT EASY AT HIGH ALTITUDES UNTIL ACCLIMATIZED!

Travel on September 4th 1960 **Information on Switzerland**

Information for School Trip abroad

> *We had lots of freedom. I do not remember having to sign in or out or even say where we were going, we just had to be at the rendezvous point at the correct time … or else! I do however remember the detailed itinerary provided which was very useful.* Roger Brown (1954–61)

> *I remember being fined 5/– (5 shillings) for going out of the hotel one evening without permission. A system of fines was one of Ivor's ways of penalizing wrongdoers.* Richard Bryan (1956–63)

Field Survey Society Trips

The Field Survey Society was formed in the Autumn of 1960 by two geography masters, 'Brett' Tussler and 'Puffkin' Templar, and two biology masters, 'Gus' Leftwich and 'Fred' Knight, working with sixth formers to bring together the Arts and Science streams in the school. There had been earlier field trips, such as a geography field trip in Shropshire in autumn 1950 but this was the first time there had been cooperation between the departments of Geography and Biology. The initial plan was to involve boys in practical field trips where land surveys and maps produced by the geographers would be used by the biologists for their own ecological surveys. They began with an earthworm survey in the iron ore quarry at Irchester and graduated in Easter 1961 to a trip taken by three masters and seven boys to the Straith of Appin in Argyll. The geographers surveyed the local Gleann-na-y-Iola stream and the biologists studied the shores of Loch Linnhe before joining together for a trek over Bein Donn and Bein Sylnich.

The club was soon in danger of being over-subscribed and a system of election of members by the committee was put in place to keep the 1962 trip to the Lizard Penninsula to a reasonable party size of fourteen boys and four teachers. Mr Alden came to the school to teach geography and was soon pressed into service as a driver.

Mr Knight left in 1962, but he was back again in 1963 to bring four boys from his new school in Colchester to swell the party to 29 for a visit to perform surveys in Wales between Portmadoc and Caernarvon.

In Summer 1964, the team increased to five staff and 25 boys divided into four teams from first and second year biologists and geographers. Now it was open-season for any interested boy to participate.

Mr Templar left in 1964, but was back again at Easter 1965 with nine boys and two other masters from his new school in Bristol, for a return visit to Wales where now there were so many keen to participate that a further trip had to be added for the additional numbers in the summer. The two trips were repeated in 1966.

Cornwall 1962, with Mr Tussler (left) and Mr Knight (kneeling)

Mr Alden left school in the Summer of 1966 for a new position in Cowbridge School in South Wales. At Easter 1967, it was his turn to bring a party of boys from his new school to participate in the field trip to North Wales. The school took two minibuses, with Johnny Hyde's mini towing a 12 ft boat loaned by Tim Tomlinson and Jock the caretaker driving his minivan. The biology projects were becoming increasingly sophisticated, including "amino acids in sea-weeds" and "fossilised pollen in peat", while geographers seemed to spend their time roaming around Snowdonia.

Field Surveys continued, joining with Kettering Technical College in Wales for Easter 1969, this time with the luxury of a coach and rooms in a hotel which gave the boys more time to complete their studies. The summer course returned to its usual haunts in North Wales.

Visits to Portsmouth to stay onboard ships

For several years three-day trips were made to see the Navy at Portsmouth. The first trip of 33 boys was led by Mr Jay. On Tuesday, the first day of the trip, the boys journeyed from Wellingborough and visited the cruiser *Royalist* and battleship *Ramilles* before being shown how to sling their own hammocks in the evening. On Wednesday morning the boys toured *HMS Victory* and the aircraft carrier *HMS Illustrious*, whilst in the afternoon they toured the motor torpedo boat base (which included a captured German E boat) and finally visited the submarine *Tantalus*. In the evening they went to the Naval Gunnery School where they saw and operated everything from 4.5 to 15 inch gun turrets.

In the Dome Trainer everyone had firing practice behind real gunsights at hostile aircraft which approached on a screen with all the fearsome noises of battle from the accompanying sound track. By an ingenious mechanism which synchronised with the sound film the number of rounds fired by each person, and his score of hits and misses, were recorded. Mr Jay was heard to mutter after learning his score that he had better remain a schoolmaster – he was clearly no good as a gunner!

On Thursday morning, the boys travelled back to WGS, stopping for lunch and an hour's sight-seeing at Oxford. (School Magazine, 1947)

In 1949, Mr Temple and Mr Sharp took a party of 27 boys to Portsmouth, having the good fortune to stay on the Royal Yacht *Victoria and Albert*. They also visited the gunnery school, the motor torpedo boat base and the naval aerodrome (where Mr Temple had been a war-time naval pilot of a 'Swordfish' plane) and were shown around a destroyer. They were, however, less fortunate than their predecessors in seeing only a small range of Naval craft. The trip was covered by *Evening Telegraph* reporter Pat Farnell and photographer Terry Rice, an old boy of the school who took the picture below.

On board the Royal Yacht Victoria & Albert

Back Row: 1: Richard Berwick, 2: Jim F. Pope, 3: Tom Wildman, 4: Peter F. 'Puffer' Jones, 5: J. C. Clayton, 6: Pat H. Hunt, 7: Glyn J. Muncey, 8: Peter White, 9: Keith Bradshaw.
Centre Row: 1: Peter Parnell 2: Steve Scott 3: Syd W. Brown, 4: T. J. Collis 5: John M. Clifton, 6: Brian H. Warren, 7: Robert Clark, 8: John Manning, 9:Roy Catling, 10:Douglas Rabbitt, 11:Graham P. Surridge, 12:E. E. Moore.
Seated: 1: R. E. Goosey, 2: Graham Norris, 3: Bob Whitworth, 4: Mr Temple, 5: Officer, 6: Mr Sharp, 7: Jim Smith, 8: Colin Cunnington, 9: Norman Redman
Front: 1: A. B. Crawford, 2: Don N. Stratton, 3: Bob Sharman

In the fifties, several more major 'Battleship' trips were made to the Royal Navy at Portsmouth.

Mr Ward and Mr Sparrow travelled with the boys in 1957, the total cost of which was 30/–. In both cases, the trip was similar in pattern to those described above, the 'hotel' was Britain's last battleship, HMS Vanguard. The beds were hammocks, slung closely together, meals were those offered to the sailors. The trip included a tour of HMS Victory, a ship still commissioned in the Royal Navy, the ship's historical background was clearly described, no doubt to the enjoyment of Mr Ron Ward, the School's history teacher. Visits were made to other ships, in particular a tour of a submarine, and a training centre where some of the boys were allowed to fire blanks using the large anti-aircraft bofors guns. The boys had to swab the decks. From the Navy's point of view the visit was presumably to attract future officers, for the boys it was a very enjoyable holiday. Graham Tall (1955–63)

H. M. S. Vanguard 1957

Back Row: 1: Mr R. V. S. Ward, 2: Officer, 4: David James, 5:Vic Ward 6: Ian Agar, 7: Roger Denton, 8:Derek Jackson, 9: Richard Lewis, 10: Terry Stratton, 11: Martin Hagger, 12: John Allen, 14: Officer, 15: 'Mr A. E. Sparrow.
Middle Row: 1: Peter Godfrey, 3: Richard Oberman, 4: Richard Buchta, 5: Roger Underwood, 6: Paul Tompkins, 6:Don Tyler, 8: Mick Newell, 9: David Jones, 10: Alan Davis.
Front Row: 1: Robert Scott, 2: Bob Mayes, 3: Jim Robertson, 4: Richard Carter, 5: Jim Penness 6: Roger Duffin, 7: Nigel White, 8: Barry Matson 9: Ted Taylor 10: Richard Bradshaw, 11: Graham Drage, 12: Roger Lines, 13: David Holder.

Chapter 13

Eminent Guests on Parents' Day

A striking feature of the Wellingborough Grammar School year was the attendance of eminent guests to present prizes at the annual Speech Day, or Parents' Day as it became known in 1946. The early years saw a sequence of worthy guests, including scholars from Oxford and Cambridge and others whose names may mean little to the reader today. Then, in the fifties and sixties, came a stream of famous men at the forefront of British Society, including Sir Alexander Fleming, discoverer of penicillin, Sir John Cockcroft, the first British physicist to split the atom, Sir Lawrence Bragg, Nobel Prize winner for work on X-rays, Lord Birkett, advocate at the Nuremberg Trials, Sir William Penney, 'father' of the British atomic bomb, author Sir Compton Mackenzie, Lieutenant General Sir Brian Horrocks, Earl Mountbatten of Burma, flying ace Douglas Bader, naturalist Peter Scott, Prince William of Gloucester, Group Captain Leonard Cheshire, old boy David Frost, and Lord King, Speaker of the House of Commons.

Over the years, society changed, from the austerity of the thirties when the school ethos was based on respect for King and Country, through the challenge of the war years and its memories, on to the later vision of a newer, more humane society.

These moods are reflected to a remarkable degree in the succession of speeches of the guests who came to present the prizes, from worthy academics, scientific innovators, popular heroes, on to internationally known personalities. Many of them left their mark through the formal naming of laboratories, lecture rooms and departments, leaving a history etched on plaques on the walls of the school. It is a remarkable tale of vision and opportunism by the third headmaster, Harold Wrenn, building on the foundations of his predecessors.

Guests 1930–1937

The first headmaster, Mr Lay, organised the first speech day in spring 1935 when he considered the school had reached the right size. His first guest was the Headmaster of his former school in Liverpool.

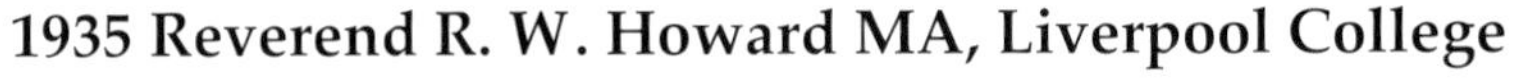

1935 Reverend R. W. Howard MA, Liverpool College

The Reverend Robert Wilmott Howard (1887–1960) studied Classics and Theology at Trinity College, Cambridge, trained for the ministry at Ridley College, and after ordination, became a tutor at St Aidan's Theological College Birkenhead in 1912. He was chaplain to the British Expeditionary Forces in the First World War, later an assistant master at Eton College, 1924–28, then Headmaster of Liverpool College, 1928–45, where Mr Lay was already on the staff as a science teacher. Mr Lay was to build the ethos of Wellingborough Grammar School on his experiences at Liverpool College and it was only natural for him to invite his former headmaster to present the prizes at the first School Speech Day.

The Reverend Howard responded with a valedictory speech:

> *Education, he said, could be set out in three stages — primary up to 10; secondary 10 to 18; and the third stage all that lay in life before them.*

In each of these stages there should be some experiences and aims:

> *Firstly there was appreciation. They should appreciate things and realise that beauty and wonder were values worth having. They should realize and appreciate the value of accuracy. Imagination, the power of seeing life through pictures, was another fine quality. Discipline too was important. When he had a boy who was sloppy, he found in many cases he had a rather too kindly mother. Adventure, also, was a spirit which should be sought by boys, especially in games.*
>
> *Secondly they could take the word appropriation as summing up the period 10–18. This was a period when boys really made things their own. They had to get, but they must never forget to give. A scholar should secure the feeling that he must never let the school down, he should appropriate the school.*
>
> *Application summed up the third stage, the putting into practice what the boy had learned. At the end of life the pupil would be able to thank God that he had been to Wellingborough Grammar School.*

Reverend Howard was later appointed Canon at Liverpool Cathedral in 1943, then Master of St Peter's Hall, Oxford, 1945–1955.

Mr Kaines-Smith makes his speech under the chairmanship of Mr Hedger Edwards (Chairman of the Governors) with Mr Lay seated to his left.

1936 Mr S. C. Kaines-Smith MBE, MA, FSA, Keeper of the Birmingham City Museum and Art Gallery

The guest in 1936 was Art Historian Solomon Charles Kaines-Smith (c.1885–1958), author of several books on art history. In his speech, he resonated with the mood of the time, declaring tradition to consist not of badges and emblems, but in the spirit of the country. He offered the example of King George as the embodiment of England's highest tradition: an English gentleman who did his duty in his job and to his fellow man. He extolled the boy who carried out his job to the best of his ability, quietly and steadily, valuing honesty and loyalty.

1937 Alderman Brigadier-General A. F. H. Ferguson JP

For his third and final guest, Mr Lay invited a member of the local gentry: Brigadier-General Algernon Francis Holford Ferguson JP (1867-1943) of Polebrook Hall near Oundle, whose great-grand-daughter, Sarah Ferguson, became Duchess of York. He served in the Boer War and commanded a regiment of Life Guards in the First World War. On retiring from the Army he became well-known locally for public service and tireless commitment as a Northamptonshire County Councillor.

At Speech Day, he urged the boys to be aware that they were citizens of a great empire to which it was their duty to contribute and not to become engrossed in their own interests. He asked them not to allow the virtue of patriotism—"the greatest thing a man can have"—to be laughed at or scorned.

He then announced he would donate a Cup to be awarded to the House that achieved the highest academic standards in each year.

Speech Day 1938–1945

1938 Sir A. C. Seward, ScD, FRS, Late Chancellor of Cambridge University and Master of Downing College, Cambridge

For his first guest of honour, Mr Woolley invited Sir Albert Charles Seward (1863–1941), a grammar school boy, educated at Lancaster Grammar School and St John's College, Cambridge. He became interested in the botany of fossil plants. He was appointed a lecturer at Cambridge in 1890, elected a Fellow of the Royal Society in 1898, was Professor of Botany at Cambridge from 1906 to 1936, and Master of Downing College 1915–1936, including a period as Vice-Chancellor in 1924–26.

1939 Sir Gilbert Walker CSI, ScD, FRS, FRAS, Late Professor of Meteorology, Imperial College of Science

Mr Woolley's guest the following year was Sir Gilbert Walker (1868–1958), a mathematician and statistician renowned for his theory of oscillating weather conditions that paved the way for weather forecasts to shift from short-term observations towards comprehensive models of world-wide climate change.

He showed interest in mathematics at Grammar School, won a scholarship in mathematics at Trinity College, Cambridge, continuing after graduation as a Fellow, researching dynamics and meteorology. In 1903 he left academia to spend the next 21 years studying the climate as the Director of the Indian Meteorological Department. He amassed a huge amount of data and used statistical analysis and mathematical modelling to propose a longer-term oscillation of weather patterns. Although this was not fully successful in his attempt to predict the future behaviour of monsoons, the underlying theory proved sufficiently robust to become the basis of modern world weather forecasting. On his return to England in 1924 he was knighted and became Professor of Meteorology at Imperial College London until his retirement in 1934. He continued to work actively at his research, publishing his last paper in 1950 at the age of 82. He was the archetypal 'renaissance man' with wide interests, seemingly unrelated to his main research, including several publications on the flight of birds he had observed in India and the mathematics of the boomerang where he achieved high levels of theoretical and practical performance.

1940 The Rt Hon. the Lord Roche PC

The guest in 1940 was The Rt Hon. Alexander Adair Roche (1871–1956). He was a Grammar School boy from Ipswich who won a scholarship to study Classics at Wadham College Oxford. He turned to law after graduation, earning his living in commercial law before being knighted and appointed a judge on the King's Bench in 1917. He was elected an Honorary Fellow of Wadham in the same year. In 1934 he was appointed a Lord Justice of the Court of Appeal and made a Privy Councillor, becoming a life peer and a Lord of Appeal as Baron Roche in 1935. He lived in Oxfordshire from 1920, rode with the hounds until he was eighty, was a competent shot and, above all, a devoted adherent of fly-fishing.

1941 The Right Reverend C. M. Blagden DD,
The Lord Bishop of Peterborough

In 1941 the focus of attention turned to the clergy, inviting the leading cleric in the Diocese of Peterborough, whose territory included Northamptonshire, Rutland and the Soke of Peterborough. The Lord Bishop of Peterborough, the Right Reverend Claude Martin Blagden (1874–1952), was in post as Bishop from 1927 to 1949. Prior to this he had followed a steady path, reading Classics at Corpus Christi, Oxford, missing a first class degree by a few marks, yet being awarded a fellowship at Christ Church, where he was ordained and spent 14 years in the Cathedral before becoming Rector of Rugby in 1912 and Bishop of Peterborough in 1927.

1942 Mr G. M. Trevelyan OM, CBE, Master of Trinity College, Cambridge, Regius Professor of Modern History, Cambridge

The next year, Mr Woolley turned his attention back to Cambridge, inviting the English historian, George Macaulay Trevelyan (1876–1962). Trevelyan studied at Trinity College, Cambridge, where he was one of the 'Cambridge Apostles', a highly select group of Cambridge intellectuals. In 1898 he won a fellowship at Trinity and lectured at Cambridge until 1903 at which point he left academic life. In 1927 he returned to the University to take up a position as Regius Professor of Modern History. In 1940 he was appointed Master of Trinity College and served in the post until he retired in 1951. He was an authoritative and opinionated writer on social history, capable of many highly quotable sayings, such as, "Education has produced a vast population able to read but unable to distinguish what is worth reading."

1943 Mr (later Sir) C. M. Bowra MA, D Litt, FBA, Warden of Wadham College, Oxford

Maurice Bowra (1898–1971) was the Warden of Mr Woolley's old Oxford college. Well-known as a wit and raconteur, Bowra was a leading light of a group of aesthetes who dominated the Oxford literary scene in the twenties and thirties. Born in China, he was educated at Cheltenham College, and studied Greek at New College Oxford from 1915, interrupting his education to serve in the Royal Field Artillery from 1917. He returned to complete his degree with first class honours and was elected a tutor and fellow of Wadham College in 1922, where he resided until his death. He became Warden in 1938, was Professor of Poetry from 1946 to 1950, was knighted in 1951 and served as Vice-Chancellor from 1951 to 1954.

Wellingborough Grammar School had links with Wadham through the earlier music teacher, Mr Appleby, and the current Headmaster, Mr Woolley, who were both undergraduates at the college.

Sir Maurice was an astute operator and took Wadham College from relative obscurity to academic excellence by the simple expedient of setting up a substantial number of scholarships. In mathematics, for example, Wadham offered 2 major scholarships of £100, 2 minor scholarships of £60 and an exhibition of £40, while most other colleges offered perhaps one or two. Wadham therefore attracted far more entrants in proportion and the college was able to take its pick of the best. Wellingborough Grammar School was to send some of its scholars to compete for entrance at Wadham. The first of these, K. R. Spencer won a major open scholarship to Wadham in 1945, and over the years several more boys were to follow in his footsteps.

Those of us who were students at Wadham during the long reign of Sir Maurice remember him with warm affection. He was a character renowned throughout the university whose verbal wit far outstripped his considerable writing power. Dinner on high table with him was a revelation, for he could eat and talk simultaneously, flinging food between his lips without interrupting his narrative, and clearing his plate before his spell-bound audience were able to eat a morsel.

My daughter was christened in the college chapel and I invited him to attend. He asked me if she would cry. I assured him she was unlikely to do so, and he smiled saying, "not a christening if she doesn't cry." As the water touched her head, she yelled heartily, with Sir Maurice standing in the ante-chapel looking in, beaming quietly.

(David Tall, WGS 1952–60, Wadham Oxford, 1960–66)

1944 Mr R. G. Routh MA, late headmaster of Bromsgrove School

Robert Gordon Routh was a replacement for the original guest, John Murray, MA, LLD, Principal of University College, Exeter. A significant headmaster of a highly regarded public school, Routh was head during the First World War when an astonishing five old boys were awarded the Victoria Cross. The Routh Hall at the school is named in his honour.

1945 Mr F. R. Salter MA, Senior Tutor of Magdalene College, Cambridge

For what turned out to be the last guest of the Woolley era, the School Hall was considered no longer large enough to accommodate Speech Day and it was transferred, for the only time to the Palace Cinema. On this occasion, the Senior Tutor of Magdalene College was invited to present the prizes. Again this seemed to be a part of the process of increasing the links between the growing academic ambitions of the Grammar School and the top universities.

Parents' Day 1946–1973

On the appointment of Mr Wrenn, as if to signify a new era, Speech Day was renamed Parent's Day and took place on the same day as the annual cricket match between the parents and the school. On such an occasion it was a happy choice to invite Mr Lay, the school's founding headmaster, to present the prizes, accompanied by his wife who had officially opened the cricket pavilion in the Summer of 1937.

1946 Mr F. C. Lay MA, BSc, City of Oxford School, the first headmaster of Wellingborough Grammar School

Parent's Day on June 20th 1946 was reported in the School Magazine as follows:

> *The combination of Parents' Day with Prize Giving was a departure from our usual practice but it was a great success. The weather caused much misgiving but at the last moment the sun rose to the occasion and half an hour after a thunderstorm we were sitting in the Quad in brilliant weather and welcoming our first Headmaster, Mr F. C. Lay, MA, BSc, now at the City of Oxford School, as principal guest, along with his wife and eldest daughter.*
>
> *The open-air ceremony of prize giving was brief and happy and parents then 'were sent to school' whilst the boys went to watch the fathers lose to the School XI at cricket.*
>
> *Exhibitions in the Labs run by the boys and stalls run by the Parents' Committee provided plenty of attraction, until tea was served in the Quad to about four hundred visitors.*
>
> *School Magazine, Summer, 1946*

1947 Mr G. H. Stainforth MA, Headmaster of Oundle School

The following year the guest was the Headmaster of Oundle School.

> *We are honoured by the presence of Mr G. H. Stainforth, MA, Headmaster of Oundle School, who distributed the prizes. Speaking after the distribution he urged the necessity of treating education, not as a commodity to be sold, but as a development of community life in which parents and School had their part.*
>
> *The full value of such community life would only be felt by continuing it beyond the School Certificate year. The qualities which he thought were given by these later years to character were unselfishness, industry and leadership, all of intense value to the country in present times.*
>
> *School Magazine, Summer, 1947*

1948 Mr G. A. Kolkhorst MA, Exeter College, Oxford

In 1948, the guest was Mr George Kolkhorst, Reader in Spanish at Oxford who had a certain reputation in the university as evidenced on the arrival of poet John Betjeman to study as an undergraduate:

> *Oxford, to which Betjeman repaired in 1925 only after twice failing the math and Latin exam required for entrance, greeted the misfit with open arms. Whenever possible he escaped the company of the uncongenially hearty C. S. Lewis and came under the benign influence — as so many of his distinguished contemporaries did — of the eccentric and iconoclastic dons Maurice Bowra and 'Colonel' George Kolkhorst.*
>
> *(Brooke Allan, The New Criterion, Vol. 23, March 2005, p. 10.)*

As a colleague of Maurice Bowra and a linguist studying Spanish, he proved to be a highly appropriate guest for the School:

> *Mr G. A. Kolkhorst, MA (Exeter College, Oxford), honoured us by distributing the prizes and by addressing an appreciative audience afterwards. He congratulated the School on affording to its members so wide a linguistic variety and urged on scholastic, business and international grounds, the increasing value of a sound knowledge of one or more foreign languages. He was particularly pleased to hear of the introduction of Spanish (his own subject) and thought our pioneering in Russian in this area a most enterprising undertaking.*
>
> *School Magazine, Summer, 1948*

G. A. Kolkhurst presents the prizes in 1948

1949 The Reverend Canon W. Francis Smith, Chairman of Northamptonshire Education Committee

The next guest, with strong local credentials as Chairman of the County Education Committee, was again a worthy individual serving the local community at the highest level. Even so, the editor of the School Magazine appeared to damn him with faint praise in the report of his speech.

> *The Rev. Canon W. Francis Smith, Chairman of Northamptonshire Education Committee, was kind enough to distribute the prizes and to give us a capable address thereafter. He viewed our present national difficulties as a challenge to modern youth and as a cogent reason for earnest devotion by everyone in and out of School to developing his powers for the solution of these problems. Only by being in the position to give of his best and by being willing so to do, can a man hope to make a worth-while contribution to progress towards a stable future.*
>
> *School Magazine, Summer, 1949*

Canon Smith presents the Ferguson Trophy for Work in School to David Law, on behalf of Gryphons House

1950 The Rt Hon. The 7th Earl Spencer

Returning to the local gentry, in 1950, the guest of honour was the Rt Hon. Albert Edward John Spencer (1892–1975), who became Viscount Althorp in 1910, served in the First World War, and became Earl Spencer in 1922. He was the grandfather of Diana, Princess of Wales.

In a brief address, after giving away the prizes, Earl Spencer emphasised the value as a cultural and character-forming influence of a school like ours. School Magazine, Summer, 1950

1951 The Right Reverend Spencer Leeson, the Lord Bishop of Peterborough

In 1951, the guest was the new Lord Bishop of Peterborough, Spencer Leeson, who gave a speech in tune with the mood of the time:

> *After the Prize Distribution, the Bishop gave, from his wealth of high scholastic experience, a pointed address on the necessity of continuing at school beyond the age of sixteen. Only then is the school's best work done both for and by the boy. Only then can he have any real inkling what his lifelong education can and should be.*
>
> School Magazine, Summer, 1951

1952 Mr G. R. G. Mure MA, Warden of Merton College, Oxford

Geoffrey Reginald Gilchrist Mure (1893–1979), a philosopher at Merton College Oxford, was invited in 1952. In his speech he questioned why he had been invited to present the prizes.

Mr Mure presents a prize to John A. Whiffing

> *Our chief guest was G. R. G. Mure, Esq., MA, Warden of Merton College, Oxford. In his address, before distributing the prizes, Mr Mure was highly complimentary to those Old Boys of the School with*

whom he had had contact. He opened his speech with a witty and light-hearted deprecation of his suitability for the duty he was then performing, but went on to warn the school of the danger in modern life of allowing all that the State was doing to improve conditions to sap self-reliance and destroy the sense of adventure.

School Magazine, Summer, 1952

1953 The Rt Hon. the Lord Luke TD, DL

In Coronation year, the school invited the Rt Hon. Ian St John Lawson-Johnston, 2nd Baron Luke (1905–1996) to present the prizes. Lord Luke was the son of George Lawson-Johnston, one-time Chairman of Bovril and noted philanthropist, who was created the 1st Baron Luke of Pavenham in 1929 and purchased the Odell Castle Estate in 1935 from the Alston family who had lived there for 350 years.

The 2nd Lord Luke used his position to good effect, as President of Lloyds Bank International with a number of honorary positions, including the British member of the International Olympic Committee preceding Princess Anne, the Chairman of the National Playing Fields Association and Chairman of the Lord's Taverners Cricket Club.

At Parents' Day, Lord Luke recalled a prize "for doing fairly hard at work and very hard at play", which he had since tried to reverse.

Lord Luke, in his address, hoped that the deep significance of the Coronation would remain with younger folk and not be remembered just as a magnificent spectacle. He congratulated the School on its successes in work and games, and was particularly pleased to see the emphasis laid on French and Spanish among other languages. The tradition of our countrymen, expecting foreigners to speak our language, died hard, and it was our business for future peace and prosperity to make real efforts to understand and talk with men of other lands in their own tongues. To build a new Elizabethan era required each to make the best possible use of his schooling.

School Magazine, Summer, 1952

Head Prefect Jimmy Hyde receives his prize from Lord Luke

A Major Change in Direction

In 1954 Mr Wrenn took a step that was to radically change the nature of the guests at Parents' Day. Before this time, although every guest was a worthy member of society who had made his mark in different ways, few could be considered 'household names'. They included three Oxford academics (plus an honorary fellow), three Cambridge academics (and another who became a professor in London), a Cambridge-educated art historian, four headmasters, two bishops, three local gentry, and the Chairman of the County Education Committee. The next guest won the Nobel Prize for discovering one of the most significant drugs in the history of medicine. He was the first of a line of national and international figures to grace Parents' Day in the coming years.

1954 Sir Alexander Fleming

Sir Alexander Fleming (1881–1955) embodied the qualities desired of the boys at Wellingborough Grammar School. In 1928, while working on an influenza virus, he observed that a mould had developed accidentally on a culture plate and created a bacteria-free circle around itself. Further experiment showed that the mould culture prevented growth of staphylococci, even when diluted 800 times. He named the active substance 'penicillin'. At the time it was difficult to produce in any quantity and his initial research publications received little acclaim until two other scientists, Howard Florey and Ernst Chain, developed a method of purifying penicillin in a practical form. It became a major weapon in fighting bacterial infections during the war and was recognised as the most effective life-saving drug in the world.

When Sir Alexander was invited to present the prizes at Wellingborough Grammar School, it was the first time he had ever been invited as a guest at a school prize day. He thoroughly enjoyed his day, presenting the prizes and declaring the new Fleming Laboratory open. In his address, he gave this advice to those seeking success:

> *"First of all there is work and more work — intelligent work and knowledge sufficient to see where the work leads. Then there is fortune which may play a major part." But he warned: "It is no good just waiting for fortune to smile on you. You must be prepared with sufficient knowledge and experience to take advantage of the good things which*

fortune puts on your plate."

"And to be successful," Sir Alexander said, "it was not only necessary to work hard. Interest in the work was required. It was essential to know what you were doing and why you were doing it."

"Fortune plays a large part in the lives of all successful men," he said. To illustrate his point he told the story of his discovery of penicillin. Of how in 1928 he was working on a very common microbe when a mould dropped from the air on to one of his culture plates, how he investigated its properties which led to his remarkable discovery.

Sir Alexander commented: "I did not want the mould and it was a purely chance happening," adding, "I suppose it had happened before to other workers and they were not interested. It may have happened to me before and I was not interested — I don't know."

Sir Alexander ended his address with these words from the Odyssey: "First the hard rowing, then the favouring breeze." He told the school, "You are doing some of the hard rowing, May you all later experience the favouring breeze."

At last a guest of international repute, known to all in the audience, was there to inspire the boys of Wellingborough Grammar School.

Sir Alexander died in 1955 and was buried a national hero in the crypt of Saint Paul's Cathedral.

Chemistry Master Mr Holmes and Sir Alexander Fleming look on as a pupil carries out an experiment in the new Fleming Laboratory.

1955 Sir Gyles Isham

Sir Gyles Isham presents a prize to Head Boy, Bill Priest, as Miss Bavin and Mr Nicholas look on.

The following year returned to the normal round of guests with Sir Gyles Isham (1903–1976), a descendant of the long line of Ishams of Lamport Hall, who had lived on the same estate since 1560.

Sir Gyles, however, proved to be an interesting character who had been an actor in films, on Broadway and at Stratford in the 20s, 30s and 40s before returning to the family estate to take up his title and settle down to manage the property and develop interests in local history.

In his speech he complimented three boys who had chosen dictionaries as prizes, and extolled the virtues of clear expression in writing and speaking. He went on to say:

> *"A prizegiving is a reminder that whatever opportunities we get, certain people make better use of them than others. They are a reminder that people cannot be equal even if they have equal opportunities." He concluded, saying: "I am most impressed with this long list of successes. This school is equally successful in playing fields and character building. It is schools of this type that are providing the country with what it must have — good brains, well used."*

1956 Mr B. L. Hallward MA, Vice-Chancellor of Nottingham University

As Mr Wrenn continued to strengthen links with the universities, the next guest was the Vice-Chancellor of Nottingham University, Mr Bertrand Leslie Hallward (1901–2003). Prior to being appointed Vice-Chancellor, he had been the Headmaster of Clifton College. The Hallward Library at the university is named after him.

Mr Hallward represented a new departure as the first university guest to formally represent a university other than Oxford and Cambridge (with the exception of Professor Walker of Imperial College London, whose *alma mater* was Cambridge, and John Murray, Principal of University College, Exeter, who was invited in 1944 but

Mr Hallward makes a presentation to R. O. Knight

did not come). Mr Hallward was himself a Cambridge man, having obtained a double first in classics at King's College in 1922. However, he truly represented the University of Nottingham, and in his speech he addressed the broader needs of the nation, speaking of a university life that needed well-rounded students rather than those who only studied single subjects.

1957 His Grace the Duke of Bedford

John Ian Robert Russell, 13th Duke of Bedford (1917–2002) was faced with paying heavy death duties on his father's estate in 1953. To solve the problem, he opened the family home, Woburn Abbey, to the public, turning the grounds into a wild animal reserve aided by the famous Chipperfield circus family. Woburn soon became a popular tourist venue for the British public and foreign tourists, including the annual excursion day from the Grammar School. In his speech on Parents' Day he told his audience that half a million visitors had been to Woburn in the first three years.

The Duke of Bedford presents the Biology Prize to A. J. (Tony) Doyle

1958 Sir John Cockcroft KCB

In 1958, with another science laboratory to name, Mr Wrenn succeeded in inviting a second Nobel Prize winner—Sir John Douglas Cockcroft (1897–1967)—who was fabled as the first man (working with his colleague Ernest Walton) to split the atom in 1932. They did this by bombarding lithium with high-energy protons, breaking it down to helium and other elements, taking the first step in the development of nuclear power. He did his best research work at the Cavendish Laboratory in Cambridge.

After working on radar at the beginning of the second world war, he spent two years in Canada in charge of the Canadian Atomic Energy Project, returning to Britain to set up the Atomic Energy Research Establishment at Harwell. He was later to be the first Master of Churchill College, Cambridge, 1959–67, and Chancellor of the Australian National University, 1961–65.

At the Parents' Day, Sir John presented the prizes, including one to sixth-former, David Frost. Following the prize giving, Sir John declared the school Cockcroft Laboratory formally open. After the ceremony he had a tight schedule and, leaving too late to travel to London in time to catch a plane to Copenhagen, he arranged for a flight from Sywell to Heathrow.

Sir John Cockcroft presents a prize to sixth-former David Frost

1959 Sir W. Lawrence Bragg OBE, MC, FRS

The next year, Mr Wrenn secured the attendance of a third Nobel Prize winner: Sir William Lawrence Bragg CH, FRS (1890–1971) the youngest ever recipient of the Prize. As a child living in Adelaide, Lawrence, aged 5, fell off his tricycle and his father, a professor of mathematics and physics, used newly discovered X-rays to study the break. His interest in science developed early and he studied mathematics, chemistry and physics at Adelaide University from the age of 14, graduating in 1908, and moving with his family to England. He completed a physics degree at Trinity College, Cambridge in 1911 and as a first year graduate, he saw how to calculate the position of atoms in a crystal by observing how an X-ray beam is diffracted by the crystal lattice. He shared the idea with his father and their joint research was awarded the Nobel Prize in Physics in 1915. During both wars he worked on sound-ranging techniques to locate enemy guns and, from 1919 to 1937, he was Professor of Physics at Manchester, being knighted in 1941. After World War II he returned to Cambridge, organising the Cavendish Laboratory into research groups and becoming interested in the structure of proteins. His X-ray methods were instrumental in the work of Crick and Watson's discovery of the structure of DNA.

In 1953 he accepted the position as Resident Professor at the Royal Institution in London where he proposed a series of lectures for children that continue to this day.

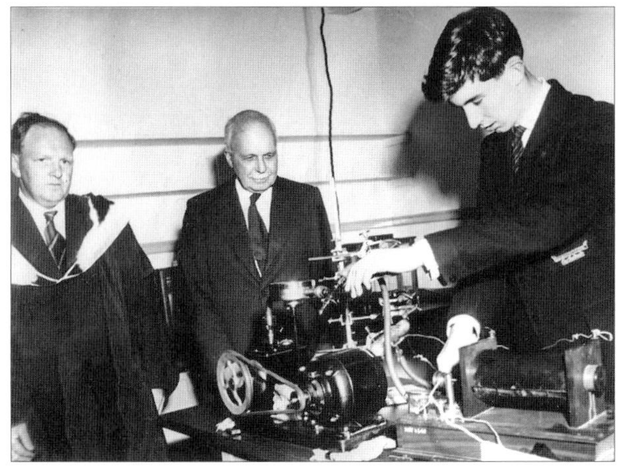

Sir Lawrence Bragg (centre) and physics teacher Mr Huddart observe a pupil carrying out an experiment

1960 Lord Birkett

Lord Birkett presents the Senior Music Prize to David Tall

The Right Honourable (William) Norman Birkett, 1st Baron Birkett of Ulverston, PC (1883–1962) was educated at the Grammar School, Barrow-in-Furness and Emmanuel College, Cambridge, where he became President of the Cambridge Union. He was called to the Bar in 1913, specialising in criminal defence, becoming famous for his persuasive advocacy, including the notorious 'Brighton Trunk Crime' of 1934, where the accused, Mancini, was faced with overwhelming evidence against him yet was acquitted by Birkett's defence. Many years later, Mancini admitted his guilt.

Birkett also represented Mrs Wallis Simpson when she filed for divorce to marry King Edward VIII. His experience of war-time trials led him to be preferred over more senior colleagues as one of two British Judges at the Nuremberg Trials. He was appointed to the Privy Council in 1947, awarded a peerage as 1st Baron Birkett in 1948, and served as a Lord Justice of Appeal from 1950 until he retired in 1957.

At the prize giving, he took an interest in each boy as he gave him his prize and began his speech by saying, "There is no success in this world worthwhile unless you become a man of integrity." He told the boys that the greatest achievement they could gain at school of the most value to them later was a mastery of English.

> *I believe that every boy in this school — and every boy in the world — has some special gift of his own. Whatever you do, put all you have into it. Do your very best.*

Following the pattern of earlier years, Mr Wrenn intended to name a room after Lord Birkett to add to the laboratories named after Fleming, Cockcroft and Bragg. However, the planned extensions had not yet materialized and Lord Birkett gave his name to a room that would become a lecture theatre when the new building scheme was completed.

A typical speech day in the quad (in 1960), with masters in their gowns, boys in their uniforms, parents in their 'Sunday best', and a largely female audience, presumably because many of the fathers were at work.

1961 Mr W. J. Penn, Chairman of the Northamptonshire Education Committee

In 1961 the guest of honour was Mr Penn, Chairman of the County Education Committee, a friend of the school who was a regular attendee at the School Parents' Days. Rather than the usual aspirational speech, exhorting the boys to greater achievements, the headlines in the next day's paper rang out his message: "BOREDOM: BOYS WARNED – One of society's biggest enemies." He went on to advise the boys to have interests of their own: "You have the right to enjoy life, including work, play and hobbies, and I advise you all to have hobbies." He continued by saying that some of the modern generation considered their elders as "squares", and advised them: "What you don't like about us discard, and what you do like, keep."

He acknowledged the need for the school to have a new hall and expressed the hope that this would happen by 1964. However, if Mr Wrenn thought the invitation would warm the relationship with the Education Committee, he was given little comfort from Mr Penn, who went on to say:

> *You may need several acres of land for playing fields. We, the Education Committee, cannot buy it but it may well be that the Wellingborough Urban Council can do something about it.*

Head boy Michael Kitson receives his prize from Mr Penn, with Chairman of the Governors, Mr Steele, and Headmaster, Mr Wrenn, looking on

1962 Sir William Penney KBE,
Director of the Atomic Energy Commission

The next year, Mr Wrenn got back on course, with Sir William Penney (1909–91), generally acknowledged as the 'father' of the British atomic bomb. A grammar school boy in Colchester, he transferred to Sheerness Technical College where he gained a scholarship to Imperial College London, graduating with first class honours and subsequently a PhD. After two years in the United States at the University of Wisconsin he was awarded a scholarship at Trinity College, Cambridge, obtaining a second doctorate in 1935 with a thesis applying quantum mechanics to the physics of crystals. In 1936, he returned as Reader in Mathematics at Imperial College until 1945.

During World War II he was loaned out to the Home Office and the Admiralty, where he investigated the properties of under-water blast waves, gaining essential insight for the design of ships and torpedoes. He supervised the development of the Mulberry harbours placed off the Normandy beaches during the D-Day landings.

In 1944 he returned to America to participate in the Manhattan Project to design the atom bomb. One of his assignments was to predict the damage effects from the blast waves of an atomic explosion. Considered to be one of the most distinguished British contributors to the work, he was flown to Japan with Group Captain Leonard Cheshire to observe the bombing of Nagasaki from the air. He later attended atomic explosions on the Bikini Atoll, enhancing his reputation when the Americans' sophisticated test gauges failed and he saved the day by calculating the blast power using observations from more simple devices.

In 1946 the Truman administration denied Britain access to US atomic research. Penney left the United States and submitted plans for a British Atomic Weapons Section to Lord Portal, Marshal of the Royal Air Force. Prime Minister Attlee decided that Britain must have an atomic bomb to maintain its position in world politics. In the words of Foreign Secretary Ernest Bevan, "We've got to have it and it's got to have a bloody union jack on it!" Project High Explosive Research was set in motion with Penney as head. The first British atom bomb was detonated on islands off the coast of Western Australia in 1952 and the first British hydrogen bomb was developed and tested in 1957. He was knighted in 1962, awarded a life peerage in 1967, and created a member of the Order of Merit in 1969. The William Penney Laboratory at Imperial College is named after him.

Speaking to the School on Parents' Day 1962, Sir William gave advice that was a model of clarity and insight as is clear from the report of his speech in the local newspaper:

> *We are living in a scientific age and are alive to our dependence on science. It was quite right that we should spend money, time and effort, teaching our young people about science.*
>
> *Although a fuse could be mended without a detailed knowledge of electricity and a car could be driven without a knowledge of thermodynamics, we couldn't live today without people understanding the principles of scientific knowledge.*
>
> *Many people were born to appreciate music and art, but nobody was born with a knowledge of science. The laws of science were difficult to understand — they had to be taught.*
>
> *The first aim of any advanced country was therefore to have science taught properly in schools.*
>
> *Sir William said that in his opinion science provided as good a training as any for management and commerce, and in so many other fields which so far it had not penetrated.*

Sir Willliam Penney addressing the audience in 1962

The increase in the number of scientists in the next decade would enable them to move into areas which at present were not manned by scientists.

"There is some way to go before we have enough scientists in these important fields of management," he emphasised.

"Pupils studying scientific subjects usually thought of research as their ultimate aim, but there were very few people engaged in pure research. The majority who worked in industry and government departments were working on applied research.

"To those young men seriously thinking of becoming scientists, they might think of the lustre that goes with research and discovery, but they should realise the greatest need is for those who develop and apply research. This is where science pays off," he said.

"This country had a great record of discovery and invention, but it was rather patchy when it came to discoveries that had not been applied."

Sir William quoted figures to show the need for more scientists. "Out of the working population today, eight in every thousand were either scientists or qualified technicians. Plans had been made to increase this figure to 13 in a thousand by 1970. Half of these people would be in industry, the remainder in educational and government establishments."

"In the next ten years these numbers would have to go up by fifty per cent, so the next decade would provide an opportunity to make a good start in the scientific world," he told students.

"The demand at the moment seems to be insatiable but according to various government predictions, the supply will meet the demand by the end of the decade. But these estimates are based on people working as full-time scientists. It does not allow for people who will go into work which is not fully scientific.

"In the past, scientific advances were usually due to the work of one gifted individual, but today, although there were still some 'extraordinary individuals', there was a movement towards teamwork.

"Scientists had not only to be good at their chosen subject, they also had to learn to work with others. They had to act in a different way from the long-haired, absent-minded types of a few years ago."

Turning to the headmaster Mr H. A. Wrenn, he said: "It seems to me this school is a very progressive one. You are training your young people in the right way."

1963 Sir Compton Mackenzie OBE

As a complete change from the focus on science in the previous year, Mr Wrenn's next guest was Sir Compton Mackenzie (1883–1972), a popular author of books such as *Whisky Galore* (which had been made into a well-known comedy film) and *Monarch of the Glen* (subsequently a TV series), he was also co-founder of the Scottish Nationalist Party, and the founder Editor of the *Gramophone Magazine* back in 1923.

At Parents' Day, Sir Compton was introduced by Alderman Steele, Chairman of the Governors, as "the most outstanding literary figure of this century," and Sir Compton amused his listeners to such an extent that he had to pause frequently for the laughter to die down as he told of his scholarly adventures

> *Sir Compton Mackenzie, in a sparkling speech at Wellingborough Grammar School Prizegiving ceremony related a number of anecdotes from his youth and said: "I'm a frightful fraud. I set as bad an example in my day as anybody and I have no right really to be talking to you."*
>
> *He advised the boys not to take up a career to please their fathers, grandfathers or uncles or they would always be wishing they had done something else. The important thing was to know what they did not want to do.*

Sir Compton Mackenzie in the school library named after him with Mrs Cox (Vice-chairman of Governors), Alderman Steele (Chairman), and Headmaster Mr Wrenn

About the school library, which is dedicated to Sir Compton, he said he was deeply touched. He would always think of the library, and it would be a precious memory. At his age it was good to think he would be remembered by the young.

"I don't think I know what it is to be old," he said. "The 'New Statesman' once said I was suffering from arrested development, and I suppose I am. I have been called the playboy of the Western world. I suppose if one has that sort of reputation, one doesn't really grow old."

One of Sir Compton's memories concerned his "nervous breakdown" at the age of 17. He was bored with school and wanted to leave, and to achieve this he decided not to sleep for a fortnight. He kept awake by reading Virgil and Edgar Allen Poe, and occasionally dozed off, but never for more than half an hour. After a fortnight he was able to give "a pretty good imitation of a nervous breakdown."

His mother sent him to one of the best doctors in London, who looked at him and said: "What's the game?" He decided to take the doctor into his confidence and explained that he wanted to leave school. The doctor wrote a letter to say it would be just as well if he left.

"And the day after, Ladysmith was relieved, I was relieved," said Sir Compton. "I was sent down to recover from this nervous breakdown at a hydro in Bournemouth, and, believe it or not, I had recovered before we passed Clapham Junction."

At the age of 17, filling in time before going to Magdalen College, Oxford, he went to a tutor in Hertfordshire and was then commissioned in the 1st Hertfordshire Regiment. "Therefore," he said, "I am the youngest man alive today with Queen Victoria's commission — should I not be stuffed and put in a museum?" Then he added: "If I'm going to name your library, perhaps I should be stuffed and put there."

Evening Telegraph, May, 1962

1964 Lieutenant-General Sir Brian Horrocks KCB

The next year it was the turn of war-hero Lieutenant-General Sir Brian Horrocks (1885–1985). He was well-known as a television presenter on military history and as Black Rod in the House of Commons.

As the son of a doctor in the Royal Army Medical Corps, he was educated in boarding school and at the Royal Military College academy where he came second to bottom in his class. Had the First World War not begun, he might never have been given a commission. As it was he joined the Middlesex Regiment and fought in the Battles of Mons and Armentiéres where he was shot in the stomach and captured. He made a number of escape attempts, at one time getting within a few hundred metres of the Dutch border before being caught. After the war, having learned Russian from his fellow Russian prisoners, he was posted to Russia as part of the mission during the Russian Civil War where he was again captured, this time by the Red Army, and spent another ten months as a prisoner. On return, he competed in the modern pentathlon at the 1924 Olympics in Paris, followed by a variety of posts in the army as an instructor at staff college and an adjutant in the Territorial Army.

In the Second World War he was posted to France to command the 2nd Battalion of the Middlesex Regiment, taking part in the retreat at Dunkirk. He was then posted to command the XIII Corps of Montgomery's Eighth Army in Africa where Rommel was currently in the ascendancy and Montgomery was preparing a major counter attack. Rommel attacked once more and, mindful that Horrocks had never commanded a division in battle, Montgomery instructed him to repel the attack without losing too many casualties. Horrocks planned a defensive battle with his army dug in around a ridge with the Germans battered by the Desert Air Force. Although the Germans won

Mr Wrenn with Sir Brian Horrocks

the position, they did so at great cost. For a time, Horrocks was reduced to leading small-scale raids as Britain's main force pursued Rommel. As the Axis forces tried to fight back, Horrocks, now in command of X Corps including the 1st Armoured division, carried out a brilliant flanking manoeuvre through a pass that the Germans considered impenetrable, forcing them to retreat. Horrocks was severely injured in an air raid and spent 14 months in recovery.

On his return to active service, he was posted to Europe in charge of XXX Corps pushing through Belgium, capturing Brussels, and making so much progress that they advanced over 250 miles in six days. However, he was overstretched and narrowly failed to reach Arnhem in an operation that became the basis of the film *A Bridge Too Far*. Despite this set-back, XXX Corps pressed on, forcing the German Army over the Rhine and capturing Bremen. Horrocks officially accepted the German surrender in the north of Germany on behalf of the Allies.

After the war he served in the British Army of the Rhine until 1949 when he retired on ill-health caused by his long-standing wounds in North Africa. Back in civilian life he became director of a construction company and presenter of several TV series covering military history, which he subsequently edited into a series of books covering the history of a number of British regiments.

At Prize day, Mr Wrenn told the parents and pupils that Sir Brian would be carrying on the tradition of naming a classroom:

> *"Henceforth", he said, "the senior history room would bear the name of one who had helped first to make modern history and then to bring the history of earlier times to life on radio and television."*

1965 David Cecil, 6th Marquess of Exeter

In the next year, the focus turned back to the nobility with a visit from David George Brownlow Cecil, the 6th Marquess of Exeter (1905–1981), styled Lord David Burghley before he inherited his title in 1956. As David Burghley, in 1927, he sprinted round the Great Court at Trinity College in the time it took the clock to strike 12 o'clock, inspiring the famous scene in the film *Chariots of Fire*. In 1928, he won the 400m hurdles Gold Medal at the Olympic Games. He later served 40 years as President of the British Amateur Athletic Association, 30 years as

President of the International Amateur Athletic Federation, and 48 years as a member of the International Olympic Committee, chairing the Organizing Committee of the 1948 Olympics.

At Parents' Day, he gave what the local newspaper described as "an inspiring pep talk", telling the boys to aim high to take full advantage of the opportunities in the world outside.

The Marquess of Exeter presenting the Ferguson Trophy to J. Forster on behalf of the Lions

> *He told the large assembly that he did not learn that all subjects he was taught were important until he left school, but the boys had the opportunity to do so now and they must grasp it. The world they were going out to was constantly changing, but amidst all the automation there would still be a need for men with skills.*
>
> *Britain had got to look to its exports and by that he meant particular European exports. If the pupils went to other countries in the course of their jobs it was important that they knew more than just one or two foreign languages. They had got to know what to say and what not to say as well as something of the background of other people. That is why it was important to pay attention to other subjects, classics in particular, as they did have more than a little bearing on the present day world and its daily round of events.*

He went on to decry the role of politics in sport, saying,

> *Sport could play a major part towards achieving world peace, by bringing together the ordinary people of the world who had the same ideals and conceptions of life.*

1966 Admiral of the Fleet, the Earl Mountbatten of Burma

With his next guest, Mr Wrenn hit the jackpot, with a major figure in the Royal family: Earl Louis Mountbatten (1900–1979), a direct descendant of Queen Victoria, born in Windsor Castle, and uncle of Prince Philip. In his distinguished career he served in the Navy in World War I, started World War II as commander of the 4th Destroyer Flotilla, famed for his daring exploits before his ship was sunk in the 1940 Crete Campaign. In 1941 he was made Chief of Combined Operations, leading a disastrous raid on Dieppe in 1942, then being assigned as Supreme Allied Commander in the South East Asia Command, overseeing the recapture of Burma from the Japanese led by General William Slim. Clement Attlee appointed him Viceroy of India (1947–8), where he oversaw the creation of the newly independent India and Pakistan in 1947. He later served as First Sea Lord (1955–59) and as Chief of the Defence Staff (1959–1965).

His visit to Wellingborough Grammar School was to formally open the new Mountbatten Hall at the School as guest on Parents' Day. Such was his popularity that the audience was packed tightly in the Hall with the overflow of boys and visitors in the gymnasium linked by loudspeaker.

In his speech, he told the boys that education does not end with school days and the most important thing to carry from school is the ability to continue learning.

> *"I knew more about the Navy than the First Sea Lord, and more about the RAF than the Chief of Air Staff when I presided at our meetings," he said, "but that was because I had spent many hours studying the papers on the subject we were going to discuss."*

He recalled that he left school at the age of 16 but continued to attend courses and to add to his knowledge by self-education. He advised

Lord Mountbatten speaks to a capacity audience at Parents' Day 1966

boys to build character by emulating the best qualities in the people they met and worked with.

> *Two important qualities which every boy should try to acquire were initiative and leadership: for those qualities the best person to emulate was Sir Winston Churchill. Quoting from three of Sir Winston's speeches in the dark days of 1940, Earl Mountbatten said that they were not only an inspiration, they gave the nation the quality of leadership which was needed.*

1967 Group Captain (later Sir) Douglas Bader CBE, DSO, DFC

Douglas Bader (1910–1982), the flying ace from the Second World War, lost both his legs in a low-flying aerobatic manoeuvre at the Reading Aero Club in 1931 when the tip of the left wing of his Bristol Bulldog fighter touched the ground. Both legs were amputated, one above and one below the knee. Invalided out of the RAF, he used his connections to rejoin when war broke out, commanding a wing of fighters, personally shooting down 23 German planes by August 1941. During an operation, he collided in mid-air with a German fighter over France and was captured by the Germans, finishing the war in Colditz Prison Camp. His biography *Reach for the Sky* was a best seller and was made into a popular film in 1956 with his role played by Kenneth More.

At the prize giving, he showed that he was not a man to bow to convention and completely shattered the formal atmosphere when he took off his jacket and sat through the proceedings with his shirt sleeves rolled up. The *Evening Telegraph* reported:

> *As the headmaster Mr H. A. Wrenn delivered his report, Group Captain Bader sat listening in a temperature of over seventy degrees. Casually he rose, apologised for interrupting Mr Wrenn and took off his jacket. Mr Wrenn told pupils they may follow suit and many were obviously grateful for the Group Captain's initiative.*
>
> *This was typical of the extraordinary way he handled himself throughout the proceedings. His refreshing speech was divided into two parts: first he had serious words of advice for the pupils. Then, on a lighter note, he gently poked fun at the school governors and other dignitaries on the stage.*
>
> *Group Captain Bader, tight-lipped throughout, and with a resolute look*

of determination, told boys to remember above all else: "Whatever you do, always remember you have to look yourself in the face afterwards. The important thing is not what you have won your prizes for today," he added. "It is not exam results or games successes. But the thing is this: when you go out from here someone will show you an easier, quicker way to do things … a dishonest way. But you learn in this school the difference between right and wrong."

Referring to the naming of a basement engineering department at the school after himself, the Group Captain said: "I didn't realise you lot were such snobs. When Earl Mountbatten visited you last year you named this hall after him. You've put me in the basement."

He was talking over a loudspeaker system which also relayed his voice to the school gymnasium where boys and parents sat who had been unable to cram into the main hall.

Group Captain Bader said the headmaster had a particularly difficult job on such occasions. "Firstly he has to present his report in an entertaining way. But he also has to suck up to the governors," he added amid laughter, "The procedure remains the same …", he continued, "but I must say Mr Wrenn's speech was one of the best I have heard … and I have heard a few."

Another unusual feature came when Group Captain Bader had

Alderman Steele, Group Captain Bader and Mr Wrenn.

finished presenting the boys' prizes. For he also had a prize for 'good conduct' for the chairman, Alderman E. A. Steele, who was apparently very surprised.

In thanking the guests, the County Chief Education Officer, Mr G. E. Churchill added a word of praise for the headmaster. "He's done it again," he said, referring to Mr Wrenn's ability to bring a nationally famous figure to the school.

1968 Lord Robert and Lady Boothby

The informal atmosphere continued the next year as Lord Robert Boothby (1900–1986) brought his wife Lady Wanda Boothby whom he had married the previous year. Lady Boothby was to present the prizes on his behalf, becoming the first and only lady to do so.

Bob Boothby was a long-serving Conservative MP from 1924–1958 and a life peer after that as Baron Boothby of Buchan and Rattray Head. In his early years as a Parliamentarian, he was the Parliamentary Private Secretary to Winston Churchill for three years and was a frequent visitor to Germany where he met Hitler in 1933. In his book *Boothby: Recollections of a Rebel* (1978), he recalled:

I received a telephone call from my friend 'Putzi' Hanfstaengi, who was at that time Hitler's personal private secretary and court jester. He told me that the Führer had been reading my speeches with interest, and would like to see me at his headquarters in the Esplanade Hotel.

It is true that when I walked across the long room to a corner in which he was sitting writing, in a brown shirt with a swastika on his arm, he waited without looking up until I had reached his side, then sprang to his feet, lifted his right arm, and shouted "Hitler!"; and that I responded by clicking my heels together, raising my right arm, and shouting back: "Boothby!"

I talked with Hitler for over an hour; and it was not long before I detected the unmistakable glint of madness in his eyes. ... He had no sense of humour. He asked me how I would feel if Germany had beaten us in the last war, and driven a corridor between England and Scotland. I said: "You forget, Herr Hitler, that I come from Scotland. We should have been delighted." He did not smile. Instead he brought his fist down with a crash on the table and said: "So! I had no idea that the hatred between the two peoples was so great." Perhaps this was one of the

> *reasons why he sent Hess to Scotland in 1940, for I am sure that he did; and why he never bombed Edinburgh.*

Lord Boothby came to the Grammar School against his doctor's advice to give his name to the School's new language laboratory. He brought his wife to present the prizes and give a speech. But then he stood up and declared:

> *Yesterday my doctor told me you must stop making speeches and drinking whisky. I said you may stop me drinking whisky — with a dash of luck — but you will never stop me making speeches.*

Never afraid to speak his mind, he went on to "cast a few pearls of sense" on the debate about immigration, suggesting that "most of the people of this country are very moderate-minded, kind, reasonable, decent and sensible," but "they want to put some definite limit on immigration in this tiny island." As a former Rector of St Andrew's University, he said:

> *"By electing Sir Leary Constantine as Rector of St Andrew's University, the students of St Andrew's have done more good for racial feeling than all the politicians put together."*
>
> *Lord Boothby then turned to education and advised his audience to be educated at St Andrew's. "Never mind Oxford or Cambridge, St Andrew's is best."*

Lord Boothby looks on as his wife speaks after presenting the prizes

Although he was not in the least opposed to comprehensive education or public schools, both were open to improvement, and both had a role to play. But the core of English secondary education lay in the grammar schools which were the great nurseries of our universities and technical colleges. "They are the core of our education generally and you are the proof of it."

1969 Mr (later Sir) Peter Scott CBE DSc LlD

Peter Markham Scott (1909–1989), who was later knighted in 1973, was the only son of the explorer, Scott of the Antarctic. He excelled in many activities as ornithologist, conservationist, painter, author, radio and television commentator and—for recreation—he was also a champion glider pilot and Olympic bronze medallist yachtsman. He was educated at Oundle and Trinity College Cambridge where he began studying biology but graduated in history of art, in preparation for a life as a wild-life painter. In the war he sailed in the Navy in light coastal ships to counter fast German torpedo-boats in the English Channel. After the war, he set up the Wildfowl Trust as Slimbridge in Gloucestershire and founded the World Wild-Life Fund, using his artistic talents to design its panda logo.

He later gave the scientific name of *Nessiteras rhombopteryx* to the Loch Ness Monster so that it could be registered as an endangered

Peter Scott looks at display material in the Scott Geography Room with his wife Phillipa

species. The name, based on Greek, means "the wonder of Ness with the diamond shaped fin" but it is also an anagram of "Monster hoax by Sir Peter S".

In his speech at Wellingborough Grammar School, he spoke about the monster, saying:

> *Some people said it was a dragon, others a griffin. I think it may be a fish, a catfish or an eel. I am prepared to think there may be nothing there at all.*

He focused on the need for enthusiasm for constructive hobbies to counteract boredom that was causing people to indulge in mindless destruction in society, then turned his attention to the great problems facing the world: nuclear weapons, overpopulation and pollution.

> *"The affluent society had become the effluent society," he said.*
>
> *Warning of dangers of lead poisoning in the atmosphere — caused by the lead from petrol fumes — Mr Scott pointed out that the incidence of lead fumes in the Arctic was already at a measurable amount.*

1970 HRH Prince William of Gloucester

Prince William of Gloucester (1941–1972) was a grandson of King George V. He spent his early childhood in Barnwell Manor, near Oundle, Northamptonshire, and was educated at Eton and Magdalene College, Cambridge, where he read history.

After graduation, he joined the diplomatic service, first in Nigeria in 1965, then transferring to Japan in 1968. He returned to Barnwell Manor in 1970 to manage the estate and carry out public duties as a member of the royal family, on occasion serving as Counsellor of State in the absence of his cousin, the Queen.

On his visit to the Grammar School in 1970, Prince William spoke about his experiences, criticising the press reporting of the tragic Biafran war in Nigeria and prophesying the future role of Japan as an economic power. He then visited the Mathematics Department to unveil a plaque in his name.

Prince William was a certified pilot and owned several aircraft. In August 1972, he died when the aircraft he was piloting crashed near Wolverhampton.

Prince William presenting the prizes in 1970

1971 Group Captain (later Baron) Leonard Cheshire VC, DSO, DFC

Mr Wrenn invited another war hero in 1971, described in the *Evening Telegraph* in the following terms:

> *World war II bomber ace and holder of the Victoria Cross, Group Capt. Leonard Cheshire, will join the long line of distinguished guests when he presents the prizes at the school's speech day on September 14.*
>
> *Group Captain Cheshire was one of the two official British Government observers in the American plane which dropped the atomic bomb on Nagasaki. The second observer, scientist Sir William Penney, has already presented the prizes at the Wellingborough school.*
>
> *Group Capt. Cheshire told headmaster Mr H. A. Wrenn he knew most of the school's previous guests and would be very happy to join his name to the list. "Naturally we are very glad to get him," said Mr Wrenn. Group Capt. Cheshire, founder of the Cheshire homes for the incurably ill, also holds the DSO and the DFC. He has written several books and a school tradition will be upheld when the English building is named after him following his visit.*
>
> *Last year's guest, Prince William of Gloucester, gave his name to the Maths department. Previous distinguished guests include Earl Mountbatten, Lord Boothby, Group Capt. Douglas Bader, Sir Compton Mackenzie, Sir John Cockcroft, and Lieutenant General Sir Brian Horrocks, who accepted the German surrender at the end of the war.*

Leonard Cheshire (1917–1992) was educated at Stowe School and Merton College Oxford where he graduated in Jurisprudence in 1939. At the outbreak of the war he joined the RAF, and in March 1943, he became the youngest Group Captain aged 25. He was awarded the Victoria Cross after completing a hundred bombing missions on heavily defended targets in Germany.

In his speech at the School, Group Captain Cheshire said:

"It is not the great campaigns and causes that count, nor doing the spectacular and great things in life, but doing the things that are within our reach and doing them well."

He did not intend to talk about his own experiences during the Second World War, but what he had learnt during the war. "We lived through those years believing that all we needed to do was win the war and then there would be a golden era of peace. But winning the war was one thing; winning peace was another."

He added: "it is no use saying 'we don't want war, we want peace.' If we are to have peace we have each got to play our part."

Group Captain Cheshire said he had thought the answer lay in joining a cause or campaign, but he had found by helping individuals who were disabled that he was playing his role. He is the founder of the Cheshire Homes which help disabled and incurably sick people all over the world.

Captain Leonard Cheshire arriving with Mr Wrenn

1972 Old Grammarian (later Sir) David Frost OBE

At last, in 1972, Mr Wrenn invited back Wellingborough Grammar School's own *enfant terrible*, David Frost. David showed enormous promise as an actor and mimic during his schooldays, with his widely known take-off of Mr Tompkins (Tonk), "Whatcha got there? A pork pie?", and his equally good voices for Mr Jackson and others. Although a model student at school, Mr Wrenn and he did not see eye-to-eye when David performed badly in his examinations at Cambridge and received a tersely worded note from the headmaster decrying his lack of effort.

David had other objectives in view: editing the literary magazine *Granta* and secretary of the *Footlights* comedy troupe, including Peter Cook and John Bird. After University, he shot into the headlines with the satirical TV show *That Was The Week That Was*, following it up with *The Frost Report*, *Frost over England*, and other programmes, conquering American television with *Frost on America*.

In his speech, David told the pupils:

Headmaster Mr Wrenn, Head of Economics, Mr Ward, and David Frost admire his commemoration plaque in the Economics Room

"It's great to be here. It's a dream come true to visit one's old school in this way. I remember my schooldays as ones of great happiness."

He recalled his correspondence with the 'Evening Telegraph' under various assumed names and recalled a letter condemning a nude statue at the Swanspool in Wellingborough as "an affront to public decency."

He said: "When I was here 15 years ago it was a different era. War was moral and sex was not."

After the ceremony, he gave his name to the Economics Room accompanied by the Headmaster and the Head of Economics, Mr R. V. S. Ward.

In later years David was knighted and continued his success in television, a household name not only in England but in the White House, America, as the only man to interview all the last seven American Presidents and the last six British Prime Ministers.

1973 The Rt Hon Lord Maybray-King, former Speaker of the House of Commons

In 1973, the guest of honour was the retired Speaker of the House of Commons, Lord Horace Maybray-King (1901–1986). Lord King was a schoolteacher in Southampton after graduation with a first-class degree in English from King's College London. Working in his spare time he obtained a PhD from King's College in 1940. He was excused military service due to a duodenal ulcer, and continued as a teacher, becoming a headmaster in 1947. He was elected to Hampshire county council in 1946 and served until 1965 with a three-year break. He won the Southampton Test seat in 1950, transferring to Southampton Itchen from 1955 to 1970. For the last five years, he was the first Labour Speaker of the House of Commons (1965–70), being awarded a peerage on his retirement, and serving as the Deputy Speaker of the House of Lords.

Lord King was to be the last guest at the last Parents' Day at Wellingborough Grammar School.

Poacher Turned Gamekeeper

David Wilson (1952–60, 1964–1975)

Several Old Boys taught at the school; some before they went to University, others were recruited after they had qualified. I was one of the latter. It began when I received a letter from Mr Wrenn offering me a position as English teacher if I wanted it. Well I wanted it and duly replied indicating my eagerness. I was invited to the School for what I expected to be a formal interview at the end of June 1964.

Mr Wrenn took me in to his office, he shook my hand and we sat down. After a couple of pleasantries he asked if I would like the job to which I replied "Yes, sir." "Good," he said. "Here's a piece of paper. Write on it, ' Today I have accepted the position of assistant master to teach English at Wellingborough Grammar School' and sign it. I'll write that I have accepted you." We wrote for a minute or so in silence. We then exchanged papers and the deal was done. "Now you can go round to staff room and introduce yourself to Mr Nicholas." I could hardly believe that I had been accepted so quickly and so easily into my old school.

Mr Nicholas knew that I was coming for interview and he knew that I would be accepted; and so it appeared did other staff who shook my hand and welcomed me. There was never any question that I was now an equal. "Hello, David, I'm Tony," said Tony Sparrow and Richard Temple simply said, "Welcome back." John Dunning approached me and shook my hand. "You'll be teaching geography but don't worry about anything, I know you're getting married soon so you worry about that and I'll take care of your lessons for next term." He did. When I took up my position in the September he simply handed me a sheaf of papers – the first month's lesson plans – including the maps I had to draw on the board.

Masters I had known as strict and even frightening as a boy were now my colleagues. We all worked together for the school and it soon became apparent that there were very few who did not contribute to the success of Sports Days, School Plays, Speech Days and the like. There were jobs for all and we did them willingly and whole-heartedly for the most part.

A good example of the corporate spirit that existed was when my first son was born. I had been made aware that there were items that parents of new-born babies would find useful available to staff. John Huddart was the co-ordinator of these items and as soon as No.1 son was born he arrived at school with a large wicker-work crib and stand with all the necessary fitted sheets, mattress etc., a set of baby scales which must have come from a maternity unit somewhere, and several other items I cannot now remember. This equipment was shared round the staff as the need arose (and since this was before teachers' pay caught up with the rest of the nation in the seventies, everything was very gratefully received.

John Huddart was a teacher I had respected and even laughed with when I was a pupil but nevertheless I found him quite formidable. When I got to know him as a colleague and a good friend I found gold. He worked hard – in and for the School, for the town and for his family and friends. He was the only member of staff with a large car/van so he was put upon whenever there was a large item to be transported. So he moved furniture, items for the Railway Club, the Scouts, and the Parents' Committee; he transported boys to matches and meetings, he would help you to move house, bringing with him his strong sons to help, he would do electrical wiring for you and sort out mechanical problems with your car. He made rope. The machinery he made himself and the raw material was usually plastic bailer twine. So good were these ropes that you could see them all round the town – in the swimming pool where they were the lane markers, at the Carnival, in and around people's houses, and of course all round the school on athletic sports days. I still have some.

John grew vegetables for his family but there was always a surplus for friends. He always supplied me with tomato, cucumber, cabbage and sweet pepper plants until the year he died. He must have collected thousands of pounds for the town swimming pool in Croyland Road by running his Tote.

His life was touched with tragedy when his oldest son was killed in a hit and run accident but he and Dot bore it bravely and his other sons did him proud.

It was a privilege to belong to that common room. There were some very bright and knowledgeable men among us. We did the *Times*, *Telegraph* and *Guardian* crossword puzzles every day, usually in a team of four or five, and on Mondays we also did the *Sunday Times* and the *Observer* puzzles. If we were really at our wits end for something to do we would tackle the *Daily Mail* but that had often been interfered with by Bob Taylor and Tim Tomlinson who were not altogether aware that you couldn't use words whose letters exceeded the number of squares.

There was a regular lunchtime Bridge four: Dr Jackson, R. V. S. Ward, I. J. Nicholas and C. A. Pine. Nick made sure that when the bell went so did the card players but if he was not there the card school continued until the Head came round and informed them, "Mr Ward, there's a class waiting for you."

You soon got to know those who opted out. Ron Ward liked to go shopping on a Wednesday afternoon so would enquire if one of us young chaps would mind refereeing game three because he had a "bit of a throat".

Alf, Spike, or 'J' as we all knew him, would avoid anything time-consuming like lessons, Staff meetings etc., if he had O-Level marking to do. I felt quite sorry for 'J'. He always wore faded clothes, jumpers with holes in, baggy trousers and a tattered gown, but I needn't have worried because he informed me that many of his garments had been given to him by his relative, "a very weathy man," JAK, the great *Evening Standard* cartoonist. In any case, 'J' had better things to spend his money on.

I once went with him and the sixth form to see the Cowper museum at Olney. He drove his newish Vauxhall and it was one of the most hair-raising experiences I have had. His eyesight was never good and when he had to take things in at speed it became quite a problem. We got there and back safely, but I never went out with him again. He parked this car next to a mini outside the Co-op in Queensway one day, carefully reversing so the two bonnets were level .... and went through the shop window. He also reversed into John Dunning's car in the front drive and in doing so flattened his own briefcase.

Mr Wrenn was quietly calm and efficient. He rarely raised his voice to boys or staff but we were never in doubt where he stood and what he expected. Staff meetings rarely lasted more than half an hour. Our main task was to promote or demote boys on the strength of the end-of-term results and this was done by staff vote and occasionally, comment. Dr Jackson once damned a boy that everyone else thought deserved promotion with, "Nar, he can't write an esshay." At the end there was always, "any other business?.. no?... thank you gentlemen."

One year Chris Cox wanted to raise the issue of whether some boys were suited to a four years to O-Level course. Chris spoke to his theme for five minutes or so, putting a sensible case. When he had finished the head simply said, "Thank you Mr Cox. Any other business?.. no?.. thank you gentlemen." And that was the last we heard of it.

Staff Sport & Social Life

Bob Taylor brought in the summer five-a-side competition and thought the staff should enter a team. In fact the staff entered two. One was a serious side with serious players like Bob himself and T. W. Lewis (who played for Irthlingborough Diamonds). They were hard, and gave no quarter to the boys, who in their turn were hard and fast too. This team was *The Experts* (always pronounced with a Beery voice and twist of the mouth). I remember 'old' Flash Bellamy being injured by a Bob Taylor tackle and I believe he never played much rugby or soccer after that. Then there was the *Experts B*, a team of less serious masters like me, Richard Oberman, and similarly less gifted footballers. We had fun on the field and in the staffroom where the names of the teams were spoken in loud, mimicking voices.

The staff also played badminton together on a Friday night. The Head usually played and perhaps six to ten others. The head was always competitive whereas some of us only went to have a bit of fun, work up a sweat and pop off to the pub afterwards. He announced to me when I played as his partner, "We'll play side to side," but I had no idea what he meant and did it all wrong and was ticked off for it.

Tennis became fairly popular with the staff, especially the Head and Nick Wills. H.A.W. told me when I joined the School staff that I should be sure to make full use of the School's facilities. He certainly did and played rugby with the boys in the winter, and cricket and later tennis in the summer. Wednesday afternoons were sacrosanct as the Head grew older. He would always play tennis no matter what else was going on in the school. When the County Auditors were due one year I heard him say to Miss Bavin "I'm playing tennis now. If they want me, tell them I'll be back at four o'clock." I suppose you can do that sort of thing when you are close to retirement and have thirty odd years of confidence behind you. The Head played tennis until he retired, if I remember correctly.

The Staff also formed a sort of cultural-cum-social group called "The Bengal Lancers". It began as a result of Speech Day having no dinner arrangements. Most staff simply brought sandwiches but some went down to the Golden Lion for a snack and a pint. Then someone thought of the Indian restaurant in

Church Street and one or two went there. Over the years the number preferring a curry rapidly increased until we took over the whole restaurant and more than 20 staff went, some ordering the special *Murg e Mussallam* which required 24 hours notice. The restaurant was owned by Mr Israil Ali who became well known to and respected by many of the staff. There was a time when we would help him to understand his tax returns and he would show his gratitude by preparing something special for us. His son Imman transferred to the Grammar School from the Public School and we made sure he was well looked after. We must have done a reasonable job because three or four years ago he returned to Wellingborough and visited Richard Temple and me, and spoke well of his time at WGS. He is now a High Court judge in Dacca, Bangladesh, and looks set to become Lord Chief Justice in a year or so.

Well, we thought the bonhomie of these lunches should be extended and we duly formed "The Bengal Lancers" which met every few weeks for curry in Mr Ali's restaurant, wherever it was (he moved to Irthlingborough for several years). There were always at least a dozen at these meetings and Mr Ali looked after us and became almost an unofficial Old Grammarian. Even after the amalgamation we continued to meet, often ending up at John Hyde's house for beer and more social chat afterwards.

The End

The two years before the amalgamation of the Grammar School and the Girls' High School were fraught. None of us liked the idea of all the good things we had built up disappearing and thought having a school on a split site was sheer folly. We opposed it rigorously at meetings with county officials but it was all cut and dried. We met the staff at the girls' school and were not encouraged. The new Headmistress's style was very different from Mr Wrenn's and her concerns were different from ours. It was not going to be easy. We saw it as the "death" of everything we had worked for and believed in and I was moved to compose parodies of the situation in the style of two of my favourite writers[†]. Many staff, even those with the top jobs, found it hard to enthuse. The change took place as a *fait accompli* but there was always a longing to turn the clock back and Howard Buchanan duly had the School's obituary printed in the *Evening Telegraph* each succeeding July.

[†] These parodies are reproduced at the end of the book, preceded by elegies for some of the masters in the style of Chaucer.

IV : FAREWELL

Chapter 14

10/65 And All That

As the Grammar School went from strength to strength in the fifties and sixties, a new mood was growing in the political make-up of the nation that led to a circular entitled '10/65' that led to the eventual change to comprehensive education. As Tony Benn summarised succinctly, by the early 1960s, "the middle class was expanding and grammar schools were not."

The tri-partite system was created after the war following the Norwood Report of 1943 that suggested there are three 'types of children', each of which required different types of education that would best be offered by three different types of schools (grammar, technical, and modern).

According to the Norwood Report, a grammar school pupil was seen as someone "interested in learning for its own sake, who can grasp an argument or follow a piece of connected reasoning, who is interested in causes, whether on the level of of human volition or in the material world, who cares to know how things came to be as well as how they are." A technical school pupil was someone "whose interests and abilities lie markedly in the field of applied science or applied art." A modern school pupil was someone who "deals more easily with concrete things than with ideas. He may have much ability, but it will be in the realm of facts. He is interested in things as they are; he finds little attraction in the past or in the slow disentanglement of causes or movements."

The Norwood Report suggested that these three types of children could be identified accurately by an examination at age 'eleven plus' (meaning having their eleventh birthday in the school year concerned). The 1944 Education Act in the following year suggested the implementation of this formulation in a tri-partite system of secondary education.

In a number of areas, such as Windermere in the Lake District, low populations meant that providing three such schools was impractical and the one school used had to be comprehensive in intake. In the early years such comprehensive schools were invariably streamed by ability but their presence and apparent success meant that the arguments for a tri-partite system could be more easily challenged.

The belief in three easily and accurately identifiable types of child became less and less viable as new information came to light and new perspectives were gaining favour. For example, a number of modern school children in the sixties were successful in the 'grammar school' GCE examinations.

The arguments against grammar schools began to grow on a variety of lines of argument:

- research questioned theories of inherited intelligence;
- errors occurred in school placements owing to the fallibility of the 11+;
- there was a wide inequality in outcome: grammar school places ranged from 10% in some LEAs (Local Education Authorities) to more than 30% in others;
- there was a profound gender inequality: many LEAs had single-sex grammar schools with many more places for boys than for girls;
- talent was being wasted with many children leaving school too early—a view reinforced by the 1963 Newsom Report *Half our Future* focusing on the education of 13–16 year olds of average and less than average ability.

Added to these general issues was the more pragmatic dissatisfaction of 'wannabe' parents who believed strongly in a grammar school education, but whose children were not selected by the 11 plus. Such parents inevitably criticised the accuracy of the test in identifying the different types of children or criticised the system for providing insufficient grammar school places.

The educational mantra of both Conservative and Labour governments before the mid-sixties was summed up by George Tomlinson, a Labour politician who was Minister of Education between 1947 and 1951. Blunt and working class, he made it clear that the government would not exercise direct control over the curriculum, being alleged to have said, "Minister knows nowt about curriculum."

The curriculum was perceived as the teachers' "secret garden" (a term first used by Lord Eccles, Minister of Education, in 1960) into which others—even those directly concerned with educational provision—were not expected to stray. By 1964 the teachers' control of the curriculum had become unacceptable to the Department of Education and Science (DES) and to politicians in general.

The Schools Council for Curriculum and Examinations was set up, representing a three-sided partnership between the DES (the paymasters), the LEAs (the organisers) and the teachers (the professionals). Whilst the partnership was intended as one of equality, the reality was that for the next ten years the teachers remained effectively in charge.

Meanwhile, left wing socialists were arguing for comprehensive schools in the 1959 *Victory for Socialism* pamphlet, so that "no longer class-divided, education would become a powerful instrument for the promotion of social and national unity." It was argued that a segregated school system divided the nation into different types of people having minimum interchange with each other.

This led to the idea of large multi-purpose schools with a joint use of facilities such as recreational space, and appropriate grouping of pupils for learning, either in mixed-ability classes in which children of different abilities could progress by learning with and from each other, or set according to appropriate criteria in different subjects. It was envisaged that a school could recognise and distinguish attainment of all types in their own right within a single system.

The Newsom Report of 1963 concentrated on the education of children in Secondary Modern schools and reported that "many of them offered their brightest children a fifth form education and the chance to take GCE." Newsom named these children, whose average IQ was very near that of the top 10% of the population, "Brown" and summarised their findings as:

> *Clearly a good many Browns have improved on their position in the eleven-plus. Indeed at fourteen John Brown has done better than a fifth of the boys in the grammar schools. It is worth noting that a quarter of the Browns managed to get their attainments up to this level, which is a national one, although they were in schools which set them no regular homework.* (*Newsom Report, paragraph 573*)

Newsom made no direct comparison of the academic achievements of these children with their equivalents who went to comprehensive schools, however, it did find both that a far higher percentage of the Brown children in a Modern school held a responsible school post, and that there was much greater difficulty making them wear school uniform:

	Responsible School Post	**School Society**	**Youth Club**	**Refusing to Wear a Uniform**
Modern	22%	35%	56%	25%
Comprehensive	6%	51%	49%	2%

Newsom Report paragraphs 622 & 623

The arguments against grammar schools were highlighted by the 1964 Labour party manifesto:

Labour will get rid of the segregation of children into separate schools caused by 11-plus selection: secondary education will be reorganised on comprehensive lines. Within the new system, grammar school education will be extended: in future no child will he denied the opportunity of benefitting from it through arbitrary selection at the age of 11.

Circular 10/65

After the election of the Labour Government in 1965, Circular 10/65 was published, and its first page declared:

It was the Government's declared objective to end selection at eleven-plus and to eliminate separatism in secondary education.

When being drafted, there was a debate in Whitehall over how strongly worded this Circular should be. The Government did not have direct control over Education; they provided the money for the Local Education Authorities to implement local decisions. In the end, a single word distinguished two quite different approaches as to whether the changes should be 'required' or 'requested'.

Those firmly in favour of the comprehensive system believed that the Circular should *require* the conversion of grammar schools into Comprehensives. Those preferring to preserve the balance of power between central government and the counties thought that the Local

Authorities should be *requested* to make the change.

In its final form, the Circular 'requested' the change although, in practical terms, the Ministry of Education used its powers over finance to make opposition to the change difficult. Local Authorities relied on central government to pay for the large number of new schools made necessary by the baby boom after the war. The Ministry of Education refused to pay for any new secondary school that was not a comprehensive. As a result, a number of counties otherwise supporting the tripartite system, such as Bromley and Surrey, found in favour of following the circular and going comprehensive.

It is worth noting that the socialists were against selection, not grammar school education *per se*. Harold Wilson answered charges that he was destroying the grammar school system by responding that he was doing the converse and offering a grammar school education to all.

Circular 10/65 offered no extra finance to change to a comprehensive system and left it completely in the hands of the Local Education Authority to determine how and when they should do so. The result was a plethora of systems with different ages of transfer. For most of England and Wales, the circular marked the abolition of grammar schools and secondary moderns.

When Labour won a bigger majority in the 1966 general election with a clear mandate for comprehensivisation, many hoped the new government would pass a new education act requiring all LEAs to go fully comprehensive. In fact, four years were to pass before the act was drafted and, when Labour lost the 1970 general election, the act was lost too.

The Education Secretary in the following Conservative Government, Margaret Thatcher, withdrew the circular at the end of June 1970, shortly after Edward Heath's government took office, but the Conservatives continued to agree Local Education Authority plans to change to a comprehensive system, with the result that the Conservatives under Margaret Thatcher established more comprehensive schools than were set up under the socialists! It also meant that the change-over took place intermittently throughout the nation.

Comprehensive Developments in Northamptonshire

Although the Labour party was in power on the Northamptonshire Council and soon put forward proposals for a change to comprehensive education, the changeover could not be immediate. It inevitably took place over a number of years because it was believed that a comprehensive school would need a viable number of 'grammar school' children implying an eight to ten form entry as compared to the three form entry in Wellingborough Grammar School.

A major pragmatic response to the development of viable comprehensive schools was to join together single-sex schools to provide a viable co-educational school system. The changes required meant that it took ten years between the publication of circular 10/65 to the eventual closure of the High School and Grammar School and the creation of the Wrenn School.

When Conservative Peer Lord Boothby presented school prizes in 1968, he rallied to the cause for retaining Grammar Schools saying:

> *:... there was a place in the English system for all types of school – Comprehensive, Public, Grammar and Modern – and that if any justification was needed for the continuing existence of the Grammar School then one had only to look at the results achieved by Wellingborough Grammar School.* *School Magazine, Autumn 1968*

When the Conservatives regained power in 1970, it seemed possible that they might save the remaining grammar schools. However, the new Government continued to accept changes proposed by local government and even more grammar schools became comprehensive.

A valedictory article appeared in the *Wellingborough News* in 1973:

> *Earl Mountbatten, Alexander Fleming, the Duke of Bedford, Peter Scott, David Frost – an unlikely selection of names. But what is the connection between these men?*
>
> *The common factor is that they have all visited Wellingborough Grammar School, reputedly one of the highest academic schools in the country. Top award for the Kitchener Scholarship, (out of 50 scholarships the grammar school got 7).*
>
> *With six hundred boys and a teaching staff of 38, the school has all the usual features of a grammar school, with its societies and various sports. But what makes the school distinctive is the happiness and directness*

of its daily work.

The emphasis is on doing things well, quickly and efficiently. At the end of last year, 67 boys passed 171 A-levels, and 90 boys ended the year with a handful of O-levels.

But the school is not merely interested in the production of the best brains in the country.

It offers a wide range of activities away from the competitive business of achieving the highest possible academic standards and this, in the words of headmaster Mr H. A. Wrenn is accomplished by getting on with the job in hand and not standing around talking about it.

Support for the School and a defence of its innate comprehensive nature was given in the article by the headboy, Gregory Hind:

Mr G. H. Pine with Ian Savage, Nicholas White and Stuart Coles in a physics lesson.

Some of the boys on the start of a cross country run.

Top grove of academe

EARL Mountbatten, Alexander Fleming, the Duke of Bedford, Peter Scott, David Frost — an unlikely selection of names. But what is the connection between these men?

The common factor is they have all visited Wellingborough Grammar School, reputedly one of the highest academic schools in the country. Top award for the Kitchener Scholarship (out of 50 scholarships the grammar school got 7), and one of the highest "O" and "A" level passes per boy in the county.

With six hundred boys and a teaching staff of 38, the school has all the usual features of a grammar school, with its societies and various sports.

But what makes the school distinctive is the happiness and directness of it's daily work.

The emphasis is on doing things well, quickly and efficiently. At the end of last year 67 boys passed 171 "A" levels, and 90 boys ended the year with a handful of "O" levels.

But the school is not merely interested in the production of the best brains in the country.

It offers a wide range of activities away from the competitive business of achieving the highest possible academic standards, and this, in the words of headmaster, Mr. H. A. Wrenn, is accomplished by getting on with the job in hand, and not standing around talking about it.

These activities range from the radio and folk clubs, to the Christian fellowship and the geology club, but towering above the other activities in the school is the TOC H, which every year provides a day-trip for some of the senior citizens of the town.

Last year's trip took them to Woburn, a departure from the traditional trip to Hunstanton, but nevertheless just as appreciated by the senior citizens.

The school was first to join the TOC H organisation, and has since then devoted itself to good causes in and around Wellingborough.

Head boy is Gregory Hind, who has been at the school since he was 14. He is taking "A" levels this year in history, English and British constitution and hopes to go to university. Ultimately he wants to find a job teaching abroad.

"The school is fully representative of a cross-section of society in Wellingborough and the surrounding area," he said, "and everyone seems to be fairly happy with the situation here. The more intelligent people are pushed — if they want to be of course — up to the highest possible standards of learning, and this, added to the fact that the grammar school gets the cream off the top of the milk as far as pupils are concerned, makes us very successful academically."

Gregory Hind is a firm believer in discipline. "It's something one must have in a community such as this one. Here the discipline is good, probably because it's not taken to extremes, and there is a lot of pupil-teacher communication.

"This is my one complaint of comprehensive education," he said. "The schools are such big mammoth efforts that personal contact becomes almost impossible.

"And, without that personal contact, I don't believe you can have a happy school, which is essential to the success of its pupils."

The school has made a recent departure from tradition with the introduction of football as a full-time sport.

Although the rugby and cricket teams have been fairly successful over the years, the football teams have outshone them all, for within a year they have become one of the top teams in the local school's league.

SCHOOL SALUTE THIS WEEK LOOKS AT WELLINGBOROUGH GRAMMAR

STORY: BRIAN BARBERTON
PICTURES: ALAN CASTLE

IT ALL BEGAN BACK IN '31

THE SCHOOL was opened by Sir Michael Sadler in 1931. Then there were 48 pupils, and five masters, including the headmaster, F. C. Lay, who was renowned for his scientific abilities.

In 1973, a gym, a new hall, new laboratories, ten new classrooms, and a music block have materialised to accommodate the quick rise in the number of pupils. But while masters, buildings and boys have changed, the one unchanging name has been that of the school secretary.

Tucked away beside the entrance hall, Nora Bavin has watched the life of Wellingborough Grammar School. Since 1931 she has seen boys settle at the school, and leave after five years.

But Miss Bavin is soon to retire. "The school has grown out of all proportion," she said, "but still at 600 it is small enough to know everybody.

"The character of the school hasn't changed very much since I came here, only the people and the buildings change. But it has always been a very happy place to work.

"It may sound corny, but happiness is very important, and our happiness and academic achievement are closely related to each other with the endless hard work of the staff. This has meant that the boys are not eager to jump on their bikes or catch a bus as soon as it's time to go home."

Miss Bavin worked part-time for the school up to 1945, until the school had grown to such an extent that it needed a full-time secretary. She was the first and only woman to become a member of the Old Boys' Association.

Valedictory article in the Wellingborough News, 1973 (selected text quoted above).

> *"The School is fully representative of a cross-section of society in Wellingborough and the surrounding area," he said, "and everyone seems fairly happy with the situation here. The more intelligent people are pushed – if they want to be of course – up to the highest possible standards of learning, and this, added to the fact that the Grammar School gets the cream off the top of the milk as far as pupils are concerned, makes us very successful academically."*

Hind's criticism of comprehensive schools relates to their size:

> *The schools are such big, mammoth efforts that personal contact becomes almost impossible, and without that personal contact, I don't believe you can have a happy school, which is essential to the success of its pupils.*

Mr Wrenn had long advocated the medium-sized school in which the headmaster and his staff could get to know every pupil. He did not publicly express this view now as he was charged with creating a successful 'mammoth' comprehensive school. When asked about the new system by an old boy, he simply said, "Look, I am headmaster of a school that is going to go comprehensive and I have to make it work."

As the Summer Term of 1975 came to an end, the Grammar School was preparing to exchange teachers with the High School and female teachers would occasionally arrive in the staff room. Every master had a key and it was not unusual to drop in during the evening or at weekends to do some marking or make some preparation for a lesson. But then a phantom female master seemed to pass through, leaving vases of flowers and women's magazines. The men were a bit put out by this and it went on for some time until the phantom was unmasked, or rather, owned up. It was Mr Wrenn himself, retaining his sense of humour to the end.

Chapter 15

Epilogue

Wellingborough Grammar School closed its doors in the Summer of 1975 and the building re-opened as part of the Wrenn School in the Autumn. Mr Wrenn, the Headmaster of the Grammar School for one term short of thirty years retired and the new school was named in his honour.

Miss Hubbard, the Headmistress of the High School became the Head of the new Wrenn School, Mr Sulch, the Wellingborough Grammar School's Second Master became the Senior Deputy Head while Mr Tussler became a Deputy Head and took over the task of planning the time-table to cope with a school on two sites with a seven-minute walk between the two.

Did the Wrenn School become a "Grammar School for all" as suggested by Harold Wilson, or did it succeed in other ways? That is for others to decide; it is not within the brief we set ourselves in recalling our memories of the Grammar School.

What is clear is that some of the Grammar School's most treasured principles were turned on their heads when the change occurred. The new mantra of the comprehensive school was to encourage every child to do his or her best to improve their own performance, not to compete against others. Competitive prizes were no longer appropriate and this led immediately to the loss of Prize Day in the form we knew it.

The immediate consequence was the end of the grand series of great men of the country visiting our little town to compliment the school on its success. The further consequence was a decision to contact all those who had donated prizes and to return their investments. This included Mr Lay, who was sent back the money he donated for the Lay Divinity Prize. What a way to treat the founding Headmaster!

The suppression of prizes had a rational reason in that it only provided a direct incentive for a few. Of the two of us, Graham Tall was inspired when the reading prizes were offered and attacked his reading with great gusto, easily winning his form prize. The following year he was again far and away the most successful in the test but was denied the prize because, as Spike explained, it was necessary to "share the prizes around." In O-level there were prizes in every subject, but each boy could have only one: the method of choice was to give the boy with the top mark the prize in that particular subject, eliminate him and repeat the process with enough flexibility to see that the prizes were well spread out. The older Tall worked the system, getting a share of prizes up to O-level, but then homing in on several prizes in the senior school, winning the Senior Mathematics Prize for the highest marks in A-level, the Senior Science Prize for the best lecture in the Scientific Society and the Senior Music Prize for being the director of the winning House in the House Music Competion.

Looking back, it all seems vanity. As so many eminent guests at Parents' Day had re-iterated, it is not the prizes that one wins at school that matter, but the life that one leads over the longer term.

The other part of Grammar School culture that has vanished from our society today is the use of corporal punishment. We should say that neither of us ever received the cane, though young Tall once went to the headmaster with three pairs of rugby shorts under his trousers. His misdemeanor was to reply to a prefect who told him to pick up a piece of paper with the retort: "You've just walked past it, you pick it up!" The padding proved to be unnecessary.

In our modern times it is an offence for a teacher to hit a child, punishable by dismissal and even legal action. In the time of Wellingborough Grammar School, corporal punishment was an ever-present sanction that was used to implement swift and short redress for those getting out of line. It was not a common occurrence for most boys, although a few who enjoyed rebellion received it more often and may have regarded it as a badge of courage. For most of us it was a normal part of life that marked the boundaries of acceptable behaviour. The vast majority of boys rarely crossed the line

We have seen in the history of the school, each of the headmasters brought a special gift. Mr Lay was a charismatic character who laid the foundations, including the House system of internal competition, the School Sports, the first School Clubs and Societies and the focus on both the academic and liberal curriculum. It took time for the school to get up to speed in academic work. The school-leaving age was only 14 in the thirties, and three in five boys left early before they took the certificate; of those who took the certificate, only half of them (one in five of the entrants) passed the necessary five subjects to be awarded the School Certificate. Mr Lay was an enthusiastic and discreet character. He had a vision that he shared with his staff, his pupils and their parents, and they all took to it with great energy, except that his call for boys to remain at school to complete their education did not have the effect he desired. The economic and social conditions of the time were such that children of poorer families may have felt the need to leave school to earn money to support the household, while the sons of businessmen may follow in their father's footsteps and had no need for paper qualifications.

Mr Woolley was a strong and focused character, who made his academic aspirations clear to all his pupils by naming those who left early and publishing form lists in order of performance in exams to highlight not only those who worked hard, but also those whose performances were less satisfactory.

The school leaving age increased to 15 in his time, and he was able to reduce the early leavers to around half the entrants and greatly increase the number of Certificate passes to include almost all the boys who took the examination.

Mr Wrenn benefited further from the raising of the school leaving age to 16 and the award of GCEs (at a higher standard) for less than five subjects. He too doubled the number of passes, this time in the number of boys achieving five or more GCE O-levels in the fifties and maintained a mature and stable system at this higher level in the sixties and seventies. The sixth form grew in size and increasing numbers of boys went on to university.

One of his major achievements was his encouragement of clubs and societies to balance high academic standards with the freedom to choose from a number of available interests and to encourage the formation of new organisations when the need arose. He had an uncanny way of building advantages for his boys. When he learned of the Kitchener Scholarships for the sons of men who had served in the forces, he quickly organised his boys to take advantage of the money available. He trusted and honoured his teachers by maintaining them in their service to the school in sport, drama, clubs and societies over long periods. He used his persuasive powers to bring a continuing sequence of boys' heroes to present prizes.

Most of all, the school owed its qualities to its masters, especially the long-serving characters who gave a special quality to the life of the boys. The twenty-nine long-serving masters with over ten years service taught more than half of the lessons over the lifetime of the school and therefore played major roles in shaping the schooling of the pupils.

In an expression of appreciation of the school in his autobiography, old boy David Frost affirmed, "I was lucky enough to go to Wellingborough Grammar School, which was a first-class school." His foreword to this book includes a valedictory statement that says it all and—as we have seen in the history of the school as a whole—it focuses on the quality of the *teachers*, which is as relevant for the life of the school before and during the war as it was in the years that followed:

> *The grammar schools, and the whole post-1944 Education Act system, gave opportunities to children of my generation that our predecessors never had. At the same time, the priorities of the system meant that anything over and above the preparation for examinations depended more than ever on individual teachers' calibre and enthusiasm. And that is where we were particularly blessed.*

It is therefore appropriate that we close our book of memories with remembrances of some of those masters, penned by an old boy who learned his Chaucer at the feet of Dr Jackson and who himself became a master at the school.

David Wilson remembers some of the characters in the school, penned in Chaucerian tones at the time that the school came to its end. He added two more at a later stage especially for publication in this book. Our journey closes as he mourns the passing of Wellingborough Grammar School in the style of Swift and sings of the changing ways of dealing with disruptive pupils in the style of Flanders and Swann.

The Grammar School is no more, but the memories linger on.

Semper Juventutis Memor!

Lines on the Passing of WGS

David Wilson

Here begynneth the Tales of the Grammar Scole at Wendlyngburg
In Homage to Chaucer

THE PROLOGUE

Whan that Septembre with hys windes stronge
Bryngs yn th'autum and the nyghtes longe;
Whan leves fall fro evri busche and tree,
And al is styl, both brid and bee;
Whan fogges eek with hir foule breth
Inspire the contree, toun and heth;
Than longen folk to maken newe scoles,
And olde maistres usen newe tooles.

But ere this tale I start to telle,
I have me thoughte it just as welle
To telle yow of the maistres, hir array,
And al hir worthynes bifor this day.

The Hedmaistre

An Hedmaistre ther was, a verray worthy man,
Who, from the tyme that he first began
To teche in scoles loved chivalrye
Truth and honour, tennis and courtesye.
In the north had he be, until he felt the colde
In forty six, and though yet thritty six yeer olde,
He cam to us and stayed for thritty yeer.
And mani wer that wished he styl wer heer.

On scole trippes had he be, mani oon,
And knew the language of ech and som,
But nevere ones in al hys lyf
He went on countie cruze and took hys wyf.

A sportynge man he was for the nones,
And played at rugbie more than ones.
At criket to, and did hys bitte
To help the staf mak the wynnynge hitte.
He practised wel, bi smyttyng on the rumpe
A score a day of scole boyes with an olde stumpe.
But tennis loved he best in special.
Wynter and somer he wolde tak hys bal
And raket eek and shew the yonger boyes
Hys skil – and sondri oother ploys.
Auditours fro countie hall he set at noght
So he coude hav hys pley upon the court.
Wel he knew the laddes in hys charge,
Their names and numbers, small and large,
And who had lost hys coot and who hys bagge,
And who went yn the stook hool for a dragge.
Er he to lesons took hys weye.
He knew hem al if sooth y seye.
Detectyf he was with sharpe imagynacioun.
Noon coude escap hys sly interrogacioun.
A good man to hys staf he was and hartie;
And now and then he gaf a sherrie partie.

The Physikian

A man fro Cumbrieland was ther also;
And he coud rol a fag and light it to,
Er it in flames burst and burnt hys lippe.
Wel organised he was, he made no slippe,
For al he got he filed in cardboard boxes
Agaynst a rainy day and sly yong foxes
Upon the staf that took awey hys thynges,
And ran awey as light as brids on wynges.
Of physics was he maistre, and he knewe
Evri art of heet and light and lodestones too.
Pulleys he hadde, som spanners and a renche,
And eek he hadde a piece of woden benche
To bete povre boyes that did nat lerne.
But honeste felawes taughte he ful yerne.
A scootmaister had he be, and gardinere,
And put hys Brussels sprouts in a freezere.

The Historieman

An humph ther was that men call'd Ron,
Who, long after second bel had gon
Was at the bridge, and oother felawes eek.
No good it was in lesons hem to seke
Biforn the laste trump was on the table.
Than wolde he goo and tel the sixte a fable
Of how the government (the partie socialiste)
Had us bitreyed and al hir chaunces miste.
He had a large figure, ful and rounde,
Which in hys youthe on mani a rugbie ground
He had displeyed, and mani a bar also.
On Wednesdaies after noon he hade to go
An do the shopping, he thought it beste.
For cross word games he wolde nevere reste,

But ratteled on until it al was done –
And then he sat and dide another one.
Wel knew he th'arte of economie,
And eek he knew in special th' historie
Of everi toun and village rounde aboute.
In oolden dayes he wolde a ladde cloute
About hys erse; but tyme had mellowed
And now twas onli hym that bellowed.
A ful solempne man he was, with large car,
And overdryve, in which he travelled far.

The mathmatikman

A butler was with us at that tyme also
Who cam to tech in scoles longe ago.
In al the land in mathematic nas hys peer,
Nor on the clarynette yf sooth I heer.
Wel coude he add and do subtractioun,
Divide and multiplye both hoole and fractioun.
He knewe the tryg and Geometrie,
The sines and tans and oother foolerie.
The calculus he knewe, integers and cos,
Hise rootes and squares, and wher hys locus was,
And where to cancel out and change hys signe,
And how to plot a graf and drawe a ligne…
But best of al he knew hys tessilacioun
And shewed hem to hys neighebor. In
computacioun.
Withouten doubt, was hys peculiar art,
And knew the hool was gretter than the part.

A gardyn he hadde, set al about with flours,
In which he worked in sunshine or in shoures,
Watchyng the yonge shootes brek thurgh the soil,
And thus he reaped the pleasure of hys toil.

An hedmystresse

An hedmystresse cam to that place also,
That unto logyk hadde longe ago.
Hir heed was farsed ful of bookes,
And of hir ire, and of hir lookes
Wer al afrayed. Wel coude she speke,
And that so longe, and hevy eek,
That mani men fel off hir benches
(And so I wene did mani wenches)
For slepe, whan passed had an hour or two
Of conferaunce – alle had to go.
In hostelrie she hadde nevere bene,
And men hir called fayre Georgene.

The following fragment, lost for some 30 years was discovered recently under the fly-leaf of a copy of Geoffrey Chaucer's "Tales of ye Grammar Schole". It was clearly written by an early scribe and was in places almost indecipherable. We have endeavoured to preserve much of the early spelling whilst aiming to make it relatively intelligible to the non-academic reader who may find the content interesting.

The Englyshman

Spyke Jackson, who was ther as wel
Had mani a wondrous tale to tel
About his past in famous London toun
And other places too, both up and doun.
He alone of al the maisters ther
Had gown of red. A hood of fur hadde he
For he was doctor of Philosophie.

He knewe th'authors of th'Augustan Age,
His Pope and Johnson; evri line and page!
In Drama was his especial art.
Non could begyn ere Tocsin bid him start.
Ful oft a gun or sword or special hat or coat
Was neded to convey a crook or pirate on a boat.
To playe the part and what yt meant,
And to excel was evryone's intent.
For that earned GOODS and GOODS meant prizes
To all that Spike had favoured or thought wisest.
At end of term when GOODS were counted
Then cam the wynner, on desk he mounted,
And Spike admired young Jones's knees
Ere he presented hym hys fees
Collected al the term just gon
From ha'penny fines from Dick or John.

Hys voice was Cockney with a spittaled 'S'.
That Englysh was hys forte, none wolde guess,
But thought he wer a gangster or a fence,
And students all, he said that they wer "gents".

One day, a first year had a go
To read "The Raven" – Edgar Allan Poe.
But when he asked the question, "What's the bird?"
They said, "An owl!" – A Bloody Owl's absurd!
The Commonroom dissolved in mirth,
Humph rocked and wobbled throughout his girth,
Nick nodded, Eddie had to smile,
Nothyng so droll they'd heard for quite a while!

With George he smote boys on the arse
Thick or thin he left up to the class.

A Maister at the Brydge, Pontoon or Rummy,
He played his cards right – he was no dummy.

His eyes wer poor. Once stopping at Co-op
Reversed his car through window of the shop.
Another day, he caused a a mighty crunch,
He parked too close hys case and squashed
hys lunch.

In tattered gown and cast-off clothes,
With black-rimmed specs upon hys nose
That hooked right forward o'er a jutty chin,
He taught boys wel that they might win
A scolarshippe to Oxford, Kent or Leeds,
Where they myghte reap the crop for which
he'd sow'd the seeds.
He served his school five years and twenty,
And H.M. said, beneath his breth, "that's plenty."
But long wil those who knew him say,
"Thanks for the mem'ry, Spike. You made my day."

The geographieman

"Out to the board," sayd Jayk,
"Mark in the River Ouse and Bala Lake.
Too slow! Sit down! Next! Yes, you!
Point to Port Harcourt, Pendembu,
Jakarta, Oslo, Ouagadugu…"

Thus with hys tests he taught us;
And to be quyck, not like a tortoise,
Or sluggard schoolboy, to be in place.
So strict he was that none dared face
Hym in argument. All with hym was black or white
And e'en when doubtful, he was right.

In olden days, before the motor car
Had come to town, hys coaches took us near and far
To coal mines, Whipsnade, Matlock, Crewe;
To Parleyment and Dovedale, Kensington and Kew.

A scoutmaister was he in trousers short,
And Toc H lamp man, who servyce taught.
At Jumbl Sales, he raised much money
For Oure scole projects; none thought it funny
That such a man as he should deal in dross.
I have no doute he never made a loss.

Honest he was, as day is long,
And ever hymned hys maker with hys song.
And though we feared hys anger and hys tongue,
We learned oure lessons well ere dinner bell had
rung.

An Elegy

On the death of the Grammar School in Wellingborough

after the style of Jonathan Swift

The Grammar School? Impossible! What, dead!
(And High School too) and nothing said?
How could such a mighty institution fall?
Was't so inglorious after all?
Well since it's gone, no matter how,
The last trump alone will wake it now!
And could it be indeed so old?
Not three score years, or so I'm told.
Three score I think is pretty high;
'Twas time, in conscience, it should die.
This world it cumbered long enough
With scholars, learning and such stuff.
And that's the reason, some folks think
It's left behind so great a stink.
Behold, its funeral appears.
No council sighs, no O.G.'s tears?
"But what of that?" its friends may say,
"It had its honours in its day."
The day will dawn, as dawn it must,
When present fancies turn to dust;
When empty thoughts and empty deeds
No more suffice our children's needs.
Honours ill-got will all be flung
And turn to dust from whence they sprung.

Pastorale

To the tune of 'The Gasman Cometh'
by Flanders and Swann

'Twas on a Monday morning
A boy was rude to me.
He told me to **** off
And it was plain to see
I couldn't really whack him
No, that wouldn't do at all,
So it was on the Tuesday morning
That the Year Head came to call.

Chorus: Oh it all makes work for the
teacher-man to do.

'Twas on the Tuesday morning
The Year Head came around.
He called the boy to stand outside
And he began to frown.
He said it wasn't good enough
It wouldn't do at all;
The boy turned round and laughed at him
And said his mum would call.

Chorus: Oh it all makes work for the
teacher-man to do.

'Twas on the Wednesday morning
His mother came to school.
She saw the Deputy's Deputy
And said she was a fool.
This really wasn't good enough
And things were getting grim,
And then she has a brain-wave
And the Deputy Head came in.

Chorus: Oh it all makes work for the
teacher-man to do.

'Twas on the Thursday morning
The Deputy Head came out.
His face was lined and wrinkled
And his hair was falling out.
The boy was unrepentant
And that wouldn't do at all.
So a call was made to Broadway
And the Head was asked to call.

Chorus: Oh it all makes work for the
teacher-man to do.

'Twas on the Friday morning
The Head was on the scene.
The boy was called to give account,
"Whatever do you mean…?"
"I meant just what I said," he cried.
"Oh, yes," she said, "I see."
…So once again on Monday
The boy was rude to me!

Chorus: Oh it all makes work for the
teacher-man to do.

Index

C

F

O

P

Q

R

S

T

U

V

X

Y

Z